Marlborough's Wars
Volume 1: 1702-1707

Europe *circa* 1700

Marlborough's Wars
Volume 1: 1702-1707

Frank Taylor

Marlborough's
Wars
Volume 1: 1702-1707
by Frank Taylor

First published under the title
The Wars of Marlborough 1702-1709
Volume 1

Leonaur is an imprint
of Oakpast Ltd

Copyright in this form © 2010 Oakpast Ltd

ISBN: 978-0-85706-086-0(hardcover)
ISBN: 978-0-85706-085-3 (softcover)

http://www.leonaur.com

Publisher's Notes

In the interests of authenticity, the spellings, grammar and place names used have been retained from the original editions.

The opinions of the authors represent a view of events in which he was a participant related from his own perspective, as such the text is relevant as an historical document.

The views expressed in this book are not necessarily those of the publisher.

Contents

Preface	7
War	11
The Exorbitant Power of France	27
The Ministry of Godolphin	64
1702	83
The Strife of Parties	101
1703	114
The March to the Schellenberg (1704)	140
The Devastation of Bavaria	176
Blenheim	191
After Blenheim	223
The Lines of Brabant	251
Schlangenberg	282
1705-1706	314
Ramillies	339
The Dutch Barrier	362
1706-1707	400

Preface

Although the *Life of Marlborough* has been written many times, and in a variety of styles, there is more than sufficient justification for writing it again.

Two biographers, and only two, have treated the subject in an adequate manner. Archdeacon Coxe's book, so far as the period subsequent to 1702 is concerned, is admirably thorough. Lord Wolseley's, which proceeds no further than that date, has quite superseded the Archdeacon's earlier chapters. Taken together these two works cover the entire field. To combine in a single volume the main results of the laborious researches of their authors would seem to be a desirable, if not a very ambitious enterprise.

In undertaking it, I have endeavoured to produce a narrative which can be read without undue fatigue by the many who are not scientific students of history. Archdeacon Coxe's book, which by reason of its burden of invaluable extracts from Marlborough's correspondence, is necessarily long, suffers, moreover, from a certain diffuseness and disorder, exasperating to all who read for pleasure. And even Lord Wolseley, in his anxiety to depict the background of his portrait in appropriate colours, exhibits a tendency towards digression and repetition, which does not make for either brevity or unity. Excepting, therefore, in a few instances, in which expansion has seemed to me to be required, I have aimed consistently at condensation.

I do not pretend to have broken fresh ground or to have discovered new facts. But a large number of contemporary documents, which were not available to Archdeacon Coxe, and some which were not available to Lord Wolseley, have now been published; and many modem historians, both English and foreign, have in recent years produced illuminating studies of the persons and events of Marlborough's time. All these I have freely consulted.

Marlborough was a soldier, or he was nothing. Even his diplomatic successes were largely attributable to his success in the field. I have therefore treated his military career more minutely than his political or private life. I have written without any claim to expert knowledge, but always ill the hope that my work may not be devoid of utility to the members of the Duke's profession.

Much of what I have written, too much as it may seem to some, is polemical in tone. But Marlborough, both in his life and after it, was pursued by enemies so numerous and so implacable, that a controversial atmosphere of necessity envelops him.

Neither Wolseley nor Coxe could escape from it, and no conscientious biographer of Marlborough would desire to escape from it. Much of the fighting has consequently been done already, and well done. But I have felt it my duty to devote considerable attention to the memoirs of the very valiant, very patriotic, but very conceited and inventive Dutchman, the field-deputy, Goslinga, whose extraordinary and repulsive allegations against the Duke, both as a soldier and a man, have not been sufficiently examined by English historians.

The functions of the 'whitewasher' I altogether disclaim. That epithet is easily applied, and not seldom misapplied. Whenever the known facts of any man's life are closely examined in their entirety, there is always a chance that the popular verdict on his conduct may be modified or even reversed. This is so, whether that verdict has been favourable or unfavourable; notwithstanding the chorus of distress which is invariably evoked, it will continue to be so till the day of judgement; and of that day's proceedings it will constitute by far the most remarkable and attractive feature.

In the case of three-fourths of the evil that is told of Marlborough (apart, of course, from deliberate lying), the facts themselves are of less consequence than the standpoint adopted by the teller. Standpoints are free to all to choose, and also to criticise. On this principle I have proceeded.

In seeking to present my countrymen with a complete yet concise account of the life and work of him, who saved both this island and the continent from a menace comparable only to the Napoleonic one, I have striven also to remind them of two things which some of them forget. One is England's place in Europe; the other is the real nature and the true significance of war. For I hold with Dalrymple that *to write history, without drawing moral or political rules of conduct from it, is little better than writing a romance.*

I desire to acknowledge my special indebtedness to my friend, the late Mr. Roderick Geikie, who shortly before his death lent me the manuscript of his treatise on the Dutch Barrier. The only other copy in existence is in the Library of King's College, Cambridge. No student of the period can afford to ignore Mr. Geikie's researches into this intricate page of diplomatic history.

CHAPTER 1

War

Geographical and climatic conditions may vary, national characteristics may differ, weapons and tactics may be incredibly changed, but the real object of all war and the true principles by which that object may be achieved remain immutable. For war, as Clausewitz insisted, is merely a strong expression, a violent manifestation of the foreign policy of a state. Whatever that policy may be, to impose it by force upon another state or states is always the end of war. And the only method by which war can certainly attain its end is the destruction of the enemy's armaments. This result may be assisted and even secured in more ways than one; but it can only be surely and swiftly wrought by battle. These conceptions of the end and means of war are universally true. They are a recognition of permanent realities, which, though at times obscured or overlooked, have given to the art of war throughout the ages an absolute identity.

Nevertheless, in military as in other affairs, history records innumerable changes and developments. Particular periods are distinguished by particular features. Thus, for example, in mediaeval warfare, when feudalism brought into the field huge levies of ill-trained footmen, nothing was more remarkable than the crushing superiority which the possession of horses and defensive armour conferred upon the aristocratic few who could afford them. But in the period which ensued, the period of the Renaissance, when the evolution of firearms was diminishing the value of the coat of mail and was profoundly complicating all tactical problems, the cosmopolitan mercenary, whether on horseback or on foot, was generally accepted as the highest type of efficiency in war.

In military history the century and a half which preceded the French Revolution can be treated as an epoch by itself. Let nobody infer that throughout that time the art of war remained stationary. For it was then that the bayonet and the bomb were invented, that fortification became an exact science, and that cavalry tactics attained to their utmost perfection. And it was then that such soldiers flourished as Gustavus, Cromwell, Turenne, Condé, Luxembourg, Marlborough, Eugène, Villars, Saxe, and Frederick. Nevertheless, during those hundred and fifty years, war, while continuing, as always, unchanged in its essential attributes, presented some peculiar and outstanding features which justify the military historian in separating that age from the ages which precede and follow it.

In studying the campaigns even of commanders so renowned as those whose names have just been cited, the modern soldier must often be astonished and puzzled by the comparative smallness of the results obtained and the comparative slowness of obtaining them. He would, of course, make large allowances for the inefficiency of the transport, the commissariat, and the intelligence departments of armies which knew not the railway, the telegraph, the motorcar, and the aeroplane. But these inventions were equally unknown in the Napoleonic era, which was nevertheless distinguished by the celerity and the magnitude of its military achievements. The material conditions under which armies moved and subsisted, and even the weapons with which they fought, underwent no extraordinary change between the age of Turenne and Marlborough and the age of Wellington and Napoleon. Yet the armies of 1800 produced far greater effects in far less time than the armies of 1650 or 1700. Indeed, from the French Revolution down to the present day, war has been remarkable for the tremendous nature of its consequences no less than for the terrifying rapidity with which those consequences have arrived.

The tedious and ineffective character of war in the earlier period is too often ascribed to nothing but the pedantry and ignorance of military men. But no armies and no centuries have ever possessed an absolute monopoly of those infirmities. In reality the causes were numerous and deep-seated. And the more important of them were not military at all, but political.

When the normal type of European government was autocratic, when even the so-called republics were but narrow oligarchies, policy was the business of the rulers rather than of the ruled. That phase of policy, which is called war, formed no exception to this law. In the past, war had been waged by savage hordes, by immense feudal levies, by huge national militias, in short by whole peoples and races in arms.

In the fourteenth, fifteenth, and sixteenth centuries these unwieldy hosts, ill-disciplined and badly organised, had proved very inferior to small contingents of highly trained mercenaries such as the free companies of English archers, the pikemen of the Swiss cantons, and the *'reiters'* and *'lanzknechts'* of Germany. The mercenaries first taught the lesson that war was neither a gallant sport for gentlemen nor a brutal pastime for the mob, but a serious profession which could not be successfully pursued without a high degree of technical knowledge and proficiency.

The strong and centralised governments of the seventeenth and eighteenth centuries understood this truth. But they also understood that an alien soldiery was expensive, unpopular, and unreliable. Accordingly they introduced the system of maintaining in their permanent service armies which were recruited in the main from such of their own subjects as were willing to adopt war as a regular trade. In England alone among the great powers of Europe this system still survives.

As every Englishman knows, armies of this kind are by no means cheap. Their numbers were consequently limited by the financial resources of the governments which paid them. A small but wealthy nation might have a larger army than a populous but poor one. The German states were rich in men, but without the gold of England or of Holland they were by no means rich in soldiers. Because such troops were few and costly, they were regarded by their employers as very precious. Moreover, they derived a special and purely political value from the fact that, in the last resort, they, and they alone, stood between those employers and revolt or revolution.

Now it is a true saying that nobody can make omelettes without breaking eggs. In war at any rate, unless you are prepared to take big risks, you cannot hope to obtain big results. But the governments of that day were not, as a general rule, prepared to take big risks. Soldiers, who in peace upheld the existing order, and at the same time absorbed so much of the fruit of the unpopular labours of the tax-gatherer, were not to be freely hazarded in war. Every government was more concerned to preserve its own army than to destroy the enemy's. The instrument came to be regarded as more important than the purpose for which it had been forged.

Thus was created an artificial and distorted view of war. But inasmuch as this view was common to all the governments of Europe, the adoption of it was fraught with no special perils to any one of them.

It was unnecessary to aim at your enemy's total destruction, since he in reality was not aiming at yours. Indeed, it might even be highly impolitic to beat him too soundly. For the international system, commonly known as 'the balance of power,' was exactly calculated to rob a belligerent of the spoils of victory. No sooner had a marked superiority been established over the enemy's forces than the intervention of some other state or states, alarmed for the equilibrium of the continent, might alter the whole character of the military problem.

Offensive plans must then be abandoned in the full tide of success, and defensive ones hastily matured. And in the end the conqueror might be compelled by a coalition to relinquish all or much that he had already won. Policy itself, therefore, in certain circumstances, might even dictate a slack and nerveless prosecution of the struggle. So long at any rate as governments, actuated by political and financial considerations, set an extreme value on the preservation of their armies, and so long as all Europe continued to exhibit a delicate sensibility towards every variation in 'the balance of power,' the presumption was that war would always proceed through half-measures to the attainment of limited results.

War being the servant of policy and not its master, it is right and natural that policy should prescribe the ultimate object of war. So too, the statesmen who furnish the generals in the field with armies necessarily compel those generals to adopt only such methods of warfare as are suitable to the numbers and quality of the troops provided. Up to this point there need be no improper interference of the civilian in the business of the soldier. But whenever the military commander is not himself an absolute monarch, whenever in fact he is not in the position of a Napoleon, a Frederick, or a Charles XII, governments have the power of imposing their own ideas of strategy and tactics upon officers who have no option but to obey or to resign.

In the period now under consideration a habit of caution, so extreme as to be often indistinguishable from timidity, was successfully communicated by the statesmen to most of the generals whom they employed. The generals were virtually forbidden to regard the destruction in battle of the armed forces of the enemy as the correct method of war. A battle was attended with such stupendous risks even to the victors that it was usually avoided and seldom sought. Other and less dangerous operations were universally preferred. The ruling idea was not swift annihilation but slow attrition. If you were the stronger of the two combatants, you might take the offensive, and endeavour by surprise to occupy some portion of the enemy's territory.

If this attempt were successful, you did not instinctively follow up the blow; you probably assumed the defensive and merely essayed to hold what you had taken until your opponent grew weary of the struggle to eject you. If however you were the weaker, you did your best to render the progress of your antagonist both tedious and expensive, in the hope that sooner or later he might tire of his enterprise or abandon it as unworthy of the cost; but in any event you strove for delay. Time was always the friend of the weaker side, for time might bring forth an ally or even a coalition of allies. In warfare of this description the capture of some rich and populous city or some powerful fortress was considered to be a triumph sufficient in itself for a whole campaign. To occupy a province and to feed your army there at the enemy's expense was a great achievement. To oblige the enemy to subsist upon his own resources was not a small one.

The military men, who were more or less compelled to adopt these false ideas of their own profession, were not necessarily ignorant of the importance of annihilating the enemy in battle. But they had imbibed their employers' terror of the risks involved. To fight, unless you were forced to fight, or unless you were possessed of some palpable advantage over your opponent, came therefore to be regarded as stupid rashness. As Sheridan remarked of the army of the Potomac, *the trouble was that the commanders never went out to lick anybody, but always thought first of keeping from getting licked"*

Feuquières, a veteran officer of the age of Louis XIV, and one of the clearest and most informed of writers upon the art of war, recognised the value of battles. A battle, he declared, will often determine the result of the whole war, and almost always that of a particular campaign. But just because it may carry with it such decisive consequences, he argues that a battle *must not be fought except under necessity and for important reasons.*[1] War, conducted upon these principles, tended to become a problem of manoeuvring for superior positions or superior numbers.

By menacing fortresses you tried to induce your opponent to reinforce the garrisons and weaken his army in the field. By affecting an inclination for battle you tempted him to strengthen his army and deplete his garrisons. For weeks and months at a time great masses of armed men marched and countermarched and encamped within striking distance of one another without delivering a single blow.

---

1. *Mémoires du Marquis de Feuquières* (1740), t. 3., p. 176.

Everybody was so afraid of making a mistake that frequently little or nothing was done. Yet even so it was necessary to eat and drink; and the army which was eating and drinking in the enemy's country was supposed to have much the better of an otherwise futile game. If, however, for reasons of state, it was desired to conciliate the civil population, supplies must be bought in open market or forwarded from previously prepared magazines, and even the advantage of free quarters was lost.

It is obvious that, when the ends of war were pursued by such spurious and pettifogging methods, war itself was bound to become both dilatory and ineffective. It is obvious also that a military system, which to modern students is apt to appear as an elaborate absurdity, originated in the political circumstances and exigencies of the time, and was accepted by soldiers either because there was no alternative, or because it was imposed on them by statesmen whose authority they were unable to defy.

The statesmen however must not be unduly censured. If they were cautious, they had also solid reasons for caution. And neither they nor the generals could accomplish the impossible. Judged by modern standards, the largest of the armies of that period were small. At Breitenfeld there were 35,000 Swedes to the same number of Imperialists; at Rocroi, 20,000 French to 26,000 Spaniards; at Enzheim, 22,000 French to 35,000 of the allies; at Blenheim, 52,000 of the allies to 56,000 French; at Almanza, 15,500 of the allies to 25,000 French; at Rosbach, 25,000 Prussians to 50,000 French and Imperialists. These were typical engagements. Battles like Malplaquet, where more than 90,000 combatants appeared on either side, were abnormal. Now a small army is relatively much weaker than a large one. A commander who assumes the offensive with a quarter or a half a million of men, and loses 50 *per cent*, or even 75 *per cent*, of his total, has still an army. He may still go forward. But a commander, who with 20,000 or 30,000, or even 50,000 men undergoes a similar experience, has nothing left, or next to nothing for offensive purposes.

How great is the wastage of war, especially for attacking armies, may be judged by three examples. In 1812 Napoleon crossed the Niemen with 442,000 men; yet he reached Moscow, three months later, with only 95,000. In 1870 the Germans entered France with 372,000 men; yet they came to Paris, after six weeks, with only 171,000. In 1878 the Russians passed the Danube with 460,000 men: yet they brought but 100,000 to Constantinople, and more than half of those were sick. Exposed to losses on a like scale, the smaller armies of an earlier age would have virtually disappeared. This consideration vitally modified the strategy of that period. But it was neither invented by statesmen nor forced upon unwilling soldiers; it was a simple truth which was apparent to all, and the consequences of which could never be eluded, as long as the numbers of the forces available remained so limited.

"The only decisive result of victory," wrote Thiebault, "is the occupation of capitals, and not that of fortresses, which only serve to weaken an army corps by the garrisons they require."[2]

And certainly a modern army, victorious upon the enemy's frontier, is expected to march swiftly upon his capital. But the generals of this earlier age regarded such a movement as a vain imagination. An army of 50,000 men, which in those days was a large army, would, in the great majority of cases, have been quite inadequate for the purpose. Suppose that it had attempted such a task, and that the constant wastage from disease and battle had been regularly made up by drafts from its base. At every stage it would have been compelled to leave behind it a guard sufficient to protect its communications against a hostile population and organised raids by the enemy.

At many of the earlier stages it would have been obliged to detach considerable contingents to mask or to blockade the numerous fortresses which guarded the frontiers . If a general neglected these precautions, he might be cut off from his base and eventually destroyed. If he observed them, he might find himself, long before the end of his journey, without any army at all. A modern general, starting with 200,000 or 300,000 men, could do all that was necessary on the march, and still retain a sufficiency of strength for the achievement of his purpose when he reached his goal. But an army of 50,000 men, or fewer, could not undertake such an enterprise.

It might indeed direct its course towards the enemy's capital. But as it could not afford to mask or to blockade the strong places on the way, it must stop to capture them. And as the art of the military engineer attained, in the second half of the seventeenth century, to a high degree of excellence, this process was a slow and costly one. Meanwhile, the enemy, who could calculate almost to a day the number of weeks or months which must be expended on a particular fortress, had abundant leisure to recover from defeat and to organise a new

---

2. Memoirs of Baron Thiêbault, ch. 10., p. 185.

resistance. Under such conditions the advance upon his capital might occupy years instead of weeks. Deprived of the terrifying effect of rapidity, the movement lost the greater part of that moral advantage which is its chief strength.

In these circumstances it is easy to understand why sieges were much more frequent than battles. And the general tendency in this direction received a powerful impulse from one special factor, the importance of which can hardly be exaggerated. It was mainly on her north-eastern frontier that France fought out her quarrel with the Spaniard; and it was there that she faced the combined armies of England and Holland. On either side this frontier was studded with fortresses of the most approved pattern, protected in many cases by natural or artificial inundations, and so disposed as to command the numerous rivers, which were then the best and swiftest highways for artillery and stores.

If the French desired to march through the Spanish Netherlands to Brussels or to Antwerp, if a coalition desired to strike across Picardy and Artois to Paris, in either case a double and even a triple barrier of fortified places must be slowly and painfully forced. In this difficult country innumerable campaigns were conducted, and many reputations made and lost. Successive generations of soldiers, trained up in such a school of warfare, were naturally impressed with the necessity of numerous sieges. Unfortunately they too often exhibited a disposition to base universal conclusions upon the special and local circumstances of a particular area. They too often failed to realise that what was right in a country where the art of Vauban and of Coehoorn had been exercised in the highest degree, might well be wrong in Germany, Italy, or Spain, where fortresses were few and mostly obsolete.

They fell into the fallacy of supposing that, just because the French were admittedly the foremost soldiers of Europe, the French method of making war on what Mr. Shandy called *the old prize-fighting stage of Flanders*[3] must be regarded as the correct method of making war everywhere. Moreover, Louis XIV, who set the mode in all things, disliked battles; but he dearly loved to besiege a place in form. Thanks to his patronage, an operation which was often necessary became always fashionable.

It may be contended that the smallness of armies was largely the result of an unsound strategy, which favoured the dispersion of fight-

---

3. Sterne, *The Life and Opinions of Tristram Shandy*, book 3., ch. 25.

ing strength over several theatres of war at the same time. Theoretically this criticism may be justified. But in practice, there were at least two formidable difficulties in the way of a large concentration of troops at a given point or on a single frontier. In the first place, the highways of that epoch were generally few, and frequently atrocious. Much of the intervening country was obstructed by impenetrable forests that have now been felled, and by dangerous morasses that have long since been drained.

The modern system, whereby an army is divided into several homogeneous corps, moving on an extensive front and utilising a multitude of parallel or converging roads, had not been introduced, because the topographical conditions were unfavourable to its adoption. The army, whatever its size, was organised as a single unit. It marched and camped and marched again as a single unit. The larger it was, the more slowly it progressed, and the more dependent it became upon navigable rivers for the transport of its artillery and stores. But navigable rivers were not always available; or if they were, they were apt to be blocked by powerful fortresses. What therefore a general gained in numbers he lost in time; and the more he increased his striking force, the more he diminished his mobility.

And secondly, with a great expansion of numbers, the problem of subsistence became soon unmanageable. The rich and fertile countries, where food was abundant, were precisely those which were most thickly garnished with fortified places of immense strength, commanding every road and controlling every waterway. The poor and sparsely populated ones could not be safely entered without the previous formation of enormous and expensive magazines, from which the troops at the front could be regularly supplied. In either case, and whether the forces were great or small, the magazine system was the normal system of the time. The Revolutionary and Napoleonic method of licensed brigandage, whereby an army swept forward like a horde of locusts, devouring all things in its path, and spurred into extreme mobility by the constant prick of hunger, did not commend itself either to the generals or the governments of that age.

It did not commend itself to the generals, because it involved the conversion of the line of possible retreat into a desert, peopled only by the spectre of starvation and a ruined and revengeful peasantry. And in any event it could not be adopted except in conjunction with that extensive front and that army-corps system, which have already been shown to have been impracticable. It did not commend itself to the governments because the theatre of war was usually the prize for which the war itself was being waged, and a devastated and disaffected province would offer but a poor return for the treasure invested in the struggle. Motives of expediency, therefore, and not of superior humanity, dictated the use of magazines. The larger the masses that were assembled at the point of concentration, the more dependent they became on this method of supply. But the range of any army which is tied to magazines is of necessity restricted.

The loss of time and loss of energy, which were the dominant features of such warfare, were conspicuously exhibited in the annual custom of suspending active operations from the middle of autumn until the ensuing spring was well advanced. Both sides withdrew into winter-quarters as if by mutual agreement, not to emerge again until the orthodox interval of six months or thereabouts had duly expired. Fantastic as this practice may appear to modern eyes, it was based upon strong and even imperative considerations. Foremost of all was, as usual, the extreme anxiety of the governments to spare their troops. History, and especially modern history, has proved again and again that campaigning in hard winter is the ruin of armies. In resolutely refusing to expose their small and valuable forces to conditions more deleterious than battle itself, the old governments displayed no more than ordinary prudence.

And in reality they had no great option in the matter. For the advent of winter virtually put an end to the mobility of armies. With few exceptions the roads of that epoch were bad at the best. Worn out by the operations of the summer months, and swamped by the autumnal rains, they passed through frost and snow-storm into a condition impassable by large bodies of men and horses, to say nothing of artillery and transport. For this reason alone some period of hibernation was almost always justifiable, and even inevitable. On the other hand, the period was often unduly extended. The opportunity offered by a fine autumn, an open winter, or a precocious spring, was rarely seized. The custom hardened into a rule of the game, a kind of military ritual, punctiliously observed by both sides to the entire neglect of the true principles of war.

But all such delay, even when it was unavoidable, was essentially pernicious. It meant that the concluding weeks of the too brief campaigning season were often devoted to the capture of some fortress which derived its sole importance from its proximity to the district selected for cantonments. It meant that a blow, struck at the close of active operations, could not be followed up, that the full fruits of victory could not be reaped. It meant also that a beaten enemy, if only he could hold out as long as the fine weather lasted, could not be crushed. Winter brought him ample leisure to recuperate, to study the causes of defeat, to levy and train recruits, to form new alliances, to solicit the interest of Europe, and to renew the conflict in the spring with recovered vigour. Thus delay gave birth to delay, and war tended to degenerate into a mere test of the financial endurance of the contending powers.

It was not in the region of strategy alone that the art of war was limited and circumscribed by conditions from which there was little or no escape. Before condemning the reluctance of both statesmen and soldiers to engage the enemy in a pitched battle, some allowance must also be made for the position of tactical science in that period. If the combats of the seventeenth and eighteenth centuries are considered in comparison with those of the Napoleonic and subsequent generations, one remarkable difference at once emerges. Victory, in the earlier epoch, was, as a rule, much more costly and much less profitable than in the later. It was more costly, because, contrary to popular and fallacious notions on this subject, the development of weapons has been accompanied by a steady diminution in the rate of slaughter.

As the power of killing has advanced, the percentage of the killed has fallen. And this is no paradox, but an easily explicable fact. When the range, the precision, and the destructiveness of musketry and artillery were comparatively small, hand to hand fighting and the terrible butchery which necessarily attends the use of steel, were common features of the combat. Moreover, at a time when the assailants never came under effective fire until they were in close proximity to the defenders, it was possible to induce troops of even moderate quality to return again and again to the attack.

But in modern war the demoralisation set up at an early stage of the advance by exposure to a deadly and concentrated lire from a distant and often unseen enemy is so rapid and so thorough that the best of soldiers cannot always be persuaded to risk more than one repulse upon the same day. War, as it has become more appalling to the nerves of men, has become less murderous to their bodies. Consequently, the generals of the older epoch had to pay, out of the smaller forces at their disposal, a heavier price for victory than their modern successors.

And victory itself, though bought thus dearly then, was apt to prove less fruitful than it is today. In all battles between disciplined armies, directed by leaders of approximately equal competence, there is usually no very marked disparity between the numbers of the casualties on both sides up to the decisive moment at which one or the other commences to retire. It is during the retreat that the victor inflicts, or should inflict, the heaviest losses on the vanquished. Above all, it is in prisoners that he earns, or should earn, the largest of his profits. Now the battles of this older period were usually fought between armies ranged in parallel lines. These lines engaged more or less along their entire length, and even simultaneously at every point.

A victory gained in such a situation, though it sometimes yielded astonishing results, was not as a rule so damaging to the beaten army as it ought to have been. Not until the time of Frederick, when the value of the oblique and enveloping orders of attack was first understood, did the conqueror obtain a fair opportunity of reaping the full fruits of his success. Battles, therefore, were gigantic lotteries, in which the fees were higher and the prizes smaller than they afterwards became. In these circumstances the cautious handling of small, expensive, and politically invaluable armies becomes easy to understand, if not always possible to justify.

The notion that a battle was no battle unless it was fought out between combatants ranged in parallel lines, with infantry in the centre and cavalry upon the wings, had other unfortunate results. It meant that the normal action must be preceded by a tedious and mathematically correct deployment, which lasted for hours, and which exposed the soldiery to a trying cannonade from the hostile guns. It meant also that, unless the country was sufficiently open to allow of this formation, armies must not engage at all. And so, by a singular perversion, the initiative was actually transferred to the commander who had little or no desire to fight, and who, as long as he chose to avoid the open, could never be attacked except in defiance of the rules of the game.

The respect, which even enterprising generals showed to fortified positions and to positions of great natural strength, was certainly exaggerated, in so far as it was based on the pedantic idea of an orthodox order of battle in parallel lines. But it was not always, or necessarily, devoid of more solid justification. The power of artillery being then insufficiently developed, and its proper application insufficiently understood, the assault had often to be delivered without that thorough preparation which ought always to precede it. When every village was a potential bastion, and when treacherous morasses abounded where scarcely a trace of them remains today, it was easy to select positions which could never be carried, or could be carried only at enormous cost, because the feebleness of the assailants' artillery had left the defenders virtually unshaken.

Moreover, the use of the spade was well understood. If time were allowed for it, what was practicable before might be rendered impracticable in a very few hours. Its abuse was seen in those immense lines, which were sometimes constructed to cover a whole province or an entire country, and which were little favoured by the greatest generals because they could always be entered by some skilful combination. But the attempt to carry such works by direct assault was usually regarded as hazardous in the extreme. And the artillery of the period being what it was, this judgement cannot be lightly treated as erroneous.

Everybody can criticise and even ridicule a military system which was so fruitful in rigid formalism and so barren in decisive results. But in many respects it was only the product of the political, social, geographical, and economic conditions of the time. Instead of being derided by contemporary opinion as feeble or absurd, it was regarded rather as a triumph of science and of progressive civilisation. And certainly, in the minute perfection of its detail, in the power of its weapons, and above all in the ample recognition which it gave to the superiority of intellect and knowledge over animal courage and physical force, it was by far the most scientific form of war that had as yet been practised in the world. And inasmuch as it restricted the miseries inseparable from warfare to theatres of very limited area, while it relieved the great majority of the people from the burden of personal service, it appeared to many observers to be singularly humane.

But its humanity was more superficial than real. It was gentle only where gentleness paid. It was capable at times of sanctioning the exercise of the most ruthless savagery upon civilian populations. For it rested ultimately, as the conduct of all war must always rest, upon expediency alone. And it was essentially cruel, because it was essentially wasteful and slow. In war mercy and efficiency go hand in hand. The most humane form of war is the one which crushes the enemy in the shortest possible time and with the smallest possible expenditure of life and money.

Every campaign is accompanied by a chronic destruction of life from exposure, exhaustion, and disease. From the first day that it takes the field every army is a dying army. In an age which knew little of medicine and nothing of sanitary science, the losses other than those inflicted by the enemy were certainly heavier than they are today. But such losses are apt to escape the public eye. A sanguinary battle excites the horror of mankind, while the insidious wastage of prolonged campaigning passes comparatively unremarked. The British forces in South Africa lost 20,721 men, of whom not more than 7,582 died by the enemy's hand. This consideration was largely overlooked by those who applauded the humanity of the military system of the seventeenth and eighteenth centuries.

And what was true of the lives of the soldiers was equally true of the pockets of the taxpayers. Because the expenditure, no less than the mortality, was spread over a term of years, it seemed to be trivial when in fact it was unnecessarily large. In the end, the intolerable strain upon the financial resources of governments and the injury done to the economic condition of peoples were usually the causes which brought about the termination of the struggle. A conclusion, which ought to have been attained by a short and severe agony, was slowly and painfully reached by the lingering process of exhaustion.

By strictly observing the rules of the game, it was possible in that age for a very inferior commander to acquire a reputation which he could hardly have acquired in any other. A general who never fought a battle, but who succeeded in feeding his army upon hostile territory, was regarded as a valuable servant who knew how to make war on safe and profitable lines. Even if he were defeated in an engagement forced upon him, he could never be censured so long as he could never be shown to have infringed the accepted maxims of his art. At the worst he would be pitied as unlucky, and perhaps superseded by some more 'fortunate' officer.

The temptation never to be original and never to assume responsibility for something not in the books was therefore strong and permanent. Moreover, most men whose profession was war were easily disposed to exaggerate and to abuse those weak and tardy methods which, under an imposing appearance of orthodoxy, tended to make the active employment of their class a perpetuity. Even so fine a soldier as Luxembourg was accused of designedly permitting a beaten enemy to escape destruction. Nevertheless, generals of the first order, generals who like Cromwell and Frederick would have shone under any system and in spite of any system, did actually appear, and from time to time amazed and confounded the pedants and the pettifoggers.

"If," said Napoleon at St. Helena, "I had had a man like Turenne to be my second in command during my campaigns, I should have been now master of the world; but I had nobody."

The genius of Turenne would have enabled him to command large armies as successfully as he did little ones.

"If he had sprung out of the earth and stood by my side at Wagram, he would have perceived my plan, and have understood everything. Condé would have understood it too."

What the same authority thought of Marlborough may be judged. Never losing sight of the true end and of the proper means of war, such generals refused to be trammelled by the maxims of a perverted school. They strove to practise their art upon right principles, in so far as the inevitable limitations of their environment permitted them a free hand. That these limitations were neither few nor slight, has already been abundantly shown. The smallness of armies involved a strategical weakness which it was not in a commander's power to remedy, and which hampered him at every point. However much he might resent the waste of time and energy inseparable from the annual retirement into winter-quarters, he was bound to recognise that often there was no alternative. The timidity of the government which employed him and of the officers who served under him was a continual drag upon his powers. If he desired to accept great risks in the hope of great advantages, he had first to extort the permission of his civilian masters, which might not arrive, if it arrived at all, until the opportunity had passed away. If however he decided to proceed upon his own responsibility, he was often confronted by the remonstrances and even the insubordination of lieutenants, imagining their own careers to be jeopardised or hoping to curry favour with the government. In either case he was worried and embarrassed at the very moment when he had need of the utmost tranquillity of mind; and in either case he was universally and un- sparingly condemned, if the enterprise miscarried.

Such was the military system of Churchill's day; and it was vastly and essentially different from that of ours. Ever since the French Revolution the dominant type of European army has been the nation in arms. Such armies are gigantic and comparatively cheap. But their action is swift and terrible. Swift at any rate it must be, for a system which summons the whole of the able-bodied manhood of the nation to the colours, and which gives thereby to every family in the land a direct and intimate interest in the speedy termination of hostilities, would be quite intolerable, if it followed the dilatory procedure of an earlier age, when only limited areas and restricted classes endured the heaviest burdens of war, and when successful war might even be self-supporting.

And swift it must be in this modern world, where the outbreak of hostilities produces such a hideous dislocation and destruction of the complex, commercial and industrial interests of the belligerent powers, that even the victor may find his victory to be worse than worthless if it be too long deferred. By reason of this very swiftness war has become more humane. And more than ever it is now the grand security for peace. Nations do not lightly appeal to the arbitrament of arms, when the stakes are so high, and the interests involved are so enormous, and when that popular sense of irresponsibility, which always accompanies, in some degree, the employment of professional armies, is replaced by the natural and honourable obligation of personal service.

In England, however, the small, professional army which was created during Churchill's lifetime still survives; and with it have survived certain of the evil traditions of that period. With the great courage which is begotten of great ignorance, the British democracy, alone in the face of Europe, still cherishes the suicidal fallacy that the forces of the twentieth century can be successfully encountered with the forces of the seventeenth. And the mass of the people still clings to the pernicious delusion that war can be waged without bloodshed, that manoeuvring is a substitute for fighting, and that the greatest general is he who never permits his soldiers to be killed. If a thousand are slain in one day, public opinion is aghast; but ten thousand may rot to death in the course of a year without greatly perturbing it.

Englishmen, at any rate, ought to be very sparing of their criticism upon the military methods of the past. Mistaken as to some extent those methods were, the universal adoption of them did at least place all belligerents upon an equal footing. But a state, which persists in retaining an obsolete system and a vicious point of view, while it ignores or even reprobates the development of its neighbours and potential foes, deliberately imposes on itself a crushing handicap fatal to the very possibility of success in the time of trial.

Chapter 2

The Exorbitant Power of France

History can be written in more ways than one—in the manner of Herodotus, for example, or in the manner of Thucydides. It can be written, and well written, by political partisans like Livy and Macaulay, or by religious partisans like Gibbon and Froude. The one qualification which is absolutely essential to the historian is the power of sympathy. If he can sympathise with, or at least understand, all the men and the things of which he has to treat, his temper is ideal. If however his powers in this direction are at once so limited and so intense that he is compelled to take a side, his work may be profitable and even admirable, so far as it goes. And it will still be history.

But early in the nineteenth century there arose a school of historical writers, whose method was fundamentally vicious and futile. They would seem to have started with the highly original assumption that, prior to the French Revolution, all the rulers of Europe were knaves and all the peoples fools. All the old governments were desperately wicked, and all whom they governed were brutalised sots, until at last the ringing of Fouquier-Tinville's bell and the crashing of Sanson's axe heralded the dawn of morality and light. This melancholy hypothesis precludes the very possibility of sympathy with anything that existed in Europe before 1789.

History, written under this obsession, is either a crazy diatribe or a complacent tract. It may gratify the palates of prigs and doctrinaires. It may flatter the vanity of an ignorant proletariat. But it possesses no sort of relation to utility or truth. It is vastly inferior to the most biased production of the most partisan historian. For the partisan historian must have an abundance, and even an excess of sympathy, to be a partisan. And he is always corrected by another of his own class. The antidote is always forthcoming. History as written by a Mitford is provocative of history as written by a Grote.

But history as written by a Michelet is provocative of derision and disquiet. By the nature of the case a partisan historian is saturated with the ideas and prejudices of some at any rate of the men and women whose actions he describes. He has therefore the virtues of his defects. But he who writes the record of a bygone age in the spirit of the present, and for the greater glorification of the present, whatever else he may be, is no historian.

To this school of writers no theme is so agreeable as the essential wickedness of

"battles long ago,"

They are prepared to prove that almost all the great struggles of the past originated in the natural depravity of kings, the caprice of concubines, or the machinations of Jesuits. The old governments existed only to plunder and maltreat their subjects. The diversion of public attention from their own misrule was therefore a supreme interest which they all shared in common. One of the best devices for attaining this end was chronic war. One of the best pretexts for chronic war was the maintenance of 'the balance of power.' The idea of 'the balance of power' is therefore to be held up to reprobation and ridicule.

It is to be represented as a piece of nonsensical jargon, invented by interested statesmen to delude the masses of ignorant dupes whom they kept in degrading servitude. And mankind is to be invited to rejoice at the thought that blood will never again be shed in Europe for the sake of a *shibboleth*, incomprehensible alike to those who framed it and to those whom they compelled to die for it. This gospel, which in some mysterious fashion is supposed to palliate the absurdities and atrocities of the French Revolution and its imitators, has possessed no finer exponent than Southey's engaging babe:

'*Why, 'twas a very wicked thing!*'
Said little Wilhelmine,[1]

It is indeed amazing that views so grotesque should ever have obtained the vogue which they enjoy today. For nothing could be simpler, saner, or more natural than the conception of 'the balance of power.' So great a logician as the Tory, Hume, declared that it was founded upon "common sense and obvious reasoning."[2] So good an Englishman as the Nonconformist, Defoe, contended that, instead of

---
1. Southey, *The Battle of Blenheim*.
2. Hume, *Essays*; "Of the Balance of Power."

being a pretext for unjust wars, it was "the life of peace."³ Whenever from any cause or variety of causes one European state of the first class becomes vastly stronger than every other of that class, a situation fraught with possibilities of peril is at once set up.

Accumulated experience has shown conclusively that a nation which has thus outstripped its peers, and is profoundly conscious of its superiority, will attempt to lay hands upon the territories of those second and third-rate powers which have the misfortune to be its immediate neighbours,

> "I question," wrote Defoe, "whether it be in the Humane Nature to set Bounds to its own Ambition, and whether the best Man on Earth wou'd not be King over all the rest if he could. Every King in the World would be the Universal Monarch if he might, and nothing restrains but the Power of Neighbours; and if one Neighbour is not strong enough for another, he gets another Neighbour to join with him, and all the little ones will join to keep the great one from suppressing them."⁴

This spirit of encroachment must almost certainly prevail, unless the larger states are willing to resist it. If it prevails, that strength, which was before excessive, becomes more excessive, and the potentiality of resistance in the remainder of the continent is diminished in proportion. The aggressor is tempted to repeat the process. With each new acquisition his resources are augmented, and the difficulty of checking his ambition is augmented too. Theoretically, by this method he might in time absorb the whole of Europe. But in practice such designs have invariably been thwarted by a coalition of the powers both big and little.

The sooner this combination is formed, the cheaper and safer is the task of reducing the common enemy to a position in which he can no longer threaten the independence of others. Indeed, prompt and resolute action upon these lines may even obviate the necessity for war at all. Too often, however, the organisation of resistance has been foolishly postponed, at the ultimate cost of a needlessly lavish expenditure of blood and money. History has invariably proved that, in dealing with disturbers of the European system, *"principiis obsta"* is the only reliable rule. But all wars undertaken for this cause, whether they be undertaken soon or late, are wars for the restoration of 'the

---

3. Defoe, *The Two Great Questions Considered* (1700)
4. *Ibid.*.

balance of power.'

The phrase, though metaphorical, is sufficiently exact. The circumstances to which it is applicable are matter of common knowledge. The ethics of the question are hardly relevant. It may, for example, be contended by the devotees of the Napoleonic cult that Europe would be better and happier today, if its thrones had been vested in perpetuity in the Bonaparte family and the Marshals of France. But, wisely or unwisely, the nations have always objected to resign their independence. So long as they retain a predilection for liberty, so long will they regard the maintenance of 'the balance of power' as a material interest and as a reasonable, and, indeed, an imperative ground for an appeal to arms.

In England, unfortunately, there are many who have persuaded themselves that, even if 'the balance of power' is admitted to concern the peoples of the continent, it has nothing whatever to do with the inhabitants of these islands. This opinion, which is by no means new, has always been a folly of the most dangerous kind. Let it be assumed that, by some magician's wand, the various nationalities which comprise the continent of Europe were welded into one homogeneous state. It is obvious that the independence of this country would not then be worth a week's purchase. A community so vast, controlling so many strategical positions, and commanding naval resources so enormous, would be irresistible. It has been well said that *the domination of Europe by one power would automatically reduce Great Britain to the political level of the Isle of Man.*[5]

Though this precise contingency is not very likely to be realised, conditions dangerously approximating to it have always been possible, and have more than once existed. Whenever a continental state, by the absorption of territory, by offensive alliances, or by the creation of a species of hegemony or suzerainty over Europe or a part of it, has obtained control of maritime forces of exceptional magnitude, the integrity of the British Isles is virtually menaced. Those who pretend that it is not, and who reason as though they were living in a world of "little Wilhelmines," are no friends to their country.

Over and over again, in modern history, this peril has arisen. And sooner or later every disturber of the equilibrium of Europe has collided with the might of England. The foreign policy of England, which it is a kind of tradition on the continent to represent as dark and tortuous, has always been marked by a severe simplicity. Whoever

---
5. *The National Review*, October, 1910.

is planning to establish a dangerous predominance upon the mainland, is, for the time being, England's enemy. No nation has played a more consistent and conspicuous part in the recurring struggles for the preservation of 'the balance of power.' Philip II, Louis XIV, the first Republic, the first Napoleon, all owed the eventual collapse of their designs to combinations of which England was often the mainspring and always an essential part. It is therefore no accident that she is now regarded as the protagonist of Europe in the conflict which must inevitably be waged against the latest aspirant for universal empire.

In the year 1700 France under Louis XIV had destroyed the equilibrium of the continent. Rapidly and surely she had risen to a position of supremacy more commanding than that once occupied by Spain. The dominion of Philip II, slowly wasting from mismanagement and from sheer neglect of its superb resources, and shattered in its military prestige by the sword of Condé, had long ceased to be even a possible match for its mighty neighbour. The Empire, loosely organised, and harassed on its flanks by the Turkish peril, was hardly in better case. France could hold her own with ease against these two combined.

And there existed no other first-class power which might restore the balance. Sweden was too weak and too remote, and Russia still too barbarous to be seriously considered. Such a situation was not unnaturally regarded by the lesser states with grave disquietude. Louis of course disclaimed all large designs against the liberties of Europe. He had always a specific pretext ready for each new act of aggression. The business of diplomacy was better understood at Versailles than at any other European court.

It is however a mistake to concentrate attention upon Louis to the exclusion of the twenty millions over whom he ruled. Louis, for all his autocratic power, was only the type and the perfect representative of a nation, which in the economic, the administrative, and the military sense was the most highly developed in Europe. Those egregious historians, who see in the France of Racine and Bossuet, of Colbert and Turenne, nothing but a horde of slaves, exploited by a self-indulgent tyrant and his gang of sycophants and harlots, have yet to explain how a people so infamously degraded could have been a model in peace and a terror in war to every state in Europe, including those which already enjoyed the supposed advantages of free and even republican institutions and of the Protestant religion.

But truth to tell, the facts were very different from the misrepresentations of a set of writers, whose sole concern is to justify the cataclysm which destroyed the ancient system.

"Go through the public services of every kind," wrote Guizot, "the finances, the roads, the public works, the military administration, and all the establishments which belong to any branch of administration whatsoever; there is scarcely one which you will not find to have had either its origin or its development or its greatest perfection under the reign of Louis XIV."[6]

Under him the French nobility was at once the most polished and the most warlike clan that the world has ever seen. The bureaucracy was exceptionally able. The commercial and industrial orders were thrifty and prosperous, and were skilfully encouraged and assisted in the production of wealth by the central government. The peasantry, though labouring under a variety of oppressive burdens, were then as always the backbone of the country. Although inferior in several respects to the yeomanry, the tenant-farmers, and the agricultural labourers of England, they were by no means the squalid serfs of modern imagination.

So close an observer as Arthur Young, who certainly held no brief for the ancient system, estimated that on the eve of the Revolution one third of the soil of France was in the hands of peasant proprietors. A race of helots could never have given birth to the rank and file of those gallant armies which broke the Spanish infantry at Rocroi, which followed Turenne in his wonderful winter march of 1674 when he chased the Germans from Lorraine, and which at Steinkirk and Neerwinden hurled back the hard fighting soldiery of England and the stubborn Dutch. For the France of 1700 was not merely populous and rich; from top to bottom she was penetrated by the military spirit.

A succession of extraordinary statesmen and soldiers had made her what she was, a unified kingdom with the most strongly centralised government in Europe. Henry of Navarre and Sully, Richelieu and Mazarin, Condé and Turenne, Colbert and Louvois, had all contributed their share. Louis himself was the last of the line. Henry of Navarre had dreamed of the hegemony of the continent; Louis' ambition assumed a more concrete form. Behind him stood a haughty and pugnacious race, equipped with immense resources and an unrivalled organisation, and bent upon the destruction of the liberties of Europe. The passion for national expansion may, or may not, be morally de-

---

6. Guizot, *History of Civilisation in Europe*, lecture 14.

fensible; but it is deeply implanted in every virile and enduring stock. It flourished strongly in the France of Louis XIV, just as it flourishes without disguise in the Germany of today.

"The great body of the people," to quote the words of Alison, "proud of their sovereign, proud of his victories, proud of his magnificence, proud of his fame, proud of his national spirit, proud of the literary glory which environed his throne, in secret proud of his gallantries, joyfully followed their nobles in the brilliant career which his ambition opened, and submitted with as much docility to his government as they had once ranged themselves round the banners of their respective chiefs in the day of battle."[7]

The contrast with the political decadence of modern France is striking; to those, whose business or pleasure it is to pretend that in 1780 she lost nothing, it cannot be other than painful.

At the peace of Westphalia in 1648 France had obtained possession of Austrian Alsace, of Breisach, and of the right to garrison Philippsburg, as well as of Metz, Toul, and Verdun. These acquisitions planted her firmly on the Upper Rhine. She also received the fortress of Pignerole on the Italian side of the Alps. At the peace of the Pyrenees in 1659 she strengthened her exposed, northern frontier by the addition of the province of Artois, and the fortresses of Thionville, Landrecies, and Avesnes. In the south she secured the territories of Roussillon and Cerdagne, where hitherto the Spaniards had maintained a footing on the wrong side of the mountain-barrier. She also established a virtual control over the duchy of Lorraine.

At the peace of Aix-la-Chapelle in 1668 she acquired a belt of fortresses in the Spanish Netherlands, Lille, Tournai, Charleroi, Audenarde, Ath, and others, which not only rendered her northern frontier as strong as it had formerly been weak, but opened the whole of the Low Countries to her attack. At the peace of Nijmegen in 1678 she obtained Franche Comté, and still further strengthened her position in Lorraine. She subsequently laid hands upon the city of Strasbourg, the fortress of Casale in Piedmont, and other places in Alsace, all of which, with the important exception of the first, she was obliged to abandon at the peace of Ryswick in 1698.

Thus in a period of fifty years, an able, arrogant, and unscrupulous diplomacy, supported always by war in its most relentless form, had

---

7. Alison, *The Military Life of John, Duke of Marlborough* (1848), p. 40.

girdled her with fortresses and carried her borders to the Pyrenees, the Alps, and the Vosges. Herself immune from attack, she could issue forth at will into the valleys of the Schelde, the Meuse, the Rhine, the Ebro, and the Po. Her expansion had naturally been watched with profound misgiving. Three times already Europe had seen fit to intervene, in 1668, in 1673, and in 1688. On each occasion the aggressor had been checked, but had nevertheless got off with a goodly portion of the spoil. And the conquests of Louis XIV were permanent conquests. He created the frontier lines of modern France.

Creasy has justly observed that "all the provinces that Bonaparte conquered, were rent again from France within twenty years from the date when the very earliest of them was acquired. France is not stronger by a single city or a single acre for all the devastating wars of the Consulate and the Empire. She has still the extended boundaries which Louis XIV gave her."[8]

Unhappily, since Creasy wrote those words, the France which affects to ignore and to despise the Bourbons has proved incapable of retaining what the Bourbons won,

William of Orange had devoted his life to the enormous labour of frustrating the designs of this ambitious and formidable power. Down to 1688 Louis had reckoned on the friendship, or at the worst, on the neutrality or the impotence of England. William, who had no fanatical attachment to the Protestant religion, and who positively detested those constitutional principles which he is supposed to have vindicated, snatched the sceptre from James II that he might cast it into the scale against the preponderating weight of the French power. In the war which followed, great exertions were made, and great losses were sustained by both sides, until at the end of eight years the mutual exhaustion of the combatants disposed them to a peace.

Louis, who had suffered more severely than the allies, was a willing signatory of the terms agreed at Ryswick. In forfeiting some of his more recent acquisitions, and in consenting at last to acknowledge William as King of England, he did but give what he had stolen, and what cost him nothing. And in return he obtained what was at that moment a necessity of his far-sighted policy, time to recuperate his forces and to prepare for a final struggle, the prize of which would be infinitely richer than any that had hitherto attracted his inordinate ambition.

This prize was nothing less than the entire dominions of the Span-

---

8. Creasy, *Decisive Battles of the World*: ch. 11., "The Battle of Blenheim."

ish monarchy, comprising, in addition to modern Spain, Naples, Sicily, Finale, the Tuscan ports, the Milanese, the Spanish Netherlands, and vast possessions in the New World. Charles II, who was rapidly sinking into the grave, had no immediate heirs. The claimants to the succession were three in number, the Emperor Leopold I, Joseph, the Electoral Prince of Bavaria, and the Dauphin. In each ran the blood of a Spanish princess. The title of each was in some respect defective.

But it was obvious to Louis and to every statesman that Europe would never permit this question to be settled as if it were a private lawsuit. It was obvious that she would not welcome a King of Spain who was also Emperor, and still less a King of Spain who was also King of France. Either arrangement would be perilously subversive of 'the balance of power.' Both Louis and Leopold recognised this fact. The Dauphin's claim was accordingly withdrawn in favour of his second son, Philip, Duke of Anjou, and Leopold's in favour of his, the Archduke Charles. But this device was more satisfactory in appearance than in reality.

The objections to the new candidates, if not insuperable, were still very grave. In the first place, by the accidents of life the kingdom of France might still revert to Philip, and the Empire to Charles. And secondly, if either France or Austria supplied a prince for the throne of Spain, either France or Austria might expect to use him as a faithful ally, if not as an obedient vassal. An overwhelming combination of forces might still result. An intimate alliance of two powers may be just as disturbing to the equilibrium of Europe as an actual union of crowns. The danger was of course far greater in the case of Philip. France was already so strong that nothing less than a grand coalition of states could curb her ambition even when she stood alone.

The secret of her success lay not so much in the wealth and enterprise of her people as in the organising capacity of her rulers. Under French direction and control the latent resources of the Spanish dominions, which needed only capital and energy for their development, might have produced incalculable riches. But the question was even more a strategic than an economic one. The armies of France, in numbers, in science, and in audacity, excelled all others. Admitted by Philip to the Spanish Netherlands, they would speedily conquer Holland, and convert it into a military and naval base against England and Germany; admitted to the Milanese, they would threaten Vienna itself through the passes of the Tyrol. Masters of Sicily, Naples, and the Tuscan ports, they would dominate all Italy south of the Po. With Philip astride of the Straits of Gibraltar, they would transform the Mediterranean Sea into "a Bourbon lake," exclusively reserved for the galleons of Cadiz and the galleys of Toulon.

The ideal solution of the problem was apparent. Joseph, the Electoral Prince of Bavaria, should have inherited the Spanish dominions in their entirety. Being but a child of five, he could have been educated as a Spaniard; and throughout his minority at any rate his subjects would have insisted on a foreign policy devoid of subservience to either Austria or France. The Spaniards themselves would have welcomed such a settlement. William also would have welcomed it. But William had a single eye to the peace and the liberties of Europe. Louis and Leopold, on the contrary, thought solely of their own aggrandisement. They would never consent to withdraw their candidates in favour of Joseph. And William was not in a position to coerce them.

But Louis at least was not unreasonable. Though he claimed the whole, he was prepared to accept a part. France was still too exhausted to renew the struggle which had forced her to accept the treaty of Ryswick. If the question of the Spanish succession could be settled peaceably on the basis of adequate compensation for the various candidates, Louis would be satisfied. Early in 1698 he sounded William on the subject. William, though at first suspicious, was soon convinced of his old antagonist's sincerity. Long and arduous negotiations ensued.

At length, in October, 1698, England, Holland, and France signed what is known as the first Partition Treaty. The three powers agreed among themselves that, at the death of Charles II, the Milanese should pass to the Archduke, Naples, Sicily, the Tuscan ports, Guipuzcoa, San Sebastian, and Fuenterrabia to the Duke of Anjou, and the residue of the Spanish dominions to the Electoral Prince.

The treaty, though secret, soon became public property. It was none too well received. The indignation of the haughty Spaniards knew no bounds. That foreign potentates should presume, though only upon paper, to dismember the Empire of Philip II was an outrage not to be endured. Leopold too looked coldly on a settlement which had been made without reference to him, and which assigned to the House of Hapsburg so much less than he judged to be its due. It is certain that effect would never have been given to the terms of the treaty without a struggle of some kind.

But it is almost as certain that the struggle would not have been of long duration. For the persons aggrieved could have offered no effective resistance. Sentimental Liberalism has wasted many tears on the cynical immorality of the three powers. But the partition of an empire, composed of various nationalities, differs essentially from the vivisection of an homogeneous state. It is true that Castilian pride was hurt; but the ethical value of Castilian pride may be overrated. The scheme was conceived in the interest of peace and of the liberties of Europe as a whole.

It yielded possibly too much to France in the Mediterranean, though even here, by leaving the Straits of Gibraltar in Spanish hands, and by introducing the Austrians into the Milanese, it established strategic checks of an effective kind. The fact that William himself supported the arrangement, is perhaps the strongest of all proofs that it would have solved a perilous problem with the smallest possible disturbance of 'the balance of power.'

But the issue was never tried. In February, 1699, the death of the Electoral Prince of Bavaria destroyed the very basis of the compromise. Louis and William however were not discouraged. They resumed negotiations, and by May they had arrived at a second settlement. It was now agreed that the Archduke Charles should take the place of the deceased prince, and should inherit the greater part of the Spanish dominions. The Duke of Anjou was to receive the same compensation as fell to him under the earlier treaty. But the Archduke was to resign the Milanese in favour of France on the understanding that France would then bestow it on the Duke of Lorraine in exchange for his duchy, which in fact, if not in law, was already French.

On paper it appeared that 'the balance of power' was better preserved by the second partition than by the first. The House of Hapsburg secured an accession of territory and of potential wealth much in excess of that allotted to the House of Bourbon. But in forfeiting the Milanese the Hapsburgs lost a strategic position of immense value. What would have been the ultimate result can only be surmised. For the second Partition Treaty met with no better fate than the first.

The great majority of the Spanish nation, without any distinction of class, were resolutely determined to uphold the unity of the empire. As soon as the contents of the first Partition Treaty were divulged, the dying King declared the Electoral Prince to be the heir of his entire dominions, and sent for him to Madrid that he might be educated as a Spaniard. The prince's death created a dilemma. The ties of blood and of friendship drew both King and people towards the Austrian claimant. A century of war had left them little love for France. But gradually the opinion grew that France was the only power sufficiently strong to maintain against all comers the integrity of the Spanish Empire.

This opinion was skilfully fostered by Harcourt, the brilliant ambassador of Louis at Madrid. France in that age was as ably served by her diplomatists as by her soldiers. The Queen, who was Leopold's sister-in-law, pleaded the cause of Austria at her husband's bedside. But her influence was neutralised by the influence of the Church, and was ultimately overborne by the passionate patriotism of an indignant nation. In November, 1700, the end came. When Charles' testament was opened, it was found that he had bequeathed his empire in its entirety to Philip, Duke of Anjou, on the sole condition that he should renounce, for himself and for his heirs, all claim to the crown of France. If Philip declined to benefit under the will, the inheritance was to pass to the Archduke Charles.

It has been suggested by some among English historians that Louis from the outset had played for this result, and that the Partition Treaties, initiated though they were by his diplomacy, were merely an elaborate device for gaining time. Louis was perfectly capable of such duplicity. But there is no convincing proof that he was guilty of it. Although the possibility of a will in Philip's favour had never been wholly absent from his calculations, it was a possibility upon which he had scarcely dared to reckon. The event took him by surprise. When the Spanish envoys arrived at Paris, he hesitated. His indecision was genuine.

It did not spring from any sense of obligation under the treaty which he had so recently signed. It originated solely in a doubt as to the true interest of France at this momentous juncture. Louis wanted the whole Spanish monarchy; but he did not want it at the price of a bloody and prolonged struggle with a coalition of the powers. That Austria would fight was certain. But the wrath of Leopold had no terrors for Louis. One man, and only one, could make him pay too dearly for the prize. That man was William of Orange.

William's health was visibly decaying. But his spirit and his brain retained their vigour, Louis was too prudent to gamble on the chance of his great antagonist's decease. He looked for a certainty, and in the military and political infirmity of England he thought that he had found one. The English people wanted peace, and the English people were unready for war. Those two circumstances determined the fate of Europe. No coalition which left out England could greatly trouble the combined forces of France and Spain. Even William could not make bricks without straw. Confident that his perfidy would not be punished, Louis broke his plighted word and dispatched his grandson to Madrid.

Of all the dangers to peace none is at once so constant and so grave as unpreparedness for war. This truth, which for most of mankind is a truism, has always been steadily ignored in England. Pursuing its fatuous policy of false economy, the English Parliament in time of peace has over and over again insisted on reducing the military forces of the Crown to something indistinguishable from a mere skeleton. Such a system is always wasteful and extravagant; in the years which followed the peace of Ryswick it was particularly perilous. Louis and William, and all who understood the European situation, knew that that treaty was only an armistice, and that the impending question of the Spanish succession would be settled, if not by an appeal to arms, at least by those and in favour of those who were obviously able to appeal to arms.

But the people of England did not understand the European situation, and they did not want to understand it. Weary of taxation and disgusted by defeat, they had compelled William to cut down the standing army to 7,000 men in England and 12,000 in Ireland, and to dismiss 5,000 Dutch and Huguenots. The King had resisted, but he had been constrained to yield. All the Tories, and almost all the Whigs, were united on this question. The English of both parties had no proper comprehension of foreign politics. They could not see the dangerous absurdity of disbanding their forces while Louis maintained his own upon a war footing. The Tories refused to listen to the warnings of a monarch, whose policy, in their judgement, involved the sacrifice of England's interests to those of Holland.

Though the Whigs at any rate had supported William in the recent war, they had been actuated more by hatred of the House of Stuart and a quixotic devotion to the cause of Protestantism in general than by any intelligent desire to redress the balance of power in Europe. These motives had now ceased to operate with their original force. At Ryswick Louis had acknowledged William's title. Nor was it a matter of vital concern to the cause of Protestantism whether the Papist who became ruler of the inveterate Papists of the Spanish Empire was a Frenchman or an Austrian.

"There is," wrote Somers to the King in 1698, "a deadness and want of spirit in the nation universally."[9]

Our forefathers' ignorance of continental politics was not with-

---

9. Macaulay's *Essays*: vol. 1., *The War of the Succession in Spain*.

out some excuse. With the exception of one brilliant interlude under Cromwell, England, absorbed in her domestic altercations, had played but a trivial part in Europe since the death of Elizabeth. And there was some excuse also for the Englishman's dislike of the professional soldier. All the great despotisms, which had arisen on the ruins of feudal institutions, maintained their standing armies and did not hesitate to use them against disaffected subjects. The idea of a standing army had come therefore to be associated with the idea of arbitrary power; and the not very logical conclusion was drawn that these permanent forces were incompatible with the existence of constitutional rule.

Bookish Whigs, familiar with the chronicles of Greece and Rome, drove home the argument with illustrations culled from the stories of the classic tyrants. Doubtless they were mistaken. Doubtless those military writers, who have so bitterly censured the traditional antipathy of the House of Commons to a standing army, have just reason for their indignation. But if ever there was a period in English history when this ignoble, but seemingly imperishable, superstition was founded upon something more worthy than unthinking prejudice, that period was the second half of the seventeenth century. In those days, at any rate, ignorance of the subject could not be ascribed to the English people.

It could not be said of that generation, as it might have been said of its predecessors, that Englishmen, with the exception of the few who had travelled or served upon the continent, had no experience of standing armies. For they themselves had seen, or their own fathers had seen, what was perhaps the most formidable and efficient body of organised, fighting men that the world has ever produced. Neither the veteran mercenaries of Tilly and Wallenstein, nor the habitually victorious soldiery of Condé and Turenne, could have stood for long, in equal numbers, before the army of Cromwell. And the conduct of that army in peace had been no less remarkable than its prowess in war. Other troops, and not alone those which were composed of hired aliens, were frequently as great a terror to their friends as to their foes.

The subsistence of even a national army on its own territories was often calamitous to whole provinces. But the behaviour of Cromwell's men in the presence of civilian populations was at that epoch unexampled in Europe. In this, as in most other respects, the 'New Model' had been a model to the world and to all time. In discipline it has never been surpassed. Moreover, unlike those gallant regiments which astonished Europe at Blenheim, at Fontenoy, and at Minden, and which in a later age destroyed the empire of Bonaparte, Cromwell's army was recruited in the main from self-respecting men of decent station and repute. It would be natural therefore to presume that an institution, so creditable to the English name, was at least popular with contemporary Englishmen. And yet, to almost all classes and parties in the state, its very name was execrable.

The explanation is simple, The 'New Model' was the product of the Great Rebellion. The Great Rebellion had been begun by a faction, who conceived themselves to be fighting for the supremacy of law. They took their stand, as for that matter did also their opponents, upon the principles, written and unwritten, of the English constitution. Their quarrel with Charles I was, in its inception, a respectable quarrel. Yet to what a grotesque issue did they, or the discredited remnant of them, ultimately bring it! Contrary to the laws, they degraded and destroyed the House of Commons and the House of Peers. Contrary to the laws, they overthrew the Church.

Contrary to the laws, though not without an insulting travesty of legal forms, they killed the King. Contrary to the laws, they substituted for the venerable monarchy of England a perpetual military dictatorship. The Rebellion had been preceded by disputes about arbitrary taxation, about the billeting of soldiers, and about the administration of justice by special commissions, disputes in which both sides were able to appeal to the indubitable records of the past. It ended in a system of martial law, which is no law, and which had no foundations in English history.

Every action in the drama had been accompanied by the clash of steel and the roll of drums. When England looked back upon that distracted period, she saw the 'New Model' like "the abomination of desolation, standing where it ought not." She saw soldiers using her cathedrals for stables, and soldiers testifying in the pulpits of her parish churches, soldiers at the doors of the House of Commons, soldiers on the floor of the House itself, soldiers innumerable about the scaffold of a King. She understood that a faction, which had not hesitated to make war upon the legitimate Sovereign because he was suspected of a dangerous desire to strain the prerogative of his ancestors, had itself set up a tyranny that beside the wildest dreams of Charles or his advisers would have seemed extravagant. And she fully realised that this tyranny was raised and supported solely by the pikes and muskets of a regular army of 50,000 men.

It was irrelevant, and it was felt to be irrelevant, to plead that in certain directions Cromwell had put his authority to noble uses. Many despots have governed well. Many more have wished to govern well. And one and all they have based their claims upon the public good. Charles himself had the best intention, and honestly declared, even with his dying breath, that he sought only the well-being of his people. All such considerations are beside the point. Those who appealed to precedent and law had themselves obliterated all precedent and all law with blood and steel. The monstrous irony of such a consummation was too much even for a people which has invariably divorced logic from its politics.

When the Great Rebellion began, it had appeared to be a solemn tragedy. Long before it ended, it was seen to be a violent and sanguinary farce. And the 'New Model' was the villain of the piece. Such were the real causes why a generation, which had witnessed so splendid and unprecedented a military portent, had no desire to see another.

After the peace of Ryswick, therefore, a House of Commons which faithfully represented the country's collective ignorance of foreign politics and its ineradicable prejudice against professional soldiers, had fixed the numbers of the regular army at the very inadequate figure of 7,000 men in England, and 12,000 in Ireland. The navy indeed was already the first in Europe. And already the nation had taken to its bosom the abominable fallacy that effective war can be waged upon the sea alone. But both Louis and William knew the truth. At this great crisis of European history England counted for nothing.

Philip was proclaimed without opposition at Naples and Brussels. His claims to the French crown were expressly reserved by Louis. The French fleet took station at Cadiz, and squadrons sailed for America and the Indies. But the peace remained unbroken. Not a shot was fired by any of those powers which had been members of the Grand Alliance. They, who in the past had freely expended their blood and treasure to prevent some comparatively trivial additions to the preponderance of France, seemed paralysed now in the presence of this sudden and gigantic peril. They looked to William for a sign; but for once the oracle was dumb.

State after state acknowledged Philip as King of Spain. But still the Emperor and the Dutch stood out. The Emperor was aiming for the assertion of his rights. But the Dutch lay open to intimidation. On the French side the frontier fortresses of the Spanish Netherlands had been garrisoned, since the treaty of Ryswick, by the soldiers of

Holland. The governor of the Spanish Netherlands was the Elector of Bavaria, who had been completely gained by Louis. With his connivance, a French army under Boufflers passed the border, and early in February, 1701, surprised the towns of the 'Dutch Barrier' with all their garrisons intact.

The flower of the infantry of Holland, 15,000 in all, became the prisoners of France. This swift and stealthy stroke, so characteristic of Louis' government, and indeed of all governments which have cherished ambitions similar to his, brought the Dutchmen to their knees. Louis, having exacted his price, released his captives. But now the north-eastern frontier of his power ran not from Calais to Metz but from Antwerp to Liège and Luxembourg. And Holland trembled.

England, so far as observers could judge, remained unmoved. The menace to her sea-borne trade and even the disappearance of the 'Dutch Barrier' and the occupation of the Spanish Netherlands by the French forces left English opinion strangely cold, so far at any rate as English opinion found expression in the House of Commons. In the course of 1699 and 1700 William had gradually got rid of most of his Whig ministers, who had proved themselves incapable of managing the Commons according to his wishes. He had given their places to Tories. Rochester Was the chief of the new Cabinet, and Godolphin, at the King's special request, had accepted the Treasury.

In November, 1700, there was a general election. The new House contained a large Tory majority. These men, country squires for the most part, disliked the notion of a continental war, because it would involve taxation of their estates and the enrichment of the financial classes which lent money to the government, and because, as they ignorantly believed, it would be waged at England's expense in the sole interest of England's ancient rival, Holland. In February, 1701, the Parliament met. Harley was elected Speaker. William desired them "to consider the state of affairs abroad."

The Commons replied by an address, in which they promised to "take measures for the interest and safety of England, the preservation of the Protestant religion, and the peace of Europe." But they declined to concur in the address of the Peers, which desired the King "to enter into alliances with all those princes and states who were willing to unite for the preservation of the balance of Europe."[10]

The Dutch, who at this time were as anxious for peace as were the English Tories, were negotiating with France with the object of

---
10. Dalrymple, *Memoirs of Great Britain and Ireland* (1790), vol. 3., book 9., p. 212.

obtaining a new barrier in place of the one which they had just lost. They begged William to support their diplomacy, and also to prepare the 10,000 men and the twenty ships of war, which England by the treaty of 1677 was bound to furnish in the event of an attack on Holland. William laid the correspondence before the Commons, who in reply charged him to keep the treaty of 1677, and to keep the peace, if possible.

Truth to tell, the Tory politicians were more eager to take vengeance on the fallen ministers than to provide for the safety of Europe. They severely censured both the substance of the now obsolete partition-treaties and the clandestine manner in which those treaties had been arranged. Yet it was certain that the King had not exceeded his constitutional powers; and it was ridiculous for men, who for the sake of peace were acquiescing in the absorption by Louis of the whole Spanish monarchy, to complain that schemes, deliberately framed in the interests of peace, had assigned too large a share to France. The object of the majority was merely factious. They wanted to discredit the last Whig ministry, and they intended to impeach it. They discovered that the Tory Jersey had been deeply concerned in the business of the partition-treaties, and that the Tory Marlborough was one of those who had been consulted.

Yet they selected the four Whigs, Portland, Halifax, Orford, and Somers for impeachment, and ignored the rest. By this procedure they stultified themselves, and exposed the vindictive nature of their aims. The two Houses quarrelled as to the time and mode of the trial. The Commons failed to appear, and a majority of the Lords acquitted the accused. A minority, siding with the Commons, protested vigorously. With this minority Marlborough voted. Both Wolseley and Coxe express regret and astonishment that one, so opposed to partisan excesses, should have identified himself with this factious cause. They also assume that his conduct must have been displeasing to William, whose favour he was anxious to retain.

And they point out that two of the accused, Halifax and Orford, were his friends. But if Halifax and Orford were his friends, Portland was his enemy. And Marlborough may also have resented the attempt of the late ministry to involve him in their responsibility. In any case it is unsafe to assume that his vote was displeasing to the King. William cared nothing for either Whigs or Tories. But he was obliged to placate one party or the other, if supplies were to be obtained. At the moment he was trying to placate the Tories. It may well have been that he desired his known friends and advisers to vote in accordance with the wishes of his new ministers and of the predominant party in the House of Commons.

While the chosen of the people were exhibiting their stupid and degraded partisanship at Westminster, France was steadily tightening her grip on Europe. William was pressed by the Cabinet to follow the example of Holland and to acknowledge Philip as King of Spain. The Dutch, in the interests of immediate peace, urged him to accept this advice. In April he yielded, and dispatched a letter of congratulation to Philip.

But at last, after its own sullen fashion, the temper of the English people was beginning to smoulder. Always deficient in imagination, and always unable to project their minds into futurity, they are seldom moved by anything short of accomplished facts. Slowly they were beginning to realise that France, by a stroke of the pen, was become mistress of half Europe, and prospective mistress of the rest. The danger to Holland was now imminent and visible. And if Holland fell, how long would England stand? Yet this was the moment which the gentlemen of the House of Commons had selected for an ignoble faction fight.

No wonder the King retired to Hampton Court and appeared to have abandoned all interest in the country's affairs. The King, after all, might well have been right from the beginning; the King understood these matters; if only the King had been permitted to retain a respectable army, the liberties of Europe would never have fallen into such grievous peril. Thus with its habitual and honest inconsistency the nation reasoned. But they did more. They spoke their minds with a loudness and a freedom that were peculiarly unwelcome to the House of Commons. The men of Kent sent up a petition, requesting that assembly to drop domestic brawls and address itself to the nation's business. The House was furious, and by a tyrannical abuse of its privileges committed the bearers of the petition to prison. Passions became more and more inflamed.

In the country it was openly alleged that certain of the Tory majority in the House were in the pay of France. The circulation of an extraordinary number of French coins lent colour to the charge. But the Tories retorted that, if Louis had really found it worth his while to bribe anybody in England, the persons selected must have been those ministers who had concurred in the partition-treaties, which France had so ardently promoted and by which she stood to gain so much.[11]

---

11. *Tom Double* (1704), p. 21.

The Speaker, on the other hand, received a singular memorial, purporting to come from 200,000 Englishmen, and threatening the Commons with popular vengeance, if they persisted in sacrificing the public's safety to the malice of partisanship.

"For Englishmen," it concluded, "are no more to be slaves to Parliaments than to a King—our name is Legion, and we are many."[12]

The House began to be frightened as well as angry. But nothing happened. "Legion" was only Daniel Defoe, who loved a hoax, especially when it conveyed and emphasised a truth. But the clamour of the constituencies grew deeper and more menacing. The full significance of Philip's succession had come home at last. The Spanish fortresses were in the occupation of French armies; the Spanish trade-routes were patrolled by French fleets; the commerce of the Indies and the Levant was declared by French proclamations to be reserved for France and Spain. By May the French had drawn defensive lines from Antwerp to the Meuse, and were drawing others from Antwerp to Ostend. They had prepared immense magazines, and were erecting forts under the very noses of the Dutch.

Louis had essayed to inveigle the States-General into a separate treaty; but the States-General had taken the dykes, and had appealed to the English people. And this time the appeal was not in vain. The Tories in the Commons awoke to the fatuity of their proceedings. The House resolved unanimously "that they would effectually assist His Majesty to support his allies in maintaining the liberty of Europe."[13]

Unanimously also they presented an address to the effect that "they would be ready on all occasions to assist him, in supporting such alliances as he should think fit to make in conjunction with the Emperor and States-General, for the preservation of the liberties of Europe, the prosperity and peace of England, and for reducing the exorbitant power of France."[14] And they voted the necessary supplies, which, as Speaker Harley declared to the King, "were more than ever were given in a time of peace, to enable him, when he was abroad, to support his allies, to procure either a lasting peace, or to preserve the liberties of Europe by a necessary war."[15]

---

12. Defoe, *Legion's Memorial* (1701)
13. *The Life of King William III*. (1705), p. 609.
14. *Ibid.*, p. 616.
15. *Ibid.*, p. 618.

Meantime, the question of the succession, which had been rendered urgent by the Duke of Gloucester's death, had been duly settled. If William and Anne should both die childless, the crown was entailed by Act of Parliament on the Protestant branch of the Stuart family, the House of Hanover. But the Commons had seized this opportunity of restricting the royal prerogative. The Act declared, for example, that henceforth no King of England should quit these islands, or engage in a war in defence of foreign territory, without the consent of Parliament. It also prohibited the admission of foreigners to the public service. Such conditions were regarded as a censure upon William's conduct. But William minded them no more than he minded the wrangling of the parties and the Houses over the impeachment of the four lords. He was satisfied that the order of the succession had been properly fixed. He was more than satisfied that addresses so encouraging and supplies so ample had been voted him at last.

He had watched with pleasure the awakening of public sentiment in England. But he had not been idle. He had been secretly encouraging the Emperor to send an army into Northern Italy. An early success in the field might arouse the martial spirit of the powers which had formerly been united in the Grand Alliance. To unite them again for the greatest conflict, and the last, was now the work to which he devoted the whole of his rapidly declining strength. But he recognised that he was no longer equal to the labour involved. It was necessary to find a man, who would relieve him of the burden of diplomatic and military preparation. It was necessary that this man should be an English-born subject, and, if possible, a Tory.

William believed that Marlborough was incomparably the best soldier and the best negotiator in the three kingdoms. But these qualifications alone were not sufficient. The struggle which was coming would far outlast the King's life. It was therefore desirable that the man whom he now selected should be one who could reasonably expect to retain the confidence of his successor. By nobody was this condition so thoroughly satisfied as by Marlborough. As Shrewsbury had foreseen, Marlborough's reversion was "very fair."[16]

He was therefore the man marked out by destiny to carry on the work of William's life. William turned to him without hesitation. In June, 1701, to the unconcealed disgust of Ormond and other important personages, the Earl was appointed Commander of the Forces in

---

16. Shrewsbury, *Correspondence* (1821), p. 220: The Duke of Shrewsbury to Admiral Russell, January 29, 1694-5.

Flanders, and also Ambassador Extraordinary and Plenipotentiary to the States of Holland. Never did William exhibit a more signal proof of greatness. All the evil years of doubt and suspicion, all the intrigue and jealousy and petty treason were forgotten. The man whom he had most feared in the past was the man whom he most trusted for the future. The power of detecting capacity in others is a rare and valuable power. But the power of ignoring the extraneous, of subordinating the accidental, of suppressing the merely personal, and of concentrating completely on a single and sublime aim, is genius.

Marlborough was equipped with ample funds, with the customary allowance of plate, and with permission to expend whatever sums he might consider necessary on secret service. On July 1 he sailed with William from Margate for the Hague. In Holland he was little known, except by reputation; but he was welcomed as the man whom William was delighted to honour. His presence, and the powers with which he was clothed, were regarded as a pledge of England's loyal support in the time of trial. The States-General assigned him the mansion of Prince Maurice as his official residence. Here he conducted conferences and received ambassadors. And here he commenced that multifarious correspondence with Godolphin, with the Duchess, and with an ever enlarging circle of princes, statesmen, soldiers, and diplomatists, both at home and on the continent, which continued throughout the remainder of his public life, and which presents to posterity an unrivalled picture of his character and work.

The immediate business before him was the reconstruction of the Grand Alliance. So far as France was concerned, he was empowered to negotiate on the basis of the withdrawal of the French troops from the Spanish Netherlands, and of the surrender of Ostend and Nieuport to England, and Luxembourg, Namur, and Mons to the Dutch. But these negotiations were not regarded seriously by either side. Unlike too many of his countrymen both then and now, Marlborough understood that, in dealing with governments such as that of Louis XIV, and indeed in dealing with any governments whatsoever, diplomacy is idle waste of time, unless it be supported by adequate force.

He therefore devoted the utmost of his energies to the renewal of that compact which was the only known check to French ambition. His task was not an easy one. England, Holland, and Austria were agreed in thinking that the power of France was exorbitant, but they were agreed in little else. Holland, provided she could secure the restoration of her barrier, and the Emperor if he could obtain the entire

Spanish Empire for the Archduke Charles, adhered to the principle of a partition. England was willing to accept any arrangement which would preserve the balance of power and guarantee the freedom of trade with the Spanish Indies and the Levant. It required both time and temper to bring the three parties to an adjustment, Marlborough's patience and tact overcame all obstacles.

Early in September the treaty was signed. England and Holland pledged themselves to demand compensation for the Emperor. If Louis proved obdurate, war was to be waged with the full strength of the three powers, and with the immediate object of conquering the Spanish dominions in Italy for Austria and of recovering the Spanish Netherlands "that they may be a barrier separating the United Provinces from France." William had been willing to restrict the Emperor's share of Italy to the Milanese alone; but Marlborough, who understood the value of sea power, and who had recognised the justice of one of the criticisms passed on the partition-treaties, insisted that, in no circumstances, should Naples and Sicily be left to France.

And it was Marlborough who, in conjunction with Heinsius, procured the insertion of a clause assigning to England and Holland respectively whatever conquests they could make in the western world. Nevertheless the completed instrument left much to be desired. It lacked precision, because the divergent interests of the signatories rendered precision well-nigh impossible. If, for example, the Spanish Netherlands should be recovered, in whom would the sovereignty rest? Although the preamble implied that it would rest in the Archduke, the silence of the treaty itself upon the point left room for Dutch pretensions. For this, and other ambiguities, the allies paid dearly at a later date.

The question of the number of troops which each of the allies should furnish had still to be determined. The negotiations were long and difficult. At length, by a subsidiary treaty, the quotas were fixed at 90,000 Austrians, 10,000 Dutch, and 40,000 English, or troops in English pay. But the Grand Alliance had other resources. The treaty was so drawn that other powers could subscribe to it, if they chose, though not as principals. Marlborough accordingly approached the King of Denmark, who agreed to furnish 5,000 men at once, and 20,000 at a later date.

Louis has been censured for permitting his enemies to organise their forces, when he might have fallen upon them unprepared.[17] It

---

17. See, for example, Feuquières, t. 2, ch. 53., pp. 261-267.

has been contended that he ought never to have released the Dutch garrisons, and that if he had followed up that stroke by the seizure of Holland, he would have held Europe at his mercy. But governments like that of Louis do not desire war for its own sake. They know that it is cheaper to win by the threat of war than by war itself. It is therefore with absolute truth that they always represent themselves as confirmed lovers of peace. Louis had got what he wanted without fighting, and he hoped to retain it without fighting. And he had excellent chances in his favour—the notorious conflict of interest between Austria and Holland, the doubtful conduct of the English Parliament, the probability of William's early decease, and above all, the imposing aspect of the united forces of France and Spain.

Furthermore, while his former antagonists were arming and confabulating, his own consummate diplomacy did not stand idle. It was busily directed to the prudent purpose of securing the alliance of certain princes, who, though comparatively feeble in themselves, ruled over territories, which, at this juncture, possessed a high strategical value. The Kingdom of Portugal was the only base from which the enemy could attack Spain by land. The Duchy of Savoy was indispensable to the maintenance of communications between France and Italy. The Electorate of Bavaria, astride of the Danube, and seated in the very heart of the Empire itself, laid bare the road to Vienna.

And the Electorate of Cologne, while it threatened the Dutch upon their flank, severed the communications of Holland and England with the Upper Rhine. These four states constituted four military positions of the first importance. Their rulers, set between the fleets and armies of the Bourbons on the one hand and the inchoate mass of unready and uncertain powers upon the other, exercised no real freedom of choice. Intimidation, blended with bribery, made them, in appearance at any rate, the satellites of France. Their adhesion to Louis, by augmenting his military superiority, still further diminished the probability of war.

In pursuance of the same wise policy Louis endeavoured to create a diversion in his enemies' rear by courting the friendship of Charles XII of Sweden. This youthful monarch had recently astonished Europe by his swift and sudden triumphs over Denmark, Poland, and Russia, which had wantonly attacked him. It seemed for the moment that Gustavus had come again. The allies, who were counting upon Danish aid, viewed with apprehension the possibility of a renewal of hostilities between Sweden and Denmark. They also feared lest

Charles should call upon England for that armed assistance, which in certain eventualities she was bound by treaty to provide. Louis was exerting himself to cajole the Swede and to corrupt his ministers, when Marlborough intervened. He too spared neither money nor fine words. And he won the game Charles, who was jealous of France, and who had good reason to value the alliance of England, agreed that he would give no help to Louis. He also agreed that England should compound in money for the men, whom at this juncture she could ill have spared.

If Marlborough's diplomacy succeeded, it succeeded in spite of obstacles, of which the conflict of Dutch and Austrian interests was only one. In Holland there were men who still believed in a pacific settlement, and whose existence encouraged Louis in his efforts to split the Grand Alliance. In England there were Tory ministers who regarded with cold suspicion the continental activities of even a Tory plenipotentiary. Marlborough was continually engaged in educating his party in the meaning and the necessities of the European situation. On the other hand, he was compelled to moderate the too impetuous temper of the King. In opposition to William's wishes, he insisted that all treaties must be submitted to the Lords Justices in London for signature, and the numbers of the British contingent must be regarded as provisional until they should receive the ratification of Parliament.

William, who never understood the English character, was impatient of these delays. But Marlborough had grasped the supreme importance of maintaining good relations between the Crown and the dominant majority in the Cabinet and the House of Commons. On the brink of a great war he realised that unity was more valuable even than time itself. Yet he knew when to break his own rules. The treaty with Sweden he signed upon his own responsibility, because he dared not allow the impulsive Charles an opportunity of changing his mind.

It is obvious that the position in which Marlborough now found himself tested to the uttermost his qualities of courage, discretion, and sagacity. Nor was he free to devote the whole of his time and energy to the business of diplomacy alone. All through the summer and autumn the British troops were steadily arriving. As commander of the forces, he was bound to supervise the arrangements for their reception. He was bound also to assist the King in organising the military establishment of Holland. Recruits must be clothed, fortresses inspected, reviews held, and every preparation made to take the field in the highest state of efficiency for war.

Meantime the policy of William had been materially advanced by good news from Northern Italy. Here a French army under Catinat had occupied the fortresses, and set a watch upon the passes of the Tyrol on the side of Verona. In May the Emperor assembled 30,000 men at Roveredo, and placed them under the command of Eugène of Savoy, the conqueror of the Turks. Instead of descending where the French expected him, Eugène struck south-east in the direction of Vicenza, and after a long and arduous march came down into the territories of Venice. He encountered no resistance, the same judicious policy which had led Louis to release the Dutch garrisons having led him also to respect Venetian neutrality. Arrived upon level ground, Eugène swept all before him.

Deceiving Catinat by skilful movements, he passed the Adige, beat the French at Chiari and Carpi, and drove them over the Mincio and Oglio. Catinat was superseded by the far less competent Villeroi, who rashly attacked the Austrians in their entrenched camp at Chiari, and was repulsed with a loss of over 2,000 men Eugène established himself firmly in Mantuan territory. Inferior in numbers, and operating without any base, he had nothing in his favour save the sympathy of the Italian population and his own genius. The spectacle of his rapid triumph had a salutary effect throughout Europe, It showed the waverers that the might of France was vulnerable, and that Austria had still the power to strike. On Prussia and Denmark and certain of the German princes the lesson was by no means thrown away.

In common with all great men who have achieved great success, Louis XIV made mistakes. Even since the death of Charles II of Spain he had made no fewer than three. It was a mistake, in accepting the crown for his grandson, to reserve the rights of Philip to the throne of France. It was a mistake to seize the 'Dutch Barrier' and to flood the Spanish Netherlands with French troops. And it was a mistake to advertise his design of excluding Dutch and English shipping from the Mediterranean and the Indies, These things were mistakes, because right policy demanded that he should lull Europe into a false security, and not alarm her by a premature and arrogant display of the power which he intended to abuse. But they were trivial errors in comparison wth the gigantic blunder which he now committed.

On September 17, 1701, James II of England died at St. Germain. By a clause in the treaty of Ryswick Louis was pledged to render no assistance to the enemies of William's title. But now, in a moment of proud and chivalrous compassion, he caused "the pretended Prince of Wales," the boy who quartered the lilies of France upon his arms, to be proclaimed King of England on French soil, by French heralds, and to the fanfares of French trumpets. Every French heart was touched by the *pathos* and the magnanimity of the deed.

When the news was brought to William at Loo, where he sat at table with some German princes, he flushed deeply, and pulled his hat low down upon his brows. The insult stung; but there was balm in the wound. At last his antagonist had played into his hand. Little as William understood his subjects, he had lived with them enough and suffered from them enough to see at a glance that Louis had done what the English would never forgive. His own immediate duty was plain. He instructed the Earl of Manchester to quit Paris forthwith. He directed the Lords Justices to expel the French ambassador. Then he quietly waited.

He was not disappointed. England was roused at last. Even those who had remained unmoved by the spectacle of violated faith and threatened commerce were profoundly stirred by the proclamation of James III on French soil. Even those who had regarded 'the balance of power' as a tiresome abstraction, and the menace of a French hegemony of Europe as a figment of interested panic-mongers, could not endure that the ancient monarchy of England should become a part of the patronage of the House of Bourbon. The nation which had repudiated 'the Bishop of Rome' trembled with fury at the thought of a suzerain at Versailles. The nation which had long been notorious for its unreasoning dislike of foreigners was all aflame at the intervention of a foreign potentate in its domestic affairs.

The fact that Louis' action had the warm approval of his subjects was in English eyes an aggravation. That the French of all peoples should affect to pose as the champions of distressed monarchy appeared to Englishmen to be preposterous. Neither the French public nor the French Court had any respectable qualifications for the part. For a century and a half the French had made war upon their kings. Huguenots, Leaguers, Frondists, nobles, churchmen, magistrates, and rabble, the whole race had lived for generations on sedition and rebellion.

Two sovereigns of France had been assassinated in the streets of their own capital with the approval of vast multitudes of their own subjects. And as for the Court, within the memory of living Englishmen it had permitted a daughter of Henry of Navarre to starve in squalor at Paris; it had expelled a King of England at the bidding of the usurper, Cromwell; it had contracted an offensive alliance with that same usurper, who was not even, like William of Orange, of the blood royal; and it had put on mourning at his death, and advertised its grief to all Europe. That France, with such a record, should undertake to give lessons to England on the duty of loyalty, was at once ridiculous and intolerable.

But in truth, nobody in England, outside the circle of the Jacobites, believed in the magnanimous and quixotic character of Louis' action. Both Whigs and Tories regarded it as an attempt by a secular power to revive in its own favour the temporal claims of the Papacy. Henceforth the King of France was to make and unmake the kings of Europe. There were many Tories, who would have welcomed "the pretended Prince of Whales," had he thrown himself upon their loyalty. But at Louis' dictation no Tory would accept him for a King. At Louis' dictation no Tory would have accepted the Angel Gabriel himself. From all parts of the kingdom addresses poured in upon the Lords Justices, Some of them were couched in language of extreme violence. Some of them suggested that, if His Majesty would only dissolve Parliament, the country would know how to choose representatives that would be careful of its honour and its safety. All of them proclaimed the indignation and resentment of the English people.

Louis was astonished, and perhaps honestly, at the fury of the tempest which he had raised. He endeavoured to explain that his recognition of the Pretender amounted to nothing, William received his advances with contemptuous silence. The affront to his own dignity he might have overlooked. But high policy required him to treat the insult to the nation as unpardonable. The game was now in his own hands. Every mail from England brought him fresh proofs that he had the people at his back. And now Sunderland, whose opinion he had always valued, began to urge him to dismiss his Tory ministers, Heinsius offered him the same advice, Marlborough, who was not consulted, was aware of the intrigue and did what he could to frustrate it.

He induced Godolphin, who had taken the alarm and wanted to resign, to continue still in office. He took every opportunity of impressing upon William the expediency of trusting the Tories, And he even ventured to suggest that, if the Whigs were recalled, his own situation might become untenable. The King listened; but his mind was virtually made up. He could not resist the temptation to select a new Cabinet and to summon a new Parliament, That such a Cabinet and such a Parliament would vigorously support the policy of the Grand Alliance could hardly be doubted. Once and for all both France and Europe would be disabused of the notion that England, though unready, was afraid to fight. These were grave considerations. It is not to be supposed that Marlborough was blind to them. Still less was he actuated by the zeal of the partisan.

But in knowledge of his countrymen he had the advantage of both William and Heinsius, and in length of vision he was very superior to Sunderland. He knew that the sentiment of a clear majority of the nation was permanently Tory. He knew that a vast and protracted conflict by land and sea could only be properly conducted by a government that was supported by an undivided people. Whatever ministers were in office, the Whigs would enthusiastically favour a war with France. But if the Tories were excluded from power, sooner or later the Tory voters, who were also the largest taxpayers, would weary of the struggle, and would clamour for a premature peace. National unanimity, as the one reliable foundation for national war, was Marlborough's aim. And national unanimity could not be preserved throughout a lengthy period of hostilities, unless the King confided the administration to a Cabinet in which the chiefs of the Tory party held a distinct predominance.

But William was determined to reap the immediate benefit of Louis' folly. Illness and adverse winds detained him in Holland till the beginning of November. Then he sailed; and England accorded him a rapturous welcome. Marlborough, whom he left behind, ostensibly to complete the work of negotiation, but in reality because the Earl was opposed to a change of government, waited anxiously for news. It soon came. Godolphin had resigned. Parliament was dissolved. For a second time within twelve months the country was on the eve of a general election. Deeply depressed by the adoption of a policy for which he anticipated no permanent success, Marlborough returned home. The contest in the country was waged with excessive bitterness on both sides. Old Evelyn, now in his eighty-second year, noted in his diary for December that there were "great contentions about elections."[18]

Greater indeed have seldom been seen. But those who had foretold an overwhelming triumph for the Whigs were disappointed. The Whig minority was much increased; but it was still a minority. And when Parliament met at the end of December, by a majority

18. *Evelyn's Diary*, December, 1701.

of fourteen votes the Tory Harley was once more elected Speaker of the House of Commons. Yet the character of the House was entirely changed. All Jacobites, all secret and corrupted friends of France, and several of the more fanatical Tories, had disappeared. And the whole assembly, without distinction of party, was pledged to support the foreign policy of William. The spirit of Parliament and of the nation was well expressed in the instructions given by the City of London to its members, who were enjoined to assist His Majesty "to make good his alliances, and in conjunction with his allies, so to reduce the French King, that it might be no longer in his power to oppress and disturb the rest of Europe."[19]

William regarded himself as a dying man. That winter he told Portland in confidence that he did not expect to see another summer. When Parliament met, he addressed them in a speech, of which it has been truly said that it "was, as it were. His Majesty's last legacy to Britain."[20]

He began with a clear exposition of the case against France:

My Lords and Gentlemen,

By the French King's placing his grandson on the throne of Spain, he is in a condition to oppress the rest of Europe, unless speedy and effectual measures be taken. Under this pretence he is become the real master of the whole Spanish monarchy; he has made it to be entirely depending on France, and disposes of it as of his own dominions, and by that means he has surrounded his neighbours in such a manner that the name of peace may be said to continue, yet they are put to the expense and inconvenience of a war.

This must affect England in the nearest and most sensible manner: in respect to our trade, which will soon become precarious in all the valuable branches of it; in respect to our peace and safety at home, which we cannot hope should long continue; and in respect to that part which England ought to take in the preservation of the liberty of Europe.

In order to obviate the general calamity, with which the rest of Christendom is threatened by this exorbitant power of France, I have concluded several alliances according to encouragement given me by both Houses of Parliament, which I will direct

---

19. *The Life of King William III.*, p. 632.
20. *Ibid,,* p. 635

shall be laid before you, and which, I do not doubt, you will enable me to make good.

Thus, having stated the grounds for action, he proceeded to emphasise its urgency:

> It is fit, I should tell you, the eyes of all Europe are upon this Parliament, all matters are at a stand, till your resolutions are known, and therefore no time ought to be lost,
> You have yet an opportunity, by God's blessing, to secure to you and your posterity, the quiet enjoyment of your religion and liberties, if you are not wanting to yourselves, but will exert the ancient vigour of the English nation; but I tell you plainly, my opinion is, if you do not lay hold on this occasion, you have no reason to hope for another.

And he concluded with an appeal for that unity, which is vital to the proper conduct of a great war:

> I hope you are come together determined to avoid all manner of disputes and differences, and resolved to act with a general and hearty concurrence for promoting the common cause, which alone can make this a happy session.
> I should think it as great a blessing as could befall England, if I could observe you as much inclined to lay aside those unhappy, fatal animosities which divide and weaken you, as I am disposed to make all my subjects safe and easy as to any, even the highest offences committed against me.
> Let me conjure you to disappoint the only hopes of our enemies by your unanimity. I have shown, and will always show, how desirous I am to be the common Father of all my people; do you in like manner lay aside parties and divisions; let there be no other distinction heard of among us for the future, but of those who are for the Protestant Religion and the present Establishment, and of those who mean a Popish Prince and a French Government.[21]

"This speech," says Dalrymple, "was translated and published in every country of Europe, and roused princes and states, some by their policy, some by their religion, but all by their sentiment, like the sound of a trumpet, against France."[22]

---

21. Boyer, *The History of William III.* (1702), vol. 3., p. 505.
22. Dalrymple, part 3., p. 235.

The impression produced by language so direct, so spirited, and so pathetic on those who actually heard it, can easily be imagined. All the treaties were at once approved. A levy of 40,000 soldiers was voted; and 40,000 seamen were ordered for the fleet. In spite of the resistance of the extreme Tories, a Bill of Attainder against the Pretender, and a Bill of Abjuration, were quickly carried. But on February 20 William was thrown from his horse at Hampton Court, and broke his collarbone. The shock was greater than his enfeebled frame could bear. Fever set in; and by the first week in March he was seen by all men to be dying. Fearless as ever for himself, he thought of nothing now save the work which he must leave unfinished.

He thought of the weakness of the little island of Britain with its divided peoples and its separate Parliaments; and his last message to the Commons was a plea for that corporate communion which would consolidate the resources of England and Scotland in the face of the foe. And he thought above all of the man whom he had chosen to take up the burden which he himself was putting off; and with his failing breath he commended the Earl of Marlborough to the Princess Anne "as the fittest person in all her dominions to conduct her armies and to preside in her councils, as being a man of a cool head and a warm heart, proper to encounter the genius of France, suppressing her designs of swallowing all Europe."[23]

Of all the wrong which he conceived that Marlborough had done him, he remembered nothing now. He remembered only the still unaccomplished purpose of his own life; he considered only its ultimate fulfilment. Truly William was of those, who, as they pass down into the shadows, do but fix their eyes more firmly on the stars.

On March 8 he died. He was only fifty-two; but he was worn out with ceaseless toil. He had given his life for the liberties of Europe. And the words of Captain Shandy should be carved upon his tomb—*Brave, brave, by Heaven!*[24]

Thus he passed; and Whiggery and Liberalism have exalted his name for ever. They could hardly have selected a more singular idol, not even excepting Oliver Cromwell himself. A soldier by instinct, an aristocrat by temperament, an architect of empire by deliberate choice, he had little enough in common with their theories and ideals. By accident alone he figured as the champion of Protestantism and of Parliamentary rule. But those were not the causes which swayed

---

23. Lediard, *Life of the Duke of Marlborough* (1736), vol. 1, p. 136. 24. Sterne, *Tristram Shandy*, ch. 19.

his passions and controlled his life. To him they were not motives but merely opportunities. Yet England's debt to him is indeed immense. He was one of the greatest of her foreign ministers. From him she first derived a just appreciation of her place in Europe and a correct understanding of the course she ought to steer in the unfamiliar sea of international politics. This was his bequest to the English people, this—and Marlborough.

A gigantic conflict was now seen to be inevitable. All Europe now realised the magnitude of the peril. The nations realised it not less than the princes, A late, and a more sheltered posterity has lectured them, and scolded them, and explained to them how, if only they had understood it, their strength was "to sit still." But they, in their perversity, believed that at a certain point the aggrandisement of a single state ceases to be compatible with the independence of its neighbours. They believed that, when that point is reached, the law of self-preservation, to say nothing of the principle of self-respect, requires that those neighbours should combine for their own defence. And they believed that the French monarchy had long since passed the point in question.

This, and nothing else, was the real meaning of the so-called War of the Spanish Succession. This had been the meaning of the wars of the preceding twenty-five years. And this, a century later, was the meaning of the struggle which began in the year of Valmy and culminated in the year of Waterloo. The same issue is destined to be raised once more, as soon as ever the new Empire of Germany shall have completed those scientific and systematic preparations which, with a cynical disregard of all concealment, she has long been conducting in the face of Europe.

Only a superficial or a dishonest student could represent the War of the Spanish Succession as a 'dynastic war.' When Peterborough sarcastically enquired whether it were worthwhile for great nations to fight for "such a pair of louts" as Charles and Philip, he was well aware that great nations did not fight in causes of that character. It was neither for this prince nor for that prince that the states of Europe drew the sword, but solely for their own liberties. For at last the scales had fallen from every eye.

"We esteem it," said the House of Lords in an address to William two months before his death, "we esteem it a further good fortune in this time of public danger that the French King has taken those measures, which will make it impossible for him to impose any more upon the world by treaties, so often violated;

neither can he hope any longer to cover his ambitious designs, or justify his usurpations, under the specious pretensions of peace."[25]

Not all the smug philosophy of the nineteenth century, nor of the twentieth, can alter the fact that the true significance of 'the exorbitant power of France' was very well understood by those who had been spectators of its growth and sufferers from its activities.

It was however so complex and so vast a structure that only by careful analysis can the modern student obtain a clear comprehension of its real character. Its elements at the time of William's death were four. The first, and the greatest, was France herself, the second was the control obtained by France over the Spanish Empire, the third was the system of alliances which France had created in Europe, and the fourth and the most immediately menacing was the strategical situation which resulted from the combination of the other three.

France herself possessed a population of twenty millions. Her soil was fertile, her industries had been greatly developed, her administration was highly organised. In that unity, which a resolute and centralised government confers, she enjoyed a great advantage over the rest of Europe. Both her rulers and her people cherished inordinate ambitions, which they promoted by a tireless diplomacy as able as it was unscrupulous. And this diplomacy was backed by a fleet, which had not been afraid to encounter the navy of England, and by an army of 200,000 men, strong in the accumulated prestige of more than half a century of victory.

The acceptance by the Spanish people of a French prince for King of Spain virtually placed at the disposal of the French monarchy the financial and military resources of the Spanish Empire. These resources were far less than they had been, and infinitely less than they ought to have been. But they were latent and undeveloped rather than extinct. And they included strategical positions of immense value. They included the taxable capacity of the Spanish Nether lands, and the fighting capacity of troops, which, whatever they had now become, had been, within the memory of men still living, the most redoubtable in Europe. Such as the Spanish Empire was, it had hitherto been found upon the side of the coalised powers. Its transference to France 'counted two upon a division,' and constituted, without any other reason, a sufficient ground for hostilities.

---

25. *Journals of the House of Lords*, vol. 17.

By the judicious employment of bribery and intimidation France had secured the alliance of the King of Portugal, the Duke of Savoy, and the Electors of Bavaria and Cologne. The combined armies of these princes, amounting to more than 70,000 men, made up a respectable addition to the total of the forces at the call of the French government. The Duke of Savoy and the Elector of Bavaria were generals of some reputation; and the soldiers of both were of excellent quality. But these allies derived their main importance from the geographical situation of their territories.

The strategical advantage which the French monarchy had now acquired in Europe was in fact the true and ultimate expression of "the exorbitant power of France." As against the armed forces of European coalitions, the French have always the advantage which attaches to the possession of interior lines. In war the combination of superiority of numbers with the element of surprise leads straight to victory. And this combination is more easily obtained for the purpose of attack, and more easily frustrated for the purpose of defence, by a power which, operating on interior lines, can concentrate more quickly than its enemy at a given point. But in 1701, the French enjoyed other and special advantages, which far exceeded in value this general and permanent one.

In the first place, they held the entire command of the Mediterranean and the Straits. In former wars the ports of Spain had been open to the fleets of England and Holland. Now even the harbours of Portugal were closed to the maritime powers. The entire peninsula was in fact a part of France. Two results followed. On the one hand, the squadrons of Toulon being free to unite with the squadrons of Brest, the naval forces of the French were no longer exposed to destruction in detail. And on the other, England and Holland, being deprived of all bases in the Mediterranean or adjacent to it, could not exert their preponderating might upon the sea either to assist the Imperialist army in Italy or to effect a diversion against the southern coast of France.

The improvident folly of the House of Commons in forcing Charles II to abandon Tangier was now apparent. The possession of Naples, Sicily, the Tuscan Ports, and Finale, tightened the French hold upon those waters, and strengthened the position of their forces in Italy. Mistress of the Mediterranean and of the gates of the Mediterranean, France was relieved of much embarrassment and peril: and the allies were robbed of the full use of their most potent arm.

Secondly, the alliance with Savoy, while it completed the picture of the Mediterranean Sea as a "Bourbon lake," ensured the communications of the French army in the Milanese. And in the possible event of the withdrawal of that army, it presented a buffer against any attempt at invasion by a victorious enemy from Northern Italy.

Thirdly, the occupation of the Milanese had several consequences of no little value. Like the alliance with Savoy, it tended to confirm the French control of the Mediterranean, while it created an additional buffer against attacks upon the south-eastern frontier of France. But for offensive purposes its importance was far greater. The French army, established there, dominated the whole peninsula of Italy. Above all, it threatened the heart of the Empire through the passes of the Tyrol. Eugène had already pressed back the forces of Catinat and Villeroi beyond the Oglio. But Eugène's situation was precarious at the best. At any moment, a determined advance, under an able commander, and in overwhelming force, might sweep him before it to the gates of Vienna.

Fourthly, the alliance with the Elector of Bavaria gave France an army and a base in the very bowels of Germany. The Elector was strong enough to bully the lesser German princes, and to intimidate some of them into neutrality at least. His position had indeed one grave defect. The territories of Württemberg and Baden, interposing between Bavaria and the Upper Rhine, cut him off from the French frontier. Unless he were properly supported from Alsace, he might eventually be isolated and overwhelmed by the combined forces of the Empire. But, assuming that he was properly supported, the offensive possibilities of his situation were of the highest order, for he controlled the course of the Danube from Ulm to Passau, and the straight road from Strasbourg to Vienna. In Germany, therefore, as well as in Italy, Louis commanded a position which menaced the capital of the Empire itself.

Fifthly, the alliance with the Elector of Cologne brought the French troops to the Lower Rhine and established them upon the left flank of the United Provinces. In the fortresses of Rheinberg, Kaiserswerth, and Bonn, they lay within striking distance of the Dutch frontier, while they severed the natural line of communication between the maritime powers and Southern Germany. The possession of Spanish Guelderland gave them in any case partial control of the Meuse; but the Elector of Cologne, by admitting them to the city and country of Liège, tightened their grip upon that river, which, excepting only the fortress of Maestricht, became theirs as far as Venlo.

And sixthly, the occupation of the Spanish Netherlands laid bare the southern frontier of the United Provinces. Here there were no strong places to obstruct the march of the invader. Only by the deliberate flooding of the country could he be held at bay. England too was directly threatened by the passing of Ostend, Nieuport, and Antwerp into her enemy's hands. Whenever a hostile power, which already possesses naval bases on one side of the Straits of Dover, acquires them on the other as well, the danger to the commerce and the safety of England is doubled, and the task devolving on her fleet is doubled also. Moreover, for defensive purposes, the Spanish Netherlands gave France what she had always lacked, an extension of that north-eastern frontier which had always been perilously close to Paris.

It was true that on the side of Holland the fortifications of Brussels, Louvain, and Tirlemont were obsolete, and the country lay open to invasion. But the French engineers were busily constructing a line of works from the Schelde to the Meuse. These works, which were strong in themselves and were covered also by rivers, inundations, and morasses, began at Antwerp at the mouth of the Schelde, and passing south-eastward to Aerschot, followed the course of the Demer, the Great Geete, and the Little Geete, till they reached the Mehaigne, whence they ran due south to the Meuse, at a point a little to the east of Namur. The line was dangerously long; but if ever it should be forced, the French had merely to fall back upon the mighty barrier of Spanish fortresses, which could only be penetrated after long and arduous campaigns.

Such was "the exorbitant power of France" at its highest pitch; and such was the strategical problem which William transmitted for solution to Marlborough and Eugène and the fleets and armies of the Grand Alliance.

CHAPTER 3

The Ministry of Godolphin

The news of William's death fell like a thunderbolt upon the members of the Grand Alliance. The controlling mind was gone, and, for aught men knew, England herself would now desert the common cause. The emissaries of France played skilfully upon the terrors of the Dutch. But the panic was only momentary. Those who yielded to it had little knowledge of the new Queen, or of the man on whom she leaned. Anne was a High Churchwoman. The dominant motive in her character was attachment to the faith of Andrewes, Laud and Ken. To save the Church of England, she had abandoned her own father in his time of need. To save the Church of England, she considered herself justified in supplanting her own brother on the English throne. If her devotion to her religion inclined her to the Tory party, it also inclined her to the policy of war.

Against that Popish power which threatened to impose a Popish prince upon the English people she deemed it her duty to stand forth as the 'Defender of the Faith.' In common too with many Tories, who had in the past obstructed the foreign policy of William, she bitterly resented the insolent recognition of the Pretender by the French King. Anne was the granddaughter of a publican's widow of Westminster, and she possessed a liberal share of that contemptuous hatred of the foreigner which is, or at any rate was, ingrained in the masses of the English people.

Moreover, she was always popular with all classes of her subjects. Her maternal sorrows, her well-known piety, her solid virtues, and her commonplace intellect went straight to the nation's heart. Then too she was English to the core; and she had been snubbed by William, whom England had never forgiven for his Dutch origin. Thus she was precisely the Sovereign to unite all parties as they ought to be united, if a great war was to be prosecuted to a successful issue. The English, externally frigid and heavy, are at bottom a chivalrous race; and, in time of crisis, as Elizabeth had discovered, they will rally to a royal woman with such fervour of devotion as no king can ever inspire.

And at the Queen's right hand stood Marlborough, the pupil of William, certified with William's dying breath to be "the fittest person in all her dominions to conduct her armies and preside in her councils." She had long regarded the Earl as an intimate friend. His political views were similar to her own. No recommendation from the dead King could raise him higher in her esteem than he already stood. "His reversion," as Shrewsbury had said at the time of his disgrace, was "very fair," And only less dearly than she loved the Prince of Denmark, Anne loved the wife of Marlborough.

Sarah was saturated with Whiggery. Her influence over the Queen was such that, as long as she retained it, the Whigs were permanently in office, if not in power. As long as she enjoyed the affection of the Sovereign, Whig opinions never lacked a voice, a shrill, persistent, diurnal voice in the royal ear. And the Whigs were all for war. In the keeping of Anne and the Marlboroughs, the policy of William was safe. Had the character and relationship of these three persons been better understood upon the continent, the loyalty of England to the obligations contracted by the dead King would never have been questioned.

Steps were immediately taken to make plain the fact that England would in nowise swerve from the line to which she stood committed. On the day of William's death, Anne assured her Privy Council of her "own opinion of the importance of carrying on all the preparations—to oppose the great power of France." Three days later she went in state to the House of Lords, where, with that "softness of voice and sweetness in the pronunciation" which Burnet[1] declares to have characterised her elocution, she spoke of the importance of encouraging the allies, while she assured the delighted Tories that her "own heart" was "entirely English."

She had already dispatched letters to the foreign governments, to announce her intention of maintaining all alliances and adopting all such measures as might be "necessary for the preservation of the common liberty of Europe" and the reduction of "the power of France within due bounds." To convince the Dutch of the sincerity of her professions, she conferred the Order of the Garter upon the Earl of

---

1. Burnet, *History of His Own Time* (1818), vol. 3., book 7., p. 340.

Marlborough, appointed him Captain-General of her forces, and, within a fortnight of William's death, dispatched him to the Hague as Ambassador Extraordinary and Plenipotentiary to the States-General. The Earl arrived on March 28. Having conferred with Heinsius and other ministers, he was received in audience by the States on the 31st. He assured them of the Queen's intention to maintain the alliance, of her willingness to renew it, and of her desire to strengthen it. He informed them that he was authorised "to concert "with them "the necessary operations."[2]

And he referred in conclusion to his own zeal for their service. Dykvelt, the president, expressed the thanks of the assembly and its "resolution readily to concur with Her Majesty in a vigorous prosecution of the common interest."[3] He added that the Earl's "person would be highly acceptable to them, not only for the Queen's choice of him and for the sake of King William, who first invested him with that character, but for his own merit." It was evident that Marlborough's capacity and charm had already impressed the stolid men who controlled the destinies of the United Provinces.

Greatly comforted, the States returned a firm and dignified answer to the threats and cajolery of Louis, who had seen in William's death an opportunity for the exercise of diplomatic arts. Marlborough continued at the Hague, settling the proportions of the allied contingents and advising on the conduct of the coming campaign. With the concurrence of the Austrian minister it was arranged that war should be declared on one and the same day at London, Vienna and the Hague. And on the Earl's advice it was decided to undertake the siege of Kaiserswerth forthwith.

Everything which Marlborough proposed seemed certain of a favourable reception from the Dutch. But in one particular he encountered their most stubborn resistance. The command of their forces in the field was coveted by various princes, including the King of Prussia himself. Prince George of Denmark was among the number; and it was only natural that his claims should be strongly supported by the Queen. Marlborough was instructed to push this candidature to the uttermost of his power. But the Dutch would have none of it. They wanted a soldier of proved ability, and above all they wanted a subject.

In war the commander of the Dutch forces was accompanied by

---

2. Boyer, *History of the Reign of Queen Anne, digested into Annals* (1703), vol. 1, p. 13.
3. *Ibid.*

agents of the government, who were known as 'field-deputies,' and who watched and controlled his conduct at every turn, A foreigner of royal blood might be tempted to treat these functionaries with the contumely which they too often deserved.

Marlborough arrived in England on April 16. He attended the obsequies of William III, and was present with his Countess at the coronation. He was one of the persons whom the Queen appointed to examine William's papers for evidence of an alleged design to exclude her from the throne. But the principal business which occupied his mind at this time was the formation of the new ministry. Anne's acquaintance with the politicians of the day did not go far. Though the Tories had affected to court her in her long retirement, and though common attachment to the Church of England disposed her favourably towards that party, she deemed herself in no way fettered in the choice of her advisers.

Marlborough, who loathed domestic politics, and who foresaw that the claims of war and diplomacy would soon absorb the whole of his energy and time, had his own conception of the kind of government which was necessary to England at the present juncture. He believed that an administration restrained in temper, representative in character, and directed by a statesman whose personality excited no special antagonisms, would inspire confidence abroad, and maintain comparative harmony at home. The statesman on whom he had set his heart was his own friend and relative by marriage, Godolphin. And certainly Godolphin possessed great qualifications. A Tory and a Churchman, he was more famous for his skill as a financier than for his zeal as a partisan.

"With the exception of Halifax," says Lecky, "he was the foremost financier of his age; an old, wary, taciturn, plodding, unobtrusive, and moderate man,"[4] he was respected by everybody and hated by none. The Queen, who had long regarded him as a personal friend, welcomed the suggestion that he should preside over her first ministry in the capacity of Lord Treasurer. But Godolphin was very reluctant to assume office. He dreaded the rage of disappointed rivals and the virulence of contending factions. Marlborough was much perturbed. He knew that the war would impose an extraordinary burden on the national finances, but he was convinced that, with Godolphin at the Treasury, they would prove equal to the strain. He wanted to feel certain that the armies which followed him in the field, and the contractors who fed them, would be regularly and punctually paid; and he even went so far as to declare that unless Godolphin accepted the Queen's offer, he himself would resign his own command.

"This man," says Macaulay,[5] referring to Godolphin's appointment at the Treasury in William's first ministry, "this man, taciturn, clear-minded, laborious, inoffensive, zealous for no government and useful to every government, had gradually become an almost indispensable part of the machinery of state." If this was true in 1689, it was still more true in 1702. Marlborough knew it, and by dint of persuasion he got his way. Godolphin became Lord Treasurer.

The Queen's affection for the Church was such that in any ministry selected by her, in the free exercise of her own discretion, the Tory element was certain to predominate. The majority of situations, and all the most important ones, were assigned to Tories. Nottingham and Hedges were made Secretaries of State. Rochester was reappointed Lord Lieutenant of Ireland, and Wright Lord Chancellor. Harcourt became Solicitor-General, and Seymour Comptroller of the Household. Halifax, Somers, and Orford were removed from the Privy Council.

Yet the party which they led was by no means ostracised. The Duke of Devonshire was continued in the office of Lord Steward; and, as Burnet says, "though no Whigs were put into employments, yet many were kept in the posts they had been put into during the former reign."[6] Burnet, indeed, has stated less than the truth. One very bitter and determined Whig was installed in close and perpetual proximity to the Queen's person. The wife of Marlborough was made Groom of the Stole, Mistress of the Robes, Keeper of the Privy Purse, and Ranger of Windsor Forest.

The ministry, moreover, was in reality much less Tory than it appeared. Every member of it was pledged to the prosecution of William's foreign policy, which the Whigs regarded as peculiarly their own. And its two most powerful personalities, Marlborough and Godolphin, though nominally Tories, laboured consistently to unite both factions in the public cause.

> "I am very little concerned," wrote Marlborough to his wife, "what any party thinks of me; I know them both so well, that if my quiet depended upon either of them, I should be most miserable."

---

4. Lecky, *A History of England in the Eighteenth Century*, vol 1. p. 39.
5. Macaulay, *History of England* (Popular Edition, 1895), vol. 1, p. 665.
6. Burnet, vol. 3, p. 346.

And again,

"You sometimes use the expression of my Tory friends. I will have no friends but such as will support the Queen and government."

And again,

"I will endeavour to leave a good name behind me in countries that have hardly any blessing but that of not knowing the detested names of Whig or Tory." [7]

A government which had just been appointed by a new and popular Sovereign, which was seen to be controlled by men so tolerant and tactful as Godolphin and Marlborough, and which, while it was committed irrevocably to the dearest policy of the Whigs, numbered in its ranks the most trusted leaders of the Tories, was assured from the outset of overwhelming support in the country at large. Its most dangerous foes were those of its own household. The Mistress of the Robes and the Lord Lieutenant of Ireland, who hated one another with inextinguishable hatred, had this at any rate in common, that they both condemned the system which Godolphin and Marlborough had decided to pursue.

Sarah considered that the Queen should have selected a Whig ministry, or one at least in which the Whig element predominated. In her judgement places should have been found for Whigs so eminent as Somers, and so rabid as her own son-in-law, Sunderland. It was not alone that her personal sympathies lay wholly with that party; she could also argue, in her downright, feminine fashion, that those who have always been known as advocates of a particular policy are presumably the most proper persons to execute it. But luckily for England and for Europe her husband's vision was both longer and clearer than hers. He had regretted William's recent breach with the Tories, because he knew that it is impossible for a clique to conduct a great war in the name of a nation.

The Whigs, as a party, were better disciplined and better led than their rivals, but they were already committed, heart and soul, to vigorous hostilities with France, It was difficult to conceive of any circumstances in which they would seek to embarrass any ministry that was prepared to fight Louis to the death. The Tories, on the other hand, though they now recognised the necessity of war, were suspected by

---

7. Coxe, *Memoirs of the Duke of Marlborough*, vol. 1, p. 235: The Duke to the Duchess, October 20, 1704; pp. 263, 264: The Duke to the Duchess, August 3, 1705.

reason of their past attitude towards the policy of William. But numerically and socially they were much more powerful than the Whigs, they included in their ranks the mass of the rural gentry, whose influence was always formidable, and they could command upon occasions the services of the most efficient organisation in the country—the parochial clergy of the English Church.

If Marlborough's ideal of a nation united in the face of the enemy was ever to be realised, the true problem was not to gratify the Whigs, but to conciliate the Tories. And the Tories could only be conciliated by employing their leaders. The Whigs could still be left undisturbed in minor posts; but a Cabinet of oil and water was impossible. To expect a Nottingham to co-operate with a Sunderland was not practical politics. It is surprising that a woman so intelligent as Sarah should ever have thought otherwise. It is only less surprising that she should have failed to comprehend the necessity of subordinating her own views to those of Marlborough and Godolphin, But her stubborn pride impelled her to follow a separate and divergent course.

"I resolved," she has herself confessed, "from the very beginning of the Queen's reign, to try whether I could not by degrees make impressions in her mind more favourable to the Whigs."[8]

This description of her policy sounds innocent enough. What part could be more womanly than to heal the breach between an amiable Sovereign and subjects so virtuous and so misunderstood as the Whig *junta*? As played by Sarah, however, it assumed a more sinister aspect.

Rochester had two grievances, one personal, the other political. He had always considered that his relationship to Anne conferred on him a natural right to the foremost place in her counsels. He looked upon the Marlboroughs as supplanters, who now by an extreme abuse of the power which they had so long usurped had foisted their creature, Godolphin, into a position which was properly the perquisite of the Queen's uncle. But if Rochester was hurt in his feelings as a man, he was equally offended in his prejudices as a Tory.

In his judgement, no Tory government was worthy of its name if it did not sweep its opponents from every branch of the Queen's service, including the very lowest. He considered that the judges, the ambassadors, the lords lieutenants of counties, and even such subordinate and local magistrates as sheriffs and justices of the peace, should one and all be members of the ruling party. This 'root and branch' theory of the

---

8. *Memoirs of the Life and Conduct of Sarah, Duchess of Marlborough* (1744), section 2, p. 135.

constitutional system was not peculiar to Rochester. It had its adherents among both Whigs and Tories. Yet Sarah, of all people, affected to be scandalised by the machinations of Rochester and his friends. She wrote to Godolphin that it appeared to her "as if everything were to be governed by faction and nonsense."[9]

Godolphin and Marlborough had no intention of permitting their colleagues to indulge in an orgy of revenge. The duty of the one was to finance a great war, and of the other to conduct it to a happy issue. In these heavy tasks they needed the support of all their countrymen without distinction of party. They knew that the Whigs were already the enthusiastic advocates of a belligerent policy; and they hoped that the responsibilities and the rewards of office would overcome the lingering scruples of the more fanatical Tories. If their hopes were disappointed, it might become necessary to call in more Whigs to the counsels of the Crown. Meantime that party must not be bullied or oppressed.

In modern eyes the system pursued by Marlborough and Godolphin seems singular enough. But at that epoch the constitution had by no means attained its present form. The doctrine of ministerial responsibility was indeed established; but the rule that ministers must be all of one political complexion, and must be selected from the party which for the time being controls a majority in the House of Commons, was not. In 1702 it was still possible to hold that the Crown has the right to criticise at all times the services of its ablest subjects without any regard to the party label by which they may happen to be designated. It was still permissible to think that, the King being King of England and not of a faction, the non-partisan character of his office should be reflected in the composition of his government.

These views were strongly held by William, whom the Whigs regarded as their own property, and by Anne, whom the Tories regarded as theirs. They were held by such Tories as Marlborough and Godolphin and by such Whigs as Shrewsbury. But they were bitterly opposed by Tories like Rochester and by Whigs like Marlborough's wife. Modern politicians would be at a loss to understand them. For the essence of the English party system, as fully developed, is the homogeneity of the Cabinet. In 1702, however, a homogeneous administration, while it was regarded as an alternative, was considered by many to be open to manifest and grave objections.

How, it was asked, would any true friend of monarchy recommend

---

9. Coxe, vol. 1, p. 82: The Countess to Godolphin, May 29, 1702.

a plan which restricted the Sovereign in the choice of his servants, and which tended, moreover, in the direction of oligarchy? And how, it was also asked, could any sincere lover of liberty advocate an arrangement which subjected one half of the nation to the tyranny of the other half? Surely, it was contended, the better way is that by which neither party is left without some representatives among the advisers of the Crown.

Queen Anne, herself a Stuart, who combined high notions of the kingly office with a conscientious conception of her duty to her people as a whole, naturally favoured a mixed administration. Marlborough took the same line. His mind rebelled, as the minds of all thinking men are still naturally prone to rebel, against the absurdities, the hypocrisies, and the humiliations of a rigid party system. As a staunch supporter of the monarchy, the son and grandson of Cavaliers who had suffered for the royal cause, he disliked any plan which facilitated encroachment on the royal prerogative.

But above all, as a soldier, he detested the idea of conducting a campaign in the name of a faction. War, and war on a gigantic scale, was to be the prime business of the new reign. The party system, as we know it, has been found the most practicable, if not the only system for a time of peace. But in the day of battle it is always seen at its weakest and its worst. England was about to take a hand in a continental conflict of stupendous magnitude. If a good understanding was to be maintained among the allies, and if a vigorous and enterprising foe was to be completely overthrown, it seemed to Marlborough that national unity, or at least a fair appearance of it, was a consideration of paramount importance.

Thus it came about that, just as William's first ministry had consisted of Whigs with an admixture of Tories, so Anne's consisted of Tories with an admixture of Whigs. Marlborough and Godolphin, who by instinct and conviction were not politicians at all, but servants of the State, were eminently fitted for the leadership of a government constituted upon this basis. But they were not unaware of the difficulty of the task which they had undertaken. William had attempted it, and not always with success. It could only be achieved by introducing into the Cabinet and the House of Commons as many men as possible of their own political temperament, and by scrupulously adhering to a domestic policy not open to the reproach of violence or vindictiveness.

Several circumstances assisted them greatly towards the attainment of their end. During the late reign so many men had notoriously changed sides or had consented to co-operate in the King's service with colleagues whose principles they abhorred that the sharpness of party distinctions had been somewhat obliterated. Then, too, some seats in the House of Commons were at that epoch virtually in the gift of the Crown and could be filled with representatives who were the nominees and the dependents of the government of the day. Moreover, the growing sense of public danger, which the seizure of the barrier fortresses and the insulting proclamation of the Pretender had enormously fomented, fostered a sentiment of national unity, which the progress of hostilities might reasonably be expected to deepen and confirm. It is obvious that a mixed administration has better chances of success in time of war than in time of peace.

"Lord Godolphin and Lord Marlborough," says Dalrymple, "who were wise and moderate men, found it easy to form a great party in the nation as well as in Parliament, consisting of moderate Whigs and moderate Tories, who met each other halfway on principles, and the whole way on the measures which the Queen should pursue in foreign politics."[10]

These statesmen recognised that the conflict with France would smooth the path for such a government as theirs; but they also firmly believed that only by such a government as theirs could the conflict with France be carried to a successful issue. Precisely as the greatest of a nation's servants, the monarch, ought to represent the whole nation and not a fragment of it, so, as they justly reasoned, the highest of a nation's acts, which is war, can only be properly executed by an undivided and unanimous people.[11]

In the country at large, the new government could rely upon the support of a considerable number of persons who were attached to no party, or whose party connections were of the frailest. But among the recognised leaders of Whigs and Tories it was none too easy to discover a sufficiency of men of a moderate and conciliatory temper to fill the high offices of State as Marlborough and Godolphin would have wished them to be filled. Partisans so bigoted and impracticable as the Lord Lieutenant of Ireland, or so vehement and vindictive as the Mistress of the Robes, were a menace to the chances of any ministry constituted, as this was, in the interest of domestic unity. It is therefore

---

10. *Dalrymple's Memoirs*, vol. 3., p. 246.
11. See Spenser Wilkinson, *Britain at Bay*. Clausewitz, *On War*, especially book 3, ch. 17.

no matter for surprise that some dissensions should have begun from the very outset.

The Queen's advisers were agreed that she should make war on France, but they were not agreed as to how and where she should make it. On these points Rochester, who was not exactly a qualified strategist, put forward some extraordinary opinions which brought him at once into conflict with Marlborough. These opinions, which were entertained by a number of Englishmen, most, though not all, of whom were Tories, originated less in party prejudice than in sheer ignorance. In 1702 the nation as a whole knew next to nothing of war.

It is not for us, their descendants, to censure them severely. Notwithstanding all the experience, glorious and inglorious, of the last two hundred years, the statesmen and the voters of today are not much better informed upon this vital topic than were the contemporaries of Marlborough. Nobody expects that the average civilian should be versed in the technical details of the military profession. But every people which claims to govern itself is morally bound, if it values its national independence, to arrive at a correct understanding of the strategical factors which should govern its action in the event of war.

The ideas of Rochester, and those for whom he spoke, could be reduced to four propositions, which, taken together, constituted a rare collection of premises that were half true and conclusions that were fallacious. The first proposition was that, England's interest in the war being much inferior to that of Holland or the Empire, England ought to participate as an auxiliary and not as a principal. But all three powers had the same high interest in the war, the maintenance of 'the balance of power.' To say that, because the French armies were already on the frontiers of the Empire and the United Provinces, but had not yet entered Vienna and the Hague, therefore England was only indirectly concerned, was to argue in the manner of the householder who takes but a languid interest in the extinction of the conflagration until the adjacent building to his own is actually in flames.

The second proposition was that, England being the foremost naval power in Europe, she ought to devote the best of her energies to the destruction of the maritime trade of France and Spain, and to the acquisition of their possessions and resources beyond the seas. These objects were certainly desirable in themselves; and had the War of the Spanish Succession been nothing better than a game of grab, they were the proper objects for England to pursue. But the war was a life-and-death struggle for the independence of the European states. So far as could be judged at the opening of hostilities the fleet would be needed in Europe to keep the seas for the passage of troops, to facilitate diversions, and to exert a steady pressure on the enemy in the Mediterranean.

The colonies of France and Spain were valuable properties; but if, while England was annexing them, France was annexing Europe, they would be useless except as a retreat for the British race when, as would speedily ensue, these islands became an appanage of the Bourbon crown. This mercantile conception of warfare is an inveterate and pernicious delusion of the English people. A numerous, martial and aggressive nation, such as the French were under Louis XIV, such as they were under Napoleon I, and such as the Germans are today, can never be humbled merely by the loss of its colonies or the destruction of its sea-borne trade.

The third proposition was that, the land forces of England being required for the defence of these islands and for expeditions to America, they ought not to be employed in operations on the continent of Europe. It was, however, allowed that a "small force" must be assigned to the defence of Holland. Of course, if the armies of England's allies were sufficient to overwhelm France, this contention might have been sound, though in that case the dispatch of even a "small force" to Holland would have been superfluous. But all the information available suggested that these allies were not even capable of defending their own territories from invasion.

That such was indeed the fact, subsequent events showed only too clearly. In the known circumstances, the only true defence of England was to throw the whole of her military strength into the continental struggle. To have retained her army at home and to have frittered it away on expeditions to America, until such time as the Bourbons had conquered the mainland and were ready to pass the Channel, would have been national suicide.

The fourth proposition was that, if the government was determined to send soldiers to the continent, it ought to send them to Spain, seeing that the war was about Spain, and not to that old manoeuvring ground of William's, the Spanish Netherlands. Obviously the Spanish Netherlands were a very undesirable theatre of operations, studded as they were with powerful fortresses. But the alternative was not necessarily Spain. Moreover, the assumption that the war was "about Spain" was incorrect. The war was not more about Spain than it was about the Milanese or the Brazils or the fortresses of Flanders. And even if the war had been "about Spain," the deduction that the fighting ought therefore to be in Spain was invalid.

It is impossible to examine the issues raised by Rochester without realising how indissoluble is the bond between policy and war. The strategy of Rochester was vitiated throughout by political ignorance and political prejudice. He was not the only Tory or the only Englishman who had much to learn. So great a statesman as Bolingbroke, writing in after life of the concluding years of William's reign, used these words:

> I have sometimes considered ... what I should have done if I had sat in Parliament at that time, and have been forced to own to myself that I should have voted for disbanding the army then, as I voted in the following Parliament for censuring the Partition Treaties.... I am forced to own this, because I remember *how imperfect my notions were of the situation of Europe in that extraordinary crisis, and how much I saw the influence of my country in a half-light.*[12]

As Bolingbroke confesses that he was then, so assuredly was Rochester. Marlborough himself, despite the illumination which he derived from his professional training, had not always been greatly wiser than they. He owed his education in large measure to William. Close contact with events themselves had completed it. He had now to educate his party.

Louis proposed to remain on the defensive, that vigilant defensive which seizes on the first mistake of the assailant as an opportunity for a counterattack. With his vast and confident armies, with the central situation which he had always held, and the commanding positions which his grandson had enabled him to occupy, he did not anticipate defeat. At the worst, he looked forward to a protracted struggle. But, if the decision were long delayed, jealousies and dissensions would probably appear among the allies, would impair their energies, and eventually dissolve their combination. To such a result nothing would contribute more strongly than the pursuit by each member of the coalition of his own immediate gain without regard to the one common and ultimate interest of the whole body, the reduction of the exorbitant power of France.

---

12. Letters on the Study and Use of History: Henry St. John, Lord Bolingbroke (1779), letter 8.

For England the temptation to devote her whole strength to the acquisition of territories in the New World was very great. But Marlborough, with the insight of the real strategist, resisted it on grounds of war and policy alike. He knew that dispersion of forces was dangerous in the military sense, divergency of aims in the political one. He knew that in any event time is never on the side of coalitions. They, of all combatants, ought to aim swiftly, and with concentrated force, at the decisive point. In this war, as in all wars against the French, that point was Paris.

Marlborough had not learned from Turenne himself how to defend France without learning also how to attack her. There were five roads to Paris—by the Spanish Netherlands, by Lorraine, by Alsace, by the Riviera, and by the Pyrenees. Of these five the last two were the worst, by reason of their remoteness from the objective on the one hand, and from the territories of the coalition on the other. The first was the shortest and the most convenient; but it was guarded by a triple barrier of fortresses which could not be taken without immense expenditure of time and lives. There remained only the second and third. For Austria the way through Alsace was the quickest and the best. But for the coalition as a whole, Lorraine was the true gate of France.

It would be necessary for a Dutch contingent to protect the United Provinces against the garrisons of the Spanish Netherlands, and for an Imperialist one to hold the north of Italy against any attempt to threaten Vienna through the passes of the Tyrol. A second Imperialist contingent would be stationed on the Upper Rhine to cover the communications of the invading army against a flanking movement from Alsace. But these dispositions having once been made, the combined forces of England, Holland, Prussia, Denmark, Hanover, and Hesse, assembling at Coblenz and advancing up the valley of the Moselle, might march to Paris in a couple of campaigns, provided only that it had capable leadership and some numerical superiority. To the attainment of this last condition it would be the function of the combined fleets to contribute. By threatening descents upon the coasts of France and Spain, by intimidating Portugal and Savoy, and by aiding and encouraging both Catalans and Camisards, they could compel Louis to move large detachments from the decisive point.

Such, in outline, was Marlborough's conception of the strategy which would most probably bring low "the exorbitant power of France." Like all great strategy, it was distinguished by simplicity of design, by unity of purpose, and by concentration of resources.

But the invasion of France by the valley of the Moselle could not be undertaken until the French had been first expelled from the angle which is formed by the Meuse and the Rhine. So long as the Rhine from its confluence with the Moselle to the Dutch frontier was in the enemy's hands, Coblenz could not be utilised as a base of operations for the allied armies. Moreover, for the sake of the immediate safety of the United Provinces, Louis must be forced to abandon his hold upon this waterway, as also upon the Meuse at least as far as Liège. This essential but preliminary work Marlborough desired to accomplish without unnecessary delay. He therefore proposed that the Dutch and English forces should take the offensive in this quarter immediately and with the utmost of their strength. This was the plan which brought him into collision with Rochester.

Marlborough's influence prevailed against that of the Queen's uncle, whom everybody knew to be a politician with a grievance. Most of the Tories and all the Whigs concurred in the opinion that Marlborough should be given a free hand, the Tories chiefly because he was a Tory, and the Whigs because, although he was a Tory, he was treading in the footsteps of William. Few politicians upon either side could lay claim to an enlightened comprehension of the strategical issues. The Whig view was simple, if somewhat crude. The King of France declined to tolerate Calvinism among his subjects; he declined to recognise the divine origin of Locke's theory of government; he extended hospitality to the family of James Stuart.

On these grounds alone, to say nothing of the growth of 'the balance of power,' he ought to be exterminated in the interest of civilisation, or, what was the same thing, universal Whiggery. William, the grand exterminator, had gone to work upon the continent; and now that he was unhappily removed from the scene of his labours, any competent successor who was prepared to go and do likewise deserved the support of all true Whigs. The attitude of the Tories, on the other hand, was as subtle as it was unconsciously amusing. In their opinion the Dutch were a race of hucksters and stock-jobbers; they were Puritans in religion and Republicans in politics; they had done their utmost in the time of Cromwell and Charles II to destroy the navy and the commerce of England, but they had failed; they had revenged themselves by sending that unlamented monarch, William, into these islands to enrich his foreign favourites with British land and British offices, and to squander British blood and British treasure in the Netherlands, solely for the aggrandisement of the United Provinces.

But, after all, 'the exorbitant power of France' had an ugly look, especially when it claimed to appoint monarchs to reign over these islands. The necessity of a war was not to be denied, and if the Queen and the general (both of whom were English and both Tories) considered that it could best be waged upon the continent, and even in the Netherlands, there was no good reason why loyal Tories should go out of their way to raise objections.

A naval expedition against the port of Cadiz, to be undertaken by the combined navies of England and Holland, had been arranged by the late King shortly before his decease. The new government, acting on the advice of Marlborough, adopted the plan. Fifty sail of the line, thirty of which were English under Admiral Sir George Rooke, made ready for this service. The expeditionary force numbered 14,000, 10,000 of whom were British under the Duke of Ormond. Both these officers were well-known, and popular Tories, And Cadiz was the naval arsenal of Spain and the centre of her West Indian commerce. The Queen anticipated that these considerations would conciliate Rochester; but she was disappointed. He merely observed that it was "a plan to have two land wars instead of one," and that "the capture of Cadiz was no attack upon the trade or settlements of France or Spain."[13]

On May 15 the Queen set her hand to a formal declaration of war against Louis and his grandson. The text of the document had been previously discussed before Her Majesty in Council, when the opinion that England ought not to engage herself in the capacity of a principal had been duly urged. But Marlborough, who was backed by Somerset, Devonshire, and Pembroke, proved too strong for the advocates of insufficiency. The Queen, having communicated her intention to the Commons, and that House having unanimously resolved that it "would, to the utmost, assist and support Her Majesty,"[14] the declaration was proclaimed with the traditional ceremony in the streets of London.

The die was cast. The armed forces of the coalition, outnumbering on paper those of France and her allies by 100,000 men, but in fact inferior by 30,000,[15] stood face to face with that strategical situation

---

13. *Dalrymple's Memoirs*, vol. 3, p. 259.
14. Boyer, vol. 1, p. 28.
15. Leadam, *The Political History of England,* vol. 9, p. 8. .

which, apart from all other advantages, conferred upon the Bourbon power an initial superiority well calculated to give pause to every friend of European liberty who understood the art of war.

But this superiority would be increased and not diminished by delay. It was now or never, if the states of Europe were to retain their independence and their nationality. The Emperor, indeed, had already been fighting for nearly twelve months in Northern Italy, where Eugène had by this time captured Marshal Villeroi and was blockading Mantua.

But the Emperor was severely handicapped by a revolt of his Hungarian subjects, who, with the assistance of French officers and French money, successfully maintained a guerrilla warfare in the heart of his dominions. Germany was deeply stirred; but Germany's resources, which in combination would have been decisive, were only partially available.

The Elector of Saxony was absorbed in the struggle with Sweden. The Electors of Bavaria and Cologne were the secret allies of France. Nevertheless, Prussia, the most powerful and the most efficient of the German states, was already in the field. And the House of Hanover, which by reason of Louis' support of the English pretender was vitally concerned in the struggle, had frustrated by armed force an attempt by the two princes of Wolfenbuttel and the Duke of Saxe-Gotha to set up a French interest in Northern Germany. The siege of Kaiserswerth had been begun by the Dutch, the Prussians, and the Palatines, and Louis of Baden was busily assembling an army for the investment of Landau. It only remained for England to take the field.

Marlborough, who in addition to his other honours had now been made Master of the Ordnance, quitted London for the Hague on May 23. He was accompanied as far as Margate by the Countess. As soon as his ship was out of sight of England, he wrote her a love-letter, the first of that remarkable series which continued unbroken throughout ten campaigns.

> "It is impossible," he said, "to express with what a heavy heart I parted with you when I was by the water's side. I could have given my life to have come back, though I knew my own weakness so much that I durst not, for I knew I should have exposed myself to the company. I did for a great while, with a perspective glass, look upon the cliffs, in hopes I might have had one sight of you. . . . If you will be sensible of what I now feel, you will endeavour ever to be easy to me, and then I shall be most

happy; for it is you only that can give me true content."[16]

This document is the first of hundreds, scribbled in the intervals of an enormous correspondence with half the courts of Europe, scribbled in barges upon Dutch canals and in travelling-coaches upon German roads, scribbled in the saddle and on the battlefield itself, and one and all breathing such a fervour of chivalrous devotion as the youngest ensign in the army, engaged in a sedulous courtship of some newfound sweetheart, could never have excelled.

Marlborough remained at the Hague till the end of June. In his capacity of Plenipotentiary he held many conferences with the deputies of the States, while in his other capacity of Captain-General he occupied himself with the organisation of the British forces in the field.

But of all the affairs which now engaged his attention the question of the supreme command of the Dutch army was by far the most important. The Earl on his arrival had renewed his petition on behalf of Prince George; but the States-General remained obdurately blind to the merits of that aspirant. Marlborough's position became extremely delicate and embarrassing. He could not be unaware of the fact, which was patent to everybody, that he himself possessed high qualifications for the very appointment which official duty and private friendship alike compelled him to solicit for another.

He was in truth the man on whom Heinsius and leaders of Dutch opinion had already set their hearts. The Dutch generals not unnaturally resented the suggestion that a foreign subject should be promoted over their heads. The claims of Ginkel, Earl of Athlone, were specially pressed upon the States. But on personal and public grounds the Dutch government decided that no candidate, native or foreign, could be compared with Marlborough. The Earl obtained the post, and with it a salary' of £10,000 a year.

Prince George was deeply mortified. But he could console himself with the reflection that the King of Prussia, the Elector of Hanover, the Prince of Nassau-Saarbrück, and the Archduke Charles were in similar case. Marlborough was troubled lest the sincerity of his own conduct should be questioned; but the excellent Prince was incapable of jealousy or malice. The facts spoke for themselves. Holland would have no sovereign prince at the head of her troops. And of subjects, the Captain-General of the English army was by far the most eligible. His appointment was sound strategy, for it united the Dutch and English

---

16. Coxe, vol. 1, p. 83: Marlborough to the Countess, May 15/26, 1702.

forces under one commander.

Moreover, it was sound statecraft, for it gratified Anne, it flattered her people, and it captivated the hearts of the Tories. Incidentally, it was a delicious revenge on all English detractors of William and his foreign generals. Marlborough himself must have winced a little at the sting of it.

The French affected to ridicule the Dutchmen's choice. They represented Marlborough as an obscure soldier who owed his new command less to his own merits than to his wife's influence. But the merchants and bankers of Holland were never the men to purchase incompetence at the rate of £10,000 a year. They knew what William thought of Marlborough's military capacity, and they needed no higher testimonial. It would have been a fortunate circumstance for them and for their allies if the wisdom which they showed in selecting a commander had been equally apparent in their treatment of him in the field.

Chapter 4
1702

The War of the Spanish Succession is a perfect example of the vices and the defects of a coalition. If the forces at the disposal of the allies had been placed under the unfettered control of a military genius of the first order, in three campaigns he would have made an end of "the exorbitant power of France." If Marlborough or Eugène had been fortunate enough to wield the political authority of a Frederick or a Napoleon, the war would have been conducted with a single eye to the destruction of the enemy. But under the conditions which in fact prevailed the opinions of third-rate generals were treated with respect, while unity of purpose and harmony of action were entirely sacrificed to the selfish and short-sighted ambitions of the various members of the vast confederacy.

Marlborough's idea of strategy was essentially modern. He utterly rejected the notion that such an enemy as France could ever be humbled by capturing a few fortresses or eating up the supplies of a few square miles of territory. From the very beginning he fixed his gaze upon the city of Paris. To crush the French armies in the field, and to pursue their demoralised remnants to the French capital itself, was his conception of the proper method of conducting such a war as was now about to be waged. Few of the soldiers and none of the statesmen of that age agreed with him. For ten years he struggled against the ignorance, the fatuity, and the malice of those who had not even sufficient understanding to know their own interest. But he never for one moment abandoned his ideal. What he might have achieved under happier conditions may be inferred from what he actually accomplished.

At the opening of the campaign of 1702, however, it was not yet time to consider the question of invading France. The immediate necessity of the situation admitted of no dispute. The French army of Flanders, though it had not as yet adopted the offensive, occupied a position so troublesome and dangerous to the allies that, until it was either removed or destroyed, nothing of importance could be undertaken in this theatre of the war. With 60,000 men Marshal Boufflers had marched down the Meuse to Xanten, in the Prussian territory of Cleves, a small Dutch force under Tilly evacuating the place on his approach. Boufflers' critics, of whom Berwick was one, alleged that he ought not to have permitted Tilly to escape, and that he had carelessly sacrificed the moral advantage which always attaches to initial success.[1]

However that may have been, the Marshal's occupation of Xanten created no little anxiety among the allies. While subsisting largely at his enemies' expense, and protecting, from his central position between Meuse and Rhine, both Spanish Guelderland and the Electorate of Cologne, he interposed between Upper Germany and Holland, threatened all the Provinces of Lower Germany, and menaced the Dutch frontier at its weakest point. He did not however feel equal to the relief of Kaiserswerth. The passage of the Rhine, which is here of great breadth, was too hazardous in the face of the enemy. But Tallard, with a separate force of 13,000 men operating on the left bank, threw both soldiers and supplies into the place by boat, and cannonaded the besiegers' quarters across the river. By these means the progress of the siege was much retarded. Tallard also contemplated the bombardment of Düsseldorf; but he was deterred by the threat of retaliation upon Bonn.

At the opposite extremity of the Dutch frontier, Coehoorn with an army of 10,000 men created a diversion by capturing the town of Middelburg, demolishing the French lines, and levying contributions in the territory of Bruges. On the approach of the Spanish general, Bedmar, he retired, opened the sluices, and sending down the waters on the enemy drove them back to Ghent.

Meanwhile, at Kranenburg, fifteen miles to the north-west of Xanten, Athlone was covering Nijmegen and watching Boufflers with an army of 25,000 Dutch and English. Despite their great superiority of numbers, the French attempted nothing of importance from the middle of April to the second week of June. This inactivity was severely censured. But in justice to Boufflers it must be remembered

---

1. *Mémoires de Berwick* (1778), t. 1, p, 174.

that, the navigation of the Meuse being interrupted by the Dutch garrison in Maestricht, which also sent out parties to harass the French convoys on the march, the supply of all things needful for a great army in the field was seriously delayed. Boufflers' post was not in fact an enviable one. He had been joined at Xanten by the Duke of Burgundy, who, though ignorant of war, exercised the titular command; and he had been instructed from Versailles that the army, which a Prince of the Blood honoured with his presence, was in duty bound to act with vigour.

Towards the end of May it became evident that Kaiserswerth must fall. Recognising that this event would set the besiegers at liberty to join Athlone, Boufflers, who had just received an important convoy, determined to march on Kranenburg forthwith. Between that place and Xanten lay the dense forest of Cleves, which, though it obstructed a direct advance, favoured the secret execution of an enveloping movement. Having summoned Tallard to rejoin, the Marshal struck his camp June 10, and, moving behind the forest in two divisions by Cleves on the right and Gennep on the left, threatened to surround Athlone and to isolate Nijmegen, which left to itself was in no condition to resist assault.

Athlone, being poorly served by his intelligence department, had a narrow escape. Almost too late he beat a precipitate retreat to Nijmegen; but, as he approached that place, the French cavalry came swiftly down upon his rearguard, while in the distance he could descry the long columns of their foot pressing forward to the chase. Fighting gallantly against superior numbers, the allied horse enabled their infantry to occupy the outworks of Nijmegen. But the Household troops of France charged up to the very palisades, and only recoiled before the fire of the artillery upon the ramparts. Athlone was saved by a short half-hour. Robbed of their prey, the French dropped back to Kranenburg and Cleves. Two days later Kaiserswerth fell, and the besieging army reinforced Athlone. Boufflers' opportunity had passed. But he had given the Dutchmen such a fright as paralysed their initiative for the remainder of the campaign.

On July 2, Marlborough arrived at Nijmegen, where he proceeded to effect a concentration of 60,000 men. On the 6th he advanced to Duckenberg, and on July 5th to Sutterburg. Boufflers in the meantime had been weakened by the loss of a detachment which Louis had ordered him to send to the relief of Landau. In numbers he was now inferior. But the disparity was slight; and Louis told him, for his consolation, that it was fully balanced by the superior quality of the French troops. This fact, if it was a fact, made no impression upon Marlborough. The new commander was determined to put an end to the nuisance of the French occupation of Cleves. His instinct told him that neither the garrisons on the Meuse nor the garrisons on the Rhine were his true objective. If Boufflers' army were destroyed the rest would be easy.

But Boufflers' army was entrenched between Gennep and Goch in a situation too strong to be attacked. And in any event the Dutch government were too terrified by their recent experience to run the hazard of a battle in such close proximity to their frontier. The very suggestion of a forward movement excited their alarm. At length they were induced to listen to a proposal of their own generals for the siege of Rheinberg. But this kind of operation had no attraction for Marlborough. He had seen at a glance the weakness of the French position in Cleves. Though a skilful and enterprising commander might have utilised that position for a bold offensive, an army located there could not hope to defend simultaneously, the province of Brabant, the Electorate of Cologne, and Spanish Guelderland. He therefore proposed to pass the Meuse and advance towards Brabant.

He told the Dutch government that such a movement could produce but one effect. Boufflers, fearful of being cut off from his base and of leaving the Spanish Netherlands exposed to invasion, would instantly abandon Cleves. He did not tell them that in that event opportunities for battle would inevitably arise. Precious days were wasted before he carried his point; but he carried it at last. At this time also he was worried by technical objections of the Prussian and Hanoverian contingents to serving under his command. When all was settled, he threw bridges over the Meuse near Grave, and, to deceive Boufflers, who was already puzzled by the long delay, sent his foragers across the river as though he intended to continue a great time in those parts. But at sunset on the ensuing day (July 25) he struck his camp, and, passing his entire army over the Meuse, pushed southward for Brabant.

Boufflers was taken by surprise. But he decided at once that he must follow Marlborough. Having dispatched a reinforcement to Rheinberg and sent word to Tallard to rejoin him as rapidly as possible, he struck his tents on the evening of the 26th, and marched up the Meuse with the utmost speed to Roermond, where he crossed the river on the 28th, and encamped at Horn upon the western bank.

Strengthened by detachments which he drew from the garrisons of Venlo and Roermond, and occupying at Horn a central position which enabled him to cover Rheinberg, Brabant, and Spanish Guelderland at the same time, he ought, in the opinion of the Duke of Berwick, to have continued in this locality.

But the difficulties of subsistence were very great; and Berwick does not explain how Boufflers could have overcome them. Boufflers, moreover, was convinced that the security of the Spanish Netherlands was the most important of the interests committed to his charge. He therefore decided to continue his march in the direction of Tirlemont and Louvain. But without a battle it seemed improbable that he could effect his purpose of interposing between Marlborough and the Belgian frontier. For, on the 28th, when the French arrived at Horn, the allies were already at Geldrop.

On the 31st, when Boufflers set out for Bree, Marlborough after capturing the castle of Gravenbroek, was advancing upon Lille St. Hubert. The two armies were marching at right angles to one another, and were steadily converging. That same evening, Marlborough was joined by nine battalions and six squadrons from Nijmegen as well as by the English artillery, while Tallard drew up to a league's distance of Boufflers' rear. The outposts of the two armies were in contact; and a collision now appeared inevitable.

On Marlborough's front, the country between Peer and Zonhoven was a vast and open heath, which the French must traverse, if they would continue their movement in the direction of Louvain. On this ideal battle-ground, the Earl proposed to try conclusions. He had reason to believe that Boufflers' men were fatigued with their long and rapid marches, and, what was even more important, depressed by the idea, which so easily springs up in the imaginative and critical[2] mind of the French soldier, that their general was somewhat overmatched.

On August 1, Tilly, at the head of 4,000 horse, reconnoitred the enemy's position, which was excellent in itself, but untenable by reason of the difficulty of subsistence. Rightly conjecturing that Boufflers would strike his camp that night, Marlborough sent back the heavy baggage to Gravenbroek, and made ready to deliver his attack at dawn. The field-deputies had consented to a battle. But during the hours of darkness their courage seems to have evaporated.

At sunrise on the 2nd, when the heads of the French columns ap-

---

2. Modern examples are many, but for '*ancien régime*' see also Mauvillon, *Leitres Françoises et Germaniques* (1740), *lettre* 2.

peared upon the heath, they besought the Earl to hold his hand. In justification of this change of attitude they laid great stress upon the fact that Tallard had now joined Boufflers. Marlborough, who knew all about the position of Tallard, was bitterly disappointed. But realising the inexpediency of friction with the Dutch government at this early stage of his command, he yielded to the agonised entreaties of the deputies, and merely requested that they would ride forward in his company to watch the passage of the enemy across the heath.

The spectacle was magnificent. Throwing up a screen of cavalry as they went the entire French army marched by in elaborate order of battle.[3] Their historians represent this movement as a daring conception executed with consummate skill. But General Kane, who was an eye-witness, has placed on record that it was marked by such hurry and confusion, that the Dutch deputies themselves were astonished, and "confessed a great opportunity was lost."

In Kane's opinion the fine French army would easily have been turned into a panic-stricken mob. But for the intervention of the deputies, he calculated, as Marlborough had calculated, that "in all human probability we should have given the enemy a fatal blow."[4] Though one chance had been thrown away, another presented itself immediately. The French encamped at Zonhoven on ground so badly chosen as positively to invite attack.

On the 3rd, "by break of day," says Millner, "all stood to arms in very good order."[5] But again the deputies opposed a stubborn resistance to Marlborough's arguments in favour of a battle.

Berwick declares that they saved the French army from destruction, "for our situation was such," he writes, "that we should have been beaten without any possibility of escape."[6]

But the opportunity passed. On August 4, Boufflers continued his march to Beeringen, where he was joined by reinforcements from the Spanish Netherlands.

Marlborough, whatever his feelings may have been, exhibited no resentment. A weaker man, or a less wise one, would have complained to the government at the Hague. But Marlborough merely reported that he had accomplished his purpose of forcing the enemy to abandon the Dutch frontier and to subsist henceforth at their own expense.

---

3. Pelet, *Mémoires militaires*. t. 2., p. 80.
4. Kane, *Memoirs of all the Campaigns of the Duke of Marlborough* (1702), p. 35.
5. Millner's *Journal* (1733), p. 22, July 22, 1702.
6. *Mémoires de Berwick*, t. 1, p. 187.

As regards the future, he wrote, that he had consulted the deputies and the generals of the States, and, with their full approval, proposed to besiege Venlo.

As several days must elapse before the preparations for this project would be complete, he advanced on the 5th to Peer, and gave orders for the ramparts of that place to be dismantled, as well as those of Bree. He likewise arranged to attack the castle of Weert, which was another of the fortified posts held by the French in that district; and for the execution of this enterprise he summoned ten battalions and seven squadrons from the garrison of Maestricht, together with six field-guns and six mortars.

But Boufflers, who saw clearly enough that Spanish Guelderland was likely to fall an easy prey to the allied army, decided now to try the effect of a blow at their communications. Accordingly on the 9th he marched northwards to Baelen, and on the 10th to Riethoven. He occupied Eindhoven with a detachment, and on the 13th pushed forward Berwick with six battalions, 600 grenadiers, thirteen squadrons, and twelve guns to that town. In this situation, he could subsist on Dutch territory, while he blocked the direct road from Maestricht to Bois-le-Duc. Though Marlborough, who could draw supplies from Maestricht, was not actually dependent upon Bois-le-Duc, he was nevertheless expecting a valuable convoy of bread and money from that place. It occurred to him that he might use this convoy as a lure to entice the enemy to battle.

Accordingly on the 12th, he returned to Hamont and on the ensuing day dispatched an escort of 2,000 horse and dragoons under Albemarle and Tilly to Bois-le-Duc, destined to take part in the investment of Venlo. To cover the march of the convoy, he ordered Opdam, who commanded a detachment of ten battalions and seventeen squadrons, to advance on the 14th towards Helmond. Opdam encamped invitingly upon the open heath of Geldrop, at a distance of less than four miles from Eindhoven.

It was Marlborough's intention, if Boufflers swallowed the bait, to support Opdam with the entire army. Berwick, who thought that a great opportunity had come, and who in any event saw no reason to avoid a general action, reported Opdam's presence on the evening of the 15th, and suggested that with the assistance of Boufflers' left wing, he could crush the detachment on the heath. Having received permission to advance, he crossed the Dommel and the Tongreloup on the morning of the 16th, while Boufflers moved up from Riethoven with the left wing.

Marlborough, who was early in the saddle, was apprised of the situation by an express from Opdam. Delighted at the success of his ruse, he drew out the army in order of battle, and pushed up his right wing towards Leende. Once again a collision seemed inevitable. When Boufflers arrived on the scene, only a mile of open heath separated the forces of Berwick and Opdam. But the Marshal's heart failed him at the last moment. Alleging that, while the action with Opdam was precisely what he desired, yet fearing that Marlborough might cut the French army in twain by a march to Eindhoven, he ordered Berwick, to withdraw behind the Dommel, much to that good officer's chagrin.

At 2 o'clock Opdam resumed his march to Helmond, while Marlborough's troops returned to camp. That night the two most disappointed men in both armies were the brother and the son of Arabella Churchill.

On the 17th the castle of Weert surrendered after a brief bombardment . On the same day, Opdam arrived at Gemert, where he met the convoy. Acting under Marlborough's instructions, he conducted it by a road which lay to the east of the road through Geldrop, and which was protected by small rivers. On the 20th, he brought it in safety to the camp. All this time Boufflers remained quietly at Riethoven, where he enjoyed the satisfaction of subsisting upon Dutch territory. But now the French government intervened. Louis was profoundly mortified by the course of the campaign.

The fall of Kaiserswerth, the failure to accomplish anything of magnitude during the siege, the vacation of Prussian territory, the desertion of the Electorate of Cologne, and the abandonment of the whole line of the Meuse as far as Maestricht, constituted in his eyes a discreditable and damaging record . In so far as his power in Europe depended upon prestige, it had certainly been shaken. He considered himself bound by the strongest claims both of honour and of policy to defend the Electorate of Cologne against all comers. But if Spanish Guelderland were lost, he could hold neither the Meuse nor the Lower Rhine. In his letters to Boufflers he made no attempt to hide his vexation.

Boufflers had proposed a diversion in Flanders as a device for drawing off the enemy from Spanish Guelderland. But Louis, who had begun to form a correct estimate of Marlborough's capacity, would have none of such futile palliatives. In a letter dated August 23rd he told Boufflers plainly that there was only one course open to him. He must dog the steps of the allies, and on the first convenient occasion, he must give them battle. On no account must they be permitted to capture Venlo. If Venlo were to fall in the presence of the Duke of Burgundy and a powerful army, France, wrote Louis, would be intolerably humiliated. Liège itself would be as good as lost, and the whole situation in this theatre of the war would be irretrievably ruined.

But before the King's letter reached Boufflers, Marlborough had done what he could to assist the unhappy Marshal to fulfil the royal will. He set out for Peer, but he left his rearguard, which consisted of the detachment under Opdam, so far behind that the enemy had every excuse to attack it. Boufflers came down from Riethoven to Exel on the same day. On the 23rd, still dangling his rearguard under the noses of the French, Marlborough continued his march over the heath in the direction of Helchteren. Boufflers dashed forward in pursuit, but he was just too late.

At the last moment Marlborough wheeled round in order of battle, and drew up to Opdam's detachment. Emerging breathlessly upon the heath, the French discovered the allies drawn up in a semicircle, upon rising ground, with the village of Spikel before their left, and a swampy rivulet in advance of their right. Their centre was covered by ponds and marshes. Extricating his army as rapidly as he could from the narrow defiles in which they were entangled, Boufflers prepared for battle. At 3 in the afternoon the artillery on both sides opened fire, and some hundreds were killed by the cannonade. Berwick inferred that the French had the better of this duel because their guns were better served, and the allied right was much exposed.

At 5 o'clock, observing that the enemy's left, which was entangled in wet and difficult ground, showed inevitable symptoms of confusion, Marlborough ordered Opdam's detachment, supported by the whole of the right wing, to advance to the attack. To the great astonishment of all who had heard the order given, it was not obeyed with alacrity. Opdam pretended that he was hindered from executing it by the marshy nature of the soil. When at length he did move, he moved so slowly that it was already too late in the day to begin a battle. The French in alarm drew off their battalions on this side, but twilight was approaching, and in any event the original opportunity had passed.

"I have but too much reason to complain," Marlborough wrote to Godolphin, "that the 10,000 men upon our right did not march as soon as I sent the orders, which if they had, I believe we should have had a very easy victory, for their whole left was in disorder."[7]

As though he had not suffered sufficiently from the imbecility of Dutch deputies, he was now confronted with the insubordination, or worse, of Dutch generals.

The ensuing day found both armies in the same position. Despite the misconduct of Opdam, which was calculated to deter the most sanguine of commanders from the hazard of a battle in which he must rely upon such officers, Marlborough was still eager to go forward. His left wing, nine battalions of which had occupied the village of Spikel, seems to have caused the enemy some uneasiness, and Boufflers, anticipating danger in that quarter, strengthened the right of his line by moving troops from its other extremity. But it was now the deputies' turn to come to the rescue of the French Marshal. They urged the advisability of waiting. If Boufflers attacked, he would have all the disadvantage of the ground. But if, on the other hand, he remained quiescent, the whole question could be reconsidered on the morrow.

Remarking merely that on the morrow Boufflers would be gone, Marlborough yielded. Nevertheless he made his dispositions for an advance on the 25th. His prophecy proved only too correct. Having carefully reconnoitred the allied position, Burgundy, Boufflers, Berwick, and all the French generals, unanimously agreed that it was unassailable. They agreed also that, as it was impossible for them to feed their army in its present situation, they must retire. Under cover of darkness therefore they struck their tents and stole silently away. Marlborough was speedily apprised of their departure; and as soon as daylight appeared he followed them with forty squadrons.

General Wood came up with the rearguard, and engaged in a running skirmish with the Household Cavalry, which after some trifling losses fell rapidly back upon the main body. Boufflers took the road to Baelen, and on the 27th returned to his old camp at Beeringen. In obedience to Louis' wishes he was continuing in close proximity to the enemy.

A French historian[8] has remarked that Marlborough might have attacked the camp at Beeringen, had he not been demoralised by the Duke of Burgundy's "audacious marches." Marlborough's private opinion of those marches has not been preserved. But all the recorded facts suggest that he had formed a very low estimate of the capacity of his antagonists. His troubles came not from the French but from the

---
7. Coxe, vol. 1, ch. 12., p. 94.
8. Pelet, *Mémoires militaires*, t. 2, p. 97.

Dutch. Opdam's disobedience was unpardonable.

In his official report to the Hague, Marlborough purposely concealed the truth, because, as he explained to Godolphin, "I have thought it much for Her Majesty's service to take no notice of it."[9] But the incident had been observed by too many competent witnesses to escape publicity.

> "My Lord Rivers," wrote Marlborough in the same letter to Godolphin, "and almost all the general officers of the right were with me when I sent the orders, so that notwithstanding the care I take to hinder it they do talk."

And talk they did. Every soldier knew that Marlborough's plan had been ruined by the Dutch general, just as every soldier suspected that previous plans had been frustrated by the Dutch deputies. Deserters from Boufflers' army (and they were very numerous) declared that the French were "so harried and famished" that they would have offered but a poor resistance to Marlborough's men, whose eagerness to come to close quarters was specially mentioned in the Earl's dispatches to the Hague.

"We ought not to have let them escape as we did," wrote Albemarle to a friend.[10] Cardonel, in forwarding to Blathwayt a copy of Marlborough's official report to the States-General, observed that if the Earl's "positive orders" had been obeyed "we could not in all probability have failed of a glorious victory." He added that the reference in the report to the marshes and the difficulty of the ground was "rather to cover the omission in not advancing as soon as they were ordered than anything else."[11] Through private letters the facts became generally notorious in England, where the greatest dissatisfaction was loudly expressed. Marlborough, for his part, was resolved to waste no more time in seeking for a battle under these exasperating conditions. He determined to devote the remainder of the campaign to the reduction of the places on the Meuse.

The French at Beeringen amused themselves, and everybody else, by the reflection that they had tried their best to bring an unwilling enemy to battle. But no one was deceived. Boufflers certainly was not. He knew that he had done what little he had done only under pres-

---

9. Coxe, vol. 1, p. 94: Marlborough to Godolphin, August 16/27, 1702.
10. Lediard, *Life of the Duke of Marlborough,* vol. 1, book 4 (Albemarle's letter, September 5. 1702).
11. Murray, *The Marlborough Despatches,* vol. 1, p. 26 (to Blathwayt, August 27, 1702).

sure from Versailles. He knew from deserters that on the afternoon of the 23rd Marlborough had ordered an attack upon the French left. And he had good reason to suspect why the order had not been positively obeyed. For Marlborough had already written privately both to Boufflers and to Berwick to explain that it was no fault of his that he had not attacked them on the heath between Peer and Bree, or in their camp at Zonhoven.

Dangeau in his diary manifests surprise that one general should make his apologies to another for failing to give battle. But Dangeau, the complete courtier, did not appreciate a soldier's instincts. Marlborough was hurt in his professional pride. Moreover, though he possessed the entire confidence of the men of his own country, he was well aware that continental opinion chose to regard him as a novice, whose military capacity was now upon its trial.

That Marlborough, in spite of Burgundy's "audacious marches," remained master of the situation, speedily appeared. The preparations of the Dutch for the siege of Venlo had been conducted in a dilatory fashion, but they were at last complete. On the 26th Marlborough sent off the Prince of Saarbrück with twenty battalions and sixteen squadrons to invest the town. Cutts, who was invaluable when fighting was to be done, and Opdam, who could well be spared, accompanied this detachment. Simultaneously a Prussian force of twelve battalions and twenty squadrons under the Margrave of Brandenburg, approached the place upon the eastern side of the Meuse.

On the 29th Venlo was invested; and on the same day Marlborough broke up his camp at Spikel and marched to Asch, where he assumed a strong position covering the siege. The effect of these movements upon Burgundy and Boufflers can well be imagined. The King had told them that the loss of Venlo would be shameful and detrimental to the French arms. But they knew no remedy. A council of war was summoned to consider the possibility of saving the place. Burgundy suggested that they should march forthwith upon the town. But opinion was unanimous that the country adjacent to Venlo could not support them.

Opinion was also unanimous that Marlborough's position could neither be taken nor turned. It was decided that nothing could be done. Boufflers explained to Louis that the army was unequal to the task of defending both Brabant and Spanish Guelderland at the same time. He reverted to his former purpose of a diversion in Flanders, and suggested the siege of Hulst. Louis reluctantly consented. And Burgundy in disgust returned to Versailles, where he was received with transports of enthusiasm by his wife.[12] In the words of an exultant English journalist, he "who was generally reported to have come to the army to be taught how to fight, learnt nothing from Marshal Boufflers but how to avoid an engagement."[13]

Boufflers indeed was unlucky in all he touched. His project of besieging Hulst was entrusted to the Spanish general, Bedmar. But the Dutch having opened the sluices, the operation terminated in a miserable fiasco. Louis was gravely dissatisfied. He realised that Boufflers, who among fighting captains was the bravest of the brave, had little talent for the higher branches of the art of war. It must however be admitted that he had been given a task which would have taxed the genius of Turenne. Against Athlone, or some other commander who proceeded by rule of thumb, he might have done sufficiently well. But even with the Dutch deputies and the Dutch generals to help him, he never had the slightest chance against Marlborough.

On September 13 Boufflers moved to Tongres, where he was in closer touch with Liège, and on the same day Marlborough drew nearer to Maestricht and encamped at Sutendael. Meantime the siege of Venlo progressed as rapidly as the quarrels of the Dutch generals with the Dutch engineer Coehoorn would permit. On the 18th a double assault was delivered. The Prussians on the right bank of the Meuse succeeded only in carrying an outwork of the town. But the English on the left stormed the fort of St. Michael, and turned its guns against the enemy, whom they cannonaded across the river.

This exploit, audaciously conceived by Cutts and as audaciously executed by the English regulars and volunteers, depressed the spirits of the French. Five days later the allied army, having received intelligence of the capture of Landau, were firing a salute in honour of the event, when the garrison, supposing this loud discharge to be the signal for another assault, instantly hoisted the white flag. In four weeks that place, upon which the French King set such enormous store, had been wrested from his grasp, while Boufflers at Tongres remained an impotent spectator of its fall.

But Boufflers had not been altogether idle. He had dispatched Tallard to the Rhine with instructions to strengthen the garrison of Bonn and to bring off the Elector of Cologne from the perilous position in which Marlborough's advance had placed that unfortunate prince. He

---

12. *Mémoires de Dangeau* (1817), t. 2., p. 191.
13. Boyer, vol. 1, p. 69.

had inspected the fortifications of Liège, and had decided that while the town itself was incapable of defence, the citadel might offer serious resistance to an enemy. He therefore reinforced the garrison, and proposed to retire with his diminished army to the shelter of the lines of Brabant. Louis and Chamillart were furious. The King wrote to the Marshal that whatever else was lost, Liège must be saved, and ordered him to encamp under the walls of the city. But Boufflers remonstrated strongly, and Louis reluctantly gave way.

Immediately upon the fall of Venlo, Marlborough ordered the besieging army to march up the river and invest both Roermond and Stevensweert. The one was taken in nine days, and the other in four. And now the entire Meuse as far as Maestricht was in the possession of the allies.

> *And every toun from Mastrick doun*
> *Our armie now hath won.*
> *We took in al both great and small,*
> *And we made the French to run.*[14]

Roermond surrendered on October 6. The French, aware that there was time to deliver yet another blow before the close of the campaigning season, anxiously wondered in which direction it would fall. The Rhine, Brabant, and Liège, lay open to the victorious allies. Marlborough, with unerring instinct, had set his heart on Liège. Much against its will, this populous and wealthy city had been forced by the Elector of Cologne into the arms of the French. The loss of it would be a severe blow to Louis' prestige. To the allies it would give increased resources and an extended control of the navigation of the Meuse in the direction of Namur. But the Dutch government hesitated. Principally because Liège was so valuable a prize, they feared lest any attempt to capture it should bring on what they dreaded most in the whole world, a battle.

Marlborough represented to them that however much importance the French might attach to Liège, Boufflers, who throughout the campaign had been afraid to fight upon approximately even terms, was not going to hazard an engagement now when the numerical odds were markedly against him . At length the Dutch were convinced . Marlborough executed his project with characteristic celerity. Having summoned the Prince of Saarbrück to follow him with a part of the army from beyond the Meuse, he struck his camp at Sutendael at 1

---

14. *The Remembrance* (Scots Brigade in Holland), vol. 3, p. 331.

on the morning of the 12th. By 4 in the afternoon his infantry were within cannon-shot of the citadel of Liège. Fifty squadrons of horse, pushing on in advance, had already invested the city.

This operation, by its suddenness and rapidity, completely disconcerted Boufflers. The allied army, marching between the Meuse and Tongres, passed close to the French camp. Marlborough, perceiving that he might attack with all the advantage of a surprise, was eager to give battle. But the Dutch deputies refused their consent. And therefore Boufflers retreated precipitately to the shelter of the lines of Brabant.

The chapter and magistrates of Liège yielded the city forthwith. But the garrison retired into the citadel, and the fortress of the Chartreuse on the opposite bank of the river. On the evening of the 18th, under the direction of Coehoorn, trenches were opened against the citadel. The batteries played for four days, and blew up no fewer than four magazines. On the 23rd the fortress was carried by assault in the most gallant fashion. Discouraged by this blow, the defenders of the Chartreuse surrendered after a bombardment of only a few hours.

And here terminated the campaign of 1702. Marlborough set out immediately for the Hague. Late on November 3 he went aboard a boat at Maestricht with General Opdam and Gueldermalsen, one of the deputies, and a guard of twenty-five men, and proceeded down the Meuse. At Roermond on the following morning he was joined by a second boat which carried Coehoorn and an escort sixty strong. A troop of fifty horse kept pace with the boats upon the bank. That evening they came to Venlo, where the cavalry having been relieved by a detachment from the garrison, they continued their course in the direction of Grave.

In the darkness of the night the boats failed to keep company, and the troopers on the shore lost their way. It happened that a party of thirty-five men from the garrison of Guelder, the only place which the French still held in those parts, was prowling on the river bank. They seized the tow-rope of Marlborough's boat, surprised the sleeping guard with a volley, and throwing in grenades, boarded the vessel and made all prisoners.

By the chivalrous custom of that age a general in time of war frequently received a passport from the enemy. Opdam and Gueldermalsen had each procured one, but Marlborough had none. He was saved by the presence of mind of an English servant, who slipped into his hand a passport which had been given to his brother, General

Churchill.

The French, who knew both Opdam and Gueldermalsen by sight, failed to recognise Marlborough, and in the hurry and darkness they did not observe that the passport which he presented was out of date. Having rifled the boat and accepted presents from Marlborough and his companions, they carried off the escort to Guelder and left the travellers at liberty to proceed upon their way. Meanwhile the news spread far and wide that Marlborough was taken. It came at once to Venlo, where the governor promptly ordered the entire garrison to march on Guelder and invest the town. It came to the Hague, where the people heard it with consternation and the States made ready to send every available soldier to Guelder and to threaten the garrison with extermination unless the prisoners were instantly delivered up. It came even to Versailles, where instructions were given to extend the most generous treatment to the English general, who was already esteemed by all Frenchmen for the exceptional courtesy and humanity which he invariably extended to prisoners of war.[15]

In these circumstances the astonishment and delight with which Marlborough's arrival at the Hague was greeted by the Dutch can well be imagined. As he passed through the streets to his hotel, he received such an ovation from that phlegmatic people as must have moved him deeply. Holland indeed regarded him as her deliverer. But Marlborough accepted official congratulations with discreet modesty. "What had been applied to him," he declared, "in justice belonged to the Queen his mistress . . . it was glory sufficient for him, to be Her Majesty's agent."[16] And he might well have added that the gratitude of a nation which permitted him to suffer such ignorant interference and such flagrant disobedience as he had already endured in the field possessed no practical value.

Judged by the standard which Marlborough had erected for himself, his campaign of 1702 fell far short of perfection. But judged by the standard of his contemporaries, it was singularly brilliant. It could hardly indeed have been otherwise. Those generals who conducted their operations in accordance with some written or unwritten book of maxims or rules had never any chance against Marlborough, for the simple reason that he had read just as much of that book as they had, and with infinitely more discernment.

When therefore, as in 1702, the pressure of extraneous causes

---
15. *Mémoires de Dangeau* (1817), t, 2, p. 194, November 11, 1702.
16. Lediard, vol. 1, p. 199.

which he could not control, compelled him to wage war upon a system other than his own, he invariably triumphed. The style was none of his choosing; but its most accomplished professors could never get the better of him at their own and only game. His superiority was clearly demonstrated by results. It was also admitted by Athlone, a typical officer of the orthodox school, who had the honesty and the generosity to declare publicly that at every important moment in the campaign his own opinion had been at variance with Marlborough's.

The Englishman's success appeared more conspicuous beside the failures of the coalition in the other theatres of the war. In September a German and Austrian army under Louis of Baden was besieging Landau, as a preliminary step to the invasion of Alsace, when the Elector of Bavaria, throwing off the mask of neutrality under cover of which he had been negotiating alternately with both sides, seized the city of Ulm and threatened to sever the communications of the Imperialists with Vienna. But Landau fell a few days later, and Louis of Baden at once recrossed the Rhine.

Left to themselves, the Bavarians might have been overpowered. Such allies however were far too valuable to be deserted. With 40,000 men Villars passed the Rhine at Hüningen in the face of Baden's army. He engaged the enemy at Friedlingen, a singular battle in which the Imperialist cavalry was routed and the French infantry ran away in the moment of victory. But Villars had the better of the exchange, and was rewarded with a Marshal's baton. The Elector, who after the fall of Landau had renewed his intrigues with Austria, ought to have advanced to meet Villars. But he refused to quit Bavaria; and the lateness of the season and the strength of Baden's army compelled the French to retire without effecting a junction.

Meantime Tallard had taken Trèves and Trarbach. These forward movements of the French on both flanks, coupled with the rising of Bavaria in the rear, rendered the Imperialist position on the Upper Rhine extremely critical.

In Italy Eugène had been confronted by superior numbers and by a general of real capacity, Vendôme. The Mediterranean being entirely at the service of the House of Bourbon, the new King of Spain crossed to his Italian dominions, and joined Vendôme with Spanish reinforcements. Eugène was compelled to raise the siege of Mantua. At Luzzara he fought a desperate and indecisive battle, of which, as of Villars' action at Friedlingen, it has been wittily remarked that "both sides claimed the victory because both were defeated." By genius alone he maintained a precarious footing in the country until both armies went into winter-quarters.

By sea Rooke and Ormond with the combined fleets of England and Holland had failed disgracefully in their attempt on Cadiz. Having done what they could by firing churches and ravishing nuns to recommend the cause of the Austrian claimant to the Spanish people, the allied forces retired ignominiously to their ships, and sailed for home. But better luck than they deserved awaited them. The Plate fleet, with its French escort, had anchored in Vigo Bay. Roused by the prospect of enormous booty, Rooke and Ormond dashed upon the place. Soldiers and sailors vied with one another in skill and daring. The enemy's ships were all burnt or taken. Part of the treasure was captured, but the bulk of it went to the bottom.

The expedition returned to England in triumph. It had struck the kind of stroke which was popular in England. It had also inflicted a damaging blow upon the resources of the enemy. But it would have better served the cause of Europe had it fulfilled its original mission of securing Cadiz as a naval base for the maritime powers. Its principal achievement, however, was as yet unrevealed. It had frightened Portugal into a distaste for the French alliance, which was powerless to protect her seaboard.

Thus at the termination of the first campaign Louis had good reason to congratulate himself upon the net result. In the Spanish Peninsula and in the Mediterranean the strategical position remained unchanged. The allies had no footing there. In Italy and on the Upper Rhine they had been forced to relinquish the attack and to assume the defensive. Only in Flanders had the House of Bourbon sustained any real loss. Marlborough had saved Holland from the peril of invasion. But that was all. The peril of invasion must be brought to the gates of France, perhaps even to the gates of Paris, ere Louis would yield. Such a contingency appeared ridiculously remote. Louis was confident that long before it could be realised, the coalition would fall to pieces. His calculations were just, but his data were defective. He reckoned still without the genius of Eugène and Marlborough.

CHAPTER 5

The Strife of Parties

The last Parliament of William was not dissolved by the mere fact of the Sovereign's death . In pursuance of a statute of 1696 it assembled immediately, and continued in being till July. The general election which ensued was accompanied by displays of bitterness and violence similar to those which had attended the contest in the preceding year. The Whigs published a black list of 167 Tories, whom they described as the friends of France. The Tories denounced the Whigs as extortionate taxers of the people and plunderers of the public treasure. The Tories were powerfully assisted by the popularity of the Queen and by her known attachment to the Church. They met the imputation on their patriotism by a straight pledge to support the war.

In the event they beat "the peevish party,"[1] as Evelyn calls their opponents, by a majority of two to one in a House of 513. Harley for the third time was elected Speaker. This result augured well for the prospects of the new ministry. But great majorities have always their disadvantages. Flushed with victory and conscious of their overwhelming strength, the Tory hosts might be tempted to pursue a revengeful policy, quite incompatible with the system of Marlborough and Godolphin. It was known that many supporters of that system had secured seats. But many of a more vehement temper had also been returned. If the Commons should be induced to enter upon furious courses, the first result would be a collision with the Upper House, where a small but reliable Whig majority was strongly entrenched.

It was evident therefore that the popular assembly would require careful management. The task was one which Godolphin and Marlborough, as members of the House of Lords, were debarred from

---

1. *Evelyn's Diary* (Chandos Library), p. 584, June 27, 1702.

undertaking, even if their other responsibilities had not absorbed the whole of their energy and time. But in Robert Harley, the Speaker, they discovered a man exceptionally adapted to this purpose.

Harley was a nominal Tory, and in old Evelyn's opinion "an able gentleman."[2] But there was little in his antecedents to suggest close attachment to either Church or King. His grandfather was a Herefordshire Puritan, a member of the Long Parliament, and a defacer of Christian art. His grandmother made good the family mansion against the Royalist forces for six weeks. His father, who also did battle for the Roundhead cause, but who detested Oliver Cromwell, supported both the Restoration and the Revolution. Harley himself was born in 1661 and entered Parliament in 1689. Exhibiting no very pronounced bias towards either party, he gradually acquired a reputation on both sides of the House for practical sagacity and profound knowledge of Parliamentary law and practice.

To these qualities, associated as they were with kindliness of disposition and an affable manner, he owed his three elections to the Speakership. At the outset of his political career he had passed as a Whig; but his opposition to a standing army of any magnitude, his advocacy of the creation of a land bank in the agricultural interest, and his refusal of a Secretaryship of State, which was twice offered him by William, rendered him extremely popular among the Tories. He was now regarded as a leader of that party. At the same time, his Puritan origin, his tolerant attitude towards Dissenters, and the natural amiability which he displayed in his public and private relations, secured him the sympathetic regard of the Whigs.

Though never a brilliant or a powerful orator, he was invariably heard with attention and respect. He had a positive talent for the manipulation of Parliamentary parties and the subtleties of Parliamentary tactics. In short he was precisely the politician of whom Marlborough and Godolphin had need. He readily fell in with their proposals; and in process of time he became a sort of ministerial 'wire-puller' and 'whip,' parts which in modern eyes must appear singular ones for a Speaker to have played. Harley played them so well that after twelve months it was arranged by Godolphin, with Marlborough's approval, that the three "should meet regularly at least twice a week, if not oftener, to advise upon anything that shall occur."[3]

---

2. *Evelyn's Diary*, p. 581, January 9, 1701.
3. Portland MSS., vol. 4: Godolphin to Harley, November 4, 1703 (Hist. MSS. Comm., 15th Report, Appendix 4).

No sooner had the new Parliament assembled than the Tory majority began to show their teeth. In an address of congratulation presented to the Queen, they declared that "the protection and security of our trade, the vigorous support of Your Majesty's allies, and the wonderful progress of Your Majesty's arms under the conduct of the Earl of Marlborough, have signally retrieved the ancient honour and glory of the English nation."[4] The use of the word "retrieved" was resented by the Whigs as a reflection on the memory of William. They moved to substitute "maintained," but they were beaten on a division by 180 to 80. In the matter of disputed elections, which the Tories regarded in the spirit of partisans rather than of judges, little consideration was shown to the minority.

But nothing was so unpalatable to the Whigs as the fixed resolution of their antagonists to investigate the public accounts. During the reign of William the control of the national finances had been mainly in Whig hands. It was notorious that great confusion existed; it was strongly suspected that malversations had occurred. Seven Tory Commissioners, of whom St. John, the youthful member for Wooton Bassett was one, were appointed to conduct the enquiry. Ranelagh, the Paymaster-General, and Halifax himself were specially selected for attack. The proceedings of the Commission in regard to Halifax culminated in a conflict between the two Houses.

But however furiously they might rage against the men and measures of the late reign, the Tory majority were as steady as the Whigs in their support of the foreign policy of Marlborough. By Burnet's own admission "the House of Commons very unanimously, and with great dispatch, . . voted all the supplies that were necessary for carrying on the war."[5] Together with the Peers, they attended the Sovereign on November 23, when she went in state to St. Paul's to return thanks for the successes of her arms on land and sea. Accompanied in her coach and eight by the Countesses of Marlborough and Sunderland, the Queen was received by the populace with remarkable demonstrations of affection and delight.

"There has not been," wrote Evelyn, "so great an union in Parliament, Court and People, in memory of man."[6]

Marlborough returned to England in the beginning of December.

---

4. Lediard, vol. 1, p. 205.
5. Burnet, vol. 3, p. 370.
6. *Evelyn's Diary*, November, 1702.

A deputation of the Commons, headed by Seymour, presented him with the thanks of that assembly. In his reply the Earl ascribed his success to "God's blessing"[7] and "the great bravery"[8] of the troops. The Queen announced that she intended to make him a duke "by the title of Marquis of Blandford and Duke of Marlborough."[9] As she had already made him a Knight of the Garter, this additional honour was criticised in some quarters as excessive; and envious voices suggested that he owed it more to the influence of his wife than to his own services.

These reflections were very unjust both to Sarah and her husband. The offer of a dukedom had in fact originated with the Queen herself. It found no favour with the Countess. Sarah considered that the family fortune was insufficient for the upkeep of so elevated a rank; she dreaded the clamour of jealous and malicious tongues, and she foresaw that the case might be used as a precedent by every importunate angler in the fountain of honour. The Queen met the first of these objections by the promise of a pension of £5,000.

But Sarah continued to discountenance the proposition, and wrote to her husband, while he was still at the Hague, to dissuade him from accepting it. He admitted the soundness of her arguments. But he also recognised that it was not so much a question of his own merits or of Anne's personal wishes as of the interest of the public service. Marlborough had taken the place of William on the European stage. He was England's plenipotentiary to the United Provinces. He was captain- general of the Queen's forces, and commander-in-chief of that Dutch army which sovereign princes had aspired to lead. He corresponded with monarchs and collaborated with ambassadors. Never before had a situation comparable to his been occupied by an English subject.

Yet there were English subjects whose social rank was superior to Marlborough's. That fact tended to impair his authority abroad, where mere titles have always been more esteemed than in these islands. In the eyes of Europe the highest grade in the English peerage was none too high for the Englishman judged worthy to complete the military and diplomatic work which William had begun. It was patent to Heinsius that a dukedom would strengthen Marlborough's hands upon the continent. Godolphin took the same view. Knowing full well that they

---

7. Lediard, vol. 1, p. 207.
8. *Ibid.*
9. *Ibid.*

were right, Marlborough yielded to their representations and accepted the Queen's offer. Those English critics who consider that according to English notions he had not yet earned the title have a right to their own opinion. But nobody has any right to say that his wife extorted this new distinction from the generous weakness of the Queen. It was in opposition to his wife's wishes, and solely in the interest of his country and the Grand Alliance, that Marlborough reluctantly became a duke.

The Queen informed the Commons that she had settled £5,000 a year out of the revenues of the Post Office on the victorious general. As she was not empowered to bind her successors, she requested the House to take the necessary steps to render the pension perpetual. This message was very badly received. It was regarded, says Evelyn, "as a bold and unadvis'd request "on Marlborough's part, "as he had, besides his own considerable estate, above £30,000 a year in places and employments, with £50,000 at interest."[10]

This judgement overlooked the two important facts that all his "places and employments" might be taken from him at a moment's notice, as had happened in the preceding reign, and that in England at any rate it was no kindness to fasten a dukedom on a man whose assured income, however respectable, was insufficient to maintain the title in the magnificent fashion traditional in this country. But those advocates of economy who dwelt upon the existing indebtedness and growing liabilities of the nation were on firmer ground. In particular, the Tories, who had so long denounced the extravagant generosity of William to his favourites, could not with any show of consistency approve the Queen's suggestion, made though it was on behalf of a Tory general.

Seymour, the Comptroller of the Household, who had headed the Commons' deputation to Marlborough on his return from the continent, spoke against the grant. Musgrave, Clerk of the Ordnance, of which Marlborough was Master, expressed the opinion that his chief's services, eminent as they undoubtedly were, had been well rewarded. Others insinuated that a single family was seeking to monopolise the royal favour. Marlborough cut short this unpleasant discussion by inducing the Queen to revoke her message. But the Commons were determined to justify themselves in the eyes of a Sovereign who possessed their true affection.

They sent her an address in which they declared their "unanimous

---

10. Evelyn's *Diary*, December, 1702.

satisfaction" at the "just esteem" which she had expressed for Marlborough's services. They reiterated their opinion that he had "retrieved the ancient honour and glory of the English nation." They alleged that his diplomatic successes at the Hague "had vindicated the gentlemen of England, who had, by the vile practices of designing men, been traduced, and industriously represented as false to Your Majesty's allies, because they were true to the interest of their country."

While lamenting the necessity of opposing her wishes, they represented the danger "of making a precedent for the alienations of the revenue of the Crown, which has been so much reduced by the exorbitant grants of the last reign." And finally they recorded their gratification that the only way to obtain the Queen's favour, as demonstrated by her treatment of the Duke of Marlborough, was "to deserve well of the public."[11]

That the party which had published the black list should join in the congratulations to "the gentlemen of England "may at first sight seem strange. But viewed in the light of that party's trafficking with France in the reign of Charles II, it becomes tolerably intelligible.

Anne replied curtly: "I shall always think myself much concerned to reward those who deserve well of me and of the public. On this account I bestowed some favours on the Duke of Marlborough, and I am glad to find you think they are well placed."[12]

The sting of this speech lay less in what it said than in what it left unsaid. Its dignified reticence showed that the Queen was hurt. The Commons had wounded her in two tender parts, her loyalty to her friends and her Stuart pride. She told the Duchess that she would increase the pension of £5,000 by a grant of £2,000 from the privy purse. But this munificence, though strongly pressed by the generous monarch, was resolutely declined.

If the Queen was disappointed in the Tories, she was soon to be incensed with the Whigs, Fearful lest, in the event of her own death, Prince George should be left without adequate provision, she requested the Commons to secure him against this contingency. Both parties concurred in voting him the unprecedented allowance of £100,000 a year. The Tories inserted in the bill an amendment exempting the Prince from the operation of that clause in the Act of Succession which prohibited future sovereigns from conferring lands and offices on naturalised aliens. This amendment was superfluous, because the

---

11. Lediard, vol. 1, pp. 208, 209.
12. *Ibid.*, p. 209.

clause in question did not refer to aliens already naturalised. But the Tories desired to suggest that it did, and to frighten the foreign favourites of William—Portland, Albemarle, Rochfort, Grantham, and Schomberg.

The Whig majority in the House of Lords were speedily in arms. They denounced the amendment as an example of the unconstitutional practice of 'tacking,' and as an attempt to give a statutory interpretation to the Act of Succession which it was never intended to bear. The bill itself was seen to be in danger. The Queen became angry and alarmed. Marlborough and his friends exerted their utmost strength on behalf of the measure. But his own son-in-law, Sunderland, was conspicuous among its assailants.

The fury of the Duchess at what she regarded as gross ingratitude towards the benefactress of the family into which the Earl had had the good fortune to marry, produced a breach which Lady Sunderland found it difficult to heal. Eventually the bill was saved by a majority of one. Many of the Whigs, including Burnet and Sunderland, set their names to a protest. Anne, whose sense of wifely duty left nothing to be desired, never forgave them for it. But she wrote to the Duchess:

> I am sure the prince's bill passing after so much struggle is wholly owing to the pains you and Mr. Freeman have taken, and I ought to say a great deal to both of you in return, but neither words nor actions can ever express the true sense Mr. Morley and I have of your sincere kindness on this and all other occasions; and therefore I will not say any more on this subject, but that to my last moment, your dear unfortunate faithful Morley will be most passionately and tenderly yours.[13]

These trials of strength however were mere skirmishes in comparison with the struggle which arose between the parties and the Houses over the bill for the prevention of Occasional Conformity. Occasional Conformity was a practice which grew out of the conditions under which Protestant Dissenters had been placed by statute. The Toleration Act of 1689 had rewarded the Dissenters for their part in the Revolution by granting them the right of public worship. But the Corporation Act of 1661, which required all corporate magistrates and office-bearers to take the Sacrament according to the rites of the Church of England, and the Test Act of 1673, which imposed the same obligation on all servants of the Crown, both civil and military,

---

13. Coxe, vol. 1, p. 104.

remained still in force.

The second of these statutes did not materially affect Dissenters; but by the operation of the first, many prosperous merchants and tradesmen were excluded from those municipal honours which were the goal of their ambition, and also from the exercise of much of that political power which centred in the corporations. Cases had occurred in which, to escape these disabilities, known Dissenters had received the Sacrament in their parish church and had subsequently resumed attendance at their licensed chapels. This practice, which was tending to become very frequent, was regarded in many quarters as a scandal, and was distinctly unpopular.

Law-abiding people disliked it as deliberate evasion of the law. The majority of Churchmen, both clergy and laity, denounced it as a sacrilege. Even the more rigid Dissenters disapproved of it as a dereliction of principle. That stalwart Puritan, Defoe, declared that nobody who differed from the Church upon essentials could conscientiously receive the Sacrament from her priests, and that all who differed from her upon non-essentials were guilty of the sin of schism.[14]

The new Parliament had not been sitting a month before a bill for the prevention of Occasional Conformity was introduced into the House of Commons by the members for the two Universities and St. John, an acknowledged free-thinker. It was a drastic measure, imposing severe penalties upon Occasional Conformists and enlarging the scope of the Corporation Act by the inclusion of freemen, who were an important section of the electorate. It passed the Commons by big majorities, and was sent to the Lords about the middle of December.

Modern opinion would excuse the Dissenters who were guilty of the objectionable practice of Occasional Conformity and would condemn the laws which tempted them to it. But modern opinion has nothing much in common with the ideas of Stuart times. In one respect indeed there has been little change. Then, as now, true toleration was rare. For the rest, indifference posing as toleration pronounces today its cheap and easy judgements on a generation which, whatever else it may have done, sat seldom at the feet of Gallio.

The men and women of that epoch really cared about religion. They cared so much that all who adopted a type of Christianity different from theirs seemed in their eyes to be in grievous peril, if not in actual perdition. From these premises it was but a logical step to the duty of persecution. A true believer was bound to discourage, and if

---

14. Defoe, *An Enquiry into the Occasional Conformity Bill* (1704).

need be, to exterminate the propagators of spiritual damnation. The government which acted otherwise was inviting God's vengeance on the people. These opinions were not merely speculative; they were generally and actively translated into practice by the faithful of all denominations. The degree of persecution was regulated mainly by the numerical and combative strength of the persecuted.

Thus in England, Roman Catholics and Unitarians were 'altogether excluded from the benefits of the Toleration Act. Miserable old women, accused of witchcraft, were tortured by the populace and burned at the stake. The Protestant Dissenters were permitted to practise their religion, but they were punished by the loss of local distinction and political power. The Church of England had endured her share of suffering. In 1702 there were those still living who had seen the head of a primate stricken off upon Tower Hill. Evelyn, and men much younger than Evelyn, would remember the years when to administer the Sacrament according to the rites of the national church was a crime.

It was matter of common knowledge that the Queen's own grandfather would never have lost his life or his crown, had he only consented to establish the ecclesiastical system of John Knox on the ruins of Anglicanism. The majority of Churchmen were convinced that, if the descendants of the Puritans were permitted to acquire political power, neither the property nor the liberty of the Church would ever be secure. Subsequent history has by no means shown that this apprehension was groundless.

Marlborough was far too good a Churchman not to sympathise with the bill, though his wife of course disliked it. A Tory pamphlet on the subject was dedicated to the Duke. But the question for Godolphin's ministry was not one of personal sentiment. The bill was ardently desired by the Queen, who induced her husband, himself an Occasional Conformist, to vote for it; it was backed by a great majority in the Commons; and it was popular in the country. The plain interest of the government was therefore to support it.

The Whig majority in the House of Lords would have rejected it, had they dared. Instead, they pursued the equally effective course of modifying it beyond all recognition. Prominent in the work were the latitudinarian bishops, headed by Burnet. One amendment, which restricted the application of the measure to evaders of the Test Act, who for practical purposes did not exist, while exempting from its operation those evaders of the Corporation Act, who were the very persons struck at, was tantamount to rejection. A great agitation arose. The pulpits rang with denunciations of the Church's enemies. Henry Sacheverell, a Fellow of Magdalen, boldly assailed the latitudinarian bishops. The mob attacked the Dissenters' chapels.

A war of pamphlets was vigorously waged. Defoe, who had exposed the Occasional Conformists as either hypocrites or *schismatics*, was provoked by the furious language of the Tory party into the publication of that brilliant satire. The Shortest Way with the Dissenters, which, thanks to its excessive irony, was at first mistaken for a Tory tract. By Nottingham's orders he was arrested and tried for libel. He was fined, imprisoned, and exposed in the pillory, where the same rabble that wrecked the meeting-houses cheered him uproariously and drank his health in pots of beer.

Defoe's action was damaging to the agitation. But the Lords lacked the courage of their own opinions. To obscure the real issue, they amended a clause relating to fines, with the object of starting the old squabble on the question of money bills. The Commons refused all the amendments. A conference between the Houses ensued. Subsequently the Lords adhered to all the amendments, though by a majority of only one in each of three separate divisions. The Commons stood firm; and the bill was lost.

The spectacle of the House of Lords as the fortress of Whiggery and the bulwark of Dissent might well be recommended to those profound students of constitutional questions, the modern electorate. They will doubtless be properly pained to observe that in destroying by majorities of one a measure which was strongly pressed by a newly chosen House of Commons, the Whig peers made no concealment of that contempt for a popular opinion which has always been characteristic of self-styled popular parties. Thoroughly to appreciate the situation, it must be remembered that no fewer than five Lords in a House of 150 were foreigners by birth and professors of that continental Protestantism which is the parent of English Dissent.

The conduct of the Whig peers had ultimate consequences which they never foresaw, but which were very disagreeable to the Whig party. The immediate effect was injurious to the government, for the loss of the bill inflamed the passion of the Tories and started an enduring discontent among the clergy at the very moment when Godolphin and Marlborough were striving to create an atmosphere of unity and peace. The irritation of the Church's friends was reflected in the temper of the Tory ministers. Rochester, happily, was no longer in office. He had resigned the Lord Lieutenancy of Ireland, because, as the Duchess of Marlborough observes, the Queen had been "so unreasonable as to press him to go thither to attend the affairs of that Kingdom, which greatly needed his presence."[15] He was succeeded by the Duke of Ormond. Anne was well quit of his insolence, Godolphin of his intrigues, and Marlborough of his "military criticism,"

But Nottingham, Hedges, Seymour, and the other pronounced Tories exerted themselves to purge the public offices and the local administration of all taint of Whiggery; and they eventually succeeded, after Marlborough's departure for the continent, in inducing the Queen to dismiss several lords lieutenant, sheriffs, and justices of the peace. She was also persuaded to make four new barons out of four strong Tories, a very considerable creation in a House of 150, where, as Burnet confesses, "things of the greatest consequence were carried only by one or two voices."[16] At the Duchess of Marlborough's request and in fulfilment of a private promise, Hervey,[17] a Whig, was added to the number. This was the only case in which Sarah's influence was exerted on behalf of any aspirant to the peerage.

It was a relief to Marlborough to turn from the contemplation of a party system which he detested to the business of the war. Supplies had been cheerfully granted; but, alarmed by the magnitude of Louis' preparations for the next campaign, the States petitioned the Queen for a fresh levy of 10,000 men. The Commons voted the money in January, but on the condition that all Dutch trade and correspondence with France and Spain should forthwith cease. The Queen in her declaration of hostilities had forbidden her own subjects to have dealings with the enemy. The Emperor and the German Princes had followed suit. But the Dutch, who desired to enjoy the advantages of both peace and war at the same time, continued to maintain a profitable intercourse with the common foe. With the assistance of the merchants and bankers of Amsterdam, which was "the financial clearing-house of Europe,"[18] Louis was enabled to pay his armies in Italy and to transmit subsidies to Bavaria.

Such suppliants did not come into court with clean hands. If Holland chose to make war upon the principles of comic opera, it was her own affair; but that she should summon the rest of Europe to her

---

15. *Memoirs of the Life and Conduct of Sarah, Duchess of Marlborough* (1744), p. 139.
16. Burnet, vol. 3, p. 382.
17. *Memoirs of the Life and Conduct of Sarah, Duchess of Marlborough*, P. 1.35.
18. Leadam, vol. 9, p. 26. 2

aid, and should then proceed to enrich herself by forging weapons to be used against all who had responded to her piercing cries, was monstrous and intolerable. At the beginning of the last campaign both Houses had addressed the Queen upon this subject. At the Hague, Marlborough had striven his hardest, but without success, to procure the prohibition of a commerce which was not only discreditable to Holland, but highly injurious to the strategy of the coalition. The Commons therefore took a necessary and proper course. The Lords could not do otherwise than support them. The conduct of the Dutch admitted of no defence.

Nevertheless the Whigs exerted their ingenuity to palliate and to excuse it. Burnet dwells upon the importance of trade to Holland and affects to be shocked at the plainness of the language used in the Lower House. The Dutch, he says, "were treated very indecently."[19] They deserved it. The special pleading of their Whig champions only aggravated the case. Such short-sighted selfishness as they had exhibited in this matter went far to justify that English prejudice against foreigners, and that English suspicion of continental alliances which had continually obstructed the policy of William.

On the eve of the Duke's departure for the Hague, an irreparable disaster befell the Marlboroughs. Their only surviving boy, John, Marquis of Blandford, had quitted Eton for Cambridge, where his natural talents, his devotion to study, and his amenability to the discipline of college life, gave promise of a brilliant future. In spite of his mother's protests, his heart was already set upon a military career; and he had undertaken to procure a commission in the cavalry for his intimate friend, Horace Walpole. But in February, 1703, he was smitten with the ubiquitous scourge of that epoch, malignant smallpox. The Duchess hastened to his side. But no remedies and no physicians could avail. Her unremitting care perhaps prolonged a life which it was powerless to save. Marlborough, who had remained behind in torturing anxiety, arrived at Cambridge in time to see the end. They buried the boy in the beautiful chapel of his college, King's. He was not yet seventeen.

Sarah, whom men have called heartless, gave way to a paroxysm of grief. It was succeeded by a settled melancholy, which impaired her health and seemed at one time to threaten her reason. She would wander for hours in the cloisters of Westminster, brooding on her loss. Neither the tenderness of her husband, nor the solicitude of her daughters, nor the sympathy of the Queen, nor the universal regret of

---
19. Burnet, vol. 3, p. 370.

innumerable friends and of the public at large, could heal her wound. In the greatness of her sorrow Marlborough forgot his own.

"You and I," he wrote, in a letter instinct with true piety, "have great reason to bless God for all we have, so that we must not repine at His taking our poor child from us, but bless and praise Him for what His goodness leaves us. . . . The use I think we should make of this His correction is, that our chiefest time should be spent in reconciling ourselves to Him, and having in our minds always that we may not have long to live in this world."[20]

The Duke found comfort also in the thought that four daughters still remained to him. The third, Elizabeth, he had recently united to the Earl of Bridgewater; and the fourth, Mary, who excelled even her own sisters in beauty, was betrothed to Viscount Mounthermer. Peterborough had sought her hand for his son, Lord Mordaunt, but Marlborough took exception to the young man's dissolute character. Having prudently made a new will, in which he besought the Queen to continue his titles in the person of his son-in-law, Godolphin, he gladly departed for another scene, where he could forget his private affliction in the service of his country.

---

20. Coxe, vol. 1, p. 111: The Duke to the Duchess, August 2, 1703.

Chapter 6
1703

Those who, on the eve of the War of the Spanish Succession, computed and compared the resources of the antagonists and endeavoured to forecast the result, omitted from their calculations the very factor which, in the event, proved to be the determining one. They omitted it of necessity, and because they did not, and could not, know it. That factor was the human one of generalship. The balance was turned against Louis, as soon as ever it became manifest that Condé and Turenne had left no heirs, while the genius of Marlborough and Eugène was at the service of the coalition.

Nevertheless, France in this time of need produced one soldier of outstanding ability, who, though, like Luxembourg, he was less than Condé and Turenne, like Luxembourg, he was only a little less. At the very outset of the struggle Louis Hector Villars came swiftly to the front, and all but crushed the combination of his country's enemies. Six years later, he stood between her and what seemed to all observers inevitable doom.

Villars in 1703 was fifty. It was exactly thirty years since he had shared with Monmouth and Churchill in the glorious assault upon the counterscarp of Maestricht. A brilliant cavalry officer, he had been noticed by Condé at Seneffe, he had ridden by the side of Max Emanuel of Bavaria at Mohacs, he had saved the beaten army of d'Humières at Walcourt, he had charged among the foremost in the famous action at Leuze. Both at Munich and at Vienna he had exhibited no little talent for diplomacy. His most obvious fault, a kind of rhetorical boastfulness of utterance, was easily pardoned in one who was ever ready to make good his words.

His proved ability, his popularity with the troops, and his personal intimacy with Max Emanuel had led to his selection, in the autumn of 1702, for the command of the army destined to relieve Bavaria. His passage of the Rhine and his victory at Friedlingen had demonstrated his capacity to handle a combined force of all arms. Owing to the duplicity of the Elector's conduct, a junction between the French and Bavarian armies was not effected that autumn. But Louis relied on Villars to effect it in the ensuing year, and left him at liberty to choose his own methods.

The new-made Marshal had other ideas of war than those entertained by the text-book generals, and by the drawing-room critics of Versailles. Ruthlessly violating the sacrosanct tradition of 'winter-quarters,' he mobilised his forces at Strasbourg and summoned his officers from their *châteaux* and their pleasures in the middle of January. He crossed the Rhine at Neuenburg, passed under the cannon of Breisach in a dense fog, marched over roads which frost had rendered practicable, in weather which the soldiers called "Villars' weather,"[1] swept the startled enemy from their cantonments, and after a siege conducted upon principles of his own took the strong fortress of Kehl in the brief space of twelve days. These unorthodox proceedings shocked the soul of every incapable officer in France. The tongue of folly and envy was loosed at once against the man who dared to succeed by breaking the rules.

Villars, it was said, conducted an army as though he were leading a squadron to the charge. The King was warned that, though for a season fortune may attend temerity, sooner or later the lucky blunderer comes to inevitable doom. But Villars inconsiderately refuted the arguments of the courtiers and demonstrated that his impetuosity was tempered by prudence by returning immediately from Kehl to Strasbourg, to rest and recruit his army. Thereupon the same critics declared that he had sacrificed a great opportunity, and exposed Bavaria to ruin; and they sought to render him ridiculous by suggesting that jealousy was the motive which had induced an uxorious husband of fifty to quit his duty and return to the side of a young and beautiful wife of twenty.

Disregarding these malicious chatterers, the Marshal continued his preparations. Meantime the Elector, assailed by the Imperialists upon three sides, was manfully holding his own. But the struggle was too unequal to continue forever. By the beginning of April Villars was ready. Baden, lying in the lines of Stollhofen, threatened the road to Bavaria. Villars would gladly have stormed the Prince's camp, but the

---

1. *Vie de Villars* (1784), t. 1, p. 135.

majority of his lieutenant-generals pronounced against the enterprise. Knowing that, thanks to the critics at Versailles, he could afford to risk no failures, he abandoned an idea which his own judgement told him was a right one, and leaving Tallard to watch the Prince's motions, plunged boldly into the mountains. The passes were held by regular troops, supported by militia, but with rare audacity and dash the French carried position after position, and at Tuttlingen on May 9 joined hands with the Elector.

This concentration of forces on German soil was an event of the highest strategical importance. Louis, who understood perfectly that war is only a department of statecraft, was fighting everywhere on the defensive, in the well-grounded hope that political causes would presently dissolve the coalition. The march of Villars, though offensive in appearance, did not in reality involve any departure from Louis' plan, which rightly enough made no distinction between the territories of his allies and the soil of France. But though Villars had been sent to protect Bavaria, he was at liberty to protect it in his own way.

Now Villars was endowed with the strategical instinct. He knew that there is no more terrible form of war than that vigilant defensive, which patiently awaits the favourable moment for a crushing counter-stroke. He knew also that the most deadly blow is the one that falls upon the centre of gravity of the enemy's power. In his judgement the time had come to annihilate Austria by the capture of Vienna. He drew his design upon the grand scale. He proposed that the French and Bavarian armies should advance along the Danube, that Vendôme, who was feebly opposed by Starhemberg's small force in Italy, should pass the Tyrol and unite his troops to theirs, and that a combined host of more than 80,000 men should then bear down upon the Austrian capital.

The shock, he calculated, would be irresistible. The Emperor, harassed as he was by the Hungarian rebels, had nothing adequate to oppose to it. The fortifications of Vienna could not endure for more than eight days. If Baden should attempt a diversion or a rescue, Tallard was at hand to hold him down. This conception, magnificent and daring as it seemed, rested upon sound and solid foundations. It captivated the wayward fancy of Max Emanuel, the experienced judgement of Louis, and the mediocre mind of Chamillart. But its execution involved the perfect cohesion of four armies and the complete co-ordination of four wills. These essential conditions of success were lacking.

More than a century later, in 1809, the efficacy of the Marshal's plan was signally demonstrated by Napoleon himself. Had Villars enjoyed that absolute power which gave Napoleon an immense advantage over most of the generals known to history, Villars would have succeeded in 1703. He failed; but the failures of genius are sometimes more effective than the petty triumphs of orthodoxy.

Down to the beginning of June at any rate all promised fair. And for more than a year the menace of his strategy was destined to hold Austria in suspense, and to fetter the energies of the coalition in every theatre of the war.

The war in 1703 is more interesting in its strategical aspect than in any other. While Villars was preparing his terrific counterstroke against the Empire, Marlborough's Mediterranean policy was already bearing fruit. The expedition of Rooke and Ormond in the preceding year had not been wasted on the Portuguese, who realised that their coasts could be either ruined or protected by the navies of the maritime powers. Judicious negotiations, culminating in May, 1704, in the famous commercial treaty which is associated with the name of Paul Methuen, detached the King of Portugal from his alliance with France.

Thus the coalition obtained a secure base for land operations in the Peninsula and for naval operations beyond the Straits, Marlborough was resolved to push this policy to the utmost. He knew the strategical value of "the noiseless, steady, exhausting pressure with which sea-power acts." The weapon which in 1703 had won Portugal for the coalition might win them Savoy in 1704. The Duke was already wavering. And he was the custodian of the road from France to Italy. It was therefore decided that the fleet should pass the Straits. Once in the Mediterranean it could at least encourage disaffection on the eastern coasts of Spain, it might even assist the rebellion of the Cevennes, and it would certainly endanger the Italian dominions of the Spanish Crown. And always it would prove to Portugal that the navy of France was impotent to punish her desertion.

Of the rebellion in the Cevennes, where upwards of 4,000 Protestants had risen in arms, little was known but much was hoped. The French government was already drafting large forces into the disaffected area, and the allies were congratulating themselves on the appearance of a counterpoise to the Hungarian trouble in the Empire. Marlborough was very desirous of encouraging the movement, but he had been forced to overcome the opposition of Nottingham, who entertained conscientious scruples on the subject of assisting rebels.

Such delicacy was singularly misplaced in dealing with Louis, who was tireless in exploiting sedition in the dominions of his enemies.

Though Marlborough may not as yet have appreciated the full magnitude of Villars' design, he knew that an offensive movement of so menacing a character could not safely be left without a strong reply. The reply which he contemplated was nothing less than the capture of Antwerp and Ostend, places the possession of which, apart from their commercial value, would have been very advantageous to the maritime powers, and would have rendered the French lines untenable. Moreover he knew by experience that the Dutch government which shuddered at the suggestion of a battle, could easily be persuaded to sanction a siege. And he hoped, as he always hoped, that before the campaign was ended, he might continue to filch from friends and enemies alike an opportunity of crushing the French army in the field.

On March 17 he arrived at the Hague. Athlone having died, it was necessary to select a new commander for the Dutch forces. Marlborough no doubt was responsible for the choice of Overkirk, an old and gallant officer, and by far the most competent of the candidates. But in the all-important matter of the plan of campaign, the Dutch government showed less compliance. They were ready of course to undertake a siege, but not the siege which Marlborough proposed. As long as the city of Bonn remained in Louis' hands, they felt that their frontier was insecure and that their communications with the Empire were obstructed. To besiege Bonn at this particular juncture was in Marlborough's opinion mere waste of time.

If Bonn were first wrested from the French, they would consent to the design upon Antwerp and Ostend, but not otherwise. The Dutch were obdurate and Marlborough, having no alternative, yielded. His principal anxiety was lest the French should utilise the opportunity, created by the absence of a large part of his forces on the Rhine, to attempt some enterprise upon the Meuse. The question resolved itself into one of time. If the allies were very early in the field, and if the siege of Bonn were swiftly pressed to a conclusion, the chances of trouble on the Meuse would be but slight. He therefore pushed on the necessary arrangements with extreme vigour.

Traversing the country, he inspected the troops in their quarters and impressed upon the officers the necessity of rapid preparation. At Nijmegen he discussed the details of the siege with Coehoorn, whom he instructed to accumulate the requisite materials as quickly as possible. Ascending the Meuse, he visited the fortresses of Venlo, Roermond, Stevensweert, and Maestricht, and on April 14 arrived at Liège, where he conferred with Sinzendorf, the Emperor's minister, and revealed to him his future projects against Antwerp and Ostend. As Louis of Baden was pressing for reinforcements, it was necessary that the Emperor should understand that none could be spared from the defence of Flanders.

Returning to Maestricht, he ordered Overkirk to concentrate the Dutch and English troops in the vicinity of that fortress, to cover the town and citadel of Liège, and to watch the motions of the French. That invaluable time might not be frittered away by the lethargic methods of Dutch or German generals, he proposed to go in person to the siege of Bonn at the head of the Prussian, Hanoverian, and Hessian forces. How necessary his presence was, appeared at once from the backward state of Coehoorn's preparations. Nevertheless, Marlborough's cavalry invested Bonn on April 25, and Marlborough himself arrived with the infantry on the ensuing day.

Meantime the French government had by no means penetrated the Duke's designs. But they made ready for all eventualities. The plan of campaign was purely defensive. It rested partly on the assumption that sooner or later the progress of Villars would compel Marlborough to dispatch a strong detachment to Bavaria. By occupying unassailable positions in close proximity to the enemy, the army was to prevent the forcing of the lines or the formation of any considerable siege. But it was on no account to fight a battle with the main army of the enemy, except for the protection of Namur or Antwerp, and then only in the last resort. It might however undertake the siege of the citadel of Liège, if an opportunity occurred during Marlborough's absence at Bonn.

The command was entrusted to Marshal Villeroi, a courtier of fine person and charming manners, but an incompetent general. He was assisted by Boufflers, who was a better soldier, but who had incurred the King's displeasure by his failure in the preceding campaign. The two Marshals entrusted the defence of the lines to small detachments, and concentrated the bulk of their forces in the neighbourhood of Tirlemont. They had more men than Marlborough had been led to believe, they had brought great guns from Maubeuge down the Sambre to Namur, and they intended to compensate themselves for the loss of Bonn by the recovery of Liège. And now was seen the value of Marlborough's inexhaustible energy.

It was not until May 8 that the Marshals were ready to move; but the trenches before Bonn had been opened on the 3rd, and the siege was being conducted with so numerous and formidable an artillery and with such astounding vigour that prolonged resistance was out of the question. Apprised of these facts, the Marshals abandoned the idea of an attempt upon Liège as altogether hopeless in the little time at their disposal. But the destruction of Overkirk's army seemed well within their means. Overkirk had assembled some 15,000 men in Bilsen and Tongres, and the country to the west of Maestricht, and he was daily expecting to be joined by 10,000 English. But the Marshals had 40,000 horse and foot, the horse in particular being of splendid quality. They did not hesitate to seize so fair an opportunity.

At daybreak on the 9th they marched from Montenaeken in eight columns. Overkirk, having early information of their advance, ordered his forces to fall back on Maestricht. Two Dutch battalions, one of which belonged to the Scots Brigade in the service of Holland, were cut off in Tongres. The mediaeval ramparts of that ancient town were indefensible against artillery. But realising that the safety of the army might depend upon the time which they could gain, these two battalions declined to yield. From 4 in the afternoon until midnight the Marshals battered the place with their field-guns, the defenders replying with "two russtie cannon."[2]

At dawn on the 10th the French reopened fire and effectually breached the wall. Thereupon the garrison surrendered. They had stood it out for twenty-eight hours. Their conduct excited the admiration of Berwick. John Scot, who was one of the prisoners, records that

The noble Duke Berwick he ther did command,
To us he proved right kinde:
'Ye are my countrie men,' said he,
'No man shal do you wronge.'[3]

And he kept his word. Overkirk's army was safe. The English had arrived, and the entire force had occupied a good position to the north-west of Maestricht. The left and centre were on rising ground and covered by the artillery of that fortress, while the right was strongly posted in the villages of Lanaeken and Petersheim. On the night of

---

2. *The Remembrance* (The Scots Brigade in Holland), vol. 3. Publications of the Scottish History Society, vol. 38.
3. *Ibid.*

the 13th the French again advanced, and by noon on the following day drew up in full view of the allied army. Villeroi and Boufilers rode out to examine the ground. At first they formed the opinion that an attack upon the village of Lanaeken was feasible, and made their dispositions accordingly.

But Overkirk reinforced the threatened point, threw up entrenchments, and saluted the French with his artillery both small and great. There were some in the French army who conceived that an attack upon the centre would have succeeded. But the more the Marshals saw of the position, the less they liked it. At 3 o'clock they ordered a retirement to Bomershoven. This decision, though humiliating to the spirit of an army which had numerical odds of nearly two to one in its favour, was subsequently approved by Louis. Overkirk's conduct stood in no need of approval. He had thoroughly justified his appointment.

In the trenches before Bonn the news of Villeroi's advance had caused profound anxiety to Marlborough. But the city was already on the verge of surrender. Attacked in three places by an overwhelming artillery, it yielded on the 15th on honourable terms.

"I think," wrote the Duke to Godolphin, "if we had not been so uneasy as we are at what is doing on the Meuse we might in four or five days more have made this garrison prisoners of war."[4]

He did not stay to see the French march out. On the 17th he was back at Maestricht.

He was now at liberty to execute what he called "the great design." But the French had so many troops in the field that, unless he could destroy their main army in a decisive action, the investment of Antwerp could only be accomplished by the most elaborate strategy. Knowing that his chances of bringing the Marshals to battle were extremely slender, he laid his plans to circumvent them without fighting. The greater part of the army which had formed the siege of Bonn followed him to Maestricht; but the residue he dispatched to Breda and Bergen-op-Zoom, where they joined the Dutch forces already established in that region. This movement appeared to threaten Antwerp or the lines that ran from Antwerp to Ostend. But on the 25th he marched from Maestricht with his main army towards the southwest, as though he intended to undertake the siege of Huy.

Yet no preparations for a siege were reported from Maestricht. The

---

4. Coxe, vol. 1, p. 118: Marlborough to Godolphin, May 15, 1703.

Marshals were puzzled. But adhering faithfully to their instructions, they took the same direction. For some days the two armies moved upon parallel lines with nothing between them but the River Geer. Once the Duke made a demonstration, as if he would attack; but on the 30th he encamped at Thys, where he remained inactive till June 9. In this position he was very close to Huy. The opinion that he was meditating an attempt upon that fortress was strengthened by the news that cannon were now being sent by water from Maestricht to Liège. On the other hand, advices which arrived continually from the Spanish general, Bedmar, created the impression that serious mischief was brewing at the mouth of the Schelde.

Bedmar's dispatches showed that, on the arrival of the contingent from Bonn, the enemy who were commanded by Coehoorn, Spaar, Opdam, and Tilly had formed two camps, at Breda and Lillo, that subsequently they had formed three others at L'Ecluse, Biervliet, and Sas van Gent, that they were perpetually in motion under cover of darkness by road, river, and sea, and that they were equally diligent in transporting cannon and in spreading all manner of rumours of their intentions and designs. Bedmar admitted that he was quite unable to determine the real object of an enemy who at one time threatened Antwerp, at another Ostend, and at another the lines between the two.

The Marshals sent him a small detachment, which raised the number of his forces to thirty battalions and twenty-three squadrons. These he distributed at various points from Lierre to Ostend. He himself, very properly considering that Antwerp was the most important part of the charge confided to his care, took station on June 8 at Burgh, which was separated from that city only by the Schelde, and which was at the same time within easy distance of the northern lines. Here he remained in no little perplexity, certain that the blow would fall, but entirely ignorant of its destination.

Thus far success had attended the execution of Marlborough's plans. Both on the Meuse and on the Schelde he had created so dense a "fog of war" that the enemy was entirely at a loss. To increase their mystification, and divert their attention from the threatened point, he moved on June 9 to Haneffe, a day's march nearer to Huy. The Marshals responded by the occupation of a strong position at St. Servais, where they could either impede the siege of Huy or march by a shorter road than Marlborough to Antwerp. Their flanks were covered by the Geer and the Mehaigne, and their front by the village of Tourinne.

They also constructed trenches and redans. They were so pleased with the ground which they had chosen that they sent a plan of it to Versailles. Less than 1½ leagues of open country separated the hostile armies, which now, and throughout the campaign, were nearly equal in numbers, though the allies had slightly the advantage. In this situation they remained for eighteen days. Except in skirmishes between foragers, not a blow was struck. The Marshals took pleasure in the reflection that Marlborough was afraid. They flattered themselves that by their skill and foresight they had reduced the enemy to impotence. They did not know then, though they subsequently discovered it, that Marlborough passed those eighteen days in fruitlessly soliciting permission from the States-General to attack the French position. But such was in fact the case. To his reiterated demands the Dutch government had only one response. The army, they declared, was Holland's "all in all." If the army were destroyed, Holland would be lost.

To argue with the panic-stricken is unprofitable. Marlborough had two good reasons for desiring to fight. But neither of them was likely to appeal to the States-General. The first was a general one, which was ever present in his mind, and which was simply the impulse of the true soldier to destroy the armed forces of the enemy. The second arose out of the particular circumstances of the moment. Marlborough had begun to entertain the gravest doubts of the success of the "great design." His plan for the investment of Antwerp depended on the combined motions of two armies besides his own.

A detachment under Opdam was to concentrate at Bergen-op-Zoom. A second under Coehoorn was to move to the western extremity of the lines and attack Ostend. It was assumed that this diversion would draw Bedmar from the vicinity of Antwerp, Thereupon Opdam, descending from the north, and Marlborough himself, rushing up from the south, would together complete the investment of Antwerp. But Marlborough's hopes of success had been diminished by the discovery that the enemy was more numerous at all points than had been anticipated.

They were still further diminished by the action of Coehoorn, who had now obtained permission from the States-General to substitute an irruption into the country of Waes for the original idea of an attack upon Ostend. In Marlborough's opinion an irruption into the country of Waes would not effect the desired object of drawing Bedmar from Antwerp. But it would enable the Dutch to levy large contributions, of which Coehoorn, as governor of West Flanders, would receive one-tenth. The capture of Ostend, on the other hand, appeared to the jealous eyes of the Dutch government to be only a selfish project of the English cabinet, conceived in the interest of the maritime supremacy of England. Such base and irrelevant motives had brought about a decision which Marlborough viewed with grave misgiving.

"Had I been at the Hague," he wrote to Godolphin, "I am very confident they would have preferred the taking of Ostend."[5]

But he was not at the Hague; and in his absence, on the suggestion of one of his own subordinates, a civilian body, intervening at the very crisis of the operations, overrode the opinion of its own commander-in-chief upon a strategic question, vital to the issue of the whole campaign. A more fatuous perversion of the art of war it is impossible to imagine.

No wonder Marlborough longed for a decisive victory. If the Marshals' army were destroyed, the problem would be simplified. The problem indeed would no longer exist. But the Dutch government was obdurate. Public opinion, ignorant of the truth, marvelled at such long inaction. Even in that age men considered it remarkable that two great armies should continue for nearly three weeks in close proximity to one another without fighting. But the question of proximity was not material. When each of two armies has been expressly forbidden to attack the other, the actual distance between them is of no account. Whether it be one mile or a thousand, there will be no battle.[6]

All this time the perpetual motions of the Dutch detachments which confronted him kept Bedmar in a permanent state of apprehension and perplexity. Towards the middle of the month the enemy showed a tendency to concentrate in force under Opdam at Lillo. Thereupon the Spanish general, more alarmed than ever for the safety of Antwerp, called in as many of his troops as could be spared from the defence of the lines, passed the Schelde, and encamped on the 17th at Deurne, in the north-eastern environs of the city. A week later Ghent and Bruges were menaced by another concentration under Spaar at the opposite extremity of the lines.

But Bedmar did not move. The crisis was now at hand. On the 26th Spaar turned suddenly eastward, while Coehoorn passing in full

---

5. Coxe, vol. 1, p. 119: Letter of May 20/31, 1703.
6. The whole of this episode is omitted by Coxe, and consequently also by the numerous historians who have followed him.

view of Bedmar's camp, crossed the Schelde below Antwerp. On the morning of the 27th they attacked the north-eastern angle of the French lines upon opposite sides. Both operations were successful, though Spaar's victory was dearly bought. The country of Waes lay now at the mercy of the Dutch, who immediately exacted contributions. Great were the rejoicings at the Hague, where the distinction between soldiering and money-grubbing was not understood. But still Bedmar remained motionless at Deurne. As Marlborough had anticipated, this kind of diversion did not greatly impress the Spanish general, who was only strengthened in his resolution to stand his ground by the appearance of Opdam's army at Eeckeren, four miles north of Antwerp.

On the 27th, the very day on which Coehoorn and Spaar invaded Waes, Marlborough struck his camp in the small hours of the morning, and passed the Geer. The French, alarmed by this sudden movement and fully expecting to be attacked, stood to their arms. But as Marlborough was presently found to be proceeding in the direction of Hasselt, the Marshals took the road by Landen towards Diest. Here on the 29th they received from Bedmar a full account of the invasion of Waes. They realised at once that the exposed position of Opdam's army at Eeckeren offered them an opportunity for a telling counterstroke. It was decided to send to Deurne forthwith a powerful reinforcement of cavalry and grenadiers under the command of Boufflers himself.

The troops set off at 8 a.m., and Marlborough, who was at Hasselt, knew nothing of Boufflers' expedition; but he knew the danger, and as soon as he heard of Opdam's advance to Eeckeren he sent him urgent instructions to withdraw to a post of greater safety, Opdam however contented himself with ordering back his heavy baggage to Bergen-op-Zoom, though his spies reported that Boufflers was on the road to Antwerp, and his colleagues entreated him to retire. It was nearly midnight when the foremost of Boufflers' men arrived at Antwerp. As fast as they came up they traversed the sleeping city, and defiling through the northern gates, joined the army of Bedmar. They had marched continuously for forty miles.

After a brief rest Boufflers and Bedmar advanced in four columns. They outnumbered the enemy by nearly three to one. Their object was to envelop Opdam's left, and to interpose between his right and his line of retreat to Lillo. Opdam, despite the warnings he had received, was virtually surprised by the French cavalry and dragoons.

The Dutch had behaved badly, but their foot, sheltered by dykes and water-courses, stood fast and repulsed the onset of the mounted men. Opdam ordered a retreat to Lillo; but at 3 in the afternoon the French infantry arrived. Some of them had been marching for ten hours, and some for more than thirty. But they flung themselves into the battle with all their well-known gaiety and dash.

A desperate conflict ensued, in which the difficult and broken nature of the ground produced no little confusion. Regiments and brigades fought independently, and supreme direction was conspicuously lacking. At an early stage in the struggle Opdam was cut off from his men, and surrounded by the enemy. He managed to slip through into the open country, where accompanied by only thirty horsemen he made his way to Breda, and wrote to the States-General that all was lost. After his disappearance the command devolved on General Schlangenberg, who exercised it boldly and well. Notwithstanding the advantage of numbers and surprise, the French made little headway. Their fiery valour died down before the stubborn courage which is characteristic of the Teutonic soldier at bay.

Slowly the Dutch drew off in the direction of Lillo. But the French had already established themselves upon the only road. Many of the Dutch regiments had exhausted their ammunition, but not their resources. With fixed bayonets and in serried ranks they clove themselves a passage. The Prussian general Hompesch, with a handful of cavalry of that nation, hurled himself upon the masses of French horse and drove them backward in confusion and disarray.

As darkness descended the whole army, glorious in defeat, marched sternly from the field. Every attack was repulsed with fury; and some of the panic-stricken assailants never halted in their flight till they were safe within the lines of Antwerp. The greater part of Boufflers' army passed the night in the belief that they had been defeated. Daylight showed them that they were masters of the field. With drums beating and trumpets sounding, they hastened to take possession of such baggage and cannon as the enemy had been unable to withdraw in their retreat to Lillo. These, with several colours, and 900 prisoners, including the Comtesse de Tilly, constituted the proofs of victory. The French had at least 2,000 casualties, and the allies no more.

Eeckeren was a soldiers' battle. It was a French victory, but a very incomplete one. It reflected little credit on the tactical skill of Boufflers and Bedmar. No amount of exaggeration could disguise the truth that an army which ought to have been annihilated had escaped after inflicting severe losses on its assailants. On the other hand, the exultation of the Dutch at the conduct of their troops did not alter the fact that the strategic object for which Boufflers fought had been achieved. The French had not destroyed Opdam's army; but they had shattered the "great design." The troops which were to advance upon Antwerp from the north, and in conjunction with Marlborough to complete the investment of the city, had been forced from their post, and compelled to retire with heavy loss. The Marshals had acted upon sound principles, and they were rewarded with the attainment of their real aim, the ruin of the enemy's combinations.

Villeroi passed the 30th in intense anxiety. He knew that Boufflers was fighting, and he knew also that he himself might be attacked. But as Marlborough merely continued his march, and encamped at Beeringen, the Marshal replied by moving to Aerschot. It was impossible for the allies to get ahead of their antagonists, who were operating on interior lines. After five days of constant marching.

Villeroi was nearer to Antwerp than Marlborough. On July I the allies rested at Beeringen, whence they proceeded on the 2nd to Baelen. Villeroi, still moving towards Antwerp, was rejoined on the 3rd by Boufflers and his men.

Opdam's dispatch from Breda turned the premature jubilation of the Dutch to grief and terror. But Schlangenberg's report from Lillo speedily restored confidence. The successful passage of their army through the overwhelming masses of the enemy was naturally regarded by the Dutch people as a gallant feat of arms. They were proud of the battle of Eeckeren. The triumphant rejoicings of the French only excited derision at the Hague. The populace did not understand that a gallant feat of arms may be also a strategical disaster. But Marlborough understood. When the first rumours of the destruction of Opdam's forces came from Breda to Baelen on July 2, he wrote to Godolphin,

> I pray God it be not so, for he is very capable of having it happen to him.[7]

Though subsequent intelligence showed that Schlangenberg and his men had given a good account of themselves, the Duke was not deceived as to the true meaning of the battle of Eeckeren. The "great design" had collapsed. His disappointment was embittered by the knowledge that he himself was being blamed for a fiasco which was entirely due to the insubordination and incompetence of the Dutch.

---

7. Coxe, vol. 1, p. 123: Marlborough to Godolphin, July 2, 1703.

The voice of the military critic, that pestilent product of ignorance, faction and private malice, was loudly raised on both sides of the North Sea. These wiseacres contended that, when Villeroi sent the detachment under Boufflers to Antwerp, Marlborough should either have sent a corresponding detachment to Eeckeren, or have seized the opportunity to attack the French army in its weakened state.

The first suggestion was manifestly absurd. Boufflers had secured a good start long before Marlborough received intelligence of his departure. But even if it had been possible, which it was not, for a reinforcement to start from Hasselt at the very moment that Boufflers set out from Diest, the map should have shown the critics that the French could not fail to reach Eeckeren many hours before their rivals. As to the assertion that Marlborough ought to have attacked Villeroi in Boufflers' absence, Marlborough would have been only too pleased to attack Villeroi at any time and under almost any conditions. But the government which had just refused his reiterated applications for leave to give battle in the open country was little likely to sanction an assault upon the moats and ramparts of the French lines.

In any case, Boufflers had fought the battle and rejoined Villeroi in much less time than was required to take the opinion of the authorities at the Hague. On those very authorities rested the main responsibility for the failure of the "great design." The rashness and stupidity of Opdam were deserving of the severest censure. But the men who had sanctioned the invasion of Waes by Coehoorn in substitution for Marlborough's original plan of an attack upon Ostend, were the principal culprits. Reasoning as hucksters reason, they concluded that Bedmar would be disturbed by the extraction of a few thousand crowns from the country of Waes.

They paid dearly for their folly. The lesson is one that has still to be learned by the English people, who imagine that great and martial nations can be brought to their knees by the capture of cargo-boats and tramp steamers. Successful war is not to be made on these lines. Those who make it like soldiers will always have the upper hand of those who make it like tradesmen.

Marlborough could afford to despise the strictures of the factious and the uninformed. But Schlangenberg belonged to neither of these categories. And Schlangenberg, who, like all the Dutch generals except Overkirk, was jealous of the Duke, had now the meanness to insinuate that Opdam's army had been deliberately exposed to destruction by the Englishman. His own dispatch, in which he had explained the impossibility of reinforcing Opdam[8] in time, convicted him of lying. But the applause of his countrymen had turned his head. He thought to damage the reputation of Marlborough; but he succeeded only in inflicting injury on the common cause and eventually in ruining his own career.

The unfortunate situation to which the affairs of the allies had been reduced by the stupidity and selfishness of the Dutch, admitted of one remedy, and only one, a decisive victory over the French army in the field. If the Marshals could be induced to fight in the open, so much the better; but if not, they must be attacked and routed in their lines. Convinced of the absolute futility of all other attempts to solve the problem, Marlborough left his army at Vorsslaer, and went to Breda and Bergen-op-Zoom to explain his views to the deputies and generals of Holland. Coehoorn, Opdam, and Schlangenberg were grumbling bitterly among themselves, but they could of course spare time from mutual recriminations to criticise the Duke's proposals. Nevertheless he obtained permission to attempt the forcing of the lines between Antwerp and Lierre, where the enemy, if they stood their ground, and were defeated, would be driven into the Schelde. He made his preparations accordingly; but by this time he knew the methods of the Dutch so well that he fully expected their decision to be reversed at the last moment. He wrote strongly on the subject to Heinsius, and while clearly exposing the merits of the project, summed up the position in a sentence:

If you have a mind to have Antwerp, and a speedy end of the war, *you must venture something for it.*[9]

But Heinsius, whose own power was insecure, could do little or nothing for his friend. Meantime, Villeroi and Bouffiers, simulating a desire to bring on that battle which they had been forbidden by their own government to fight, had marched boldly out of their lines and occupied an excellent post at St. Job. Marlborough proposed to summon Schlangenberg from Lillo, and attack the French, though he had little hope that they would stand their ground. The Dutch government consented. On the 23rd Marlborough marched from Vorsslaer to Brecht, and sent his heavy baggage to Breda. Only four miles separated the armies.

---

8. See General Schlangenberg's account of the battle of Eeckeren (Lediard, vol. 1, p. 241, July 2, 1703).

9. Coxe, vol. 1, p. 125: Marlborough to the Pensionary, July 4/15, 1703.

The Duke rode forward to reconnoitre, whereupon some of Villeroi's officers advised him to retire. But Villeroi, who guessed that Marlborough would not attack till he had been joined by Schlangenberg, and who was anxious to play out the farce as long as no danger attended the performance, continued in order of battle at St. Job. That night Schlangenberg moved rapidly up to join hands with Marlborough.

At daybreak the allied forces began to converge upon St. Job. Villeroi observed them until 9 a.m., when he hastily retired by ways which he had specially prepared to the shelter of the lines. Marlborough summoned a council of war to discuss the plans of attack. But so many objections were raised by the Dutch that he realised the utter hopelessness of achieving his purpose with such allies. On the 27th he rode with an escort of 4,000 horse to view the works between Lierre and Antwerp. The sight of the fosse, which was 27 feet wide and had 9 feet of water in it, settled the matter, so far as the Dutch were concerned. There was no more spirit in them.

Marlborough was drinking the cup of mortification to the dregs. Conscious of his own ability to sweep the French from Flanders and Brabant in less than a fortnight, he was condemned by solemn nonentities to play the most humiliating of parts in the ridiculous tomfoolery which they called war. The injury which the Dutch were doing to themselves was entirely their own affair; but the injury which they were doing to the common cause was not. Solely on the ground that he intended to create such a diversion in the Netherlands as would speedily relieve the pressure on the Empire, Marlborough had over and over again refused to dispatch reinforcements to Bavaria, where they were sorely needed.

Yet ten weeks of summer had elapsed since the fall of Bonn and he had accomplished nothing. No wonder that he was anxious lest his own reputation should suffer in the eyes of Europe. No wonder that he wrote letters to Sinzendorf which told the brutal truth about the Dutch. Some of these letters unfortunately fell into the hands of Villeroi, who gleaned from them how much he owed to the States-General. Also, he gleaned something of Marlborough's ideas and plans. But the information could do him no good, and Marlborough no harm. So long as the English general was prohibited or prevented by his allies from fighting the French army, nothing really mattered.

It was necessary now to decide upon the future course of the campaign. Coehoorn was anxious to pursue his lucrative operations in

Waes. But Marlborough, who from the time of the battle of Eeckeren, had never ceased to declare that they must either fight the Marshals' army or return to the Meuse, absolutely refused to remain in the vicinity of Antwerp. He intended to besiege Huy, a small place with a strong castle, the possession of which by the allies would cover Liège while it uncovered Namur. He knew that the Marshals would follow, and "if they give occasion," he wrote to Godolphin, "I hope we shall venture, by which God may give us more success in three or four hours than we dare promise ourselves."[10]

Taking Schlangenberg with him and leaving Coehoorn to sulk in Flanders, he started on August 2. The road was that which he had already traversed .Villeroi, after pausing to satisfy himself that this movement was not a feint intended to cover a sudden return upon Antwerp, moved down within the lines in the direction of Huy. The importance of that fortress was fully recognised by Louis, who wrote to Villeroi to impress upon him the necessity of preserving it. Villeroi was greatly troubled by the King's letter, which virtually required him to solve the very problem that had baffled Boufflers in the preceding campaign. To protect with one and the same army both the lines of Brabant and the places on the Meuse, and to accomplish these two objects without fighting except in defence of a chosen position of immense strength, was a task which he saw no prospect of achieving.

In company with Boufflers he studied the country with the minutest care, but without result. And Louis was constrained to prepare himself to learn with resignation of the loss of Huy. Marlborough arrived on the 14th at St. Servais, whence he sent a detachment over the Meuse below Huy to invest the place upon the right bank. On the 15th he moved to Vinaimont, where he posted himself strongly to cover the siege. The trenches were opened on the 17th. On the 20th the great guns arrived by water from Maestricht, and on the 21st the batteries opened on the castle and the three forts. On the 22nd the defenders of the forts were driven to take refuge in the town, where they were all made prisoners. The whole of the artillery of the allies was now turned upon the castle.

On the 25th the governor, alarmed by the preparations for an assault, beat a parley. He was willing to surrender on condition that the garrison should march out to Namur. The Duke refused these terms, and ordered the assault to be delivered. But the French soldiers, after

---

10. Coxe, vol. 1, p. 128: Marlborough to Godolphin, July 26, 1703.

some resistance, declined to continue a struggle which could only terminate in a massacre. Thereupon the governor yielded, with 900 men, whom Marlborough proposed to exchange against the two battalions that were lost at Tongres.

All this time Villeroi had remained within the lines, which he had been strengthening and extending in the direction of Namur. In the north Bedmar was repairing the damage which Spaar and Coehoorn had inflicted on the works that covered Waes. Coehoorn himself was now too weak to attempt anything. But Marlborough was once more at liberty. What use would he make of the remainder of the season? His intentions were variously reported to Villeroi, who saw with surprise that for ten days he remained idle at Vinaimont. This waste of valuable time was due, of course, to the attitude of the Dutch. Marlborough had once more insisted that the lines should be attacked.

He was supported by the English generals, and by the generals commanding the contingents of Denmark, Hesse, and Lüneburg. He was convinced, from personal inspection and from the information of his spies, that the operation was perfectly practicable, and nowhere so practicable as on the side of Vinaimont. His troops were in splendid condition, and more numerous than the French. Above all, he was moved by the strategical consideration "that the enemy being superior in Italy, and in the Empire, and being outnumbered nowhere but here, the eyes of all the allies are fixed upon us, and they will have cause justly to blame our conduct, if we do not do all that is possible to relieve them, by obliging the enemy to call back such succours into these parts, which is not to be done but by pushing boldly."[11]

The Dutch generals and deputies, faithful to the narrow policy of that government and nation, ignored entirely the question of high strategy. But they expressed their doubts as to the alleged weakness of the lines, and they argued that, even if the enemy were beaten from his works, he could find other and stronger positions in his rear. As an example they indicated the field of Ramillies, the very ground on which, three years later, Marlborough routed a French army in two hours.[12] As an alternative to the forcing of the lines, they urged the siege of Limbourg, the possession of which would increase the security of the United Provinces. They were supported by the Prussian and Hanoverian officers.

All the arguments on both sides were reduced to writing and for-

---

11. Lediard, vol. 1, p. 262.
12. Burnet, vol. 4, p. 129.

warded to the Hague, under cover of a letter[13] in which the Duke repeated and emphasised his own opinions. He told the States that, in his judgement, the French would retire rather than endure an assault, but that if they resisted, his soldiers were so numerous and good, and so extraordinarily keen to come to grips with the enemy, who were for the most part raw and untried troops, that the result could not be doubted.

He dwelt in particular on the necessity of relieving the pressure on the Empire by a powerful diversion at the only point where the coalition enjoyed a superiority of numbers. The allies, he said, expected it. England, he knew, expected it, and he presumed that the Dutch people, who would reap the greatest advantages from it, expected it also. He assured the States that, if this campaign were to terminate without any considerable result, the winter would be marked by bitter grumbling across the Channel. As for the Dutch generals, their reasoning, he said, appeared to presuppose that the army was acting on the defensive. But if that were indeed the case, what, he asked, would be the situation in the ensuing year?

The Duke had spoken and written like a true soldier, who looked with a single eye to the attainment of the true end of war, the destruction of the enemy. Surveying every theatre of the immense conflict, he perceived what was necessary to the success of the common cause, and he asked for nothing better than to be permitted to do it. The States on the other hand saw naught but the one area in which their own forces were engaged, they considered no interest save that which to their dim and defective vision appeared to be their own, and they gave their decision accordingly. They declined to risk their army against Villeroi's earthworks. Despite his long experience of their folly and selfishness, Marlborough seems to have been astonished. For once, his indignation found a voice. Hitherto he had suffered them and their unspeakable officers in silence. But this time the provocation was intolerable.

His reply, eloquent in its obvious restraint, contained this passage:

Since I had the honour of writing to you, I have been more and more convinced by the information which I have daily received as to the enemy's situation, not only that this enterprise was practicable, but that it could even be expected to yield all the success which I anticipated from it; and now in the end

---

13. Murray, vol. 1, p. 166: Marlborough to the States-General, August 26. 1703.

(*enfin*) the opportunity is lost, and I pray with all my heart that no mischief come of it, and that we may not have cause to be sorry for it, when too late.[14]

In all the circumstances such language seems sufficiently mild; yet nothing so severe had ever before escaped him.

It only remained to besiege Limbourg. To conceal his purpose from Villeroi, Marlborough marched on September 5 to Avennes and set his men to cut fascines as though he would attack the French lines. At the head of 200 horse he rode to view the enemy, who saluted him with musketry and round-shot. On the 6th he visited them again, and after a last, wistful glance at the long barrier of earth and water and iron that shut him out from Brabant and Flanders, filed off in deep dejection for St. Trond. Here he left the main army to Overkirk, and went in person to the siege of Limbourg. The investment was effected on the 9th. Bad weather was the cause of some delay; but the town surrendered on the 23rd, and the citadel two days later. Villeroi, affecting to be reconciled to the loss of the place, made no attempt to relieve it.

With the fall of Limbourg active operations terminated. In the beginning of November both armies went into winter-quarters. Before the end of the year Guelder, which had been blockaded for many months by a Prussian force, surrendered. Thus in the course of two campaigns the whole of the territories of Spanish Guelderland, Cologne, and Liège, had been wrested from the French; and the peril of invasion by the Meuse and by the Rhine no longer threatened Holland. These results were well pleasing to the Dutch, who with little risk and trifling loss had obtained what they regarded as virtual security.

Their jubilation and their flattery left Marlborough cold. He was well aware that the safety of Holland was an essential preliminary to a successful attack on France, and in England he had maintained this very truth in the face of the bitterest criticism. But with the strategist's instinctive knowledge of the value of time, he realised that an expenditure of two years was too heavy a price to pay for what had been achieved. Against an enemy who conducted his operations on the same principles as the Coehoorns and the Opdams, Dutch methods might be attended with no special disadvantages. But when a soldier so intrepid and enterprising as Villars was running loose in the very

---

14. Murray, vol. 1, p. 173: Marlborough to the States-General, Septembers, 1703.

heart of Germany, it was no longer safe to fritter away the energies of splendid armies in futile promenades. The Dutch standpoint was the very antithesis of the Duke's. From Holland to South Germany was a far cry. What Villars did upon the Danube concerned Vienna and not the Hague. Such selfish blindness, which is the vice of all coalitions, was the hope of Louis and the despair of Marlborough.

And Marlborough realised that the evil consequences of Dutch stupidity would not be restricted to the military situation alone. His knowledge of his countrymen told him that this abortive campaign would weaken Godolphin's government and diminish the popularity of the war. Already the refusal of the States to prohibit correspondence with France and Spain, and the backwardness of their naval preparations, had revived the old Tory mistrust and jealousy of Holland. Already the treatment which he had received in the previous summer had excited the disgust of the English people without distinction of party.

It would now be open to Rochester to say that, whether his principles of strategy or Marlborough's were the more correct, the spectacle of 50,000 men fiddling in Flanders while the Empire burned, could be justified on no principles of strategy whatsoever. Ever since he quitted England in March, the Duke had been harassed by Godolphin's complaints of the obstruction and the intrigues of Nottingham and Seymour. Writing from Haneffe to the Duchess he had said of Nottingham, "I wish with all my heart the Queen were rid of him, so that she had a good man in his place, which I am afraid is pretty difficult," and of Seymour, "We are bound not to wish for anybody's death, but if 14 (Sir Edward Seymour) should die, I am convinced it would be no great loss to the Queen nor the nation."[15]

On the other hand, the Whigs out of spite at his refusal to employ them, borrowed the "military criticisms" of Rochester, accused him of deliberately prolonging the war in his own interest, declared that he was hostile to the succession of the House of Hanover, and joined him in their lampoons with Harley and Godolphin under the nickname of "the *Triumvirate*." The Duchess aggravated the situation by pestering both her husband and the Queen in favour of that party. In utter weariness the Duke expressed a wish in one of his letters to resign. Sarah showed this passage to the Queen, and hinted that she and Godolphin entertained a similar inclination. Anne was greatly distressed.

---

15. Coxe, vol. 1, p. 133: The Duke to the Duchess, June-3/14, 1703.

"You should," she wrote, "a little consider your faithful friends and poor country, which must be ruined if ever you put your melancholy thoughts in execution. As for your poor unfortunate faithful Morley, she could not bear it; for if ever you should forsake me, I would have nothing more to do with the world, but make another abdication; for what is a crown when the support of it is gone? I never will forsake your dear self, Mr. Freeman, nor Mr. Montgomery, but always be your constant and faithful friend; and we four must never part till death mows us down with his impartial hand."[16]

Such language only encouraged Sarah to maintain the pressure on behalf of the Whigs. But Anne was obdurate. Marlborough, though fearful that most of the Tories would do more harm out of office than in it, admitted that Nottingham and Jersey might with advantage be removed.

"But who," he wrote, "is there fit for their places? I do protest before God I know of none."[17]

He was resolute in his adherence to that system on which Godolphin's ministry had first been formed. But he clearly perceived that neither Godolphin's ministry nor any other could reconcile the English people to the policy of William, if the Dutch conception of the art of war were any longer permitted to prevail.

Fortunately for Europe the alliance between France and Bavaria was not exempt from the defects of other alliances. Villars, who had planned to be before Vienna on July 1, found in the Elector himself an antagonist more formidable than the generals of the enemy. The views of Max Emanuel differed as widely from the Frenchman's as the views of the Dutch government from those of Marlborough. Max Emanuel, who had set his heart upon the title of king and a dominion enlarged by the acquisition of the Palatinate, the Tyrol, and the Milanese, thought only of consolidating his position and extending his borders, while Villars, like Marlborough, had no other aim than the destruction of the enemy.

Conflicting purposes produced divided counsels. The march upon Vienna was postponed, and ultimately, so far as the campaign of 1703 was concerned, abandoned. The Elector invaded the Tyrol, entered Innsbrück in triumph, and was advancing to the passes with the object

---

16. *Ibid.*, p. 132: The Queen to the Duchess.
17. *Ibid.*, p. 134: The Duke to the Duchess, June 10, 1703.

of joining hands with Vendôme and the French army of Italy, when the peasantry rose in his rear, and after a savage struggle forced him to retire to Munich. Villars continued to hold the line of the Danube against Louis of Baden and Count Styrum, and at Höchstädt on September 20 he struck a fierce blow against Styrum, whom he routed utterly with severe loss. But his grand aspiration was as far as ever from fulfilment.

At the conclusion of the campaign he resigned his command in disgust. He was succeeded by Marsin, whom he himself had recommended for the post. Meantime the concentration of forces on Bavaria had left Tallard at liberty to act upon the Rhine, where he had taken Old Breisach, beaten a German army by accident at Spires, and recovered Landau. Thus, the winter found the French still established in Bavaria, and their communications with the Rhine still undestroyed. And the menace of the strategy of Villars, though suspended, still remained.

When Marlborough turned his gaze from Germany to the Mediterranean, he beheld a prospect distinctly more encouraging. The combined fleets under Sir Cloudesley Shovel had sailed in July, with a large convoy of merchantmen under their wing. Having called at Lisbon and Tangier, Shovel passed the Straits, and watered on the coast of Valencia, where he published a proclamation in favour of the House of Austria. He sent two ships into the Gulf of Narbonne to communicate with the Camisards, and to supply them if possible with arms and money. But this attempt, though it greatly alarmed the French, was unsuccessful. The main fleet sailed for Leghorn, where its appearance made an excellent impression on the Italians. All this time the French never dared to venture out of Toulon.

Consequently, when Shovel returned to England in November, the people grumbled because he had no showy exploits to his credit. They did not understand the moral value of the process which is familiarly known nowadays as 'showing the flag.' Yet this process, which had already been largely responsible for the Portuguese alliance, was not the least among the causes which in October, 1703, produced the defection of Savoy from France. Victor Amadeus had long been negotiating with the allies.

Louis, who had discovered his duplicity, ordered Vendôme to disarm the Piedmontese contingent in the French army and to invade the territories of the Duke. The Duke retaliated by arresting all the French in his dominions, and joining the Austrian army under Starhemberg. The rupture was complete. To France this loss was at least as serious as the loss of Portugal. It meant that the war in Italy, which at the best had been difficult and expensive enough to maintain, must now be conducted with weakened forces and insecure communications.

The favourable aspect of affairs in the Mediterranean suggested to the coalition the possibility of action on the soil of Spain. It was understood that there were Spaniards ready to revolt against their Bourbon sovereign as soon as the Hapsburg claimant should appear; and it was thought that, with the assistance of Portugal and the support of the naval forces of England and Holland, a strong diversion might be made upon the Spanish mainland. In deference to the doctrine of the balance of power, the Emperor and his heir resigned their claims to the succession in favour of the Emperor's second son, the Archduke Charles. Charles was proclaimed King of Spain, and was formally acknowledged by the allied powers.

It was arranged that he should proceed to England, whence an English fleet would convey him to the Peninsula. Nottingham and the Tories who followed Rochester approved the project, because they wanted to transfer the British army from Flanders to Spain. Marlborough approved it also, but upon different grounds. The forces of the coalition, operating as they were on the Meuse, the Rhine, the Danube, and the Po, were already too dispersed. At this juncture concentration rather than dissipation was the crying need of the allies' strategy.

A fifth attack at a point so remote from the centre of the Bourbon power, which was Paris, could not be justified except as a diversion. The essence of a diversion is that the forces which are employed to create it should be much inferior to those which it obliges the enemy to withhold or to detach from the decisive point. During the Seven Years' War this system was successfully applied by Pitt, at the urgent request of no less a strategist than the great Frederick himself. In 1703 it recommended itself also to Marlborough. Had the Portuguese troops and the Spanish adherents of Charles been strong enough, with the help of the navies of the maritime powers, to maintain the struggle, the situation would have been an ideal one. But they were not; and by the treaty with Portugal 10,000 Dutch and English soldiers were promised for service in the Peninsula.

Marlborough assumed that new levies would be raised for this purpose; and it was therefore with no little vexation that he learned, after the fall of Limbourg, that Nottingham was detaching some of his best regiments from Flanders without his knowledge or consent. Whatever degree of success attended the movements of King Charles, they could fairly be expected to operate as a valuable diversion. But Spain was a mysterious country, and Spanish opinion an unknown quantity. The expedition must, at the best, be something of an adventure.

In Marlborough's judgement, so long as it was mainly self-supporting, it might act as a dangerous drain upon the enemy's resources without materially weakening those of the allies. But he was strongly opposed to the drafting of veteran troops from the principal theatres of the war to this new and problematical enterprise. Such a procedure was foreign to the nature of a true diversion. The Duke's vexation was shared by the Dutch, though for less enlightened reasons.

The new King of Spain arrived at Düsseldorf on October 16. Marlborough quitted the army and hastened to congratulate the young monarch. Charles received him very graciously, and remarking that he was only a poor prince, unbuckled a sword, set with diamonds, and presented it to the Duke, who kissed the hilt. They travelled together to the Hague, whence Marlborough sailed for England, which he reached on November 10. Before his departure Charles handed him his portrait, also set with diamonds. They met again at Christmas, when the King arrived at Portsmouth, and the Dukes of Marlborough and Somerset were deputed to meet him and accompany him to Windsor. During his visit at the castle, Charles exhibited marked deference towards the Duchess, and gave her a ring valued at a thousand pounds.

But the favours of the House of Hapsburg were as impotent as the plaudits of the Dutch populace to allay the anxieties of Marlborough, The safety of Holland and the adhesion of Portugal and Savoy to the common cause were indeed solid achievements, calculated to provide a firm foundation for an offensive system of war against the exorbitant power of France. But time was now the essence of the question. The Bavarian peril was instant, threatening, and big with doom. Long before France could be stricken in a vital part, Austria might go down in hopeless ruin. Such was the strategical problem which at the close of 1703 the genius of Villars and the fatuous policy of the Hague presented for solution to Marlborough and Eugène.

CHAPTER 7

The March to the Schellenberg (1704)

The gravity of the situation in which the Emperor found himself at the outset of the year 1704 was patent to all Europe. With forces, the essential inadequacy of which was enhanced by their dispersion, he was confronted by enemies converging along three separate lines upon the capital itself. In the east the Hungarian rebels, whose elusive tactics defied the efforts of disciplined armies, were overrunning Silesia and Moravia, and carrying desolation and terror to the very walls of Pressburg and Vienna. In the south it was doubtful how long the skilful Starhemberg and the valour of Savoy could hold their own upon Italian soil against the superior numbers of so able a commander as Vendôme. But the darkest cloud of all was in the west.

Here the Elector of Bavaria and Marsin, with an army of 45,000 men, against which the Emperor could oppose no more than 20,000, were masters of the Danube from Ulm to Linz. They were in communication with the Hungarian rebels, and they were supported by Tallard with a second army of 45,000 in Alsace. Holding the fortresses of Landau and Breisach, Tallard could dispatch a reinforcement over the Rhine, and masking the lines of Stollhofen, which were weakly guarded by the Margrave of Baden, could send it across the Black Forest, which was very insecurely defended by militia and a mere handful of regular troops.

Eugène, who, as President of the Council of War, had spent the year 1703 in endeavouring to reorganise the military administration of the Empire, realised the necessity of opposing to the design which Villars had inaugurated a new and vigorous strategy. His views were shared by Marlborough. Before the close of the campaign of 1703, private correspondence on the subject began to pass between the two commanders. Both were agreed that the mischief could only be cured by a twofold remedy, a concentration of the allied forces, and an offensive movement against some vital part of the enemy's system.

It was obvious that Bavaria was such a part; and it was natural enough that the Emperor's general should wish to divert the forces of England and Holland to the point where his master's dominions lay exposed to a decisive blow. Marlborough understood that the coalition could not hope to survive the downfall of the Austrian power. But knowing by bitter experience, the selfish and stupid timidity of the government of the Hague, he must have doubted the feasibility of an operation which would involve the departure of Dutch soldiers from the Meuse to the Danube. Yet what was the alternative? The only conceivable alternative was such an invasion of French soil as would place Paris in jeopardy at least as great as that of Vienna.

If the blow at the heart of the Empire could be anticipated by a blow at the heart of France, the Bavarian design would collapse. Indeed, the war itself would be finished. It was thus that Marlborough had always planned to finish it. He knew the road. It ran from Coblenz up the valley of the Moselle to Metz and Thionville. He had always intended that, as soon as ever the Dutch frontier was cleared, he would follow that road into the plains of Champagne. Moreover the States could be more easily persuaded to dispatch their forces to the Moselle than to the Danube. But the Germans, on the other hand, were unlikely to consent to a concentration in Lorraine while the enemy was in occupation of Bavaria.

And even assuming that a large and well-found army could be assembled in the valley of the Moselle in the early spring, time, which would then become the deciding factor, would still be greatly in favour of the French. The probability was that Vienna would be taken before Paris was even afraid. If therefore Marlborough considered his cherished project of invasion as a possible alternative to a concentration in Bavaria, he must have considered it only to dismiss it. But the position was provoking in the extreme. He had spent two campaigns, which was one at least too many, in securing the Dutch frontier. And now, when at last he had hoped to assume the offensive against the true centre of the enemy's power, he was compelled to devote a third to the safety of the Empire.

Some historians appear to regard the conception of a march from the Meuse to the Danube as a flight of genius, to be proudly ascribed by the biographers[1] of Marlborough to their hero, and by those of Eugène[2] to theirs. Doubtless the daring and the magnitude of the operation must have astonished many contemporary soldiers of the orthodox school. A flank march[3] of that description was also a breach of the rules. But these two generals, who never quarrelled over anything, would certainly not have disputed for the honour of originating a plan which seemed to both of them to be the obvious, necessary, and only possible solution of the strategical problem confronting the allies in the winter of 1703-4.

"Everything is very simple in war," says Clausewitz, "but the simplest thing is difficult."[4] And so it now appeared.

From the nature of the case the execution of the project devolved almost entirely upon Marlborough. He applied himself to the task with consummate cunning and address. By the irony of circumstances the notorious stupidity of the Dutch government was now become his principal asset. The necessity of a concentration in Bavaria might be patent enough to the strategical mind; but that the Dutch government would ever consent to it no sane observer of European politics would easily believe. Certainly the French, who had had thirty years' experience of the military methods of the Hague, would never believe it.

Secrecy therefore was to a great extent assured, unless the preliminary arrangements should be so mismanaged as to excite suspicion even in the minds of an enemy predisposed to suspect anything rather than the truth. But Marlborough was determined to take no risks. He had hit upon an excellent device for deceiving everybody, whether friend or foe. A march on Paris by the Moselle was not, as has already been seen, the correct reply to the French movement on Vienna; but the idea of such a march was sufficiently specious to impose upon all parties. The French would readily believe in it, and the Dutch might be induced to consent to it.

Operations on the Moselle would naturally be based upon Coblenz. But if Marlborough could only effect a great concentration of men and stores so far up the Rhine as Coblenz, he would have accomplished an important stage upon the road to Bavaria, while the French were expecting him at Metz and Thionville. He decided therefore that

---

1. Lodiard, Coxe, Fortescue, Creasy, Alison.
2. Malleson and German writers, and also Burnet.
3. Lieut.-Colonel F. N. Maude, *The Evolution of Modern Strategy*. ch. 3, p. 25.
4. Clausewitz, On War, book 1., ch. 7.

he would openly advocate a campaign upon the Moselle and would publicly urge the Dutch government to prepare for the invasion of France upon an adequate scale.

So far as it went, this plan promised well. But success depended in the long run on Marlborough's own willingness to accept responsibility. For assuming that on the pretext of threatening Paris, he got permission from the Hague to carry his army up the Rhine valley to Coblenz, and even beyond Coblenz, the cross-roads must ultimately be reached, the moment must ultimately arrive when, on his own authority and at his own peril, he must call upon the soldiers of the States to follow him not to Paris but to Munich.

Marlborough, who possessed in full that rare courage of the mind which even the most famous soldiers have sometimes lacked, contemplated that eventuality with quiet confidence. In the same spirit he resisted the very human temptation to share the burden of his secret with a crowd of sympathetic advisers, whose enthusiasm might easily outrun their discretion. It was known of course to Eugène and to the Emperor. There is no absolute proof that it was ever revealed in its entirety to any other persons. But Marlborough's contemporaries believed that he communicated it also to Heinsius and Godolphin, as well as to Queen Anne and to the Prince of Denmark. He could hardly have ventured to proceed without the willing connivance of Heinsius, whose support would be essential to him at the most critical junctures in the game he was about to play.

Godolphin too, though in a lesser degree, could do for him in England what Heinsius could do in Holland. But in the case of Godolphin, and still more in the case of the Queen and the Prince of Denmark (with whom in this connection the Duchess ought surely to be coupled) there was no necessity to be very explicit. He probably told them that it was imperative to march to the relief of the Empire, and that, once he had quitted the United Provinces, he should not consider himself bound to adhere to the advertised scheme of a campaign upon the Moselle, since circumstances might arise which would render Alsace or even Bavaria a better theatre of operations than Lorraine. He may, of course, have said more; but this much would have been ample for his purpose.

"Mr. and Mrs. Morley" had too little knowledge of the art of war, and too much confidence in the talents of "Mr. Freeman," to say nothing of "Mrs. Freeman" and "Mr. Montgomery," to create difficulties. The Queen is called by the historians stupid; but that is a useful form of stupidity which never interferes with the man who, being in authority, understands his business. Moreover she was both brave and loyal; if her general failed, she would never repudiate or disavow him.[5]

The fate of Godolphin's ministry hung upon the issue of this secret project. When Marlborough returned to England at the conclusion of his last campaign, he was determined to resign a position which had become well-nigh unendurable. Although in contact with Godolphin and the Queen he had abandoned this unworthy resolution, he saw clearly that domestic politics were going from bad to worse. The clergy were still sulking over the rejection of the bill for the prevention of Occasional Conformity, while the Tory squires were beginning to grumble at taxation for which no solid results could be shown. When Parliament met in November, the Queen in her speech expressed a strong desire that all her subjects should live "in perfect peace and union among themselves," and that the two Houses "would carefully avoid any heats or divisions."[6] But the conflict of parties was immediately renewed in its most violent form.

A measure for the prevention of Occasional Conformity was again introduced into the Commons, and was again carried by a large majority. The more violent Tories proposed to "tack" it to a money bill, till Marlborough intimated that the Queen would view this step with grave disfavour. Despite her detestation of the hypocritical practice which the bill was intended to suppress, Anne was sincerely anxious for peace, and on this occasion she authorised Prince George to absent himself from the House of Lords. Godolphin and Marlborough were in a dilemma. In their hearts they approved of the bill; but they feared to oppose it lest they should lose more ground with the Tories than they had already lost, and they feared to support it lest they should alienate the Whigs.

They adopted the line of condemning its introduction as unreasonable, which obviously meant inconvenient to themselves. In these circumstances Burnet and his men did not hesitate to strike. The bill was rejected by a dozen votes. Marlborough and Godolphin neither spoke nor worked on its behalf; but they voted with the minority, and signed a protest of the Tory peers. This 'trimming' pleased neither side. It was now the avowed aim of the clergy and their friends to oust Godolphin in favour of Nottingham. In February, 1704, the Queen

---

5. Coxe takes this view (see vol. 1, pp. 149, 153). For others, see Burnet, vol. 4, p. 48, and Lediard, vol. 1., ch. 5, pp. 283, 284, 285.
6. Boyer, vol. 2, p. 163.

announced her intention of restoring to the Church the first fruits and the tenths, which Henry VIII had appropriated. She proposed to devote the money to the augmentation of the poorer benefices. This generous act of restitution increased her own popularity, but it did nothing for the government. The ministry of Godolphin came into existence "to reduce the exorbitant power of France." By the outcome of its foreign policy it must stand or fall. Judged by the results of two years of warfare and taxation, it appeared to be falling.

Nevertheless, the necessary preparations for a third campaign were not obstructed by the House of Commons. An additional force of 10,000 men was voted, and in fulfilment of the treaties with Portugal and Savoy, supplies of money were granted to these impecunious allies. On the suggestion of Heinsius, the States invited Marlborough to visit Holland in January and to confer with them upon the critical position of the coalised powers. Traversing the North Sea in weather of exceptional severity, the Duke landed at Rotterdam on January 18, 1704. Without delay he unfolded to the States his proposal for the invasion of France upon the side of Lorraine. He suggested that he himself with the British troops should undertake this enterprise, that Overkirk with the Dutch should remain behind to guard the frontiers, and that the foreign auxiliaries should be shared between the two armies.

His arguments were strongly supported by Heinsius. But although Marlborough continued in the country over a month, the timid Dutchmen would neither promise nor refuse their consent. They were persuaded however to vote supplies of money to the Prince of Baden, the Circle of Suabia, the Elector Palatine, and the Duke of Savoy, and to hire 4,000 Württemberg troops in place of the detachment under orders for Portugal. At the same time Marlborough was skilfully flattering the vanity of the King of Prussia. Having sent to Berlin, in confidence, a detailed plan of the imaginary campaign upon the Moselle, he succeeded in obtaining an augmentation of the Prussian forces in the field. The management of the States was now left in the hands of Heinsius and his friends; and in the last week of February the Duke returned to England, where he made his report to the Queen, and induced her to forward pecuniary assistance to the Circle of Suabia and the Margrave of Baden forthwith.

To facilitate the business of recruiting, which was now become extremely difficult, a bill empowering the justices of the peace to press the idle and destitute was carried through Parliament. Rochester's Tories protested against the measure as a violation of the liberties of the subject. Nottingham also adopted an obstructive attitude, which finally exhausted the patience of Marlborough and Godolphin. Marlborough in particular perceived that, before committing himself irrevocably to his momentous enterprise, it would be expedient to purge the ministry of elements antagonistic to the proper conduct of the war.

The Queen was unwilling to lose the services of a man whose high character and attachment to the Church she much admired. But Nottingham himself left her no option. By insisting that she should choose between Whigs and Tories, and declining to sit in council with the Dukes of Somerset and Devonshire, he forced her to accept his resignation. With him went Jersey, Seymour, and Blathwayt. Nottingham's place was bestowed upon Harley, whose young and brilliant disciple, St. John, received at the same time the secretaryship for war. Mansell, a strong Tory, was made Comptroller of the Household, and the Earl of Kent, a moderate Whig, became Lord Chamberlain.

These changes were in accordance with the system of government upon which Godolphin and Marlborough had hitherto proceeded. But they gave great offence to Rochester's party on the one hand and to such bigoted Whigs as Sunderland on the other, while the Duchess, who, in addition to her pronounced Whiggery, entertained an instinctive mistrust of both Harley and St. John, protested strongly to her husband against the new appointments.

To fortify his position both at home and at the Hague, Marlborough would appear to have entered into an arrangement with Eugène that the Emperor should transmit a written request to the Queen of England for her assistance in his great extremity. On April 2, the envoy, Wratislaw, presented this document. After reciting the imminent perils to which the Empire was exposed, it prayed Her Majesty "to order the Duke of Marlborough, Her Captain General, seriously to consult with the States General of the speediest Method for assisting the Empire; Or, at least, to conduct Part of the Troops in Her Majesty's Pay beyond Sea, to preserve Germany from a total Subversion; it not being just in itself, nor any ways advantageous to the Common Cause, that Her Majesty's Troops should tarry on the Frontiers of Holland; which were not in the least threatened by the Enemy, and were defended by great Rivers and strong Places, whilst the Empire was destroyed by the French Troops, by Fire and Sword."

To this very cogent reasoning the Queen replied that, "the Duke of Marlborough, Captain General of Her Armies, had received Orders from Her Majesty, to take the most effectual methods with the States General of the United Provinces, Her good Allies and Confederates, to send a speedy Succour to His Imperial Majesty, and the Empire, and to press the States to take the necessary measures to rescue Germany, from the imminent Danger it was now expos'd to."[7] An instruction to this effect was issued to Marlborough by the Cabinet. Orders at once so forcible and so vague were exactly what he wanted. They gave him immense authority over others while they left him an entire latitude for himself.

Accompanied by Churchill, Orkney, and other officers, the Duke sailed from Harwich on April 19, and reached the Hague on the 21st. Fearful lest the enemy should deliver a decisive blow in Bavaria before his own preparations were completed, he wrote at once to the Margrave of Baden to impress upon that somewhat lethargic commander the need for activity and vigilance. The Margrave had prepared a plan for a campaign upon the Moselle; and to gratify one who might at no distant date become his colleague, Marlborough affected to adopt it. But for the moment it appeared that neither to the Moselle nor anywhere else outside the Netherlands would the States-General consent to send their troops.

The efforts of Heinsius and his friends had not prevailed against the narrow views and nervous apprehensions of a people who knew how to make money but not how to make war. Marlborough now took a hand in the game. The discussions were lengthy, and not devoid of heat. At last the Duke was constrained to play his trump-card. He let it be known that, if their High Mightinesses were content to remain idle spectators of the "total subversion" of Germany, the Queen of England was not, and that, with or without the co-operation of their High Mightinesses, every man and horse in the service of Her Majesty should march with him to the rescue of the Empire. The threat was sufficient. Their High Mightinesses preferred safety to honour; but if the Duke kept his word, (and they knew that he would,) neither safety, as they understood it, nor honour would be theirs. On May 4 the requisite powers were granted. And Marlborough was free to turn his attention to the movement of his columns towards the Rhine and the accumulation of material and stores at Coblenz.

The troops which he had obtained from the States were foreign auxiliaries. The native Dutch were to remain behind with Overkirk.

---

7. Lediard, vol. 1, pp. 286, 287.

By this arrangement he escaped from the insufferable incubus of the field-deputies, who had ruined his first two campaigns. His plans were developing rapidly, and the prospect of success seemed fair. But he was far from happy. He had left the Duchess in a sullen mood, if not in a fury; and the oppressive shadow of her wrath was always at his side. To many it will seem a monstrous and intolerable thing that a man whose single brain controlled the strategy of mighty empires, whose time was occupied by a thousand details and a thousand duties, whose mind was burdened with the secrets and gigantic enterprises upon which the fate of his country and of the whole civilised world depended, should, at this the most anxious and exacting moment of his whole career, have been harassed by the evil temper of the woman whom he loved best on earth.

It may be that Sarah never realised in full how profoundly her displeasure could make him suffer. It may be also that, on this occasion at any rate, her anger was not wholly without excuse. For if, as seems probable, it originated in the recent appointments of Harley and St. John, she honestly believed those appointments to be fraught with peril to her husband's interest. Whatever may have been the occasion of her wrath, Marlborough felt it, as he always felt it, intensely. On May 5, however, he received from her a letter in a different strain. At once his depression was transformed to an almost childlike joy. He was about to start for Utrecht; but before his departure he sent her a reply which, when considering in what hour and in what circumstances it was written, is one of the most pathetically human documents in history:

> For I am going up into Germany, where it would be impossible for you to follow me; but love me as you now do, and no hurt can come to me.[8]

So, in the midst of his labours, wrote the soldier of fifty-four to the middle-aged woman of society who had been his wife for twenty-six years. And so might a young knight errant in the days of chivalry have written to his queen of love on the eve of some high adventure. That same night the Duke embarked upon a yacht for Utrecht, and upon one of the greatest enterprises in the annals of war.

Having spent one night with the Earl of Albemarle at his seat of Vorst, the Duke arrived at Roermond on the 8th, and Maestricht on the 10th. In both places he occupied himself with the inspection of

---

8. Coxe, vol. 1, p. 155: The Duke to the Duchess, April 24/May 5, 1704.

troops and the instruction of his subordinates. The Dutch and English forces were marching from the various garrisons and cantonments in the direction of Cologne. Though the actual business of concentration was entrusted to his brother, Churchill, there were not many details that escaped the vigilant eye of Marlborough. After a week of incessant labour, his arrangements were complete. On the 16th he quitted Maestricht to assume command.

At Bedburg, between Roermond and Cologne, Churchill had assembled the army. On May 18 Marlborough reviewed them, and found them to consist of 51 battalions and 92 squadrons. The English contingent numbered 16,000 men. The Dutch and Prussians, quartered on the Rhine, were to join at a later date. On the 19th the march began. The route lay through Kerpen, Kühlseggen, and Meckenheim to Sinzig, which was reached on the 23rd. From the very beginning, Marlborough was harassed by the nervous terrors of the allies. At Kerpen he received a dispatch from Overkirk, who was alarmed by the movements of Villeroi.

The French Marshal, who had 40,000 men in the Netherlands, had left his lines, passed the Meuse with a large force at Namur, and was demonstrating against Huy. At Kühlseggen came news from Louis of Baden, who was in momentary expectation that Tallard would cross the Rhine and attack the lines of Stollhofen. Overkirk pressed the Duke to halt and Baden urged him to quicken his pace. Unshaken in his own purpose, but realising the necessity of calming their anxieties, Marlborough ordered the Dutch and Prussians on the Upper Rhine to make a motion in support of Baden, while he wrote at once to the States-General to assure them that they had nothing to fear from Villeroi, who would certainly follow him in his march towards the Moselle. He even begged them to send him reinforcements, which, on his view of the situation, they could easily spare.

On the day that the army encamped at Sinzig, the Duke rode over to Bonn, and inspected the garrison and the fortifications. This he did on purpose to strengthen the general impression that he was preparing for a campaign upon the Moselle. On his arrival at Sinzig, he learned that Tallard had succeeded in passing a detachment of 10,000 recruits for Marsin's army through the Black Forest, in spite of the efforts of the Imperialist forces under Baden to frustrate the operation. The Duke was not perturbed by this intelligence. For the fact that Tallard had subsequently returned with his army to Strasbourg, conclusively showed that the French had not yet divined the great secret.

He was also informed that, in accordance with his anticipation, Villeroi was pressing forward towards the Moselle. These circumstances enabled him to renew his petition to the States-General for reinforcements. They also furnished him with an excuse for accelerating his own movements.

On the 25th he quitted Sinzig and took the road to Coblenz. He was accompanied by all the cavalry and dragoons in the army. Churchill was instructed to follow as rapidly as possible with the infantry, artillery, and baggage. On the 26th, while his horsemen were passing the Moselle and the Rhine at Coblenz, the Duke visited the Elector of Trèves at the fortress of Ehrenbreitstein, which welcomed him with a triple discharge of all its cannon. Pushing on that night to Braubach, he was visited in his camp by the Landgrave of Hesse-Darmstadt. And here he wrote a letter to the King of Prussia, complimenting the Prussian troops and urgently soliciting reinforcements.

On the 27th he marched to Nastätten, and on the 28th to Schwalbach, where he learned that the government at the Hague were dispatching 8 battalions and 21 squadrons to his assistance. On the 29th he reached Kastel, a village on the right bank of the Rhine, over against Mainz. Leaving the men to the enjoyment of a well-earned rest, the Duke and his retinue crossed the river, and entering the carriages of the Elector of Mainz were conducted amid the thunder of artillery to the palace. The Elector entertained his guests with lavish hospitality, and was loud in his praises of the English soldiers, who exhibited that smart appearance which has always distinguished the British Army. From Mainz the Duke wrote to Godolphin to explain that he was endeavouring to arrange with Frankfurt bankers "to take up a month's pay for the English." He added that "notwithstanding the continual marching, the men are extremely pleased with this expedition."[9]

They had every reason to be pleased. Never before had the army of an English monarch been seen in Germany. And never before had any army, native or foreign, conducted itself as this one. For Marlborough had issued the strictest injunctions that nothing was to be taken from the inhabitants without payment. He saw to it also that the men had always the wherewithal to pay. In the German peoples, who were gazing now for the first time upon the regular forces of the British Crown, curiosity was soon succeeded by astonishment. So the barbarous islanders were not barbarous at all.

In a country which had long been habituated to regard all sol-

---

9. Coxe, vol. 1, p. 160: Marlborough to Godolphin.

diers as robbers, ravishers, and assassins, the soldiers of the Queen of England were conducting themselves as correctly as at Windsor or at Kensington. To the burgher and the boor alike, such moderation seemed nothing less than a portent. Certainly the gabled villages and steep- roofed cities of old Germany had never looked down upon its like. Moreover these righteous men were good to gaze upon, and they rode their beautiful horses with consummate ease, considerations not unavailing even against the solid breast of the feminine Teuton.

"The Electors of Trèves and Mayence," wrote an English officer, "have seen us on our march, and at least 200 ladies, some of them much handsomer than we expected to find in this country."[10]

In short, the English had not been many hours on the German side of the frontier before they were popular. And as they advanced, they became more than popular. For why, it was asked, had they crossed the northern sea and ridden so many weary miles through dust and sun? They had done it to save Germany from the French tyrant, to save German wealth and German women from that atrocious treatment which too often fell to the lot of any civilian population that found itself at the mercy of a profligate soldiery. Therefore the English were deliverers, and they were heroes. And for heroes, and virtuous heroes at that, nothing was too good. The march, fatiguing as it was, became a sort of triumphal progress. Marlborough and his troopers were not only fed but feasted, not only welcomed but acclaimed.

No wonder therefore that the men were "extremely pleased." It was not in human nature, and certainly not in the very human nature of the British soldier, to be anything else than "extremely pleased "in a land flowing with beer and resounding with benedictions. Those who know him as he is today, and as he has ever been, can imagine how he rose to the occasion, and with what valiant stolidity he played the part thus surprisingly thrust upon him. His happiness indeed was deep and unalloyed. He was sick to death of damp and dreary Holland. Adequate language, in which to describe his sentiments towards Dutch deputies and Dutch generals, had long been to seek even in his opulent vocabulary. But now at last he had escaped from the irritating jurisdiction of their "High Mightinesses."

His general too had escaped with him, such a general as could

---

10. Coke MSS. belonging to Earl Cowper, vol. 3, p. 36: R. Pope to Thomas Coke, June 4, 1704 (Hist. MSS. Comm., 12th Report, Appendix, part 3).

not be matched in all Europe, if only he were freed, as now at last he was free, from the meddling of impertinent fools. Together they would show these neglected foreigners how war was understood in England.[11]

Thus reasoned within himself the British soldier. And so with the wonderful joy of the truant in his heart, with a new and extremely beautiful country to explore, with plenty of hard work, an abundance of the finest food, a superabundance of alcoholic liquors, and the delicious certainty of a big fight at the finish, he rode radiantly on through guttural plaudits and the smiles of massive beauty, following, he knew not whither, but always in devoted confidence, that gracious and serene commander. While he was at Mainz, Marlborough persuaded the Landgrave of Hesse, who had prepared artillery for a campaign on the Moselle, to send it up the Rhine to Mannheim. This operation, which appeared to threaten Landau, was intended to increase the mystification of the French generals. Marlborough had indeed been eminently successful in creating that 'fog of war' which was essential to the execution of his plan.

At first, his declared intention of a campaign upon the Moselle had imposed upon Villeroi, who had hastened across Luxembourg in pursuit. But the march from Coblenz to Mainz, though not incompatible with operations in Lorraine, suggested that Alsace was the real objective. The dispatch of the Hessian artillery to Mannheim and the construction of a bridge at Philippsburg confirmed this new impression. With sentiments akin to relief, Villeroi and Tallard made ready to unite their armies. Hitherto they had been sorely puzzled. The rapidity of Marlborough's march had greatly added to their embarrassment.

Their constant interchange of views with one another, and with the government at Versailles, had been rendered nugatory in the most exasperating fashion by the perpetual arrival of intelligence which upset from hour to hour their most recent calculations. Every possibility of the situation had been considered, every solution of the problem had been examined, even the right one. The right one however appeared so unlikely that it received but scanty attention. And now when the truth was so soon to be revealed, the two Marshals laid firmer hold than ever on a wrong conclusion.

On the 31st, Marlborough's troopers got once more to horse, and passing the Maine, continued their march towards the south. With every step, the beauty of the country grew more wonderful. They

---
11. Coke MSS., *ibid.*

were riding now over the broad and sunlit plain of the Rhine, and under the shadow of that mysterious mountain-land of Odenwald. From Weinheim, on June 2, the Duke dispatched a letter to his wife, who was still pressing for permission to join him.

"You could hardly get to me and back again to Holland," he wrote, "before it would be time to return into England. Besides, my dear soul, how could I be at any ease? For if we should not have good success, I could not put you into any place where you would be safe.

"I am now in a house of the Elector Palatine, that has a prospect over the finest country that is possible to be seen. I see out of my chamber window the Rhine and the Neckar, and his two principal towns of Mannheim and Heidelberg; but would be much better pleased with the prospect of St. Albans, which is not very famous for seeing far."[12]

On the following day he came down through the apple-orchards to the Neckar at Ladenburg. The troops crossed the river on a bridge of boats and encamped on the opposite bank. And here the Duke permitted a halt of two days, not only to refresh his men and horses, but also to afford an opportunity to Churchill to lessen the widening gap between the main body and the mounted arms. Never for one moment, as he dashed forward with his brilliant squadrons, had he banished from his memory the long files of toiling infantry and guns. He had impressed upon his brother, before they parted, the prime necessity of speed; but he had also insisted that speed must not be secured at too heavy a cost. The reasonable comfort of the men must be consulted; their physical fitness must be preserved to the very end.

The recruits, whom Tallard had sent to Marsin, had been so cruelly overdriven that half of them were dead or in hospital. Marlborough had no desire to reach the Danube with an army incapacitated for active service. He had therefore instructed Churchill to begin every day's march at sunrise, and to have all the troops in camp before high noon. Churchill had punctually obeyed these orders, and was bringing up his men in fine condition and at a splendid pace. They reached the Maine at Kastel on the 3rd, the day of Marlborough's arrival on the Neckar.

That same day the Duke wrote to his brother, enquiring as to the state of his forces and directing him to proceed straight to Heidelberg,

---

12. Coxe, vol. 1, p. 161: The Duke to the Duchess, May 22/June 2, 1704.

as the road by Ladenburg was not an easy one. It was in a dispatch from Ladenburg, that Marlborough at last disclosed his true intention to the Dutch government.

The Queen, he wrote, had commanded him "to march to the relief of the Empire." He begged them to permit their troops "to share in the honour of that expedition."[13] The States-General putting the best possible face upon the matter, consented with unusual promptitude. But the secret was still hidden from the French. Though the passage of the Neckar excited their suspicions, it was not inconsistent with a projected advance to Philippsburg or the lines of Stollhofen. But on the morning of the 6th, when Churchill was only a couple of marches from the Neckar, the truth was made manifest to all.

On that day the Duke and his cavalry, taking to the road once more, wheeled off from the valley of the Rhine, and struck south-east upon the way to Heilbronn. They camped at Wiesloch; and on the morrow, riding on through the legendary Neckarland, past Turenne's old battlefield of Sinsheim, a name redolent to Marlborough of the memories of his youth, they came to Eppingen. Here the Duke wrote to Churchill, who was now at Weinheim, warning him that the road from Wiesloch to Sinsheim was a hilly one, urging him to spare his artillery horses as much as possible, and authorising him to shorten his marches if the men showed signs of exhaustion.

On the 8th, having been joined on the road by some of the auxiliaries, Marlborough pushed on to Gross Gartach, whither the Duke of Württemberg sent to compliment the English general and to promise him any assistance in his passage through the ducal territory. And here, still mindful of the long columns of men and guns that were trudging in his wake, he wrote to his brother to impress upon him the imperative necessity of finishing each day's work while the morning was still cool. He also urged him to see that the colonels provided their regiments with proper boots, of which a good supply at reasonable prices could be procured from Frankfurt.

On the 9th he passed the Neckar a second time, and advanced to Mundelsheim. Here on the ensuing day he was joined by Wratislaw and Prince Eugène, who was closeted alone with the Duke for three hours;[14] and here was laid the foundation of that famous and singular friendship, so honourable to both commanders and so fatal to "the exorbitant power of France."

---

13. Lediard, vol. 1, p. 303.
14. Coke MSS., *ibid.*: Letter of June 13, 1704.

The next day's march was over the hills and down into Gross Heppach, a picturesque village in the lovely valley of the Rems, Eugène accompanied the column, and in conversation with Marlborough expressed a desire to inspect the British cavalry and dragoons. So in the fair, green meadows by the riverside, the English general drew up his squadrons. Both men and horses were perhaps a trifle lean, for they had travelled fast and far; but the fineness of their condition was unmistakable. Conspicuous also was that trim smartness of uniform and that correctness of bearing and perfection of movement which have ever been characteristic of the British Army. None of these details escaped the practised eye of the Prince. Nor did he fail to remark the alert and proud demeanour of the men.

"My Lord," he said, "I never saw better horses, better clothes, finer belts, and accoutrements; yet all these may be had for money; but there is a spirit in the looks of your men which I never yet saw in any in my life."

The Duke was pleased. "Sir," he replied, "if it be as you say, that spirit is inspired in them by your presence."[15]

He was never at a loss for the language of compliment. But in his ears at any rate the words of Eugène sounded as no idle flattery. In those days English horses were easily the best in the world; and English troopers were real horse-masters, and knew how to preserve the fitness of their chargers through all the fatigues of a prolonged campaign. Moreover, from his youth up Marlborough had mingled with the fighting men of all nations. He had confronted the tough barbarians of Northern Africa, he had served among the French when the military prestige of France was at its zenith.

Germans, Dutchmen, Flemings, British—he had fought against them all and with them all. Both as a comrade and a foe he had intimate knowledge of the military qualities of most of the armies of Europe. And he had formed the deliberate opinion that the British Isles produced the finest soldiers in the world. The subsequent history of war by no means proves that he was wrong. Yet everybody today has the misfortune to know Englishmen who, in the fullness of their ignorance both of what war is and what it has been, affect to despise the judgement of Marlborough as a vulgar and a puerile prejudice.

At Gross Heppach the two commanders awaited the coming of Louis of Baden, who arrived on the 13th. They received him with every mark of consideration and respect. The Margrave was a general

---
15. Lediard, vol. 1, p. 307.

of the orthodox school, but he represented that school at its best. Inferior as he was to Marlborough and Eugène, he was vastly superior to such officers as Opdam. Unfortunately, declining health had begun to paralyse his energies both of mind and body. The criticisms passed upon his recent failure to prevent the passage of recruits to Marsin's army had rendered him extremely sensitive. Conscious of the progressive decadence of his powers, he was anxious only to conserve a reputation which he had little hope of increasing.

Such a man, jealous and suspicious to the last degree, deficient in nerve, and fearful of fresh responsibility, was little better than an embarrassment to Marlborough and Eugène at this most critical juncture. Marlborough had hoped that by delicate tact and judicious flattery, the Margrave might be induced to take command of the army on the Rhine, and to leave the Imperialist forces on the Danube to Eugène. Eugène, who knew the Margrave's character thoroughly, anticipated difficulties. And he was right. For it speedily appeared that the Margrave had no intention of abandoning the principal theatre of the war in favour of a younger rival.

Taking his stand upon his right of seniority, he insisted upon remaining in person on the Danube. Marlborough acquiesced at once. He had been well coached by Eugène, who had told him forcibly that the Margrave would require most careful management. He therefore left nothing undone to humour and conciliate the man with whom he would presently be forced to co-operate in the field. On one point only he was firm. Imperialist generals claimed precedence of all others within the Empire. But as commander-in-chief of the forces of the Queen of England and of the States-General of Holland, Marlborough declined to become the Margrave's subordinate. It was therefore agreed that the old, unsatisfactory compromise of a dual command upon alternate days should come into operation as soon as a junction had been effected between the allied armies.

Early on the 14th, the cavalry set forward on the road to Ebersbach. Marlborough remained behind at Gross Heppach, to entertain his two colleagues at dinner at the Lamm Inn, a great, old hostelry where the tradition of that famous day is still preserved. After this farewell meal, Eugène departed for Philippsburg, and the Margrave for the army on the Danube. Marlborough reached the camp at Ebersbach the same evening. Here he was informed by Wratislaw that the Emperor desired, with the Queen's consent, to create for him a principality in the Holy Roman Empire. Marlborough had all the English gentleman's contempt for mere titles.

"I did assure him," he wrote afterwards to his wife, "that I was very sensible of the honour his master intended me, but in my opinion nothing of this ought to be thought on till we saw what would be the fate of the war."

But Wratislaw insisted. "What already had been done," he said, "had laid obligations on his master above what he could express, and that if the Queen would not allow him to do this, he must appear ungrateful to the world, for he had nothing else in his power worth giving or my taking. What is offered will in history for ever remain an honour to my family. But I wish myself so well that I hope I shall never want the income of the land, which no doubt will be but little, nor enjoy the privilege of German assemblies. However, this is the utmost expression that they can make, and therefore ought to be taken as it is meant."[16]

It was eventually decided that the Emperor should write to the Queen, and that in the meantime the matter should continue in abeyance. To Ebersbach came news from the army of Flanders, such news as astonished nobody, and Marlborough least of all. Overkirk having outwitted the French by a rapid march and passed the lines at Wasseiges had been robbed of the fruits of his enterprise by those suicidal methods which were making war, as conducted by the Dutch, the laughing-stock of Europe.

"Our friends there," wrote Marlborough to Harley, "have lost a very great opportunity. If they had made a good use of it, we might have found the effects in these parts and everywhere else."[17]

The Duke no doubt was thinking of Villeroi. Pressure on the Meuse might have compelled Villeroi to return to that quarter, or at least to detach a considerable contingent. But as it was, he and Tallard were now drawing together in the neighbourhood of Landau. Their combined armies might carry the lines of Stollhofen; or they might mask the lines, while they threw a powerful reinforcement into Bavaria. Marlborough had immense confidence in Eugène. But Eugène could not perform the impossible.

A diversion in the Netherlands would certainly have diminished the peril beyond the Rhine. But as Marlborough expected nothing from the Dutch, he was not disappointed. He relied in fact upon him-

---

16. Coxe, vol. 1, p. 166: The Duke to the Duchess, June 4/15.
17. *Ibid.*, p. 165: Marlborough to Harley, June 15, 1704.

self alone, upon himself, that is, and Eugène. His responsibility at this moment was overwhelming. Both in England and Holland, foes more vigilant and cruel than any he would ever encounter on the field of battle, were waiting and hoping for his ruin. Nothing but victory, shattering, dazzling, reverberating victory, could save him from their vindictive machinations. And that victory must be gained with heterogeneous forces and a feeble colleague.

Alone in the heart of this great, strange land where no British army had ever before set foot, with mighty and numerous enemies as yet unbeaten on his front and on his flank, and with the vultures of faction croaking hoarsely in the distant north, he had need of all his courage. It could not fail him, though as the sense of solitude grew greater, he leaned the more upon his absent friends. Harley's appointment to the Secretaryship of State had been gazetted at the end of May. In writing to congratulate him from Gross Heppach, the Duke had also congratulated himself on "having so good a friend near Her Majesty's person to represent in the truest light my faithful endeavours for her service and the advantage of the public."[18]

Now, as always, slanderous voices and the intrigues of malice were infinitely more terrible to Marlborough than all the Marshals of France. War was his proper business; and in war he could trust himself. Louis of Baden might not be a soldier after his own heart; but Louis of Baden at his worst was a thousand times better than Coehoorn and Opdam and the pettifogging meddlers of the Hague. And always there were those 16,000 Englishmen, with that "spirit in the looks" of them, the like of which Eugène had never before set eyes on. Whatever of doubt or misgiving may have visited the heart of their leader in moments of depression, to them at any rate he made no sign that might dim that splendid confidence which was at once the omen and the instrument of certain victory.

On the 16th Marlborough continued his advance. He halted at Gross Sussen; and at the same time auxiliary troops of Hesse, Hamburg, and Hanover encamped in the vicinity. Here he remained until the 21st. It had been raining heavily for several days. The roads were becoming impracticable; and the Duke was greatly concerned for his infantry and guns. He wrote to Churchill to urge him to be careful of the men's health, and as sparing as possible of the artillery teams. He arranged for the formation of magazines at Heidenheim and Nördlin-

---

18. Murray, vol. 1, p. 307: Marlborough to Harley, June 13, 1704.

gen. He directed the Danish infantry, which had reached Frankfurt, to proceed to Stollhofen. And to pacify the States-General, who were terrified by a rumour of Villeroi's return to Flanders, he ordered boats to be prepared as if for the rapid transport of guns and baggage down the Rhine. At the same time he wrote to Heinsius:

> I beg you will take care that I receive no orders from the States that may put me out of a condition of reducing the Elector, for that would be of all mischiefs the greatest.[19]

He of course was well aware that whatever plan was ultimately adopted by French generals in concert with Versailles, the return of Villeroi to Flanders was out of the question. For the crisis was now at hand. The Elector of Bavaria was sending his baggage to Ulm, and was passing his army across the Danube. He evidently intended to defend that river from its northern side. Louis of Baden with the Imperialist army was approaching Westerstetten, which is only eight miles north of Ulm. On the 21st Marlborough advanced to Ursprung, the auxiliaries falling in upon the march. On the 22nd the allied armies joined hands at Westerstetten. On the 23rd the two commanders reviewed their forces, and on the 24th they advanced to Elchingen and Langenau.

Thereupon the Elector retired to the impregnable position of Lauingen and Dillingen, midway between Ulm and Donauwörth. Here he had prepared himself a camp, strongly entrenched and almost surrounded by water. On the 26th the allies moved to Herbrechtingen and Giengen, where only two leagues separated them from the enemy. On the 27th the infantry and guns marched in. And Marlborough saw with joy that, though the continual rains had caused some little sickness, the columns swung by with a proud and vigorous air that would certainly have earned them from Eugène the same commendations as he had already bestowed upon their comrades of the mounted arm.

The hour, for which he had toiled and planned so long, had come at last. He was face to face with that prince, who, to gratify a private ambition, had gambled with the safety of Europe. And there were no Dutch deputies to come between them. Max Emanuel knew well that the game had taken a dangerous turn for him and for his unfortunate subjects. He at any rate had always feared lest Marlborough's ultimate goal might prove to be upon the Danube. And all through May and June the dread of such a possibility had held him back from the Vienna

---

19. Von Noorden, vol. 1, p. 538: *Marlborough an Heinsius*, 19 *Juni*, 1 704, *Heinsiusarchiv*,

road. That was Wratislaw's meaning when, in the Emperor's name, he declared to Marlborough that "what already had been done, had laid obligations on his master above what he could express."

And now the Elector's forebodings were realised. His enemy was at the gate. So profound was his disquiet that he had already begun to negotiate for terms with Marlborough, who in anticipation of such a contingency had been furnished by his government with full powers to treat. But the demands which the Elector advanced were ridiculously high. Only by defeat would he be persuaded to lessen them.

From the very outset of his march Marlborough had fixed his eye upon the town of Donauwörth. It was here that no less a soldier than Gustavus had passed the Danube. Almost the last words of Villars when he quitted the Elector at the end of the campaign of 1703, had been these:

> You are still master of the Danube; take Passau. Fortify your towns, above all the Schellenberg, that fort above Donauwörth, the importance of which the great Gustavus taught us.[20]

Passau had been taken, but down to the end of the third week in June, nothing had been done to strengthen the defences of Donauwörth. The town itself was surrounded by mediaeval walls, which in the age of Vauban were already obsolete. But it was covered on the south by the Danube, and on the north by the Schellenberg, a steep and lofty hill, terminating in a broad plateau which was capable of receiving an army of 20,000 men. Such an army, properly entrenched, could not be easily dislodged. For as the ascent began from the very fosse of Donauwörth, the flanks of the position which were the most accessible to attack could be enfiladed from the ramparts of the town, while the defenders could be both supplied and reinforced from the garrison itself and from Bavarian armies beyond the river. But it was not until June 20 that the business of fortifying the plateau had been begun by a small body of infantry and dragoons, assisted by a multitude of peasants from the surrounding country.

On the 30th, which was Marlborough's day of command, the allied army, in full view of the Elector's camp, made a march of two leagues in the direction of Donauwörth. To this move the Elector replied by ordering a detachment of Bavarian infantry and guns under Count Maffei, to proceed along the right bank of the Danube towards the threatened point. On July 1, the allies continued their advance as far as

---

20. *Vie de Villars*, t. 1., p. 289,

Amerdingen, which is fifteen miles from Donauwörth; and the Elector dispatched a force of Bavarian cavalry under Marshal D'Arco in support of Maffei. This cavalry encamped on the southern side of the Danube, opposite Donauwörth. But early in the evening of the 2nd, D'Arco and Maffei, with all the infantry and artillery, passed over the river and joined the troops and labourers already at work upon the Schellenberg.

The allied commanders were well informed by spies and deserters of all that was passing at Donauwörth. The Elector's plan was not difficult to understand. His own position was at present unassailable. But if once the allies secured the bridge of Donauwörth, he would be forced to retire immediately. If, on the other hand, they could be either intimidated or repulsed at Donauwörth, they might be compelled to fritter away their time upon the northern bank of the Danube until the French army, which Villeroi and Tallard had pledged themselves to send, arrived in Bavaria.

This design could only be frustrated by prompt action. Donauwörth must be taken before the operations of the engineers and the arrival of reinforcements rendered the position on the Schellenberg impregnable. Both Marlborough and the Margrave realised this truth. On the evening of the 1st the Duke visited his colleague's quarters. What passed between them is unknown. But apparently they agreed that the Schellenberg should be attacked on the ensuing day. For at 10 that night Marlborough sent an express to Nördlingen, with a letter from the Margrave to the authorities of that town and full instructions for the collection of surgeons and the preparation of a hospital on a considerable scale.

Between Marlborough and the Margrave there existed at this time, in the words of Cardonnel, "a pretty good harmony."[21] The Margrave, moreover, was no fool. He understood the situation perfectly. It was not in intelligence, but in moral courage that generals of his stamp could be trusted to fall short. Marlborough knew well that, as soon as ever the allied troops came in sight of the Schellenberg, his colleague would begin to perceive objections to an attack. Fortunately the Duke would be in supreme command. He made up his mind that, before the Margrave's day came round again, the Schellenberg should be his.

Before daylight on the 2nd, Cadogan set off with a body of cavalry, pioneers, and pontoons, to prepare the way. The distance to be traversed was fifteen miles; the roads, such as they were, had been ruined

---

21. Letter from Mr. Cardonnel to Mons. —— at Zell (Lediard, vol. 1, p. 315).

by perpetual rains; and, a league from Donauwörth, it would be necessary to cross the River Wörnitz, At 3 a.m. Marlborough marched with 35 squadrons of horse and 5,850 selected foot of his own army, and 3 regiments of Imperial Grenadiers. At 5 the main body followed. It was almost 8 when watchers on the Schellenberg descried the scarlet coats of Cadogan's troopers on the heights beyond the Wörnitz. At first they imagined that it was nothing but a reconnaissance. But as the scarlet patches continually increased in number, and the Bavarian outposts were seen to be rapidly falling back upon the village of Berg, D'Arco concluded that the allies were on the march towards Donauwörth.

At 9 he dispatched an express to the Elector with an urgent request for reinforcements; and at the same time he ordered the whole of his infantry to fall to work with pick and shovel on the western side of the Schellenberg, where the trenches were still in an unfinished condition. Then he and Maffei rode down towards the Wörnitz to take a nearer view of the enemy. Having formed the opinion that Cadogan was merely marking out a camp, and that the attack would not be delivered until the following day, the Bavarian generals returned to Donauwörth, and went forthwith to dinner. Had they known that Marlborough in person had already joined Cadogan, they would not have sat down with so excellent an appetite.

The Duke had quitted his columns on the march, and had overtaken the quartermaster at 9 . Pressing forward towards the Wörnitz, he obtained a good view of the Bavarian position. He also noted that the camp beyond the Danube, where D'Arco had left his *cuirassiers*, was constructed to receive a large contingent of infantry. And he drew the correct conclusion that additional reinforcements were expected from the Elector's army. Presently he was joined by the Margrave; and the two commanders, accompanied by a crowd of officers, rode closer to the enemy, who opened a sharp fire upon these daring intruders. By noon the reconnaissance was completed. And now the selected detachment appeared upon the banks of the Wörnitz. So foul were the roads that nine hours had been spent in marching twelve miles.

Marlborough's decision was taken. He knew that fortified camps, supported by the artillery of towns, were reported to be unassailable. But he was resolved to storm the Schellenberg before nightfall. No general in Europe, except Eugène, would have ventured such a throw. Without exception they would have argued that the troops were too fatigued to attempt so arduous a task, and that a disastrous repulse in a difficult country and with the Elector close at hand, would probably involve the whole army in a catastrophe.

Marlborough was not a desperate gambler. He reasoned correctly, and upon sound premises. A day's delay would mean the completion of the enemy's works and the arrival of reinforcements. It would then be represented that what was dangerous before had become quite impossible. The Margrave would assuredly refuse to venture an attack in such circumstances. If Marlborough, when his day came round, insisted upon making the attempt, the price of success would be enormous. Unless he were prepared to pay that price, or to abandon the whole line of the Danube to the Elector, he must fight at once. The fact that the men were tired did not greatly weigh with him. They were his own men. He knew them; and he judged them by no ordinary standard.[22]

Accordingly, after a brief halt the troops began to pass the Wörnitz. The enemy had broken down the bridge; but Cadogan repaired it, and also threw pontoons across the river. While Marlborough was regarding the passage of the mud-splashed columns, an officer galloped up with a letter from Eugène. It contained intelligence which only confirmed him in his present resolution. Tallard and Villeroi were at Strasbourg, preparing to dispatch an army through the Black Forest.

Marlborough's decision had one advantage, to which he attributed great value, the advantage of surprise. He knew that the Bavarian generals, reasoning upon orthodox lines, would not anticipate attack that day, and that if attack came, it would find them startled, embarrassed, and perhaps unnerved. The event justified his anticipations. D'Arco and Maffei were still sitting at table in the town, when news arrived from the outposts that the allies had begun to pass the Wörnitz. They hurriedly mounted their horses, and rode out to see for themselves what was doing. Arrived at the summit of the Schellenberg, they perceived the enemy in great force upon the heights beyond the Wörnitz, and the heads of his columns advancing from that river towards the foot of the mountain.

Even now they refused to believe that an immediate attack was in contemplation. But D'Arco had serious misgivings. He ordered the work upon the trenches to proceed with unremitting vigour, and he dispatched another express to the Elector. To his subordinates he spoke but little. Sunk in a gloomy and forbidding silence, he contemplated the motions of the enemy. As battalion after battalion came rapidly

---

22. *The Accomplished Officer* (1708), pp. 136, 231, 232.

across, he realised at last that, contrary to what he regarded as the rules of the game, he would be compelled to fight before nightfall. The one alternative was retirement. To abandon to the enemy a bridge over the Danube and a base for the invasion of Bavaria, was out of the question. He must stand his ground till help came. The chances seemed greatly in his favour. The size of his army has been variously reported. The lowest estimate is 7,000, which is certainly too small; the highest is 32,000, which is absurd. It seems most probable that he had over 10,000 men upon the Schellenberg, and that in Donauwörth town he had 2,000 more. Of those upon the Schellenberg, about 8,000 were Bavarian infantry, soldiers of the very finest quality.[23]

Such troops would not be easily driven from a strong position. And that the position was exceedingly strong is not to be denied. The works upon the western side of the Schellenberg were still unfinished; but considering the time and labour that had been expended on them, and judging from the remains which still exist, they must have been respectable. They were certainly not so contemptible as they are represented to have been by French and Bavarian writers, anxious to excuse defeat. For a considerable distance, moreover, they could be swept by a flanking fire from the walls of Donauwörth. That fact alone had been assumed to confer comparative immunity upon the western side of the mountain.

On the north-western slope of the Schellenberg a dense wood runs up to a point within a few yards of the angle where the line of D'Arco's trenches turned towards the east. An attack from the wood itself, which was practically impenetrable, seemed very unlikely. But if, as appeared probable, the allies intended to assault the western side of the position, they could only escape the enfilading fire of the town by advancing on a narrow front, with their left flank hugging the wood as closely as possible. Accordingly, D'Arco planted eight of his fifteen cannon at this threatened angle, and concentrated the bulk of his foot in the same quarter. At the same time, he ordered Du Bordet, the French governor of Donauwörth, to man the palisades, which did duty for a counterscarp, with French infantry. And for the sake of appearances the French regiment of Nectancourt was stretched out in a feeble fine along that part of the trenches which approached the town, and which was supposed on that account to run no risk of serious assault.

By 4 o'clock Marlborough had drawn up the attacking force at the

---

23. "*A la verité bons et forts*," *Mémoires de La Colonie* (1748), t. 1., p. 305.

extremity of the lower slopes of the Schellenberg. It consisted of the detachment of 5,850 foot, supported by 30 battalions, the whole being arranged in four lines. A fifth line was composed of 18 squadrons under Lumley, and a sixth of 17 under Hompesch. The command of the attack was entrusted to the Dutch general, Goor, a brave and skilful officer in whom Marlborough had the utmost confidence. At this time the Bavarian artillery began to play. But under cover of the smoke from the village of Berg, which had been fired by D'Arco's outposts, an English battery came swiftly into action, and drew all the attention of the Bavarian gunners to itself.

The regiment of the Bavarian infantry were shielded by their earthworks from the English balls. But fifty paces to the rear, D'Arco had stationed in reserve a regiment of French grenadiers in the service of the Elector. The officer who commanded them, La Colonie, a cool and hardy veteran, had been instructed by the Marshal to watch the development of the attack, and in particular to keep a vigilant eye upon the wood. This regiment, which by its situation on higher ground got little protection from the earthworks, soon attracted the notice of the English gunners. Their first shot killed an officer and twelve men. As the assault was momentarily expected, La Colonie dared not quit his exposed position. His grenadiers endured the punishment with wonderful firmness. Every time that he saw the flash of the English cannon, he saw some of his people on the ground. This regiment alone lost five officers and eighty men before it had an opportunity of firing a shot.

A little before 6, Marlborough gave the word; and the infantry, carrying fascines which the cavalry had cut for them in the woods, stepped briskly forward, the squadrons of Lumley and of Hompesch keeping pace with their advance. Lord Mordaunt, Peterborough's son, and Colonel Munden, of the English Foot Guards, led the way at the head of a chosen band of Grenadiers. At once, every gun on the Schellenberg was trained upon their front, while the artillery of Donauwörth directed a converging fire against their right flank. The English, who were nearest to the wood, were out of range of the town; but they suffered severely from the battery of eight pieces in the angle of the works.

But nowhere was there any check, or any confusion. The whole line went forward without wavering and without firing. Soon the steepness of the ascent concealed them from D'Arco's men; but the fire of the Bavarian artillery never slackened. At 200 paces from the works they emerged, and still strode on, steady and silent, through the rushing balls. And now La Colonie and his men moved down into the angle, and the gunners loaded with case. Then the English, says Maffei, cried "God save the Queen,"[24] and with a thundering shout, charged forward at the double.

Few, if any, of the defenders of the Schellenberg had ever heard the islanders cheer. The astute La Colonie did not like the sound ("truly terrifying"[25] he calls it); and he dreaded its effect upon the troops. So, to drown it, he ordered his drums to beat. Straight for the trenches went the English and the Dutch, Mordaunt and his Grenadiers dashing on before. The cool and disciplined veterans of D'Arco waited till the range had dropped to eighty paces. Then the word was given; and over the western face of the Schellenberg broke a crashing tempest of musketry and grape. The effect was terrible. Officers and privates went down in heaps.

The gallant Goor was one of the first to fall. The whole line reeled and staggered. But as the smoke lifted, Mordaunt and Munden were seen conspicuous in the forefront, unwounded, and cheering on the men. Closing the gaps, the survivors pressed forward, while the Bavarians plied them with every gun and musket in the trenches, as fast as they could load and fire. The allies, blinded by the smoke, mistook a hollow way for the ditch, and flung down their fascines. This error resulted in confusion. Those who actually reached the works and exchanged thrusts with the defenders across the parapet, were too few and scattered to force a passage. The charge had spent itself. Then at several points, whole companies of Bavarians leapt out, and dashed furiously forward with the bayonet, sweeping the mountain clear for eighty paces. But the English Guards, unshaken by a cruel loss of officers, stood firm as the Bœotian hoplites on the slope at Syracuse. At length the Bavarians drew off, and panting but triumphant, returned into their works.

The allies dropped back into the dip of the hillside, where they were no longer visible to the enemy's marksmen. But the tops of their standards showed that they were stationary and close at hand. They were in fact re-forming. Fresh men, and above all, fresh officers, were taking the places of the fallen. Meantime the Bavarian artillery poured a perpetual rain of round-shot on their unseen ranks. And D'Arco, still further weakening his left and centre, concentrated every available

---

24. *Mémoires de Maffei* (1741), t. 2, p. 37.
25. *Mémoires de La Colonie*, t. 1., p. 319.

man on the angle by the wood. Wagon-loads of hand-grenades were distributed in the trenches; and every preparation was made to maintain the most obstinate resistance until nightfall, when the situation of the allies would begin to be precarious.

The breathing-space was short. Soon the Bavarians beheld once more the serried[26] ranks of blue and scarlet, proudly and steadily advancing. General officers, who had dismounted from their horses, were leading, sword in hand. But the veterans in the trenches remained undismayed. Once more, at the proper distance, they delivered their murderous volleys with the utmost coolness; and once more the oncoming line was torn and riddled by the hurricane of lead and iron. But still it surged onward to the trenches, and sword and bayonet clashed across the breastwork in a savage grapple. The defence was too strong to be broken. Back went the baffled remnants of the second charge; and after them came the exultant Bavarians with lowered steel. This time the repulse was more serious. The ground was already heaped with the slain.

The Austrian general, Styrum, had been mortally wounded. Here and there appeared indubitable signs of panic. The retreat rolled down into the dip, and on towards the lower slopes, when Lumley riding calmly forward with his eighteen English squadrons, checked the movement at his horses' heads. At once the broken infantry began to rally. Maffei, who rightly dreaded the risks attaching to these counter-strokes, recalled his men to the trenches, and forbade them to sally out again. Then the Bavarian cannon reopened once more. Some of Lumley's saddles were emptied, and some of his chargers sank shuddering to earth. But his troopers, contemplating these things with a stolid and impassive air, infected the dispirited foot with something of their own unshaken confidence.

Though D'Arco had been astonished and perturbed by Marlborough's decision to attack that evening, the brilliant success of the defence had revived his hopes. But there was one officer, who at the first shot had lost his head, and who never recovered it. That officer was Du Bordet, the French governor of Donauwörth. He must have been aware that, if the Schellenberg were captured, the town would immediately become untenable, and that therefore it was his primary duty to support the defenders of the mountain to the utmost of his power. Yet in deliberate defiance of D'Arco's orders, he left his palisades un-

---

26. *"bien serrez," Mémoires de Maffei*, t. 2, p. 38.

manned, and kept his infantry in idleness behind the ancient ramparts. Presumably he imagined that the allies would attempt to carry the place by storm, a not impossible feat. Whatever were his motives, his disobedience had fatal consequences. Recoiling from the unendurable fire of the trenches, the right wing of the assailants spread out towards the town.[27]

Though they suffered badly from the cannon on the walls, they were astonished to find that no musketry galled their flank. Nor did they fail to notice that the trenches in this quarter were but thinly lined. The news was carried to the rear. Half an hour after the beginning of the first assault, the main body of the Imperialist army had arrived. Louis of Baden immediately placed himself at their head, and led them to the point which ought to have been so strong, but which was credibly reported to be so open to attack. The gunners on the ramparts smote them with an enfilading fire as they passed; but the infantry of the garrison, shooting at an ineffective range, did them but little damage. Splendidly led by the Margrave, they still held on towards the meagre defences where the solitary regiment of Nectancourt beheld with consternation the advent of a whole army.

Too soon the Frenchmen fired one ragged volley, and hastily filed off into the town. The Imperialists swarmed over the trenches, and formed in perfect order on the inner side. D'Arco saw them, and swept down like a whirlwind with his nine squadrons of Bavarians and French. It was a bold and timely charge; but it shivered into fragments before the close and well-aimed fire of the Imperialist infantry. The beaten horsemen broke madly off towards the town, the Imperialist cavalry riding hard upon their heels. D'Arco himself was borne onward with the rush. The frightened governor was with difficulty induced to open his gates to the Marshal.

It was now a little after 7. Marlborough's men were again preparing to advance. Lord John Hay's regiment of dragoons (the "Scots Greys") had dismounted, and joined their comrades of the infantry. Maffei, La Colonie, and the valiant defenders of the height knew nothing of the Margrave's passage through the lines. His movements were concealed from them by the steepness of the ground. The tenacity of the enemy had shaken their confidence. The explosion of some powder-magazines had caused a momentary panic. But they still had faith in their ability to hold their own till nightfall.

Unconscious of their danger, the thin flank watched intently for

---

27. *Mémoires* de *Feuquières*, t. 4, p. 110.

the coming of the third assault upon their front. Presently it came. But simultaneously the troops upon their left were startled by the apparition of a line of infantry slowly advancing from the direction of the town. At first La Colonie imagined that reinforcements were arriving. He was swiftly undeceived by a bullet in the jaw. The mass of the Bavarian army still stood fast; but this new peril on their left disturbed and weakened their defence. The English and Dutch pressed on against the front. It was evident that these converging attacks must ultimately annihilate the defenders of the angle.

Suddenly the whole Bavarian army broke, and raced for their lives across the broad plateau, the Imperialists pouring deadly volleys into the demented throng as it passed across the front. Marlborough's men rolled over the trenches like a flood. The Greys had quickly remounted; and horse and foot swept forward side by side. Marlborough himself rode in among the foremost. The infuriated infantry, thirsty for revenge, would have scattered in pursuit of the enemy, had not the Duke forbidden it. But every sabre in the thirty squadrons of Lumley and Hompesch was loosed upon the fugitives.

"The word," says a contemporary writer, "was 'kill, kill, and destroy.'"[28]

Little, if any quarter, was given. Scrambling over the parapets on the northern and eastern faces of the Schellenberg, thousands of the fugitives made for the plain and river. Many were cut down as they ran. Some, like La Colonie, escaped by swimming, but more were drowned. Others fled towards the town, where the governor denied them all admission. A bridge of boats, which D'Arco had constructed some days before, gave way beneath the weight of the crowding masses, and precipitated them into the Danube.

And always the exasperated horsemen drove furiously upon the terrified mob, their merciless steel flashing hither and thither in the twilight as they hunted with shrill halloos through the standing corn, or galloped with a menacing thunder of hoofs and curses along the reedy banks of the river.

Marlborough had won. He had risked all, and he had won. His own conduct during the engagement was much admired.

"The Duke of Marlborough," wrote Hompesch, "gave orders throughout the whole action with the greatest prudence and

---

28. *MSS. of the Duke of Rutland*, vol. 2, p. 181: Lord Gower to the Duke of Rutland, July 6, 1704 (Hist. MSS. Comm., 12th Report, Appendix, part 5).

presence of mind."[29]

But his was a higher courage than that of the mere fighter. He had known the big price to be paid, and he had not shrunk from paying it. For that reason alone, the story of the Schellenberg deserves to be read and reread by every British general today. Over 1,400 of the allies were killed, and nearly 4,000 wounded. The loss in officers, and particularly in officers of high rank, was extraordinary. Eight generals, including Goor and Styrum, eleven colonels, seven lieutenant-colonels, three majors, twenty-six captains, and forty-six subalterns lay dead or dying. Among the wounded were nine generals, including the Princes of Baden and Hesse-Cassel, seven colonels, nine lieutenant-colonels, fifteen majors, sixty-two captains, and one hundred and eighty-one subalterns.

On both sides, veterans who had grown grey in war unanimously declared that such fighting had never been seen. On both sides also it was admitted that the British had set a new standard of devoted and enduring valour. Their casualties (they had more than 1,500) exceeded, both actually and relatively, those of any other contingents engaged. When darkness fell, the rain came down in torrents, drenching the wounded where they lay. There was work and enough for Marlborough's hospital at Nördlingen.

It was not to be expected that in an action of this character the defenders should suffer as severely as the assailants. Maffei alleges that before they broke, their casualties did not exceed 400; but he admits that 2,000 were slain or taken in the chase, which was certainly ruthless. Marsin, writing to Tallard, fixed the casualties at 1,500; but a German record of the time declares that the Bavarians alone had 1,755 killed and wounded. The rout was so complete that accurate figures could never be obtained. When due allowance is made for the killed, the wounded, the drowned, the prisoners, and the deserters, their losses probably equalled those of the allies, if they did not actually exceed them. Dr. Hare asserts that not more than 3,000 of them rejoined the Elector. And the majority of these, having thrown away their arms to facilitate their flight, were not effective.[30] The very flower of the Bavarian infantry was ruined. Fifteen or sixteen cannon, thirteen standards, and all the tents and baggage remained in the hands of the victors.

---

29. Letter of General Hompesch to the States (Lediard, vol. 1, p. 327).
30. Pelet, *Mémoires militaires*, t. 4, p. 532: *Tallard au Roi*, 18 *juillet*, 1704.

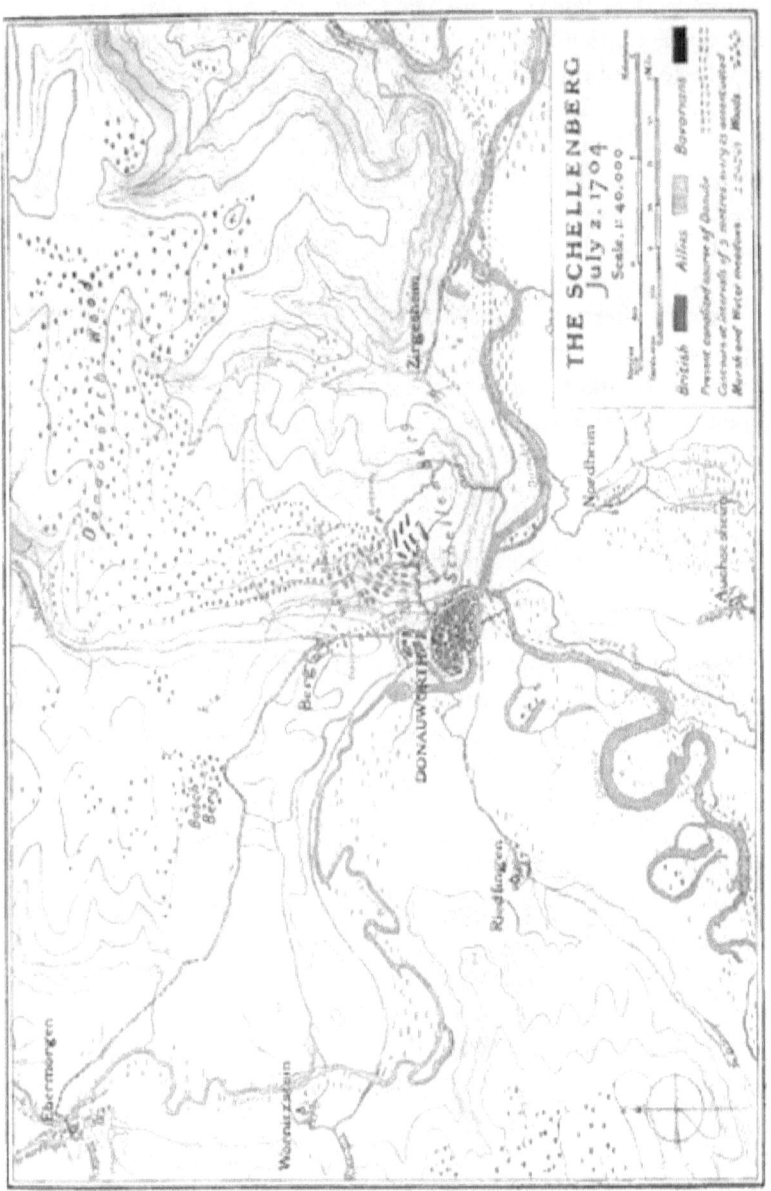

In Holland the news was received with rapture. But Marlborough's enemies in that country insisted on assigning all the glory to the Prince of Baden, and embodied their opinion in a medal. The Margrave had behaved with perfect loyalty to his colleague, and he had borne himself like an excellent tactician and a brave man. But the whole conception and, above all, the whole responsibility had been Marlborough's. To ascribe to another the winning of a battle which but for Marlborough would never have been fought at all, was an act of petty malignancy which deceived no one. Least of all did it deceive the English people. The English have never been a nation of soldiers; but they have always been a nation of fighters. And here at last was fighting.

At last, after two years of war, as war apparently was understood upon the continent, a British army had been permitted to show how fighting was understood in the British Isles. The populace had no doubt as to which general and which soldiers had won the battle. Wherever two or three Englishmen were gathered together, it was proudly told how Her Majesty's soldiers had lost 33 *per cent*, of their numbers, and had still gone forward, how in the Guards only five officers out of seventeen remained unhurt, how Mordaunt with three bullets in his clothes and Munden with five in his hat, had come off unscathed as by a miracle, and how of the eighty-two heroes whom they had led, but twenty-one had returned. Men told with enthusiasm of the patient fortitude of the Greys. They dwelt with grim satisfaction on the details of the stern pursuit. And with exultation, not untinged with anxiety, they acclaimed the general whose only fault was the most noble weakness of despising personal danger too much.

But the Jacobites, who were the friends of France, and the recalcitrant Tories and the discontented Whigs, who were the enemies of Marlborough, had much ado to conceal from the mass of their countrymen the rage and vexation of their embittered souls. They had hoped that Marlborough's audacious march would end in a catastrophe, and they had been woefully disappointed. But they were not without resources. If they could not with safety proclaim their sorrow for their country's triumph, they could nevertheless inject a little poison into the cup of national rejoicing. They could speak with the respectable voice of 'the military critic.' This pernicious type, compounded in equal proportions of military ignorance, personal spite, and the malice of ignoble faction, is only too familiar in modern times. He had plenty to say upon the subject of the Schellenberg. Such a victory lent itself especially to those insidious forms of detraction and misrepresentation, which are his stock-in-trade when he caters for a people profoundly uninformed on military affairs. What, after all, it was asked, did this victory amount to? The conquest of a barren mountain and a paltry town. The enemy were reported to have suffered heavy losses; but the enemy denied it, and the fact was at best problematical.

On the other hand it was certain that 5,500 of the allies were killed and wounded, and that the British casualties were out of all proportion to those of the other nations. It was suggested that the British general who ordered the attack was a blunderer who had only been saved from the consequences of his own incompetence by the skilful intervention of a foreign colleague. It was insinuated that by a turning movement, or some other movement familiar to the youngest student of the art of war, the whole of the sacrifices incurred might have been easily avoided. It was argued that the real honours remained with the enemy who for an hour and a half had withstood the onslaughts of an army nearly ten times as numerous as their own. And it was calculated that, if 8,000 Bavarians could inflict such losses on 80,000 of the allies, Marlborough and the Margrave would soon find themselves without any army at all.[31]

These splenetic chatterers obtained a certain audience. The ordinary Englishman understands little of strategy, and even less of those spiritual forces which in war are more potent than any other factor. In the coffee-houses of London, in the ale-houses of the shires, they could read the lists of killed and wounded; but they could not see the black care at Max Emanuel's heart. A battle is not a boxing-match decided upon points. The victory does not necessarily belong to the side which can show the fewer casualties on balance. Heavy losses may mean, as they meant at the Schellenberg, a great price deliberately paid for a great strategical advantage. They may also mean, as they meant at the Schellenberg, such a moral gain as cannot be calculated in any material terms. A general who has once shown that he has the resolution to demand of his men what Marlborough demanded that day,[32] is a general who will be obeyed by all beneath him and dreaded by all against him.

Recruits that have proved themselves capable of conquering under most abnormal punishment, are recruits known henceforth to be re-

---

31. Steele, *The Tatler*, No. 65.
32. See Maude on Napoleon, *The Evolution of Modern Strategy*, ch. 2, p. 20.

doubtable beyond the average, and knowing themselves to be so. The Bavarian soldier is second to none in Germany. On the Schellenberg he had fought well, and he knew that he had fought well. He had seen his assailants suffer more cruelly than it was the wont of the bravest and most disciplined troops to suffer without breaking. He had seen them return again and again to the attack; and in the end he had seen them victorious. Every survivor of D'Arco's detachment could draw the obvious conclusion. They drew it, and their comrades and commanders drew it; and from the time of that desperate grapple above Donauwörth there set in among the armies of France an insidious demoralisation, which contributed to every fresh disaster, and to which every fresh disaster contributed.

It was a great ending to a great march. Right across the enemy's front, from the North Sea to the Danube, Marlborough had passed without let or hindrance, while in three theatres of the war at once three hostile armies, doubtful and perplexed, did nothing. Six weeks the sword of England hung suspended; and when it fell, all Europe rang with the stroke. The Elector's finest regiments were ruined, the river barrier of his dominions was forced, the military prestige of France was rudely shaken, and the courage of every soldier of the coalition was braced with that irresistible confidence which springs from proved superiority. These truths, obscured and denied as they might be by Dutch malcontents and English traitors, could not be hidden from the eyes of Austria. The Emperor Leopold, "the most virtuous and pious monarch of his line,"[33] at whose very throat the sword of Louis had so long been pointed, wrote to Marlborough with his own hand, "an honour rarely shown to any but Sovereign Princes." He addressed him as "Illustrious, Sincerely Beloved."[34] He dwelt in particular upon the swiftness and the vigour of the blow at Donauwörth. And he showed himself to be under no delusion as to the real author.

"My generals themselves," he said, "and my ministers declare that this success (which is more gratifying and, at the present time, more opportune than almost anything else that could befall me) is principally owing to your judgement, foresight, and execution, and also to the wonderful ardour and constancy (*miro ardori et constantiæ*) of the forces under your command."

It was well said, and it was well that he should say it. No monument marks the resting-place of England's dead at Donauwörth. But

---

33. Malleson, *Prince Eugène of Savoy*, p. 9.
34. Lediard, vol. 1, p. 344.

for them whose feet had marched so many German miles to make their last halt upon the slopes of the Schellenberg, what fitter epitaph could be devised than the Emperor's own?—

"*MIRO ARDORI ET CONSTANTIÆ.*"

Chapter 8

The Devastation of Bavaria

The stupid attempts, which were made in various quarters, and from various motives, to disparage the victory of the Schellenberg, did not impose upon the Elector. He was soldier enough to realise instinctively and at once that his system of holding the Danube by means of his fortified camp upon the northern bank had failed disastrously. On the morning of the 3rd, the day after the battle, he abandoned the position at Lauingen and Dillingen, passed the river, and retired towards Augsburg. Marching in full view of Donauwörth, he sent word to the governor to burn the town with its magazines and bridge, and to rejoin him with the garrison. But the governor had not yet sufficiently recovered from his attack of nerves to execute any orders with resolution and alacrity.

While the soldiers were piling straw into the houses, the anxious magistrates contrived to apprise Marlborough of what was doing. The allied troops, who were already in the suburbs, set to work forthwith to construct pontoons. Fearful lest his retreat should be cut off, Du Bordet set fire to some of the stores that night, and hastily marching out in the small hours of the morning, destroyed the bridge behind him. The allies entered immediately and extinguished the flames. They were fortunate enough to find the enemy's powder magazine intact. They also captured 2,000 sacks of meal, a quantity of oats, and an arsenal containing three great guns.

Protected by the cannon of Augsburg, the Elector and Marsin entrenched themselves behind the River Lech. In this situation they awaited the coming of Tallard. But Tallard had not yet crossed the Rhine. Assuming that Eugène did nothing to impede his march, some weeks must elapse before he could arrive at Augsburg. In the meantime, the Elector's country lay open to the allied army. It was the purpose of Marlborough's strategy to terminate the Bavarian peril once and for all. This purpose could be accomplished in one of two ways, either by destroying the armed forces of the enemy, or by detaching Max Emanuel from the French alliance. The one alternative was impracticable, so long as the enemy continued in his position at Augsburg.

But the other, in the Elector's present mood of profound dejection, held out every prospect of success. It seemed to be a question only of the precise degree of pressure which would be requisite to reduce him to submission. Marlborough and the Margrave proposed to penetrate into the heart of Bavaria, to feed their men and horses, as far as possible, at the expense of the inhabitants, and if time allowed, to possess themselves of the capital itself.

The army passed the Danube on the 5th, and marched to Medingen. The 6th was kept as a day of thanksgiving for the victory of the Schellenberg; and by the Margrave's orders the *Te Deum* was sung in the churches of the neighbouring towns. That day the Danish horse arrived in camp. The army was now complete. Active preparations were made for the passage of the Lech. On the evening of the 7th a detachment crossed at Genderkingen, the enemy offering no resistance. They were joined on the 8th by a reinforcement of 6,000 men. The same day the main body advanced to Genderkingen. Meantime the garrison of Neuburg, a post upon the Danube between Donauwörth and Ingolstadt, which was menaced by these movements, abandoned the town.

As the possession of this place materially strengthened the communications of the allied army, it was occupied at once by 4,000 Imperialists. On the 9th and 10th the main body passed the Lech. But it was impossible to continue the advance until the little town of Rain, where D'Arco had left 500 regular troops and a body of militia, had been captured. Owing to the late arrival of the artillery, the ground was not opened till the night of the 13th. The place surrendered on the 16th. In it were found twenty-four cannon and a valuable supply of corn.

During this pause events of the first importance occurred. A messenger arrived from Eugène on the 12th, with certain intelligence that the French had passed the Rhine at Fort Kehl on the 6th. Eugène, who was observing their motions, desired a reinforcement of cavalry. On the 13th thirty squadrons of Imperialist horse were dispatched to his assistance. And Marlborough sent him word that as many more should follow as he might deem necessary. At the same time, diplomacy was not idle. The relations, which had been broken off before the battle, were renewed. The Elector himself had asked for an interview with Wratislaw.

Wratislaw held a preliminary conference at Aichach with Max Emanuel's secretary, who expressed the opinion that the terms proposed by the allies would be accepted by his master. No news of Tallard's coming had reached Augsburg. Provisions were already running short. Marsin himself convened a council of war, at which the desirability of arranging for the neutrality of Bavaria was seriously advocated by French officers. The Elector was surrounded by advisers who were favourable to the Austrian Court. The Electress also was a powerful advocate of peace.

In these circumstances, the negotiation gave rise to the most sanguine hopes. But they were hardly shared by Marlborough, and they were doomed to speedy dissipation. On the 14th came a dispatch from Tallard with the welcome intelligence that he was already in the Black Forest. Thereupon the Elector declined to meet Wratislaw, and explained that in view of the powerful assistance which the King of France was sending him, it would not consort with his honour to abandon his ally.

Having established magazines at Neuburg and Rain, Marlborough and the Margrave now resumed their advance. On the 18th they came to Aichach. The garrison fled to Augsburg; but 900 peasants, who offered some resistance, were either killed or taken, and the town was plundered by the soldiery. Here also a magazine was set up. On the 21st, the army turned aside from the Munich road and moved towards the Lech. The following day, a detachment of horse and foot under Marlborough in person made a dash on Friedberg. The garrison fled precipitately to the Elector's camp, Marlborough captured a hundred of their horses, which were grazing in the meadow, and occupied the town. On the 23rd the entire army followed, and took up its station on the hills within a league of Augsburg. Here they remained for eight days, and here they were joined by many of the wounded who had recovered their health in the hospital of Nördlingen and the villages adjacent to that town.

The two armies were now face to face, the Lech alone dividing them. The strategy of Marlborough's march from the Meuse to the Danube had attained its culmination. With a superior force he stood between Vienna and the enemy. The road which Villars had proposed to follow, was blocked and barred.

But the situation was deficient in finality. Though Wratislaw had once more attempted to reopen negotiations, the Elector had haughtily refused to renounce his alliance. The French and Bavarian armies had not been destroyed. And Tallard was coming. His arrival would change the whole condition of the game. Meantime it was necessary to act. Marlborough had abandoned his original idea of capturing Munich, for though the defences of the place were poor, its garrison was powerful, and the requisite guns and stores, which the Margrave had promised, were not forthcoming.

An attack upon the fortified camp at Augsburg was out of the question. But if the enemy could not be forced out of their position, they might be starved out of it. From the beginning the allied generals had aimed at this result. Large armies had now been living in Bavaria for nearly two years. The resources of the country had been greatly diminished. When Marlborough and the Margrave passed the Danube, they found themselves dependent upon Nördlingen and Nürnberg for the bulk of their bread. But whatever of food and forage existed in Bavaria was theirs to take.

The enemy, on the other hand, was cut off by their advance to Friedberg from his natural supplies, and was reduced to living on his magazines at Ulm and Augsburg. These accumulated stocks were being rapidly depleted. Every day that passed without the advent of Tallard brought nearer the moment when Marsin and Max Emanuel must either famish in their camp or march out to give battle at a hopeless disadvantage.

To attain this end the allied armies had subjected Bavaria to the most rigorous treatment. Everything which they wanted, they seized. Everything which they did not happen to require for their own use, or which they were unable for lack of carriages to transport to their own magazines, they ruthlessly destroyed. But the harvest was plentiful that year, and it was still unreaped. The allied generals were determined that it should remain unreaped. As their armies advanced, towns and villages were fired on every hand. The terrified peasantry sought refuge in Munich, where the churches rang with their prayers and lamentations. The spectacle of their sufferings had been almost more than the Elector could endure. Marsin was convinced that, if Tallard's letter[1] had not arrived on the 12th, a treaty would have been concluded.

The story of this tragedy spread quickly over Europe, and it lost

---

1. Pelet, t. 4, p. 524: *Marsin à Tallard*, 14 *juillet*, 1704

nothing in the telling. But the allied generals were deaf to criticism. To the Elector's indignant protests they coldly replied that the remedy was in his own hands. To the magistrates of certain towns which sought to save themselves by the offer of enormous contributions, Marlborough, who is popularly supposed to have lost no opportunity of procuring gain, sent answer that "the forces of the Queen of England were not come into Bavaria to get money, but to bring their Prince to reason."[2]

But the Elector held doggedly to his post, and would neither fight nor yield. On the 26th the allies made a general forage in full view of his camp. That evening came a message from Eugène. Tallard, after wasting six days before Villingen, had abandoned the siege, and on the 24th had got as far as Tuttlingen. He had 26,000 men with him. Eugène, who had been obliged to leave a garrison in the fines of Stollhofen, was observing him from the opposite bank of the Danube with a greatly inferior force.

These combinations left the ultimate issue more than ever in doubt. But on one thing Marlborough and the Margrave were firmly resolved. If the French were determined to go to Vienna, they must go by some other road than the Bavarian one. Rather should that unhappy land be turned into a desert where neither man nor horse could exist till at least another winter and another spring had passed. On the 28th no fewer than thirty squadrons under Dutch and Imperialist officers were detailed upon the dreadful service. East and south they rode, foraging and burning to the very suburbs of Munich . On the 31st they were reinforced by the Duke of Württemberg, with 2,000 horse and dragoons. For six long summer days this tempest swept through the tormented countryside. Everything that an army could eat was either taken or destroyed. Whole villages were laid in ashes. Not until August 3 did the smoke-blackened columns return to Friedberg.

For the devastation of Bavaria, Marlborough has been unsparingly denounced by German writers. And English historians,[3] with the Englishman's excessive anxiety to do more than justice to the other side, have lent their voices to swell the clamour. The indignation of Bavarians at the ruin of their country is natural enough. And all men, whether English or Bavarian, are free to form, and to express, their own opinions on the morality of the measures adopted by the allied

---

2. Lediard, vol. 1, p. 350.
3. Alison, p. 74.

generals. But they are not free to speak as though the responsibility for those measures attached to one of those generals alone. The command was equally shared between Marlborough and the Margrave.

On alternate days each of the two enjoyed sole authority. It is therefore absurd to ascribe operations, which extended over a period of more than three weeks, to Marlborough alone. Indeed, a little reflection should have shown the critics that, if any distinction can be made between them, it must be made in favour of the Englishman. For military executions, systematically inflicted on a territory of the Empire, an account would naturally be rendered by the Emperor's own general and the Emperor's own ministers, rather than by a foreigner commanding the forces of two foreign powers. The facts, so far as they are known, support this view. The work of destruction was actually begun by the Margrave;[4] and it was largely carried on by the Imperialist troops. Moreover, in writing to the Duchess on the subject, Marlborough used language which suggests that, while he fully concurred in what was done, he was not the instigator of it.

"Nothing," he said, "but absolute necessity could have obliged me *to consent to it.*"[5] He was never the man to shirk responsibility. But there is no reason why he should be saddled with more than his share, and least of all by his own countrymen.

Historians[6] have also misrepresented the motive and purpose of the devastation of Bavaria. According to some, these vigorous measures were coercive; according to others they were retributive. In one version they appear as aids to diplomacy, in another as the penalties of obstinacy. A little more attention to facts, and especially to dates, would have corrected both these errors. The executions began on the 12th, immediately after the passage of the Lech. They continued steadily for three weeks and three days. They were most extensive and severe between July 28 and August 3. Now on July 12, the negotiations were already in a delicate and very promising condition. Two days later they collapsed. Except for one short-lived attempt to reopen them, this collapse was final.

It is evident therefore that the executions of the first four days were not retributive, for at that time the Elector was momentarily expected to break with France. It is evident also that those of the last ten days were not coercive, for at that time it was certain that he would not

---

4. *Millner's Journal,* July 1, 1704.
5. Coxe, vol. 1, p. 183: Marlborough to the Duchess, July 30, 1704.
6. Not excluding Coxe (see vol. 1, p. 183).

be coerced. These theories are not satisfactory. They are also superfluous, seeing that the truth is known. On July 29, Marlborough writing to Stepney, stated in a few words what the real object was. It was a twofold one—"to deprive the enemy as well of present subsistence as future support on this side."[7] In the first place the allied generals were endeavouring to starve their antagonist out of his fortified camp at Augsburg; and secondly (and this was the more important part of their strategy) they were seeking to render Bavaria incapable of sustaining the combined forces of Max Emanuel, Marsin, and Tallard.

These were purely military aims. No doubt it was hoped that the Elector's heart might be softened by the sufferings of his people. And no doubt the Germans at any rate experienced a vindictive pleasure in punishing a German who did not scruple to introduce the armies of France into their common country.[8] But such considerations were subsidiary and incidental. The severities which the allied generals exercised upon Bavaria, they exercised in their military capacity, and primarily for the attainment of military ends.

This kind of warfare was neither a diabolical invention of Marlborough's nor a reversion to obsolete "methods of barbarism." Nor was it a proof of incapacity. In the Palatinate, in 1674, it was employed by a general so capable and so humane as Turenne himself. Of that classic example Marlborough had been a witness. Modern sentiment may affect to be shocked at it; but even modern sentiment can give no security that it will never be employed again. In 1704 it was, to a certain extent, the logical outcome of the military system of the time. But in 1810 Wellington wasted Portugal to the lines of Torres Vedras, and as late as 1812 the Russians devastated their own country for strategic reasons. The Napoleonic system largely depended for its success upon authorised brigandage.[9]

The indignation of the Elector was peculiarly inept. That Donauwörth might not be used as a base for the invasion of Bavaria, he himself had given instructions to lay the town in ashes. That Bavaria might not be used as a base for the invasion of Austria, the allies applied to it the very treatment which its ruler had thought appropriate to Donauwörth. In the circumstances his indignation was somewhat inconsistent. That of his French allies was merely ludicrous. Tallard

---

7. Murray, vol. 1, p. 379: Marlborough to Stepney, July 29, 1704.
8. "The rage of the Germans" (see letter to the Duchess, after Blenheim, August 21, 1704: Coxe, vol. 1, p. 217).
9. Maude, *Evolution of Modern Strategy*, ch. 8, p. 76.

wrote to Louis that the allies had been guilty of "cruelties which the Turks would not be willing to commit."[10]

Tallard, like all his colleagues in the French service, was certainly a good judge of atrocities. And Louis himself was not an amateur. In 1689, in the depth of winter, Marshal Duras, acting on the orders of the King and Louvois, had sacked Heidelberg, Mannheim, Speyer, and Worms, had burned Ladenburg and Oppenheim, and had mercilessly ravaged all the country of the Palatinate, with portions of. the Electorate of Trier and the Margravate of Baden. Castles, cathedrals, and even hospitals had been given over to the flames.

"Many," says Macaulay, "died of cold and hunger: but enough survived to fill the streets of all the cities of Europe with lean and squalid beggars, who had once been thriving farmers and shopkeepers."[11]

What Duras did was not only horrible beyond imagination; it was also, in the judgement of no less a soldier than a Frenchman, Villars himself, strategically unsound. The memory of it was not dead in 1870; it was painfully fresh in 1704. In 1704 also, the barbarities, inflicted by French soldiers on French Calvinists after the Revocation of the Edict of Nantes, were matters of common knowledge. Similar barbarities had been employed against the Camisards in the Cevennes, and had only been terminated that very summer by the authority of Villars. It is little wonder that the criticisms of an enemy who possessed so black a record, left Marlborough and the Margrave totally unmoved.[12]

Marlborough, like his master Turenne, was a man of gentle and humane temper. The work of destruction, which he himself ordered, he loathed with an intense loathing.

> "You will, I hope, believe me," he wrote to the Duchess, "that my nature suffers when I see so many fine places burnt, and that must be burnt, if the Elector will not hinder it. I shall never be easy and happy till I am quiet with you."

And again,

> "This is so contrary to my nature, that nothing but absolute necessity could have obliged me to consent to it, for these poor people suffer for their master's ambition. There having been no war in this country for above sixty years, these towns and vil-

---

10. Pelet, t. 4, p. 547: *Tallard au Roi*, 4-5 *août*, 1704.
11. Macaulay, *History of England*, vol. 1, ch. 11.
12. On the day of Blenheim the French and Bavarians, for tactical reasons, burned seven villages (see chapter following).

lages are so clean, that you would be pleased with them."[13]

The Duke's distress was natural and proper. But from the public standpoint it was not entirely justified. A German state, which had made common cause with the comrades of Marshal Duras, had small claims on German sympathy. And a petty power, which, regardless of the common danger, was using its strategical position to promote its own aggrandisement, could not be permitted indefinitely and with impunity to gamble with the liberties of Europe.

There is one test, and only one, by which to try the action of the allied generals.[14] Did it achieve the ends to which it was directed? It certainly failed to force the Elector to a battle. But it brought him so low[15] that, had Tallard delayed another week, he must either have fought or starved. It certainly succeeded in rendering Bavaria untenable by great armies for at least a twelvemonth. Thanks to the victory of Blenheim, the magnitude of that advantage has been overlooked. But the allied generals could not foresee the victory of Blenheim. One historian says that their action was "wholly unnecessary." They did what prudence dictated at the time. Had there been no Blenheim, or had Blenheim been a French triumph, the injustice and absurdity of this criticism would have been signally revealed.

"It is expediency," says a modern writer, "that alone conditions the degree of violence which can be usefully employed in war."[16]

And the sentiment which affects to be shocked at the devastation of Bavaria must explain how it is that the contingency of war between modern England and a continental power is invariably and universally discussed upon the unchallenged assumption that the enemy will make it a principal aim to destroy the food-supplies and the raw materials of industry of a civilian population of forty millions. If beggary and starvation are legitimate weapons, when the victims are Lancashire operatives and London clerks, it has yet to be shown why the exercise of similar methods upon Bavarian hinds must be regarded as atrocious barbarism.

The advance of Tallard compelled the allied generals to resolve upon a new course of action. To remain at Friedberg was impossible.

---

13. Coxe, vol. 1, p. 183: Marlborough to the Duchess, July 30, 1704.
14. This was Marlborough's test, "I take pleasure in being easy when the service does not suffer by it" (Coxe, vol. 1, p. 217, August 25, 1704).
15. Pelet, t. 4, p. 527: *Tallard au Roi*, 18 *juillet*, 1704.
16. Maude, *The Evolution of Modern Strategy*, ch. 2, p. 18.

The ruin of Bavaria had left them totally dependent on their communications for supplies. And these communications might easily be cut, as soon as Tallard arrived. They therefore decided to fall back upon the Danube and lay siege to Ingolstadt. This movement offered two advantages. On the one hand by shortening their communications with Nördlingen and Nürnberg, it would render their situation less vulnerable to annoyance or attack. On the other, by securing them the possession of the principal magazine and strongest fortress in Bavaria, it would confirm their hold upon the highway to Vienna. The most daring soldier would not dream of marching through that desolated land, with his flank exposed to numerous and enterprising foes, who gripped the Danube at Donauwörth, Neuburg, and Ingolstadt, while they drew unlimited supplies from the rich countries in their rear.

The Margrave volunteered to undertake the siege with 15,000 men. Marlborough was to cover it, in conjunction with Eugène. This arrangement was well pleasing to the Duke. Though he could ill spare 15,000 men from the fighting-line, the departure of the Margrave was cheap at the price. He was eager to fight, and he wished, when he fought, to have Eugène at his side. He knew that all things were tending towards a decisive conflict. But there was always the possibility that the enemy would endeavour to avoid one. In that event, he was confident that, with Eugène for a colleague, he would speedily find a way of forcing them to the arbitrament of battle.

On August 4 the allies struck their camp and marched off towards Ingolstadt, still burning as they went. The pillars of smoke which marked their path were seen on the horizon by Tallard's men, who came that day to the banks of the Lech at Biberbach, midway between Donauwörth and Augsburg.

"*Monseigneur*," wrote Tallard to the Elector, "I here present to you this invincible army, which has taken Landau, which has beaten the enemy at Speyerbach, which has passed the lines in spite of every effort to protect them, and which will place you in a position to achieve your aims by enabling you to surmount all difficulties with the valour of our troops."

On the 5th the allies encamped at Schrobenhausen; and the Margrave went to Neuburg to inspect the preparations for the siege. On the 6th Eugène, who had followed the march of Tallard like a shadow, quitted his army at Höchstädt and rode over the Danube to take counsel with his colleagues. On the 7th Ingolstadt was invested.

The same day the Margrave returned to Schrobenhausen, where he found Eugène very ready to concur in the proposed division of forces. Marsin and the Elector were now known to have joined Tallard on the Lech. To view the camp and to examine such defensive positions as the intervening country might afford, Marlborough and Eugène rode out upon a reconnaissance.

But they had nothing to fear in this quarter. The enemy had no intention of passing the Lech. Their actual decision was soon to be disclosed. The allies resumed their march upon the 8th, and halted on the 9th in the vicinity of Rain. Here the Margrave departed for Ingolstadt with 15,000 men, while Eugène set off to rejoin his army in the neighbourhood of Höchstädt. A few hours later came intelligence that the enemy was moving towards Lauingen and Dillingen. Eugène, who had received the same tidings on the road, returned at once to consult with Marlborough. It was evident that the enemy intended to cross the Danube, and strike a blow against the allies' communications. Eugène's small army lay across their path. If it remained, it might be destroyed by forces outnumbering it by three to one. If it withdrew, the enemy might dash upon the magazines of Donauwörth or Nördlingen, carry the mediaeval ramparts by assault, and send their raiding horsemen far and wide into Franconia.

After a consultation lasting two hours, the allied generals decided that a concentration of their forces should be effected at the village of Münster on the Kessel, a small tributary of the Danube, four miles westward of Donauwörth. Eugène's army had already fallen back from Höchstädt to this point. Thither Eugène at once repaired, while Marlborough made ready to support him with the utmost speed. At 2 a.m. the Duke of Württemberg took the road with twenty-eight squadrons of cavalry and dragoons. He was followed by Churchill with twenty battalions of foot. At 3 the main army was in motion.

At daybreak on the 10th Eugène reached Münster. There he found that Leopold of Anhalt-Dessau, an excellent officer who commanded in his absence, had ordered the troops to strike their tents, and fall back upon the Schellenberg. These orders were at once countermanded. The baggage only was dispatched to the Schellenberg. But five squadrons rode off towards Höchstädt to ascertain the movements of the enemy. They returned with the intelligence that the French and Bavarians had passed the Danube, and encamped at Lauingen. Eugène naturally assumed that he would be attacked at the latest on the ensuing day. Having sent an express to Marlborough to acquaint him with the news, and to urge him to expedite his march, the Prince now commanded his infantry and a portion of his horse to retire to the Schellenberg. He himself, with twenty-two squadrons of dragoons, remained at Münster.

Late that evening he was joined by the twenty-eight squadrons of the Duke of Württemberg. All through the night of the 10th, 6,000 horsemen kept watch and ward upon the banks of the Kessel. But the enemy made no move. On the morning of the 11th the express returned from Marlborough, with tidings that Churchill was close at hand, and that the Duke himself was continually upon the march with the main army. Thereupon Eugène recalled his men from the Schellenberg. He was presently joined by Churchill. By 4 p.m. Marlborough was at Donauwörth, by 6 he was in council with Eugène, and by 10 that night the two armies were concentrated on the line of the Kessel. The baggage and artillery came in at daybreak, after an unbroken march of twenty-four miles.

This performance was in all respects an admirable one. Though the distances traversed by Marlborough's men were not extraordinary, the roads had been spoiled by rain, and no fewer than three rivers, the Lech, the Danube, and the Wörnitz, had been traversed on the way. The energy and skill exhibited by the Duke were worthy of the vigilance and audacity displayed by the Prince. In these qualities they showed themselves very superior to their opponents, who seem to have been as ill informed of Marlborough's movements as they were certainly negligent of the opportunity afforded them by the isolation of Eugène, whom they might have attacked on the night of the 10th, or at any time on the nth, with odds immensely in their favour.

Even on the morning of the 12th it was not too late, for Marlborough's men were so exhausted with their efforts that they would have fought at a considerable disadvantage. But beyond capturing the unimportant town of Höchstädt on the nth, the Elector and the Marshals did nothing. They appear to have assumed that at the mere rumour of their approach the allies would abandon Bavaria without a blow.

It was a fatal assumption. What was applicable to the average general of that epoch was not necessarily applicable to Eugène and Marlborough. The orthodox officer preferred anything to fighting; Eugène and Marlborough preferred fighting to anything. The destruction of the enemy in battle was ever the grand passion of these great commanders. Moreover, in the immediate circumstances of the moment, a decisive engagement was to them essential. It was true that by occupying a strong position, they might have covered the siege of Ingolstadt without a combat. But the enemy could have retaliated by overrunning Franconia and cutting off supplies. Villeroi too might make an irruption into Württemberg. And in the end they might be driven by hunger to raise the siege and to abandon Bavaria and the Danube altogether. Eugène and Marlborough had no intention of making war on these lines. Whether the enemy came to them, or they went to the enemy, they intended to fight a decisive battle.

They would have fought on the 12th, had Marlborough's men been less fatigued with their exertions on the road. But as it was, the troops remained that day in camp, while the two generals with an escort of twenty-eight squadrons rode out to reconnoitre. They soon discovered the enemy's cavalry, and with the help of glasses they descried his whole army moving forward from Dillingen through Höchstädt. Ascending the church-tower of Tapfheim village, at 1 o'clock that afternoon, they clearly saw the French and Bavarian quartermasters marking out a camp between Blindheim and Lutzingen.

Thereupon Marlborough and Eugène returned to Münster, and ordered out the pioneers and pontoon-train to bridge the Reichin at Tapfheim and prepare the roads for a general advance on the ensuing day. No sooner had the work begun than it was interrupted by the enemy's cavalry. The alarm was given, the allied army stood to arms, and Marlborough and Eugène, leaving their meal unfinished, rode back to Tapfheim with their twenty-eight squadrons, supported by dragoons and infantry. But the enemy's horsemen, who were only seeking information, galloped swiftly away as soon as they had made a few prisoners.

Having strengthened their dispositions for the maintenance of Tapfheim and the line of the Reichin, the allied generals once more ascended the steeple. It was now 4 o'clock, and the French and Bavarian armies were plainly discernible in their new camp.

The valley of the Danube between Donauwörth and Dillingen is bounded on its northern side by a range of wooded hills, which is "a continuation of the lower level of the Schellenberg." This range, not running parallel to the river, but pursuing an irregular course, gives to the intervening plain an uneven breadth, varying from less than a mile at Tapfheim, which is the narrowest point, to three miles at Blindheim, which is the widest. The plain is intersected by three little streams, the Kessel at Münster, the Reichin at Tapfheim, and the Nebel at Blindheim, which running from the base of the mountains empty themselves into the Danube.

Insignificant as that may now appear, streams were at that time a formidable obstacle to the march of an army, because, in an age when drainage was neglected or little understood, they generally indicated the existence of difficult and treacherous ground. And this part of the Danube valley formed no exception to the rule. When therefore Marlborough and Eugène examined the enemy's position through their glasses, they came to the conclusion that it was not one to be despised. The right flank was protected by the Danube, which in this region flows circuitously but fast, between steep and bushy banks, through a bed one hundred yards in width, abounding in shoals and islands, and bordered by a fringe of reedy marsh. The left was secured by the mountains and the woods.

Along the entire front ran the swampy line of the Nebel. Behind the Nebel and seated on a gentle slope were three villages, Blindheim on the right, Oberglauheim in the centre, and Lutzingen on the left. Immediately behind these villages the French and Bavarians were encamped on the plateau. It was obvious that the ground which the enemy had selected was very defensible. The approaches to the Nebel on the Tapfheim side were covered by the village of Unterglauheim, through which the highroad ran from Donauwörth to Höchstadt, and over against Blindheim by two water-mills. To attack it at all, the allies must defile over the Kessel and the Reichin, and must deploy in full view of a foe who, with forces numerically superior and flanks that could not be turned, awaited them at his leisure behind a triple screen of marshes and villages. Critics, wise after the event, discovered a variety of defects in the French position. To Marlborough and Eugène these defects were not particularly apparent.

Nevertheless, their determination to give battle was in no wise shaken. They meant to fight, and to fight without delay, lest the enemy should entrench himself. As against these advantages of ground and numbers, which the enemy undoubtedly possessed, they relied upon their own tactical skill and upon the excellent quality and spirit of their troops. Moreover, the moral superiority which belongs to the assailant would be theirs; and it was augmented in the case of Marlborough's men by the confidence inspired by the recent victory at the Schellenberg. And once more, as at the Schellenberg, the allied generals by doing what their methodical antagonists would never expect them to do, would secure the advantage of a virtual surprise.

These considerations made them hopeful of success. Their optimism was by no means shared by their subordinates.[17] Certain officers remonstrated openly with Marlborough on the rashness of his project. He heard them with attentive courtesy. When they had finished, he told them that he was fully sensible of the difficulties and dangers of the attempt, but that a battle was "absolutely necessary."[18] Thereupon, the requisite orders were issued to the army, which received them in a fashion that boded ill to the prospects of Bavaria and France.

The march was to begin at two hours after midnight. The time was short. The Duke devoted a portion of it to prayer. He then received the Sacrament at the hands of his chaplain. After a brief interval of slumber, he rejoined Eugène. The Prince had been writing letters; but his active brain had rejected all repose. Together they applied themselves to the work of final preparation.

---

17. "Almost all the generals were against my Lord's attacking the enemy" (Francis Hare to George Naylor, August 14, 1704: Hist. MSS. Comm., 14th Report, Appendix, part 9, Hare MSS., p. 201).

18. "There was an absolute necessity for the good of the common cause to make this venture" (Letter to the Duchess, August 18, 1704: Coxe, vol. 1, p. 314. Barnet, vol. 4, p. 51).

Chapter 9

Blenheim

When the Elector and the two Marshals encamped between Blindheim[1] and Lutzingen, they flattered themselves that the game was in their own hands. They assumed that the allies would immediately withdraw from the Danube, and would sacrifice without a struggle the grand object of the whole campaign.[2] The Elector, ardent by nature and thirsting for revenge, was eager to fall upon an enemy whom he regarded as already in retreat. Tallard apparently had some misgivings. He wanted at first to remain at Höchstädt, but he deferred to the opinion of Max Emanuel and Marsin, who knew the country, and also of those French officers who had served in it under Villars.

None of the three commanders had any certain intelligence of the allies' movements or designs. Letters from Donauwörth to the Elector declared that the Margrave of Baden was still at Ingolstadt. Having no independent evidence by which to check the veracity of this statement, Marsin and Tallard recommended that some prisoners might be captured and interrogated on the point. For the purpose of this somewhat unscientific test of truth, the skirmish at Tapfheim was arranged. It produced four witnesses, who unanimously deposed that the Margrave and all his men had joined the army of Eugène and Marlborough.

Possibly the Elector regarded the statements of these hardy liars as a complete confirmation of the news which he had received from Donauwörth. But Tallard was somewhat nervous, and proposed the

---

1. In the MS. I found only the form Blindheim. but Blenheim being more generally known I have distinguished between the name of the battle and the name of the village, by using in the one instance the English version Blenheim, and in the other the German form Blindheim.—G.W.T.
2. Feuquières, t. 3, pp. 364, 366, 367.

construction of a redoubt on the highroad which runs from Donauwörth to Dillingen. The Elector begged him not to disturb the earth. D'Arco, untaught by his melancholy experience at the Schellenberg, dismissed the idea of an assault upon the French position with contemptuous ridicule. Had Tallard been absolutely convinced of the fact that the Margrave was still at Ingolstadt, he too would have been quite easy in his mind. For Tallard was at least as incapable as his colleagues of believing that Eugène and Marlborough could be so neglectful of the rules as to deliver a frontal attack upon a numerically superior force occupying a strong position.

The whole situation is a good example of the paramount importance in war of understanding the mentality of your antagonist and of procuring reliable information as to his numbers and probable intentions. When the Elector and the Marshals went to their beds that night, they were already half beaten. They imagined that the campaign was as good as over. But all their hopes and plans were built upon a rotten foundation of assumption and conjecture.

The French and Bavarians took their suppers gaily. The Comte de Mérode-Westerloo, a Flemish officer, who was serving in Tallard's army, and who survived to realise the tragic irony of that last evening, has recorded with what hearty appetites and in what exalted spirits his comrades sat down to eat and drink in the village of Blindheim. He has recorded also how he himself slept better than he ever slept before.[3] But only five miles away, on the banks of the Kessel, there was joy of a sterner kind. And Marlborough in his tent was on his knees.

At 2 o'clock the allied forces were in motion. Unencumbered by their baggage, which had been sent back towards Donauwörth, they passed the Kessel at 3, over bridges previously prepared, and advanced towards the Reichin. Marlborough's army marched upon the left, and Eugène's upon the right, and each in four columns. Arrived at the Reichin, they halted, whilst the Duke with the help of the troops that had been posted at Tapfheim drew out a fifth column on his extreme left. The advance was then resumed until Schweiningen was reached, when Marlborough and Eugène rode forward with an escort of forty squadrons to observe the enemy.

A dank, white mist lay thickly on the plain; but at 6 this party was discovered by the French outposts, who immediately fell back and alarmed the detachments stationed at Unterglauheim and in the

---

3. *Mémoires de Mérode-Westerloo* (1840), p. 298.

water-mills before Blindheim. Meantime, assisted by a Prussian officer who had fought at Höchstädt in the preceding year, the allied generals surveyed the ground before them, so far as it was visible through the clinging haze. They had decided that Marlborough's army, which numbered 34,000 men, should attack from the Danube to Oberglauheim, while Eugène's, which numbered only 18,000, should attack from Oberglauheim to the mountains.

As therefore the nine columns moved slowly forward from Schweiningen over the ever-broadening plain, their lines of march continually diverged, until the whole array, 52,000 in all, spread out towards the French position like the ribs of a gigantic fan. So unconscious of their peril were the Elector and the Marshals that at daybreak they had dispatched some considerable parties of cavalry to forage. They had early intelligence that the enemy was stirring; but their attitude was one of "perfect tranquillity and infinite satisfaction at having forced M. le Prince Eugène and M. de Marlborough to quit Bavaria."[4]

The reports of the outposts, who had been startled by the appearance of the forty squadrons, did not disturb them. Assuming, as they had all along assumed, that the allies must now retire to Nördlingen, it was only natural that the movement should be masked by a screen of cavalry. In those early morning hours, Tallard himself, the least complacent of the three, was actually writing to Versailles that the enemy were on the move, and that according to "the rumour of the countryside,"[5] they were bound for Nördlingen.

But now the mists began to roll away, and by 7 the landscape stood revealed in the radiance of the August sun. The allied army was plainly visible; but even now its intentions were not apparent to commanders blinded by their own preconceptions. Eugène's infantry, marching in two columns along the skirts of the mountains, and protected on the side of the French by the two columns of his cavalry, was at first assumed to be the vanguard of the allies on their way to Nördlingen.

But the direction taken by the five columns under Marlborough did not coincide with this hypothesis. Coming steadily on towards the French right and centre, they halted and began to deploy. At last the reality of the situation was recognised. The silent camp sprang instantly to life. Drums beat, and trumpets pealed. The soldiers poured from their tents and hastily assumed their places in the ranks. Cannon were discharged to recall the foragers from the fields. The baggage-

---

4. Feuquières, t. 3, p. 367.
5. *Campagne de Tallard* (1763), t. 2, p. 140,

wagons of Tallard's army rushed precipitately out of Blindheim to seek a safer position in the rear. The Elector and the two Marshals ascended the steeple of that village to view the dispositions of the enemy. And here and there upon the plain the smoke of flaming hamlets rolled up against the blueness of the sky.

To impede the march of the allies and to deprive them of all cover, the French and Bavarians set fire to Schwenenbach, Berghausen, Wolperstetten, Weilheim, and Unterglauheim, and also to the mills before Blindheim. This operation forms a curious commentary on the horror which its authors had so recently expressed at the devastation of Bavaria. The ethical distinction between destroying private property for strategical, reasons and destroying it for tactical ones is not easy to detect.

The three armies drew up in the order in which they had encamped. Tallard's on the right, Marsin's in the centre, and the Elector's on the left. Numbering in all some 56,000 men, they had an advantage of at least 4,000 over the forces of their assailants. The space between Blindheim and the Danube, which measures about a furlong, was secured by a barricade of wagons, and defended by twelve squadrons of dismounted dragoons, whose horses had perished of a malady contracted in Alsace. Blindheim itself was occupied by sixteen battalions of Tallard's foot and half a battalion of artillery, who fined the palisades and hedges, loop-holed the walls, and closed the openings with improvised obstacles of every kind. In rear of the village stood eleven more battalions, in readiness to reinforce the garrison, or to expel the enemy, if by any chance he should succeed in capturing the post.

On the brow of the slope, from Blindheim nearly to Oberglauheim, Tallard's cavalry, 5,500 strong, were ranked in two lines. They were supported by the infantry behind Blindheim, and by nine battalions and four squadrons of dismounted dragoons, drawn up behind their centre. Towards Oberglauheim they came into touch with thirty-two squadrons of Marsin's cavalry, which, likewise in two lines, extended behind and beyond that village. Oberglauheim itself was defended by fourteen battalions of Marsin's foot. To the left of the thirty-two squadrons the line was continued by seventeen battalions of infantry and terminated in front of Lutzingen by fifty-one squadrons of French and Bavarian horse.

The extreme left was protected against a flank attack by nine battalions of Bavarian foot, thrown back *en potence*. The artillery, consisting of eighty-two field-guns and eight pieces of heavier calibre, was judiciously distributed from end to end of the entire line. This order of battle has been censured by judges, both competent and incompetent, with an almost unparalleled severity. Feuquières[6] professes to have detected in the tactics of his countrymen no fewer than twelve specific blunders, of which six at least may be described as errors of disposition. But in justice to both victors and vanquished it must be admitted that this form of criticism has been somewhat overdone. Louis' generals had already committed grave faults; but neither Tallard nor Marsin was a fool, and the Elector was an experienced, and even a distinguished soldier.

All three acted in concert and were jointly responsible for the preliminary arrangements. The Bavarian officers and many of the French ones were thoroughly acquainted with the ground, which indeed was recognised by both sides to have been well adapted for the purposes of defence. The presumption is that the dispositions made must have been suitable in the main to the line of country which it was proposed to hold. That presumption is not greatly shaken by the arguments of the critics. It is said, for example, that Tallard ought not to have shut up twenty-eight battalions of foot in the village of Blindheim. He ought not; and he did not. The battalions which he placed in Blindheim numbered sixteen. Yet this untruth, accompanied by appropriate commentary, is to be found in almost all the writings on the subject. It is said that Tallard's army ought not to have encamped and fought as a separate unit. But Tallard's horses were infected with a dangerous disease, which would have been communicated to those of Marsin and the Elector, if the troops had coalesced.

It is said that, as a result of this division, the centre of the whole line was composed of the cavalry of the inner wings of both armies. But though it was usual at that period to form the centre of infantry, the rule was not so *sacrosanct* that it could not be broken, if the nature of the ground or other circumstances favoured such a course. The Elector and the Marshals had plenty of time to make whatever dispositions they considered proper; and the fact that they adopted an exceptional formation suggests that, in their judgement, the occasion was exceptional. That they should have ventured under any conditions to depart from one of the cast-iron customs of the orthodox school, is evidence that they were soldiers of a less pedantic order than most of their contemporaries.

Moreover, it is not strictly accurate to say that their centre was

---

6. Feuquières, t. 3., pp. 382-387.

composed of cavalry alone. For behind this cavalry were nine battalions of Tallard's foot, while before it, in the village of Oberglauheim, were fourteen of Marsin's. It is evident that the Elector and the Marshals considered that, from Unterglauheim to the mills, their line was so well protected by the Nebel swamps that no serious attack was to be anticipated in that quarter.

While Marlborough's columns were deploying, and Eugène's were still filing toward their appointed places on the right, the two commanders made a careful scrutiny of the enemy's line. Whether they discovered at this time, or at any time, those numerous mistakes which subsequently became apparent to the critics, may well be doubted. They could not fail to observe, however, that the distance between Blindheim and Oberglauheim was too great to be entirely swept by a converging fire from the cannon in those villages. On the other hand, officers whom they had sent to examine the Nebel and its banks, reported that the ground from Unterglauheim to the mills, though superficially hardened by the summer sun, was difficult for infantry and well-nigh impossible for horse. Below the mills the stream could be easily forded; but there the village of Blindheim, which the enemy appeared to be converting into a fortress, barred the way.

Above Unterglauheim a similar obstacle was presented by the village of Oberglauheim. From this point onward to the mountains there seemed to be some opportunity of engaging the enemy upon terms of comparative equality. His left flank, though shielded by the wooded heights, was certainly less secure than his right. Marlborough and Eugène concluded that the quarter, in which he derived least advantage from the nature of the ground, was exactly the quarter in which he would expect to be assailed most strongly. Determined to encourage him in that idea, they agreed that Eugène should deliver a vigorous attack upon the hostile left. If it succeeded, the position would be turned. But whether it succeeded or not, it would serve as a feint, which would distract the attention of the defenders, while Marlborough sought to strike a decisive blow at the point where it was least anticipated.

That precise point the Duke had still to ascertain. But he was disposed to find it on the long low ridge where he saw the squadrons of Tallard stretched out in a double line from Blindheim to Oberglauheim. He knew that the marshes were a formidable obstacle; and he inferred, from the unorthodox arrangement of the enemy's army, that Tallard, who of course knew it also, relied too strongly on this fact. He therefore resolved to traverse the marshes as best he might, and endeavour with superior forces to pierce the enemy's line upon the ridge beyond.

But Marlborough did not assume, as the critics have assumed, that his opponent was an idiot. On the contrary, he took it for granted that Tallard had a rational plan, and that his own business was to penetrate that plan. Now, there are four ways of defending a stream, and each of the four may be justified by success. Firstly, you may occupy positions upon the enemy's side, and resist his approach. Secondly, you may hold the bank upon your own side and dispute the actual crossing. Thirdly, you may permit him to attempt the passage and fall upon him in the midst of the operation. And fourthly, you may allow him to come over and to thrust himself into a prepared position from which he will not easily escape. It was plain that Tallard had not adopted the first of these methods. And judging by the distance of his lines from the brink of the Nebel, he did not propose to adopt the second, or even the third.

Apparently, he had selected the last. Apparently, if the allies should after all attempt to pass the Nebel in force (a contingency which Tallard deemed improbable), the Marshal would wait till they were safely over, only to charge them in the front with horse, while the infantry of Blindheim and Oberglauheim sallied out upon their flanks. Attacked on three sides, they would be pushed back into the marshes and there annihilated. Such in reality was Tallard's plan. It was conceived in the true spirit of defensive warfare. Had it succeeded, the critics would have compared it to Hannibal's manoeuvre at Cannae, and would have acclaimed its author as a masterly tactician.

Because it failed, they denounce him as a criminal blunderer. Marlborough fell into no such error. He saw the trap, or the risk that there was one. He saw also what was necessary to be done. Blindheim and Oberglauheim must be assaulted so strongly that the infantry which held them would be far too busy to participate in the combined movement necessary to the success of Tallard's tactics. If either or both of those villages could be carried, so much the better. But, in any event, their garrisons must not be permitted to assail the flanks of that force which was to pass the marshes and hurl itself against the cavalry upon the ridge.

Although the Duke must have suspected that he might be allowed to pass the Nebel without serious opposition, he did not rashly take it for granted. In anticipation of every eventuality, he deployed his troops, other than those of the column on his extreme left, in a fashion not recommended in the text-books.[7] He arranged them in four lines, the infantry in the first and fourth, the cavalry in the second and third. The infantry in the first were destined to traverse the stream and secure the opposite bank, while the cavalry of the second and third were crossing; and the infantry of the fourth were to line the hither bank in support of the operation. The engineers were ordered to the front. Five pontoons were laid; the stone bridge at Unterglauheim, which the enemy had broken down, was hastily repaired; and the thirty-five squadrons of the second line of horse were commanded to collect fascines.

The opportunity, which the motions of the allied army presented to artillery, did not go unobserved by the enemy's gunners. Between 8 and 9 they opened fire by the right; and in quick succession, all their ninety pieces, from Blindheim to Lutzingen, came into action. Marlborough's batteries, working under the eye of the Duke himself, replied at once; but Eugène's, which were greatly impeded by difficult and broken ground, were very late in opening. The allies had only fifty-two guns in all, and on the whole they had the disadvantage of position. In these circumstances, the odds in such a duel were at least two to one in favour of the French, who moreover exhibited all their traditional skill in the manipulation of this arm. Men were falling fast, when Eugène took leave of the Duke and rode off to superintend the deployment of the columns of the right.

For Marlborough and his army there now ensued a long and anxious pause. Their artillery was splendidly served, but it was overmatched; and horse and foot were constrained to endure the slow torment of the French cannonade through hour after hour of galling inactivity. They bore their punishment as only troops, in which the Teutonic strain predominated, could have borne it. The Duke's example consoled and inspired them all. He commanded the chaplains to conduct a service of prayer and intercession at the head of every regiment. He instructed the surgeons as to the proper stations for the field-hospitals.

In full view of the enemy's gunners he cantered slowly down the lines, observing with satisfaction the order and the spirit of the men. A round-shot struck the earth beneath his charger's hoofs. With a thrill of horror the soldiers saw him vanish in a cloud of dust. But graceful and serene as ever he emerged unscathed; and a great sigh of relief

---

7. "*Bizarre*," Feuquières, t. 3, p. 370.

went up from the thousands that had given him their love and trust.

"He told me," says Burnet, "he never saw more evident characters of a special Providence than appeared that day."[8]

The Duke had need of all the strength that he could derive from his natural resolution and his religious faith. It is "a truth of the first importance," said Clausewitz, "that to attack an enemy thoroughly inured to War, in a good position, is a critical thing."[9]

To the allies the strategical consequences of failure would be appalling. To Marlborough himself the personal consequences would be ruin and disgrace. And the material circumstances, artillery, numbers, situation, homogeneity of forces, the unexpected and costly delay upon the right wing, all appeared inimical to the prospects of success. But in war the things that are seen count for far less than the things that are not seen. The story of the Schellenberg was still fresh. It was common talk among the soldiers upon both sides. The confidence of the French, founded though it was upon long years of triumph, had been shaken. The confidence of the allies had risen to great heights.

Moreover, as Clausewitz also has observed, "one of the most important principles for offensive War is the surprise of the enemy. The more the attack partakes of the nature of a surprise, the more successful we may expect to be."[10]

This advantage Marlborough and Eugène had already secured. The popular idea of a surprise is an ambuscade like Sanna's Post, or a nocturnal scramble like Sedgemoor. But the word has a far wider interpretation in war. The French and Bavarians had six hours to prepare for action. Nevertheless they were effectively surprised. When an army which is assumed not only to be afraid to give battle but to be actually retreating on its base, is suddenly discovered to be marching boldly to the attack, a moral surprise of immense value has been achieved. Working on the imaginative and mercurial temperament of French soldiers, such a surprise may produce great results.

Totally unmoved by any sense of personal danger, the Duke completed his inspection. He then permitted himself to take some refreshment. But every minute his anxiety increased. Until Eugène informed him that the right was in position, the attack could not begin. But the columns of the right were still wading through streams, and stum-

---

8. Burnet, vol. 4., p. 51 (compare the remark of Wellington, after Waterloo, "The finger of God was upon me").
9. Clausewitz, *On War*, vol. 3, book 7, ch. 9.
10. *Ibid.*, vol. 3 Summary of Instruction.

bling over shallow ways, and painfully extending themselves under the fire of Marsin's artillery and the Elector's. Horseman after horseman dashed off from Marlborough to his colleague; but always the answer came back that the time was not yet. The sun shone brilliantly on acres of yellow grain, slashed with long, glittering lines of scarlet, blue, and steel. The music of both armies rose and fell in challenging *pæans*. And always the cannon boomed across the marshy stream, and men and horses were cut down, now singly, and now in swathes, and the dismal procession of wounded trailed slowly to the rear. The heat became intense, for it was now high noon. The day was half spent, and already the casualties of the allies amounted to 2,000, when an *aide-de-camp* of Eugène's came racing from the distant right. The moment had arrived.

Down by the Danube that ninth column, which Marlborough had formed at Tapfheim, had deployed into six lines, four of infantry and two of horse. Most of the troops were British. The Duke commanded Lord Cutts to launch them against Blindheim. At a quarter to 1, Rowe's Brigade, which formed the first line, and a brigade of Hessians, which formed the second, inclined a little to the right, marched briskly down to the mills, and passing the fords under a heavy fire from the cannon posted in and about Blindheim, halted for a moment on the opposite bank. Here they obtained some partial shelter from the ground, which swelled up towards the village. At the same time, the remainder of Marlborough's army, directed by the Duke in person, moved slowly towards the Nebel.

He, who beyond all others should have been a vigilant spectator of this advance, saw nothing of it. Prepossessed, like his colleagues, with the notion that the real attack was to be made at the opposite extremity of the position, and imagining that the deployment of the enemy was still far from completion, Tallard had ridden to the left to observe the preparations of Max Emanuel and Marsin. A quarter of an hour after his departure Marlborough's men were observed to be in motion. It was precisely at this juncture that the moral advantages possessed by the allies bore deadly fruit.

The officer entrusted with the defence of Blindheim, Lieutenant-General the Marquis de Clérembault, seems to have been one of those whose firmness had already been shaken by the confident and wholly unexpected strategy of Marlborough and Eugène. For now when he beheld the scarlet lines descending to the Nebel and realised that he himself was actually confronted by the very troops, whose astonishing resolution at the Schellenberg was in the mouths of all men, he lost his head. Although the forces in Blindheim were already adequate, and more than adequate, for its defence, in an access of nervous apprehension he called in to their assistance the eleven battalions which Tallard had disposed in rear of the village.

This movement dangerously weakened the French army in the open, while in Blindheim it produced inconvenient and unnecessary congestion. But the Marshal was not there to see and countermand it. Clérembault's fault was gross, and more than any other committed on that day contributed to the loss of the battle.

General Rowe dismounted, and sword in hand stepped to the front of his brigade. Straight up the slope he went, and after him in perfect order and silence went the five British battalions. The French, well covered by their defences, and outnumbering their assailants by five to one, waited like the veteran troops that most of them were, till the distance had dropped to thirty yards. Then all the crowded front of Blindheim village broke into long sheets of spluttering flame. The redcoats fell like leaves; but tightening their ranks, and fixing their eyes upon the figure of their leader, erect and shadowy amid the blinding smoke, they still held on. From those tortured lines no answering shot leapt back, for Rowe had ordered that not a trigger should be drawn until he reached the palisade. Unscathed he reached it. He struck his sword into the timber, and looked round. It was the signal. The English volley crashed, and fortunate indeed were Tallard's men that they did not receive it in the open field.[11]

The officers sprang forward. Steel clashed on steel across the hedges and stockades. But the odds were too overpowering. Some of the finest regiments in the French service were in action here. Their unshaken volleys swept the English down. Already one-third of Rowe's brigade were slain or disabled. Already Rowe himself had got his mortal wound. Sullenly the shattered ranks receded. But they had still to reckon with the mounted arm. On the right of the foremost line of Tallard's horse rode that illustrious body of troops, the *Gendarmerie*, three squadrons of whom now passed the village at the trot, and driving in upon the English flank, captured the colour of the 21st.

But their triumph was a brief one; for the Hessian foot, moving smartly up to the support of comrades, of whom they were well worthy, hurled back these splendid cavaliers with ringing volleys. By German hands the English banner was torn from its captors. The three

---

11. Fontenoy, Quebec.

squadrons recoiled, and never rallied till they had passed the Maulweyer. But seeing that others were now in motion, and realising that the attack on Blindheim could not be prosecuted under such conditions, Cutts sent back an urgent request for cavalry. By General Lumley's orders, five English squadrons from the left of Marlborough's line, fording the stream and struggling through the marsh, drew up in good order on the threatened flank.

Thereupon eight squadrons of *Gendarmerie* rode out as if to charge them; but to the astonishment of the English, these resplendent horsemen, who had the double advantage of numbers and of ground, stopped short, and opened fire with carbines from the saddle. They were instantly taught the futility of such tactics in the face of a well-trained cavalry. Marlborough's troopers went through them sword in hand, and chased them from the field. But the infantry in Blindheim poured in a galling fire upon the flank of the victors, who simultaneously were charged by fresh squadrons from the right of Tallard's second line, and driven backward almost to the Nebel. Here, however, the Hessian infantry again intervened, and by steady shooting compelled the pursuers to retire.

The remainder of Cutts' infantry now passed the stream; and Rowe's brigade, reinforced by Ferguson's, resumed the attack on Blindheim. The French guns, which had been firing on the fords, were hastily withdrawn. The English forced their way into the outskirts of the place, but they could make no permanent impression on the body of it. Three times they tried, and three times were driven out with cruel loss. Then Marlborough stopped the slaughter. It had not been in vain. It had convinced the defenders of Blindheim of the serious nature of the attack on their position and of the resolute character of the men engaged in it. So long as Cutts' brigades remained within striking distance, it was unlikely that any of the garrison, very excessive though it was, would be permitted to quit the village.

How very excessive it was, Marlborough could now conjecture. He did not know the exact numbers of the foot that were masked by Tallard's horse, but he was assured now that they were few. For it was evident that a small army had been placed in Blindheim. In the Duke's mind the probability that Tallard's squadrons on the ridge were the vulnerable part of the enemy's line, had now become almost a certainty. To augment his own preponderance at the decisive point, he now withdrew the Hanoverians from the fourth line of Cutts' detachment, and re-formed them behind the centre. But to impose upon the defenders of Blindheim and hold them always at their post, he instructed Cutts to maintain a false attack upon the village. This order was skilfully executed. Continually advancing and firing by platoons, these sixteen or seventeen battalions occupied the attention of twenty-eight of the enemy besides twelve squadrons of dismounted dragoons.

During the four assaults on Blindheim and the cavalry charges which followed on the first repulse, the main body of Marlborough's army had drawn down towards the Nebel. With the assistance of pontoons and planks, the infantry of the first line picked their way across the rivulet and marsh at various points between Oberglauheim and the mills, and drew up as rapidly as possible on the opposite bank. The cavalry followed. Some dismounted and led their chargers; others threw in fascines; each in his own way endeavoured to effect a crossing. The operation was necessarily attended with some disorder.

But Tallard, whom the echoing thunders of the attack on Blindheim had recalled to his own command, did not yield to the temptation to depart from his original plan. He permitted the French artillery to concentrate its fire upon the disorganised groups of men and horses; but apparently he still adhered to his opinion that nothing serious was to be anticipated from the allies in this quarter. If however they insisted upon thrusting themselves into his trap, the more of them he could catch, the better he would be pleased. Unfortunately for himself he neglected to recall to their proper position the infantry which Clérembault had ordered into Blindheim.

Riding on the left of the line, the English squadrons were compelled to cross two arms of the Nebel and the swampy island between. But so keen were they to come at the enemy, that they were the first of the allied horse to pass through the intervals in the infantry and ascend the rise. No sooner were they perceived by Zurlauben, the Swiss veteran who commanded Tallard's cavalry, than he charged them in person at the head of the *Gendarmerie* and some contiguous squadrons. This movement in no way contravened the general plan of the French Marshal. For Zurlauben must naturally have regarded the advance of the English as merely a renewal of the previous attempt to cover the flank of the brigades assaulting Blindheim.

Aided by the fire from the village, he drove them back upon their foot, who shooting steadily at thirty paces brought him at once to a standstill. Thereupon he was charged in turn by cavalry from Marlborough's second line, supported by five English squadrons, drawn from the fifteen under Lord Cutts. The French were chased to the farther side of the Maulweyer; but a tremendous fire of musketry from Blindheim forced the allied horsemen to relinquish the ground which they had gained.

At the opposite extremity of Marlborough's line the Danish and Hanoverian cavalry under the Duke of Württemberg furnished the gunners in Oberglauheim with an excellent target as they struggled across the stream. Before they had time to recover their order, Marsin, who did not adapt his system of defence to the plans of Tallard, launched the squadrons of his right upon them, and drove them backwards to the very brink of the Nebel and even beyond it. But Churchill's infantry repulsed the pursuers; and Württemberg quickly rallied his troops. Returning to the charge, he found it impossible to endure the flanking fire from Oberglauheim. This post had been long and vigorously cannonaded by Marlborough's artillery; and eleven battalions under the Prince of Holstein-Beck had been chosen to attack it. At the head of his men the Prince now passed the Nebel a little above the village.

Blainville, who commanded there, was a stronger tactician than Clérembault, and he knew how to execute Marsin's idea to perfection. No sooner had the two leading battalions of the allies set foot upon dry ground than he drew out of the village as many as nine, including the Irish Brigade in the service of France, and prepared to charge. Perceiving his peril, the Prince sent instantly to the nearest squadrons of Eugène's cavalry for aid. By a rapid advance they could have saved his right flank, which the enemy's longer line was threatening to envelop. But they refused to stir. Blainville gave the word; and dashing furiously down the slope, the torrent of Keltic valour carried all before it. One of the Prince's two battalions was annihilated. He himself was mortally wounded, and captured by the victors.

The allied army was now in grave danger. Blainville's brilliant counter-stroke was cutting it in twain at its very centre. If Marsin could follow up the movement more rapidly than Marlborough could stem it, the battle might be won for France. The Duke galloped instantly to the scene of the disaster, and leading forward three fresh Hanoverian battalions in support of the detachment of the Prince of Holstein-Beck, he passed the Nebel and engaged the infantry of Blainville with superior numbers. Reinforcing Württemberg with some Dutch squadrons, he effectually covered his own left while he threatened Blainville's right. At the same time he dispatched an urgent request to Eugène for mounted men.

Eugène had need of every trooper; but knowing that his colleague would ask no more than imperative necessity required, he sent him, without a moment's hesitation, a powerful body of Imperialist *cuirassiers*. Blainville was already falling back, when by Marsin's orders a detachment of French cavalry rode out to his assistance, and formed upon his left. This was the movement which Marlborough had dreaded, and had sought to anticipate by his message to Eugène. Marsin was just too late. Even as his squadrons bore down upon the Duke's defenceless right, the *cuirassiers*, coming up at the gallop, charged them in flank. The situation was saved.

Blainville withdrew in haste to the shelter of the village. The Prince of Holstein-Beck, bleeding profusely from several wounds, was abandoned by his captors. Württemberg continued to advance. And Marlborough, having ordered up some cannon to secure the ground which had been gained, instructed the officers upon the spot to imitate the tactics of Cutts at Blindheim, and content themselves with holding the garrison of Oberglauheim in the strictest check.

It was now past 3 o'clock. The Duke dispatched his *aide-de-camp*, Lord Tunbridge, to ascertain exactly how matters stood upon the right wing. All this time Eugène had been loyally executing his share of the compact. He had formed the whole of his infantry on the right and the whole of his cavalry on the left. When Cutts advanced against Blindheim, Leopold of Anhalt-Dessau led forward the Prince's foot to the attack of Lutzingen. Covered by the fire of a battery, which had with difficulty been posted on the heights, seven battalions of Danes and eleven of Prussians moved down towards the Nebel, which here breaks up into numerous streamlets. The rough and boggy nature of the ground delayed their progress; and a good half-hour elapsed before they came into contact with the enemy. But as soon as the right of the Imperialist horse had passed the stream and formed upon his left, Leopold charged.

At first all went well. On the extreme right the Danes attacked the Bavarian foot, while the Prussians, driving the enemy back 400 paces, stormed their great battery in front of Lutzingen and captured it. The cavalry broke the Elector's first line of horse, and chased it to the shelter of the second. But the second fell furiously upon the victors, and swept them back across the Nebel. Wheeling sharply to the left, the Bavarian Life Guards rode in upon the flank of the Prussian foot. These splendid soldiers faced the onset without flinching. Not until the Bavarian infantry came pouring back from Lutzingen did they at length give way. The Danes, whose left flank was now exposed, retired also. The guns were relinquished to their rightful owners, and ten colours were lost. Leopold exerted himself to the utmost to restore order; but only when the fringe of the wood was reached, did discipline reassert itself. Eugène in the meantime had been rallying his cavalry. Strengthened by their own left, which had not hitherto been engaged, they returned towards the Nebel. Thereupon the Elector's squadrons prudently retreated. Eugène led on his men to a second charge.

Again they were successful at the first; but the infantry were not yet ready to support them, and the converging fire from the battery before Lutzingen and the cannon of Oberglauheim, was too hot to be endured. The Imperialists faltered, broke into utter confusion, and fled back across the Nebel. It was now, when his infantry had been once repulsed and his cavalry twice, that Eugène was asked for that assistance which he rendered with such unquestioning promptitude.

A second time the Prince rallied his beaten horsemen. Then ensued a long and awful pause. For three-quarters of an hour, at a distance of no more than sixty paces, the cavalry of both sides sat still upon their panting horses, while in full view of the hostile lines Max Emanuel and Eugène rode up and down the ranks with words of exhortation and encouragement. Away on the right Leopold was still re-forming the Danes and Prussians.

It was now 4 o'clock. Both armies had been under fire for more than seven hours, and in physical contact for three. The heat was intense. The allies, in particular, who had been afoot before sunrise, and none of whom had marched fewer than five miles before coming into action, were feeling the full effects of their exertions. The lull upon the right extended also to the left. All along the Nebel, from the mountains to the Danube, the combat hung suspended for a time. It was evident that the crisis was at hand. The defenders assumed that they were winning. Four times upon their right they had repulsed the assailants of Blindheim.

Twice upon the left they had swept back the cavalry of Eugène, while his infantry, victorious at first, had been ultimately crushed and driven to the shelter of the woods. In the centre, with one brilliant charge they had all but split the allied army in twain. And now, in this prolonged hesitancy of the attack, they not unnaturally detected the approaching paralysis of exhaustion.

Lesser men than Eugène and Marlborough might have fallen into the same error.

"Before 3," wrote the Duke's chaplain, "I thought we had lost the day."[12] But the Prince of Savoy was a soldier of unconquerable heart. The more he was disappointed by the failure of his efforts, the more determined he became to resume them. He knew that, in the teeth of superior numbers, well posted and gallantly led, he himself could expect no dazzling triumphs. But he knew also that, if only he could absorb to the full the attention of the forces immediately opposed to him, his colleague might be trusted to strike the decisive blow elsewhere. With equal wisdom and unselfishness he did the hard and thankless duty allotted to him.

There is an essentially English phrase for that form of enlightened self-sacrifice, which is one of the grand secrets of success in sport and war. It is 'playing the game.' And no Englishman ever played the game more superbly than this French-Italian in the service of the Court of Austria that August afternoon beside the blood-stained waters of the Nebel.

His confidence in Marlborough was not misplaced. After driving Blainville back into Oberglauheim, the Duke had steadily continued to pass his troops across the marshes. By 4 o'clock his entire army, including the cavalry of Cutts, was over at last. His plan was drawing to maturity. The repulses before Blindheim, the disaster to the Prince of Holstein-Beck, the discouraging reports from the right wing, all left him unperturbed. In a sense he welcomed them, as tending to drug his opponents with a false security and blind them to their real peril. He himself saw through the appearances of failure and the symptoms of collapse into the very soul of things, and he knew that he could win.

Between Blindheim and Oberglauheim he had now a combined force of all arms, outnumbering in every branch the troops which Tallard could oppose to them. His men were such as he could trust implicitly. In the centre and rear they were comparatively fresh; and even on the wings, where they had been previously involved in the fighting round the two villages, they had borne themselves well and were in excellent spirits. Nothing could save Tallard but a combined movement by Clérembault and Blainville against the Duke's flanks, or a powerful reinforcement from the Elector. But Clérembault and Blainville were already held fast, and the Elector was anxiously regarding the preparations of Eugène.

---

12. Hare MSS.: Francis Hare to his cousin (George Naylor), Augnst 14, 1704 (Hist. MSS. Comm., 14th Report, Appendix, part 9., p. 200).

The Duke maintained his formation in four lines; but now his cavalry composed the first and second, his infantry the third and fourth. To guard against a sortie by the numerous garrison of Blindheim the bulk of the infantry were drawn towards the left. To facilitate the retirement of broken squadrons, intervals were allowed between the battalions. About half an hour after 4 Marlborough set the whole body in motion. Very slowly and in beautiful order they began their advance. At the same time, far away on the extreme right, the Danes were working round the Elector's flank, and Leopold of Anhalt-Dessau, waving a colour above his head, was leading his Prussians a second time on Lutzingen. And simultaneously the squadrons of Eugène followed the Prince himself across the Nebel to a third and final charge. From end to end of the allied line the last great movement had begun. If it succeeded, the victory was gained; but if it failed, there could not be another.

The leisured and majestic march of Marlborough's men conveyed to the French beholders of it a wonderful impression of conscious power. Tallard took the alarm at once. His cavalry, inferior in numbers, and already despondent or fatigued, could never by itself endure the oncoming shock. Hastily he ordered forward those nine battalions of foot, which had hitherto stood idle in rear of his centre. To the left of his line, in the direction of Oberglauheim, they now formed between the squadrons. But Marlborough's officers upon the spot responded promptly. They brought up three battalions of Hanoverian infantry, supported by cannon, and set them among the horse at the threatened point. And still, though every available French gun was trained upon so fair a target, the slow and stately ranks rolled on.

The Marshal had never believed that they would attempt to pass the swamp. Owing perhaps to his defective eyesight, he had never realised till now in what numbers they actually had passed it. It was too late to withdraw infantry from Blindheim by the rear of the village. It was impossible to withdraw them by its flank, for Cutts' platoons could shoot them down like sheep as fast as they emerged. For Clérembault's folly, and for Tallard's failure to prevent it and neglect to repair it, the price must now be paid.

But to France even now one last opportunity was given. She owed it neither to the discipline of her veterans nor to the daring of her nobles nor to the resource of her commanders. She owed it entirely to the simple valour of her youngest soldiers. In the hour of trial, the nine battalions, recruits for the most part in their first battle, bore themselves like men grown old in war. Already they were falling fast; but they closed their ranks at the word of their officers and stood up unflinchingly before the lacerating grape-shot. Their steady shooting overpowered the musketry of the Hanoverians, and brought the cavalry of Marlborough's right to a sudden standstill. Those of the left, smitten cruelly by the fire of Blindheim, halted at the same time; and then, to the delight of Tallard, the whole line of horse recoiled upon the foot.

"I saw," he wrote, "an instant in which the battle was gained."[13]

One swift and concerted charge by every French sabre from Blindheim to Oberglauheim might indeed have saved the day. But no such charge was ever executed. Here and there well-led troops and squadrons rode resolutely forward; but for the most part, Tallard's horsemen, fearful of the infernal fire of Marlborough's supporting foot, hung timorously back, or moved, when they did move, in feeble, ineffective fashion.

Marlborough saw at a glance that the moment was come. His guns were pouring grape into the nine battalions, when he called upon his cavalry for a decisive effort. With trumpets blaring and kettle-drums crashing and standards tossing proudly above the plumage and the steel, the two long lines, perfectly timed from end to end, swung upwards at a trot, that quickened ever as they closed upon the French. At the sight and the sound thereof two-thirds of Tallard's horsemen went shamelessly about and galloped for their lives. But the heave of that strong, deliberate wave caught every isolated group that dared to breast it, and flung them all in shattered ruin from the field. It caught those nine battalions of gallant boys, whose professional knowledge did not embrace the art of running away.

They stood, said Orkney afterwards, "in the best order I ever saw";[14] but it caught them, and engulfed them, and one who on the morrow rode past that fatal place counted their corpses as they lay in their ranks, preserving in their deaths a faithful record of the discipline which they had maintained so admirably in their lives. And on it swept, still roaring and devouring, to the very tents and baggage-

---

13. Pelet, t. 4, p. 568: *Tallard à Chamillart*, 4 septembre, 1704.
14. *English Historical Review*, April, 1904: Letter from the Earl of Orkney to Lord Bristol, August 17, 1704 (copies of four letters written by George Hamilton, first Earl of Orkney, who served as Lieutenant-General in Marlborough's army, have been preserved at Craster Tower, Northumberland. It is not known if the originals exist).

wagons of Tallard's camp, where it stayed awhile. Then the cavalry of Marsin, apprehensive for their own imperilled flank, changed front to the right. From Blindheim to Oberglauheim the whole line of the defence was rent asunder as by a giant's hand.

Tallard was well-nigh at his wits' end. He dispatched a messenger to Marsin with an urgent request that reinforcements of infantry should be sent him, or else that a strong offensive movement should be made against Marlborough's right. But Marsin and the Elector were already fully occupied. The first line of their horse had gone down before the squadrons of Eugène; but the second, by a timely charge, had swept the Imperialists back across the Nebel in ignominious rout. The shame of this third repulse stung the Prince to fury. Two of the fugitives he shot down with his own hand. But the panic of the troopers was irremediable. In disgust he left them to their officers, and galloped away to the right, where his infantry was moving grandly to the attack.

"I wish to fight among brave men and not among cowards,"[15] he cried, as he dashed up to the steady battalions of Brandenburg. His wish was gratified. Magnificently the Prussians bore themselves against heavy odds. The ground was rough and broken, the fighting close and murderous. The assailants were mown down with devastating blasts of grape-shot. But once more the great battery was taken. The outskirts of Lutzingen were carried. The Elector's left was forced inward by the Danes. Eugène exposed himself in the foremost ranks.

A Bavarian dragoon levelled his carbine at the Prince, and took a careful aim; but just as he was about to discharge the weapon, he was killed by a Danish soldier. Tenaciously this superb infantry clung to every inch of ground that it had won, though it had no more than two squadrons of horse to shield its left flank. Marsin in the centre felt the pressure of its slow but obstinate advance. He began to be afraid for his own left. Already everything upon his right was crumbling into space.

When Tallard sent to him for aid, he refused it. Feuquières and other critics declare that he should have fallen on the flank of Marlborough's horse. Promptly made, this daring and difficult manoeuvre might conceivably have been attended by considerable success. But Marsin and the Elector thought otherwise. Rejecting all tactics of heroism or despair, they determined to play for safety and to extricate their own armies with the smallest possible loss. Their decision, whether good or bad, is entitled to that consideration which always

---

15. For the account of this incident see *Memoirs of the House of Brandenburg* (1757)

belongs of right to the opinions of the men in touch with actualities. In some essential respects the knowledge upon which a general acts in battle is necessarily greater than that of mere critics; in others it is often less. They ought therefore to be careful how they try him by a standard which cannot fairly be applied. And always he must choose, and choose quickly, under conditions which are in the last degree unfavourable to tranquil thought.

Behind his camp Tallard rallied the remnants of his broken horsemen as best he could. He conceived the idea of forming a new front from Bhndheim to Sonderheim, parallel to the Danube. Thrusting out his right to keep touch with Clérembault's infantry, he was instantly charged on that exposed flank by Marlborough's triumphant squadrons. This time the French did not await the shock. They delivered one futile volley from the saddle, and fled. Behind Blindheim the ground falls steeply to a loop of the Danube. Down into this deathtrap went thirty maddened squadrons, the allied cavalry thundering at their heels. Many were sabred here, but many more perished most miserably in the river and its marshes. Another large body took the road to Höchstädt.

At Sonderheim they made a stand; and Taflard dispatched a messenger to Clérembault with orders to evacuate Blindheim and join him forthwith. But the allied horse were advancing rapidly along the Höchstädt road. The messenger was captured; and when Tallard set off in person to execute his own commands, he found himself surrounded. He was taken by an *aide-de-camp* of the Prince of Hesse, who conveyed him to the Duke of Marlborough. The Duke received him with the most delicate consideration. Many French officers of high rank suffered the same fate as the Marshal. On the approach of Hompesch with the allied cavalry the troops at Sonderheim resumed their flight. Beyond the Brunnen they essayed to rally; but before Hompesch could charge them, they scattered over the country in irretrievable ruin.

It was now past 7 o'clock. Away to the northward Marsin and the Elector were already in full retreat. These purists in the rules of civilised warfare had fired the villages of Oberglauheim and Lutzingen, (thereby raising the number of inoffensive places destroyed by them that day for tactical reasons to seven,) and under cover of the smoke and flame had abandoned their positions. In three columns, one of foot and two of horse, they retired along the base of the hills. Eugène followed; but the exhaustion of his infantry and the disappearance of many of his cavalry diminished the ardour of the pursuit. Two Bavarian battalions, overtaken by superior numbers, laid down their arms. But Marsin and the Elector, despising an enemy whom they considered they had well beaten, turned furiously at bay, and wrenched the two battalions from the hands of their captors. Then they resumed their retreat, which was conducted, on the authority of an English witness, "with great dexterity and expedition."[16]

Out on the Höchstädt road, Marlborough in the failing light perceived the conflagrations of the villages, and the black columns creeping westward under the shadow of the hills. Recalling Hompesch from the chase, he assembled as many cavalry as possible, and led them across the dusky plain towards the flank of the retiring columns. But in the twilight and the smoke he mistook the foremost division of Eugène's army for a Bavarian force threatening his own right. He hesitated, and the enemy made good use of the delay. Their steady and well-ordered march impressed the Duke. He wisely decided that it would be dangerous in the gathering darkness to fling his jaded horsemen on an army so ably led and so little demoralised. Thus through the summer night Marsin and the Elector pursued the road to Dillingen, collecting as they went the drifting wreckage of Tallard's host.

Many of the flying cavalry drew rein for a while in the little town of Höchstädt. It was after 8 when a bruised and mud-stained horseman rode wearily up to a group of officers who were slaking their thirst at the fountain in the market-place. He was recognised as Mérode-Westerloo (he who has written of the merry supper at Blindheim twenty-four hours before). "You are very late," said one, with astonishing ineptitude.

The haughty Fleming, conscious that he had 'played the game' that day for France when too many of her own children had failed her, eyed the speaker coldly. "You are very early," [17] he answered. And that, before long, was the verdict of the nation.

Meanwhile, the village of Blindheim had become the theatre of one of the most poignant tragedies in the history of war. When Marlborough's decisive charge hurled the cavalry of Tallard beyond the French camp, Churchill with the bulk of the allied foot closed in upon the place, taking his station between Cutts' men and the Maulweyer brook. Ingoldsby and Orkney with the infantry from the right of the line passed the Maulweyer and began to extend towards the Danube.

---

16. Kane, p. 55.
17. *Mémoires de Mérode-Westerloo*, p. 316.

At first they were embarrassed by the right of Tallard's cavalry; but Marlborough's last charge cleared the field in that quarter, and left them free to complete the investment of the village. The powerful garrison did nothing to prevent its own isolation. Clérembault, having witnessed the destruction of the entire line from Blindheim to Oberglauheim, lost what little nerve he may have still possessed. Judging that he and his men were doomed, and reahsing perhaps that his own misconduct was largely responsible for the loss of the battle, he seems to have become temporarily insane. Accompanied only by a groom, he slunk away to the Danube bank, where he urged his horse into the dangerous current, "apparently," says Saint-Simon, "with the intention of becoming a hermit afterwards."[18]

The groom got safely over; but, by the mercy of Providence, Lieutenant-General le Marquis de Clérembault perished in the stream. Blansac, on whom the command devolved, was in ignorance of his general's fate, and at a loss to account for his disappearance. Not a word came through from Tallard. An officer of the *Gendarmerie* rode past the village, and Blansac requested him to go to the Marshal for instructions. He went, but only to be captured by Marlborough's cavalry. A wise and resolute leader would now have taken upon himself to order the immediate evacuation of the village by the rear. But Blansac at this juncture showed himself neither wise nor resolute.

The precious moments sped by. Orkney and Ingoldsby drew tight their net. Before 6 o'clock, from the Danube on the east to the Maulweyer, and from the Maulweyer to the Danube on the west, Blindlieim was girdled with a semi-circle of bayonets and cannon. Crowded and overcrowded there under the lengthening shadow of the village steeple, were some of the finest regiments in the service of the great King. Four times they had repulsed their enemies with scanty loss to themselves. The sloping ground upon their front, all littered with scarlet-coated bodies that writhed in agony or else lay very still, bore witness to the disciplined accuracy of their fire.

Throughout the day they had been in the highest spirits. But now with strange and ominous swiftness depression fell upon their ranks. In all ages the French soldier had possessed, in an exceptional degree, the military instinct. Often he divines the part which his own particular unit is playing in the total combination. Frequently, before he receives his orders, he knows what they will be. And when he has received them, he executes them with that skill and confidence which

---

18. *Mémoires de Saint-Simon* (1842), t. 7, p. 250.

only understanding can bestow.

But this popular genius for war has grave and obvious defects. It can make the soldier mistrustful of his general in circumstances of which none save the general can adequately judge. It can make him critical of his officer almost to the point of insubordination. And in the moment of adversity it leaves him weaker than the men of less intelligent and less imaginative races. It was not a French commander who declared that he could always rely upon his soldiers to extricate him from the consequences of his own mistakes. And it was not the infantry in Blindlieim that could save Tallard now. They could not save themselves.

They had witnessed, or those of them posted to the left and rear of the village had witnessed, the rout of the cavalry and the annihilation of the nine battalions. They had exchanged a few scared words with passing troopers, whose demoralisation infected all with whom they spoke. They could see the allied troops closing rapidly in upon their left and rear. They knew instinctively that it was time to be moving. Yet nothing was done. Their leader was nowhere to be seen. His lieutenant was silent. The orders, which every soldier expected, remained unspoken. And soon it would be too late. Already they foresaw the end; and black horror gripped their souls.

The businesslike methods of Marlborough's officers, who were aware that they had to do with a numerous and veteran enemy, left little to chance. No sooner was the place surrounded than Lord Orkney rode over the Maulweyer to report to Churchill, who was arranging for simultaneous attacks on every side. While the gunners cannonaded the village from the north, Cutts delivered his fifth assault on the east, and Orkney and Ingoldsby essayed to force a passage on the west, where no preparations had been made for a defence. Cutts was again repulsed; and Orkney and Ingoldsby, after effecting an entry, were presently driven out with the bayonet.

But the pursuers' rush was checked by the fire of the British dragoons, who easily shot away the head of every column that sought to debouch by the narrow avenues. Soon the attack was vigorously resumed on this side. Orkney's men penetrated as far as the churchyard, the high stone wall of which served the French as an excellent breastwork. The shooting from the houses greatly galled the assailants, who eventually fell back, while guns and howitzers played upon the obnoxious buildings. Several were speedily in flames. And now the closely packed French began to find their situation unendurable.

Two brigades under Dénonville pressed forward to charge. The astute Orkney seized the occasion to beat a parley. He called out to the French soldiers that, if they would yield, they should have "good quarters";[19] and his *aide-de-camp*, Abercrombie, actually rode up to the Royal Regiment, and snatching the colours from the ensign, who gave him a slight wound over the arm, demanded to know if they did not hear the general's offer.

Dénonville conferred with Orkney. He was willing to surrender on condition that his men should not be plundered. Orkney agreed; and the two brigades laid down their arms. At the same time a third capitulated to Ingoldsby. Orkney enquired of his prisoners what force remained in the village. He was told that there were more than twenty battalions, besides twelve squadrons of dragoons, "which," he says, "I owne, struck me, since I had not above seven battallions and four esquadrons." But the Hamilton's face betrayed no secrets. "I maid the best countenance I cou'd,"[20] he says.

Abercrombie was now sent into Blindheim under a flag of truce, and Dénonville, at Orkney's request, accompanied him. The *aide-de-camp* explained the situation to Blansac. His statements were confirmed by Dénonville, who then proceeded to harangue the soldiers, arguing that it was the King's interest that their lives should be saved. Blansac, by his own account, indignantly cut short this scandalous oration, and amid the cheers of Navarre and the sombre silence of the other regiments exhorted the men to remain firm in their duty. But he went out of the village with Abercrombie, and he promised Orkney that he would consult his officers. The *aide-de-camp* returned with him, and quitting the place on the eastern side, informed Cutts that the enemy were about to capitulate.

Cutts, whose losses had been very severe, was astonished and incredulous. But Abercrombie was right. After a hasty council of war, Blansac went a second time to Orkney. Opinion had been divided, and the unhappy man could come to no resolution. The older officers had favoured a surrender, but the young ones had sworn to cut their way out sword in hand. In these circumstances the Hamilton played his cards perfectly. He told Blansac that Tallard was taken, that Marlborough was a league away in pursuit of the flying horse, and that twenty fresh battalions and all the artillery of the allied army were close at hand.

---

19. See *English Historical Review*, April, 1904.
20. *Ibid.*

It was, in his own words, a "little *gasconad*,"[21] but it sufficed. Blansac agreed to surrender on the same terms as Dénonville. When the decision was communicated to the troops, it was accepted by many with gloomy resignation. But some wept, and others gave way to paroxysms of fury and despair. Certain of the officers refused to set their hands to the capitulation. And the regiment of Navarre destroyed its colours.

Between 8 and 9 that night the tragedy was played to a finish. In the summer gloaming they marched out, those old illustrious bands whose very muster-roll sounded like the history of France. Navarre, and Artois, and Provence, and Languedoc, and Rohan, and La Reine—they all marched out, and piled their weapons in the darkening fields. And now, when they saw for themselves the actual numbers of their conquerors, some said that Blansac had been fooled by Orkney's judicious 'bluffing.' Yet Orkney honestly believed that the French could never have escaped.

Many years afterwards he explained to Voltaire his professional reasons for holding that opinion. In his judgement, no troops in the world could ever have issued from the narrow lanes of Blindheim and deployed under the converging fire from the broad front of the allied fine. But there were others present, both English and Dutch, who thought otherwise, and who considered that with resolute leadership at least one-half of the garrison of Blindheim might have forced a passage. Before the last of this melancholy procession had defiled into the plain, a horseman dashed up with a message from Marlborough. Doubtless the Duke had learned from his prisoners what forces were in Blindheim. He at any rate was not anticipating so easy a capture, for his orders were that the troops blockading the place should lie upon their arms till dawn, when they would be reinforced by the entire army.

Tidings of victory were already on the wing. Through the cool of the summer night Marlborough's *aide-de-camp*. Colonel Parke, was galloping hard into the north. He carried one of the most singular and unconventional dispatches in the history of war. The general in supreme command of the forces of Great Britain and the United Provinces reported the destruction of the French army and the ruin of French strategy in the manner of a knight-errant announcing to his mistress the accomplishment of a true lover's vow. On a scrap of paper, torn from a notebook, and bearing on its reverse side a memorandum of an inn-keeper's account, the Duke had scribbled with a lead-pencil

---

21. *Ibid.*

to the woman whose smile was more to him than the eulogy of princes this pregnant message:

> August 13, 1704.—I have not time to say more, but to beg you will give my duty to the Queen, and let her know her army has had a glorious victory. M. Tallard and two other generals are in my coach, and I am following the rest. The bearer, my *aide-de-camp*, Colonel Parke, will give her an account of what has passed. I shall do it in a day or two, by another more
>
> Marlborough.[22]

Parke, a heavy man and a tall, was no respecter of horseflesh. Within ten days he was at Windsor. The Duchess read the letter and took him to the Queen.

"Without vanity," said Orkney, "I think wee did our pairts."[23]

They did indeed. Considered without reference to its strategical results, the actual victory was stupendous. The casualties of the allies amounted to 12,000 killed and wounded, of whom more than 2,000 were British. The exact losses of the enemy could never be ascertained. But out of a total of 56,000 men, at the very lowest 14,000, and probably some thousands more, were killed, wounded, or drowned on the field of battle. The prisoners, including Marshal Tallard and many generals, besides 1,200 officers of subordinate ranks, amounted to 15,000, of whom 3,000, being of German extraction, took service with the allies.

The deserters were computed at from 3,000 to 5,000. But for many days the wastage of the beaten army continued. Writing a fortnight later, Marlborough declared that he had intercepted several letters to the French Court, "by which the enemy own to have lost 40,000 men, killed, taken prisoners, and deserted since the battle."[24] Apparently, these enormous figures, five-sevenths of the total arrayed for France at Blenheim, did not conflict with his own observations. As for the spoils, they were immense, and comprised no fewer than "100 pieces of cannon, great and small, 24 mortars, 129 colours, 171 standards, 17 pair of kettle-drums, 3,600 tents, 34 coaches, 300 laden mules, 2 bridges of boats, 15 pontoons, 24 barrels, and 8 casks of silver."[25]

---

22. Coxe, vol. 1, p. 206.
23. Athol MSS.: Letter from George Hamilton, Earl of Orkney, giving his account of the battle of Blenheim, August 14, 1704 (Hist. MSS. Comm., 12th Report, Appendix, part 8., p. 62).
24. Murray, vol. 1., p. 435: Marlborough to M. Bothmar, August 27, 1704.
25. Boyer, vol. 3, p. 87.

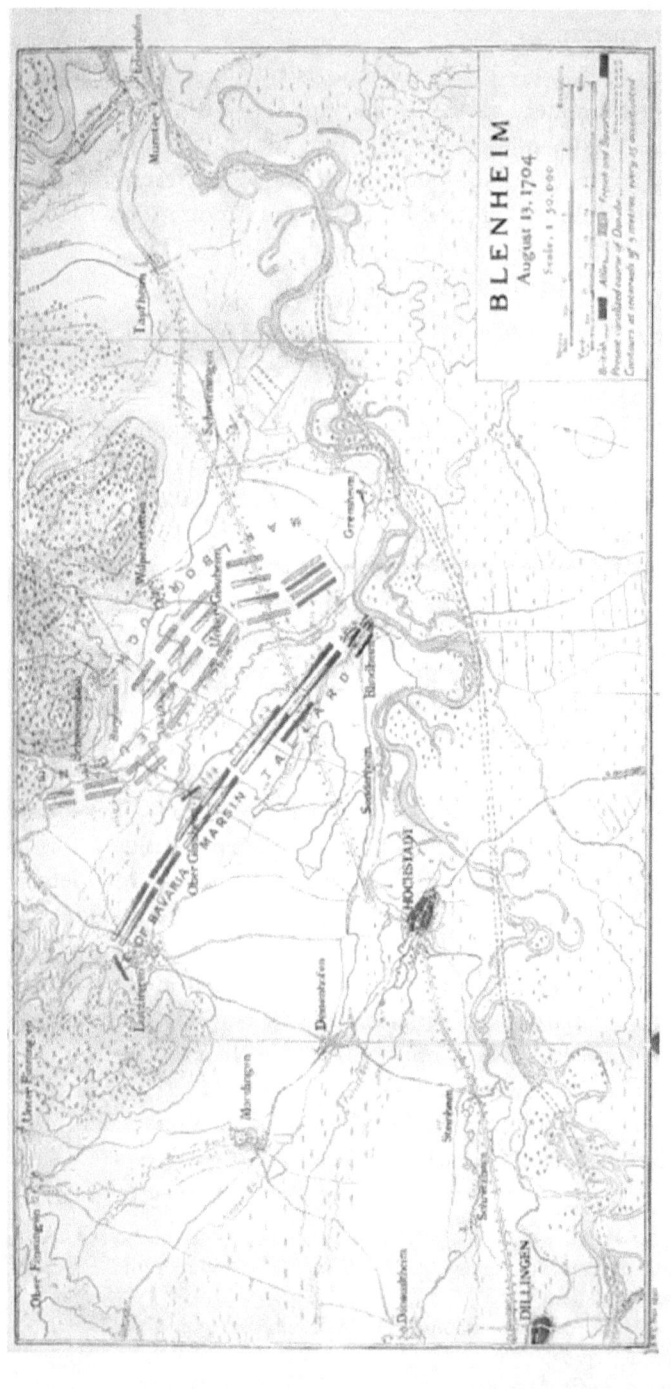

"It is," wrote one[26] who was present, "a very entire victory in all parts of it."

"It is perhaps," wrote another,"[27] "the greatest and completest victory that has been gained these many ages."

Marlborough himself, in writing to his "dearest soul," observed that it was "as great a victory as has ever been known,"[28] and again that "never victory was so complete."[29] And in words that show him unmistakably as the lover of his wife and the generous friend of Eugène, he said, "I am so pleased with this action, that I can't end my letter without being so vain as to tell my dearest soul, that within the memory of man there has been no victory so great as this; and as I am sure you love me entirely well, you will be infinitely pleased with what has been done, upon my account as well as the great benefit the public will have. For had the success of Prince Eugène been equal to his merit, we should in that day's action have made an end of the war."[30]

But something incomparably more valuable than 40,000 men with cannon and equipment was lost to the French monarchy. More than sixty years had elapsed since Condé on the field of Rocroi had shattered the ancient prestige of the Spanish arms. For more than two generations the French had been regarded as the most formidable soldiers in Europe. Their conquests had increased their reputation, and their reputation had facilitated their conquests. Their enemies, habituated to defeat, met it because they expected to meet it. But at Blenheim the idol was ruthlessly broken and trodden in the dust.

It was not merely that French generals had been hopelessly outwitted. It was not merely that a French army, holding distinct advantages in numbers and position, had been practically annihilated. These things were startling, and serious enough. They could however be explained; they might even be explained away. Their effects could always be minimised by official reservations and denials. But no sort of ingenuity could minimise the incompetence and cowardice of a Clérembault, or the feebleness of a Blansac, or the misconduct of a Dénonville, or the spiritless behaviour of so many of Tallard's cavalry, or the failure of those dashing horsemen, the *Gendarmerie,* from whom

---

26. Hare MSS.: Francis Hare to his cousin (George Naylor), August 14, 1704 (Hist. MSS. Comm., 14th Report, Appendix, part 9, p. 201).
27. *English Historical Review,* April, 1904.
28. Coxe, vol. 1, p. 213: The Duke to the Duchess, August 14, 1704.
29. *Ibid.*, p. 214.
30. *Ibid.*

so much was invariably expected, or the complete demoralisation and the enduring dejection of the mass of the survivors.

These were circumstances witnessed with their own eyes by the soldiery of the allied nations, and symptomatic, in their judgement, of an all-pervading rottenness where they had been taught to expect the most minute efficiency. The reaction was excessive. The men who had been the bullies of Europe were now despised by their former victims. The work, so well begun at the Schellenberg, was consummated at Blenheim. Henceforward the moral advantage rested always with the armies of the coalition. More for this reason than for any other, notable as the others were, this victory was rightly considered at the time to mark an epoch. In France the news was received at first with incredulity, which rapidly turned to indignation.

"We were not accustomed to misfortune,"[31] says Saint-Simon. Marsin and the Elector supplied no details. But the broad facts were undeniable. They were also, for a long time, incomprehensible.

"We no longer," says Clausewitz, "take twenty-seven battalions in a village, as they did at Blenheim."[32]

Nor did they then, as a general rule. Little by little, however, a connected narrative was extracted from the private letters of officers, who one and all were loud in their criticisms of particular persons other than themselves, and particular regiments and divisions other than their own. These recriminations made a very bad impression. The relatives of certain of the prisoners and the slain did not venture to appear in public. To the anguish of bereavement was added the intolerable bitterness of disgrace. Every ignorant layman was demanding to know why this or that elementary maxim of the art of war had been disregarded by those who were paid to observe it. And others besides ignorant laymen were unable to keep silence. On no one did the blow descend with more crushing severity than on Villars, who in this catastrophe beheld the destruction of his grand design.

> "I am ashamed," he wrote, when he learned that there were Frenchmen who sought to justify the capitulation of Blansac, "I am ashamed for our nation upon account of so base a surrender, and I see with a grief that I cannot express, how short we come of the ancient Romans, and of French that I have known."[33]

---

31. *Mémoires de Saint-Simon*, vol. 7, p. 265.
32. Clausewitz, *On War*, vol. 3, ch. 9.
33. Vogüé, *Mémoires de Villars*, t. 2, p. 330, *Appendice*: Villars à l'abbé de Saint-Pierre, September 2, 1704.

The government put the best face they could upon the matter. Recognising that it is easier to replace old generals by new ones than to restore self-respect to an army publicly convicted of misconduct, they prudently decided that the whole responsibility for the disaster should be ofilcially ascribed to the unhappy Tallard .

And in England? Small wonder that in England the hearts of men should have burned within them. Not for three hundred years, not since the miracle of Agincourt, had the islanders struck such a resounding stroke upon the continent of Europe. And this thing was not done in a corner. It was done in the very centre of the civilised world, and at a moment when the eyes of all the peoples were riveted upon the combatants. The nation was intoxicated with pride and joy. On every peak the bonfires blazed; from every steeple the joy-bells clashed. From borough and shire addresses of congratulation poured in upon the Queen.

The Jacobites were stricken dumb. The Tories of the Rochester school, and the military critics of the armchair and pothouse schools, found it convenient, for a season, to simulate a pleasure which they did not feel. Anne appointed a solemn thanksgiving to be observed throughout her dominions. On a fair September day, with her councillors and peers, with her great officers of state and her resplendent household cavalry, with Norroy and Garter and all the superb pageantry of Britain's kings, she passed amid the acclamations of her people and the thunder of her cannon from her palace of St. James's to the glorious new cathedral of St. Paul's.

Through Temple Bar she passed with stately ceremonial, through Fleet Street, gorgeously draped, and lined with glittering train-bands and the banners of the ancient guilds. All eyes were fixed upon the royal carriage with its eight goodly steeds; but for once it was not the amiable countenance of their beloved Sovereign, but the beautiful and proudly smiling face of Marlborough's wife that the spectators sought. The Queen of England was ablaze with jewels; but with that affectation of humility, which is the uttermost expression of pride, she, who knew herself to be the queen of the hour, wore but "a very plain garment."[34]

Well indeed might Marlborough hope that his "dearest soul" would be "infinitely pleased." Glory such as now was his no private Englishman had ever before enjoyed. The dispatches from the seat of war, the

---

34. *Evelyn's Diary*, September 7, 1705.

letters from officers to their friends, and the gazettes of the European capitals were unanimously agreed that England had produced a military genius of the first magnitude. But there are spots upon the sun. The Duke, it appeared, had been guilty of one mistake; he had been careless of his own safety.

> "He exposed himself," wrote one who was in the thickest of the fighting, "as much as any officer or soldier in the army, and much more than most of the generals."[35]

> He was "everywhere, from one attack to another," wrote Orkney, "and ventured his person too-too much that day."[36]

> "My Lord Marlborough," wrote Hare, "was everywhere in the action, to encourage our men, and exposed to infinite dangers."[37]

The valiant Hompesch reported to the States that the Duke "exposed himself in the most dangerous places, during the whole action, giving directions with a presence of mind amidst the hottest fire."[38]

But this splendid weakness, if it was a weakness, did but endear him all the more to the countrymen of Cœur de Lion and the Black Prince. War, as the masses of the English people pictured it, was not the scientific thing that Vauban and Turenne had made of it, but the Homeric hurly-burly of the ballads and the chronicles. They loved to imagine their hero, like Achilles impervious to death and wounds, and like Samson butchering his thousands with his own right arm. But fantastic notions of the victor of Blenheim were not confined to his own compatriots.

To the wives and mothers of France he appeared as the destroying angel. In the olden time they had imposed a fearful calm upon refractory babes with one whisper of the name of Talbot. But long was Talbot dead; and now were the Bluebeards, giants, dragons, ogres, and hobgoblins of the night incontinently deposed, and a legendary "Malbrook" came to his own in the kingdom of all childish terrors.

---

35. Pope (Coke MSS.): Captain Richard Pope to Thomas Coke, August 16, 1704 (Hist. MSS. Comm., 12th Report, Appendix, part 3, p. 40).
36. *English Historical Review*, April, 1904.
37. Hare MSS.: Francis Hare to his cousin (George Najdor). August 14, 1704 (Hist. MSS. Comm., 14th Report, Appendix, part 9, p. 201).
38. Lediard, vol. 1, ch. 7, p. 404: Letter from General Hompesch to the States-General.

CHAPTER 10

After Blenheim

All through the night of the 13th Marsin and the Elector marched unmolested on the road to Ulm, collecting the wreckage of Tallard's host as they went. Before daybreak they had safely passed their baggage across the Danube at Lauingen. As soon as it was light, the infantry followed, while the cavalry continued its retreat upon the northern bank. A detachment of 1,000 men was left at Lauingen with instructions to burn the bridge on the first appearance of the enemy.

It is an axiom of war that the victorious army, resisting every temptation to relax its energies, must pursue the foe with unrelenting vigour. The night-ride of Gneisenau's Prussians through Genappe to Frasnes is a classic example of what such an operation ought to be. In this respect the battle of Blenheim offers no analogy to the battle of Waterloo. But the circumstances were not analogous. At Waterloo the combined armies of Wellington and Blücher considerably outnumbered the French. It was therefore possible to entrust the chase to troops which had been only partially, or not at all, engaged in the actual combat.

It was not upon the weary and decimated cavalry of Lord Uxbridge that the work devolved. But at Blenheim the allied army, numerically inferior to the French, and already fatigued by long marching, had been under fire for twelve hours, had been closely engaged with the enemy for seven, and had sustained casualties amounting to 23 *per cent*, of its total strength.

Under such conditions every man had been needed in the fighting-line, and no reserve could be retained for the purposes of pursuit. The combatants themselves, and particularly the cavalry, the pursuing arm, were too exhausted to undertake the task.

"I have not a squadron or a battalion which did not charge four times at least,"[1] said Eugène. Moreover it must be remembered that, whereas Napoleon's entire army was nothing but a panic-stricken mob when it fled from Waterloo, the troops of Marsin and the Elector withdrew in excellent order from the positions which they had held throughout the day. They could never have been broken without a determined struggle, the issue of which, in the obscurity of the night, was by no means assured.

Whatever forces could have been brought against them must have been considerably diminished by the necessity of providing a strong detachment to guard the prisoners, who numbered already nearly one-fourth of the unwounded survivors. It must not, therefore, be assumed that Marlborough and Eugène knew less of their business than Wellington and Blücher. They very properly declined to compromise a splendid victory by pushing it too far with inadequate resources. If only the 15,000 men, who were with the Margrave at Ingolstadt, had been present at the battle, not a Frenchman or a Bavarian could have escaped. But if the Margrave had been there as well, the battle would never have been fought.[2]

The soldiers slept upon the ground which they had won. An abundance of vegetables and a hundred fat oxen ready skinned having been discovered in the French camp, they did not lack for immediate refreshment. In a water-mill outside Höchstädt Marlborough, who had been seventeen hours on horseback, allowed himself three for slumber. Daybreak found him once again in the saddle. Accompanied by Eugène, he rode into the town to inspect the magazines which the enemy had abandoned, and which were likely to prove useful to the allied army.

Thence they proceeded to the quarters of Marshal Tallard, whom they found in deep dejection and with a wound in one of his hands. Marlborough showed himself extremely anxious to render his unfortunate captive such services as might be in his power. Tallard having expressed a desire for his own carriage in preference to Marlborough's, which the Duke had offered him, a trumpet was instantly dispatched to the enemy with a passport for the Marshal's coach. Though Marlborough endeavoured to avoid the topic of the battle, Tallard, with a pathetic eagerness to justify himself, insisted on discussing it.

"At this interview," says Hare, "many of the French generals crowded about his Grace, admiring his person as well as his tender and

---

1. A. von Arneth, *Prinz Eugen*, vol. 1, p. 272. 238
2. See *Mémoires de Mérode-Westerloo*, p. 324, ch. 12, and Burnet, vol 4, p. 53.

generous behaviour. Each had something to say for himself, which his Grace and Prince Eugène heard with the greatest modesty and compassion."³

From the day when he first took the field against Burgundy and Boufflers in 1702, Marlborough's reputation for courtesy and humanity had stood high among the armies of France.⁴ The delicacy which he displayed on the morrow of Blenheim, and the thoughtful consideration which he subsequently showed for the numerous prisoners without distinction of rank, enthroned him for ever in the hearts of a nation, very quick to appreciate chivalry in its most redoubtable foemen. Whatever else they may have thought of Marlborough, the people of France regarded him always as "a very perfect gentle knight."⁵

The army now advanced beyond Höchstädt, and encamped at Steinheim over against Lauingen and Dillingen. Marlborough, having traversed the field of battle and viewed the bodies of the slain, came to Steinheim at noon. He immediately occupied Lauingen and Dillingen with detachments, and ordered the bridges over the Danube to be repaired. In this situation he remained for four days and a half, while the army rested and arrangements were made for the proper disposition of the prisoners and the wounded.

The wounded were carried back to Donauwörth and thence to Nördlingen, while the prisoners, having been equally divided between the two commanders, were dispatched by road and river to various fortresses. Those who were assigned to Marlborough's share were envied by their less fortunate comrades, who received from Eugène a treatment that was harsh in comparison. The Duke suggested that Tallard and the general officers, whom he had reserved for himself, should be taken to England; but pending the receipt of instructions from home, he sent them northward on the road to Frankfurt.

The number of captives was increasing hourly, for isolated Frenchmen went in peril of their lives among the peasantry, and freely surrendered to the allied troops to escape assassination. They were a great embarrassment to Marlborough and Eugène, who were likewise hampered by a deficiency of provisions, and of vehicles for the transport of the army's bread. Two hundred wagons however were obtained from Württemberg. The 17th was observed as a day of solemn thanksgiving; and on the 19th the advance was resumed in the direction of Ulm.

---

3. Coxe, vol. 1, p. 211, extract from *Hare's Journal*.
4. See Chapter 4, "1702."
5. See Saint-Simon, vol. 2, p. 255.

The halt at Steinheim has been criticised as a reprehensible waste of time.[6] If two commanders, so enterprising as Marlborough and Eugène, both deemed it inadvisable to attempt a rapid advance, there is a strong presumption that they were right. For they were in contact with the actual circumstances, our knowledge of which is necessarily imperfect. Had the enemy been utilising the respite allowed him in preparing a strong, defensive position on the Iller, the delay would certainly have proved injurious. But the Austrian hussars, who hung upon the rear of the retreating French, cutting off stragglers and keeping touch with the movements of the main body, reported that to all appearances Max Emanuel and Marsin were abandoning Bavaria.

It was known that they had ordered the evacuation of Augsburg on the 17th. That same night they set their columns in motion towards the Black Forest. Though they carried with them no fewer than 7,000 wounded, many of whom died on the way, they marched with such celerity that on the 20th they reached Tuttlingen, where they were joined by the garrisons of Augsburg, Memmingen, and Biberach. Steadily as the troops of the left and centre had quitted the field of battle, contact with the fugitives of the right soon told upon their nerves.

At Ulm, "the whole army," according to an eyewitness, was in "terrible consternation."[7] On leaving the town, the waggons and heavy baggage, including the greater part of the officers' possessions, were deliberately burned that progress might not be delayed. On the road to Tuttlingen a great part of the soldiery got completely out of hand and committed many excesses. The line of march was black with the smouldering ashes of villages and castles. The cruelty of the French was the measure of their terror. At every stage they expected to find that Marlborough and Eugène had outmarched them and cut them off from France. Their horses were dying of disease; the peasantry murdered all laggards; and the Austrian sabre was seldom far behind.

Such a runaway rabble would never have allowed itself to be overtaken in a straight race with a hostile force comprising all three arms. But Mérode-Westerloo, who saw with amazement the depths of demoralisation to which a beaten French army could descend, expressed the view that, if Marlborough and Eugène had pushed forward a strong detachment of dragoons to occupy Moesskirch and to fight a delaying action, a passage would never have been forced. If the main

---

6. See Lediard, vol. 1, p. 447, and Malleson's *Eugène*, p. 113.
7. See a letter printed in Alison, from an officer in the French Army, vol. 1, p. 183.

body of the allies had subsequently appeared, capitulation must in his judgement have ensued.

This opinion is not to be lightly set aside, though its author's unconcealed disgust at the misconduct of the French in the battle and at their indiscipline in the retreat may have somewhat obscured his vision. Others besides Mérode-Westerloo have considered that the allied generals let slip a great opportunity. In so far as this idea was maliciously put forward by the enemies of Marlborough, it may be disregarded. When a general has done so much that the world is astonished, that is a silly sort of detraction which insinuates that, if he had done still more, the world would have been still more astonished.

In so far, however, as this criticism was genuinely advanced by those who understood war, it certainly deserves attention. The verdict must be left to experts. But in judging the inaction of Marlborough and Eugène, the words of Clausewitz in his chapter on those insidious and innumerable forms of "friction," which oblige generals to achieve less than they propose, should not be forgotten.

"Everything," he wrote, "is very simple in war, but the simplest thing is difficult."[8]

It should not be forgotten also that, besides the questions of supply, of transport, of the multitude of prisoners, and of the physical capacity of their own men to undertake the forced marches which would be essential to the success of any grand strategy against the flying enemy, Marlborough and Eugène had no knowledge of the whereabouts of Villeroi. They knew that he had been in the vicinity of Strasbourg. They naturally assumed that he would march to the rescue of the army of Bavaria. And they may well have hesitated to expose exhausted troops to the hazards of an encounter in difficult country with a fresh and unbeaten foe. It was Clausewitz also, who, in dealing with pursuit by parallel march, observed:

> Such marches tell upon the pursuer as well as the pursued, and they are not advisable if the enemy's army rallies itself upon another considerable one.[9]

In point of fact, when the news of Blenheim reached Alsace, Villeroi, who had been demonstrating against the lines of Stollhofen, had wasted no time in sending for orders from Versailles. He had promptly moved towards the sources of the Danube, and on the 23rd he was in

---

8. Clausewitz, *On War*, vol. 1, book 1, ch. 7.
9. *Ibid.*, vol. 1, book 4, ch. 13.

the neighbourhood of Villingen. Marsin and the Elector, not daring to enter the mountains until they were assured of Villeroi's co-operation, left Tuttlingen on the 24th. Communication was established on the 25th. Villeroi's men took over the duty of rearguard; and on the last day of the month the whole body came down to the banks of the Rhine and to the bridge of Strasbourg, where they found safety at last under the cannon of the fortress of Kehl.

Meantime the allied army had reached Söflingen on the outskirts of Ulm on the 21st. In every village that they traversed they saw the new-made graves of French officers. A garrison of four French and five Bavarian battalions had been left in Ulm with the object of delaying pursuit. But pursuit was not contemplated. Louis of Baden in his camp at Ingolstadt had received the news of Blenheim with incredulity, which quickly turned to jealous rage, when he recognised the trick that had been played upon him. Against Marlborough in particular he cherished from this time onward a petty resentment, which became the common talk of Europe, and which had evil consequences for the allied cause. But with the help of Wratislaw he was persuaded to abandon a siege, which had ceased to have any importance, and to rejoin the army at Söflingen, where the arrival of his detachment made good the deficiency resulting from the battles. Concealing his indignation as best he could, he discussed with his colleagues the measures to be taken for improving the victory.

There were officers in Marlborough's army who considered that enough had already been accomplished for one campaign. And there were people at home, including apparently Godolphin, who shared this view. But it was never for a moment entertained by the three commanders. They were all agreed that the allied forces must follow up their success by marching to the Rhine and beyond it. But as to the course of action to be subsequently pursued, there arose a difference of opinion which illustrates well the essential antagonism between the orthodox strategy of that age and such a mind as Marlborough's. Louis of Baden proposed the siege of Landau. The advantages of the operation were obvious.

This fortress, which had been wrested from the French in 1702, and recovered by them in 1703, was a nuisance in winter and a menace in summer to Southern Germany. Its capture, by enabling a large part of the allied forces to take their quarters beyond the Rhine, would relieve the governments of the neighbouring states of considerable expense. But in Marlborough's opinion the opportunity created by the known demoralisation of the enemy could be utilised far better on the Moselle. Now was the time to secure that river from Coblenz to Trèves, and even beyond Trèves.

If by the end of the campaign the allies were firmly established in the valley of the Moselle, in the ensuing spring they could begin that great offensive movement upon Paris, which, as Marlborough believed, would assuredly end the war. In comparison with this design the siege of Landau was mere pettifogging. But the Germans were set upon the capture of the place; and Marlborough suspected that, as long as it remained in the enemy's hands, they would never follow him across the French frontier. Nobody ever understood better than he that the art of war consists, as Moltke said, in "adapting the means at hand to the attainment of the object in view." He yielded therefore to the representations of the Margrave; but he did so in the reasonable expectation that a fortress, which had just endured two sieges in as many years, would quickly fall, and that he would still have time to establish a footing on the Moselle before the termination of the campaign.

The future of Bavaria was now engaging the attention of the allied generals and their governments. Marlborough and Eugène had already proposed to the Elector that, if he would furnish 8,000 men to the common cause, he should be restored to his dominions and should receive an annual allowance of 400,000 crowns from England and Holland. But Max Emanuel's notions of honour forbade him to desert the fortune of France in the hour of calamity. The lamentable situation of the Electress and her children appealed strongly to the chivalry of Marlborough.

"It has made my heart ache," he wrote to the Duchess, "being very sensible how cruel it is to be separated from what one loves."[10]

He showed his sympathy by facilitating correspondence between the husband and wife, and by exerting his influence to promote such a treaty with the Electress as would secure to her an adequate revenue and the liberty to reside at Munich. But her own pride and the resentment of the Emperor were formidable obstacles to an accommodation.

On August 26 the army began to move in four columns and by separate routes. The rendezvous was Philippsburg. Under the com-

---

10. Coxe, vol. 1, p. 217: The Duke to the Duchess, August 21, 1704.

mand of Churchill the English infantry and artillery returned by the way they had come, over the Rems and through Gross Heppach to Mundelsheim. What manner of reception they got from the friends they had made in those fair villages of Württemberg two months before, it is easy to imagine. The horse remained at Söflingen with Marlborough, who was expecting a definite communication from the Electress. But after a delay of three days, the Duke entrusted the conduct of the negotiations to Wratislaw, and taking a circuitous road to the right, rejoined Churchill at Mundelsheim. General Thungen, with twenty-three battalions and fifteen squadrons, was left behind to form the siege of Ulm.

On September 1 on the invitation of the Duke of Württemberg, Marlborough and several of his officers proceeded to Stuttgart, where they were magnificently entertained. On the 2nd he passed the Neckar at Lauffen. On the 5th he encamped within easy distance of Philippsburg, where Eugène had already arrived. That afternoon the two commanders crossed the Rhine to reconnoitre. Villeroi lay behind the River Queich; but he showed his cavalry beyond it. Fearful lest the French should forestall them, Marlborough and Eugène threw a detachment over the Rhine on the morning of the 6th, and occupied the strong position of Speyerbach. The rest of the army followed on the same, and the ensuing, day. By the 8th, when the Margrave arrived with the Imperialist horse, the concentration was complete.

Villeroi and Marsin, who were supposed to be preventing the siege of Landau, made no attempt to oppose the passage of the Rhine. For some days they had been entrenching themselves upon the southern bank of the Queich, and constructing palisades across the fords. But they could not impose upon the victors of the Schellenberg and Blenheim. The situation now was governed, not by maxims, but by realities. The moral factor was now omnipotent.

One army was convinced that it could not lose, and the other that it could not win. When, therefore, on the 9th, the allies advanced against the French position, Villeroi commanded an immediate retreat. The movement was executed with such alacrity that it could hardly be distinguished from a rout. The allies passed the river, and occupied the French lines, while Villeroi halted at Langencandel, which, according to Marlborough, had been "in all times famous for being a strong post, it being covered with thick woods and marshy grounds."[11]

---

11. Coxe, vol. 1., p. 220: Marlborough to Godolphin, September 12, 1704.

All night the French lay on their arms; but no sooner were they apprised, on the morning of the 10th, of the continued advance of the allies, than they resumed their disorderly retreat. That day they passed the Lauter, and subsequently they retired as far southward as Hagenau and the line of the Motter. This precipitate flight from approved positions of defence was the highest compliment that could be paid to Marlborough and Eugène and the troops under their command. As Marlborough himself said, "if they had not been the most frightened people in the world, they would never have quitted these two posts."[12]

The siege of Landau was entrusted to the Margrave. It was covered by the forces of Marlborough and Eugène, which encamped at Cron-Weissenburg. Unfortunately the defences of the place proved to be far stronger than had been anticipated, while the Imperialist troops were found very deficient in all the necessaries of a besieging army. Marlborough exerted himself to supply what was needed; in particular, he ordered up the Hessian cannon from Mannheim, and he improved communications across the Rhine by the occupation of Lauterburg.

The fall of Ulm, which occurred on the 11th, not only released Thungen's detachment, but also provided the allies with a valuable store of munitions and artillery, discovered in that fortress. The trenches were opened on the 16th, but the operation was attended with considerable loss. From the very outset the garrison showed itself to be exceptionally vigilant and active. The commander, Laubanie, understood the greatness of his opportunity. Winter was approaching; and every day that the victors of Blenheim could be detained before Landau was a day gained for France.

On the 21st, the Emperor's heir, the King of the Romans, who was an enthusiastic admirer of the Duke of Marlborough, arrived in the Margrave's camp, and assumed the nominal command of the siege. Here he was visited by Marlborough and Eugène. On October 2 he honoured them with his company at Cron-Weissenburg, where he reviewed the covering army and dined with the Duke. The Emperor was at this time writing to Marlborough under the title of "Prince of the Holy Roman Empire."

In the eyes of the grateful monarch this dignity, which had been proffered even before the Schellenberg, seemed after Blenheim to be greatly overdue. Anne's consent had now been obtained. But the Duke represented to Wratislaw that, until the Emperor assigned him

---

12. *Ibid.*

an imperial fief and formally gave notice of the new creation to the other princes, he would prefer that the matter should continue in abeyance.

Ever since the battle of Blenheim the state of the Duke's health had caused some anxiety to his friends. Fever, induced by bodily fatigue and mental strain, had rendered him so weak that amid the autumnal damps of the Rhine valley he fell an easy victim to a severe attack of ague.

"Your care," he wrote to the Duchess, "must nurse me this winter, or I shall certainly be in a consumption."[13]

And to Godolphin he declared,

"You will find me ten years older than when I left England."[14]

But no solicitations could induce him to quit the army. The situation at Landau was far from satisfactory. Though Villeroi made no attempt to intervene, operations were obstructed by continual rain and by the ingenuity of the garrison. To Marlborough, impatient as he was to seize the line of the Moselle before the French could recover from their present panic, the delay was exasperating, especially as it was in part attributable to the mistakes of the besiegers.

"Our people," he wrote to Harley on October 6, "are advancing by the sap, in order to make a lodgment on the counterscarp. This method may save a few men, but will cost the more time, and it may be a great many more men in the end by sickness."[15]

Unlike so many inferior commanders in all ages, Marlborough never forgot that in war the swiftest way is usually the most humane.

But neither vexation of spirit, nor bodily infirmity, nor the remonstrances of those he loved, could turn him from his project. Whether Landau fell or not, he was resolved that, before the campaign closed, the Moselle from Coblenz to Trèves should be in the possession of the allies. In a sense the project was greatly favoured by the siege of Landau. For the French assumed that, until one important operation had been terminated, another would not be commenced, and that in any event the numbers at the disposal of the allies were insufficient for the conduct of two such undertakings at the same time. But this very campaign had already demonstrated in striking fashion that the gen-

---

13. Coxe, vol. 1, p. 226: The Duke to the Duchess, October 10, 1704.
14. *Ibid.*, p. 225: Marlborough to Godolphin, August 23, 1704.
15. Murray, vol. 1, p. 497: Marlborough to Harley, October 6, 1704.

erals who make the most assumptions are those who suffer the most surprises. Marlborough, whose intelligence department was usually very efficient, was aware that the enemy regarded the siege of Landau as the concluding act of the campaign.

He decided therefore to leave Eugène at Weissenburg, and with a small detachment to make a rapid dash on Trèves, which was a place incapable of serious defence. If Trèves were taken, the fortress of Trarbach, which dominated the Moselle between that city and Coblenz, would then be isolated; and with the co-operation of the Dutch government and the German princes, it could be besieged in form. Having arranged that twelve battalions of Overkirk's infantry should march towards Trarbach, while the Elector Palatine, the Elector of Trèves, and the Landgrave of Hesse were to push forward artillery and supplies in the same direction, Marlborough occupied Homburg on the 13th with a small force.

On the 19th, he dispatched fourteen guns, four howitzers, and three battalions to the same place. Twenty-two battalions followed on the 20th, and forty-eight squadrons on the 21st. He himself arrived on the 24th. On the ensuing day he set off for Trèves. The country was rough and barren; but he marched with speed, for his little army numbered no more than 12,000, and rumours were reaching him that the French had divined his object and had dispatched considerable detachments from Hagenau and Flanders to anticipate him on the Moselle.

In reality, his movements had perplexed Marsin, who was at first inclined to think that the allied troops were setting off for their winter-quarters. Not until the 26th, when the truth was known, did the Marshal order a detachment to take the road to Metz. Marlborough had nobody to fear save the Marquis d'Alègre, who had quitted Flanders to organise a force (at Consaarbriick) for the protection of the frontier. But d'Alègre was no better informed than Marsin. After traversing what he described as "the terriblest country that can be imagined for the march of an army with cannon,"[16] the Duke arrived at St. Wendel on the 26th.

Fortunately the weather was fine; otherwise the ways would have been impassable for guns and baggage. Disquieting stories of the enemy's movements continued to come through. Although he was hopeful of capturing Trèves before the French could effectually intervene, he was fearful lest they might destroy the city and leave him only the

---

16. Coxe, vol. 1, p. 228: Marlborough to Godolphin, October 26, 1704.

ashes. His letters from St. Wendel reveal his anxiety.

"I should be very unwilling to be beaten at the end of this campaign,"[17] he confessed to Godolphin.

And to the Duchess he wrote:

"This march and my own spleen have given me occasion to think how very unaccountable a creature man is, to be seeking for honour in so barren a country as this, when he is very sure that the greater part of mankind, and may justly fear, that even his best friends, would be apt to think ill of him should he have ill success."[18]

But he still went manfully forward. On the 28th he came to Hemerskeil within six leagues of Trèves. That was a night of terror in the ancient and famous city. Three hundred of King Louis' soldiers garrisoned the fort of St. Martin; and notwithstanding the politic tears which the French had so recently shed over the sufferings of Bavaria, it was very well known that "the barbarous method which they had long practised" was "to burn the places they forsook."[19] The citizens dispatched three deputies to Marlborough's camp to represent to the English general the horror of their situation. Before daylight the Duke was in the saddle. Accompanied by all his cavalry and dragoons and followed by four battalions of infantry, he took the road to Trèves.

By 11 the anxious watchers in the town espied his vanguard. Thereupon the French abandoned the fort, flung their ammunition and stores into the Moselle, and retreated precipitately across that river, burning the bridges behind them. Quick as they were, the Duke's dragoons were quicker, and captured some prisoners and baggage. Marlborough had won, but by a very narrow margin. That same day d'Alègre appeared at the head of a body of 500 horse within two leagues of Trèves. He was supported by a little army of 5,000 men; but on learning that the Duke had already arrived, he promptly retired.

Having billeted his infantry in Trèves and the neighbouring villages, Marlborough collected 6,000 peasants and set them to work on the defences of the city. His cavalry encamped in a strong situation on the Saar, where they protected the whole country against possible raids from Thionville, Metz, and Saarlouis. Saarlouis was a post which the Duke had designed to secure before the conclusion of the cam-

---

17. *Ibid.*
18. *Ibid.*, p. 229: The Duke to the Duchess, October 26, 1704.
19. Burnet, vol. 4, p. 54.

paign; but the forces at his disposal were inadequate to the task, and the prolongation of the siege of Landau destroyed all hope of adding to their numbers.

The rocky fortress of Trarbach had still to be reduced. On November 1, having arranged the distribution of the troops in their winter-quarters, Marlborough set off with 300 horse over the mountains to Berncastel, which he reached on the 3rd. All was going well. Overkirk's detachment had already arrived, and the siege-train was coming up the river from Coblenz. He therefore entrusted the conduct of the siege to the Prince of Hesse-Cassel, and departed on the 4th for Landau, where he was disappointed to find that the resources of the defence were not by any means exhausted.

But some consolation awaited him. His intervention in the business of Bavaria had borne good fruit. On November 10 a treaty was concluded by the King of the Romans and the Bavarian representatives, whereby the Electress undertook to disband her husband's army, to surrender his fortresses, and to restore his conquests. In return she was permitted to reside at Munich, to receive a sufficient revenue, and to maintain a personal guard of 400 men. The country was placed under an Austrian administration.

Neither at this time, nor at any other, could Marlborough devote his undivided attention to his own command. Knowing that whatever was done in one theatre reacted sooner or later on the operations in every other, he always regarded the immense contest as an organic whole. His own marches, battles, and sieges never absorbed so much of his energy that he had none to bestow on the problems arising out of the higher strategy of the war. Indeed, the more his outstanding genius came to be acknowledged, the more he grew to be regarded as strategist-in-chief to the Grand Alliance.

At the present moment the infirmity of the Empire was his main concern. Though Blenheim had saved the power of Austria from the destruction which threatened it from the first day that Villars crossed the Rhine, the Hungarian rebellion, like a chronic ulcer, continued still to drain those resources which ought to have been concentrated against the might of France. Blenheim indeed had done more harm than good to the cause of domestic peace. For while the rebels appeared to be very little depressed by the collapse of their French and Bavarian allies, the Emperor and his ministers, relieved from pressing danger, exhibited no genuine inclination to come to terms.

Both sides had accepted the mediation of the Dutch and English governments, which had instructed their envoys to promote a settlement. Marlborough had long been exerting himself to the same end. The task was both difficult and delicate. Questions of civil and religious liberty being involved, the English Whigs and Nonconformists loudly proclaimed their sympathy with a movement which menaced the very existence of England's ally, and which notoriously flourished on the pay of England's foe. This characteristic indiscretion by no means strengthened the Duke's hands. But the Austrian government gave him a respectful ear, thanks entirely to his personal prestige at the Court of Vienna and to the obvious sincerity of his efforts, inspired as they were by a single-minded anxiety for the interests of the coalition and not by any pretension to impose the principles of the "Glorious Revolution" on a foreign state.

Before the battle of the Schellenberg he had spoken his mind very freely to Wratislaw on this subject. He was in constant communication with the English ambassador, Stepney, in regard to it. At Weissenburg he took advantage of the presence of the King of the Romans and Eugène to urge his views in quarters where they were always assured of a friendly reception. And he even summoned Stepney from Vienna to assist at the deliberations. But his labour was in vain. The demands of the malcontents were pitched too high, and the interests arrayed against the policy of compromise proved to be too powerful. Late in October, to the delight of the French and to the great detriment of Europe, the negotiations ended in hopeless failure.

Marlborough was constrained to resign himself to the indefinite continuance of this wasteful conflict. Already it was responsible for that lack of money and material which had hampered the siege of Landau, while in Italy it had paralysed the forces of the coalition throughout the summer. In Italy, indeed, the French had easily recovered the whole of Eugène's conquests except Mirandola; and though the Duke of Savoy stood firm, he was greatly overmatched by Vendôme, who captured Vercelli and Ivrea, laid siege to Verrua, and threatened Turin itself. Early in October an envoy from Victor Amadeus arrived at Weissenburg to solicit the assistance of Marlborough and Eugène.

"We expect salvation from no side but from your Grace," wrote Hill, the British agent at Turin, "but from thence we do expect it."[20]

The English commander was profoundly conscious of the strategi-

---

20. Coxe, vol. 1, p. 242.

cal importance of the territories of Savoy, which constituted the very gates of Italy. But he was at his wits' end to provide a remedy. The only power which appeared capable of making the necessary effort was Prussia. Marlborough accordingly suggested to his government that he should go in person to Berlin to solicit succour for Savoy. Anne and Godolphin, who desired his presence in England, disliked the proposal; Sarah, who knew how uncertain was the state of his health, discouraged it; and the Duke himself, who sorely needed repose, hated the idea of a long and tedious journey in November. Moreover, the prospects of success seemed none too bright. But the public interest prevailed; and on October 16 he wrote to the King of Prussia to announce his intention of visiting Berlin.

In Portugal the expectations founded on the advent of the Austrian claimant had not been realised. The King of Portugal was an invalid. His generals were incompetent, his fortresses decayed, his magazines empty. His army was a destitute, licentious, and cowardly rabble. Schomberg, who commanded the English contingent, had not inherited his father's virtues. Deficient in energy as well as in tact, he preferred the amusements of Lisbon to the care of his soldiers, while he quarrelled with Fagel, the general of the Dutch, at the outset of the campaign. In these circumstances Berwick, who commanded on the Spanish frontier, had an easy task. The allies, who, like the French in 1870, had intended to invade, were themselves confronted with invasion.

Their forces, which were dispersed when they ought to have been concentrated, suffered defeat in detail; and several of their places were taken. Fortunately for them the intense heat and the mortality among his horses compelled Berwick to withdraw from Portugal on July 1. Schomberg, at his own request, was recalled. The campaign in itself had been discreditable. But considered as a diversion, it was not unpromising. England and Holland had detached a force of 10,000 men to this new scene of operations; but 12,000 French, 23,000 Spaniards, and one of the best generals in Louis' service had been withheld from Italy, Germany, and Flanders. Before nominating a successor to Schomberg, the government consulted Marlborough, who recommended his old friend and companion-in-arms Rouvigny, Earl of Galway, the hero of Aghrim.

The brilliant success of his Mediterranean strategy consoled Marlborough for all other disappointments. On May 8 Rooke sailed from Lisbon with the combined fleets of England and Holland. Hesse-

Darmstadt and 2,300 marines accompanied him. Their orders were to pass the Straits, and proceed to the assistance of the Duke of Savoy, whose coast towns of Nizza and Villafranca were supposed to be besieged by the French. Off Barcelona, where Charles had many partisans, they made a demonstration; and Darmstadt went ashore with 1,600 marines. But the governor arrested the principal malcontents, and prepared for a vigorous defence. Having thrown a few bombs into the place, the fleet continued its voyage.

Its appearance in the Gulf of Lyons excited the hopes of the Camisards, and alarmed Villars, who was engaged in pacifying the disturbed area. On June 4 the news arrived from Lisbon that Nizza and Villafranca were not besieged, but that the Brest fleet under Toulouse and d'Estrées was making for Toulon, and had already passed the Tagus. Thereupon Rooke started for Lisbon, where he hoped to find Shovel with a squadron from England. On the 7th he sighted the Frenchmen and gave chase, but without avail. Knowing that the combined fleets of Brest and Toulon would be too strong for him, he returned to Lisbon, where he found Shovel.

Methuen now sent him reiterated instructions to surprise Cadiz; but Rooke, whose caution was as great as his courage, refused to make the attempt without the aid of an army, and remained cruising near the Straits. Darmstadt suggested an attack on Gibraltar. Rooke concurred. On July 31 he sailed into the Bay. Darmstadt landed with the marines; Byng cannonaded the fortress from the sea; and the sailors gallantly stormed the New Mole Fort. On August 6 the garrison marched out, and Darmstadt took possession of the Rock in the name of Charles III.

The enormous importance of this acquisition was by no means realised in England, where public opinion had not sensibly advanced since the evil day when it forced Charles II to abandon Tangier. But Marlborough's mature judgement, confirming the impressions of his early youth, told him plainly that without a secure base on the Mediterranean England's naval strength could never be properly applied in those waters. And of all possible bases none had a strategical value so high as Gibraltar. For whoever holds the Rock severs both the French and Spanish sea-power into halves.

In Paris and Madrid this truth was understood; and the extreme anxiety of both the Bourbon governments to recover the lost position first drove into the minds of Englishmen some comprehension of its worth in war. No sooner had Darmstadt occupied the fortress than the enemy began to move both by land and sea. The bulk of the Spanish troops in Berwick's army prepared to march towards the Straits, while Toulouse and d'Estrées descended upon Rooke.

Off Malaga, on August 24, the navies met in an obstinate and bloody grapple. The French had more ships, cleaner bottoms, and a better stock of ammunition. All day the fight continued; but on the morrow, when Rooke offered to renew it, the enemy made for Toulon. Though their casualties were heavier than those of the allies, Malaga was little better than a drawn battle. And yet, in a sense, it was decisive.

"From that day until the end of the war," says Clowes, "the French never again allowed their grand fleet to risk a general engagement."[21]

Henceforward they conceded to England and Holland the command of the sea, and devoted their energies to the fitting out of single ships and small squadrons which preyed upon the commerce of the maritime powers.

Moreover, the immediate strategical advantage rested with Rooke. Had he been beaten, Gibraltar would have been shut up by sea as well as by land. The Spaniards were already blockading it by land; but on the 30th Rooke anchored once more in the Bay and began to furnish the garrison with all things needful for the defence. Provisions for three months, sixty heavy cannon, gunners, marines, carpenters, and bomb vessels having all been supplied by the allied squadrons, Rooke set sail for England on September 21. Sir John Leake with sixteen ships of the line remained at Lisbon for the winter.

The siege of Gibraltar began almost immediately. The Spanish troops were arriving daily, and on October 4 a French squadron under Pointis sailed in from Toulon, and landed 4,000 men with guns and stores. On October 21 the trenches were opened. Darmstadt had improved the fortifications of the place, and his garrison numbered 2,500, mostly English. But it was evident now that Gibraltar could not be held without a great expenditure of men and money. The task ought properly to have been undertaken by Charles III and the King of Portugal. But the Queen's government foresaw that the burden would in fact devolve upon England, and before deciding to add to their responsibilities the maintenance of what the majority of Englishmen regarded as a barren and unprofitable cliff, they consulted Marlborough.

---

21. Clowes, *Royal Navy*, vol. 2, p. 404.

His reply, written from Berncastel on November 3, was unequivocal. The place must be relieved by sea, and "no cost ought to be spared to maintain it."²²

The soundness of this opinion was endorsed by the obvious embarrassment of the enemy in the Peninsula, where the departure of 8,000 Spaniards for Gibraltar left Berwick so weak that the allies in Portugal ventured to pass the frontier and advance against Ciudad Rodrigo. Berwick took up a strong position on the Agueda, and obliged them to go back, But he himself was recalled, because he wisely had refused at this critical moment to detach French troops from the army on the frontier to the siege of Gibraltar.

Marlborough, on his return from the Moselle, did not stay long at Weissenburg. Having arranged the winter-quarters for his army, he went to Landau, where he made a last appeal to the King of the Romans and the Austrian ministers on behalf of the Duke of Savoy. "They gave me," he said, "fair promises."²³ On the 14th he started for Berlin. He slept that night at Heidelberg, where he had a long conference with the Elector Palatine. Next day he came to Frankfurt.

At every stage he was greeted "with extraordinary marks of respect."²⁴ Passing by Cassel and Brandenburg, he reached Berlin on the 22nd. The British ambassador, Lord Raby, and the high officials of the Court of Prussia met him outside the gates. The same evening he was received by the King of Prussia "with great kindness."²⁵ He was nobly lodged and splendidly entertained. The royal family and the representatives of foreign states combined to do him honour. Dinners, suppers, balls, and even "a combat of wild beasts"²⁶ were organised for his diversion.

"The King of Prussia," he wrote to the Duchess, "did me all the honour he could."²⁷

But the Duke made it clear to his courteous hosts that he was come to Berlin for business. In several interviews with the King and the ministers he exposed his project for the succour of Savoy, and discussed the difficulties in the way of its realisation. Frederick, whose aim was always to exalt the prestige of the new monarchy of Prussia, had been very gratified by the eulogies universally bestowed on that

---

22. Murray, vol. 1, p. 526: Marlborough to Sir Charles Hedges, November 3, 1704.
23. *Ibid.*, p. 538: Marlborough to Harley, November 13, 1704.
24. Lediard, vol. 1, p. 463.
25. Coxe, vol. 1, p. 244.
26. Lediard, p. 463.

steadfast infantry, which had served Eugène so loyally on the day of Blenheim. It flattered his pride that the illustrious Englishman, who had just saved the empire, should travel in person to his Court to solicit a fresh contingent of his fighting-men.

Above all, it was a triumph for his policy that the coalised powers, not excluding the haughty and jealous House of Hapsburg itself, should turn in their necessity to a kingdom that was only four years old. Marlborough understood the situation to a nicety, and played his part to perfection. Frederick was entirely captivated.

But Prussian statesmen were naturally afraid lest their country, denuded of its choicest troops, should tempt the ambition of Charles XII, who had already humiliated Denmark, Russia, and Poland. At this very time a Polish envoy was seeking the assistance of Frederick against the Swedish invader, and he even addressed himself to Marlborough with a request for the intervention of England. Marlborough replied that he had no instructions, but that the Queen was very desirous that peace should be kept in the North. England, indeed, and all the members of the coalition against France were directly concerned in isolating this quarrel.

Marlborough readily met the Prussian ministers with an undertaking on behalf of Anne that she would use her best endeavours to pacify the North; and he announced that England, Holland, and the Empire were prepared to guarantee by treaty the integrity of Prussian soil. Satisfied on this vital point, Frederick came speedily to terms. Eight thousand men should be dispatched to Italy, if England would pay two- thirds of their upkeep, and Holland one-third, and if the Emperor would furnish them with bread. An agreement on these lines was quickly framed.

In certain details Marlborough exceeded somewhat the instructions he had received from Vienna; but his influence at that Court sufficiently protected him. He also seized the opportunity of arranging a dispute which had arisen between the King of Prussia and the Dutch in regard to the estate of the late King of England. These services to the common cause he performed in a manner very pleasing to Frederick, who, though he was never famous for liberality, presented the Duke on his departure with "a hat, with a diamond button and loop, and a diamond hat-band, valued at between twenty and thirty thousand crowns, and two fine saddle horses with rich furniture, besides

---

27. Coxe, vol. 1, p. 246: The Duke to the Duchess, December 2, 1704.

other rich presents."²⁸ To M. Cardonnel and the rest of the Duke's suite the King was proportionately generous.

Marlborough quitted Berlin on the 29th, and travelling in the company of the Crown Prince of Prussia, came on December 2 to Hanover, where the reigning family received him as the greatest of their future subjects. "I have so much respect shown me here that I have hardly time to write,"²⁹ he told the Duchess.

At Hanover he learned that Landau had fallen on the 26th of the preceding month. Resuming his journey on the 5th, he turned aside by express invitation to visit Amsterdam, where a magnificent reception awaited him. On the 12th he arrived at the Hague. The capital accorded him a fitting welcome. He was publicly thanked by the States-General; and private citizens, no less than the populace at large, took every occasion of displaying their gratitude and joy. Marlborough held many interviews with the principal persons in the government and the state.

The result of his negotiations at Berlin gave universal satisfaction. But the Emperor's treatment of the Hungarian question was freely censured. Knowing how deeply the sensitive Austrians resented Republican and Whig criticism of their domestic affairs, Marlborough laboured to persuade the Dutch that the government of Vienna was entirely sincere in its policy of pacification. He laboured also to convince them of the decisive advantages that might be expected from a vigorous offensive movement on the Moselle in the ensuing spring.

Those who in the past resisted the departure of Dutch troops from the Netherlands, had now been silenced by the logic of recent events. During Marlborough's absence in Germany nothing terrible had happened at home. On the contrary, the French magazines at Namur and Bruges had been partially destroyed by bombardment, while the French army had remained quietly within its lines, which Overkirk had threatened at various points.

Consequently Marlborough experienced no difficulty in procuring the adoption of his plan. It depended largely for success upon the prompt formation of adequate magazines on the Meuse, the Rhine, and the Moselle. The Dutch government embarked upon this work with energy and zeal. Their activities were sensibly quickened by a pledge from Marlborough that Holland should be reimbursed her extraordinary expenses out of the first requisitions levied upon French

---

28. Lediard, vol. 1, p. 464.
29. Coxe, vol. 1 p. 246: The Duke to the Duchess, December 2, 1704.

soil.

All this time the Duke had never ceased to urge upon the Emperor and the German princes the necessity of thorough and rapid preparation for the invasion of France. From the Hague, moreover, he wrote to both Harley and St. John, deploring the fact that "nothing has been offered yet, nor any care taken by the Parliament, for recruiting the army."[30] He was resolved that the breathing-space, which he was compelled by the military system of that age to allow to the enemy, should be as brief as possible.

"An early campaign "he declared to be absolutely essential. "Without it," he said, "we may run the hazard of losing in a great measure the fruits of the last."[31] He had a right to command the exertions of others, for he never spared himself. No detail was too trivial for his personal supervision. To his advice every minister resorted; to his arbitrament every disputant bowed. Very characteristic was his answer to Harley, who had consulted him on a proposal to purchase horses at Hamburg for the British cavalry.

"I should not think it for the Queen's service," he wrote, "having always been of opinion that English horses, as well as Englishmen, are better than what can be had anywhere else."[32]

Doubtless these Hamburg chargers were a little cheaper than the homebred kind. And they cost nothing for shipping. But in Marlborough's day the gospel of cheapness had not been fully revealed. Moreover, it is evident that, if, in his fifty-fifth year, with all his accumulated experience of diplomacy and war, Marlborough could present these old-fashioned notions in the form of considered advice to a minister of the Crown, he was still as impenitent a 'jingo' as when at Beaumont, in 1691, he had suggested to the Count de Dohna that English soldiers were invincible.

During his journey to Berlin the situation of the allied forces, newly established on the Moselle, had caused the Duke some uneasiness. But the enemy was too weak and too depressed to attempt a raid from Thionville or Metz. On December 20 Trarbach surrendered after a prolonged defence. From Utrecht to Trèves a clear passage by water was now open to the commissariat and siege-train of the invading army.

---

30. Murray, vol. 1, p. 556: Marlborough to Harley, December 16, 1704.
31. *Ibid.*
32. *Ibid.*, p. 344: Marlborough to Harley, November 25, 1704..

Thus terminated one of the most remarkable campaigns in all history. In a few months Marlborough had destroyed the prestige which France had enjoyed for forty years. This is not the place in which to attempt an analysis of the genius by which he accomplished such a result. But it is necessary here to note one fact. The idea of transferring an army from Flanders to Bavaria, though it passed for a bold one in that epoch, was not, of itself, an evidence of extraordinary powers. The execution of it was all in all. And in the execution of it Marlborough showed that one of the greatest of his resources was the surprise, both strate- gical and tactical. He surprised the enemy, when, instead of marching up the Moselle from Coblenz, he took the road to Mainz.

He surprised them again when, after crossing the Neckar, he made for Bavaria instead of for Alsace. He surprised them a third time when he assaulted the Schellenberg. He surprised them a fourth time when he countered the arrival of Tallard by a juncture with Eugène. He surprised them fifthly when he gave battle at Blenheim, and sixthly when he selected the least accessible portion of their line for his decisive stroke. And seventhly he surprised them, when in the middle of the siege of Landau he made his dash upon Trèves and Trarbach.

On the 22nd Marlborough embarked for England. Tallard and twenty-six French officers of high rank accompanied him. He landed at London Bridge on the 25th. The Duchess, who had gone as far as the Tower to meet him, joined him at the "Old Swan" in Bishopsgate; and together the triumphant lover and the mistress who, on this occasion at any rate, was surely kind, proceeded to Whitehall. The Queen and Prince George received him at St. James's. On the following day he took his seat in the Upper House, which complimented and thanked him in a very laudatory address. His reply was short, but remarkable:

> I am extremely sensible of the great honour your lordships are pleased to do me; I must beg, on this occasion, to do right to all the officers and soldiers I had the honour of having under my command; next to the blessing of God, the good success of this campaign is owing to their extraordinary courage. I am very sure, it will be a great satisfaction, as well as encouragement to the whole army, to find their services so favourably accepted.[33]

The British soldier of the period was frequently a criminal; he was commonly regarded as a blackguard. But when in his foreign

---

33. Lediard, vol. 1, p. 470.

quarters at Breda or his favourite pot-house at Westminster he heard some scholarly comrade read out the words which this beautiful and gracious personage, the darling of the proudest courts of Europe, had used of him and his kind in the presence of the Peers of England, he rose superior to himself and to the opinion of society. These men had not the gift of tongues. But they could think and feel; and for seven years they registered their gratitude in deeds, the like of which are only done for generals who possess the key to the self-respect and pride of simple hearts.

A committee of the House of Commons having waited on the Duke with an address of congratulation and thanks, to them also he replied in a similar strain.

> "I beg leave," he said, "to take this opportunity of doing justice to a great body of officers and soldiers, who accompanied me in this expedition, and all behaved themselves with the greatest bravery imaginable."[34]

For two nights Tallard and his comrades remained unheeded in their ship upon the Thames. It was considered politic to offer this deliberate affront to the Marshal, because in the course of certain negotiations he had declined to recognise the Queen's title. The prisoners were subsequently conveyed by Churchill to Nottingham and Lichfield, where they took up their residence under generous conditions of liberty and comfort. On January 3 the thirty-eight standards and one hundred and twenty-eight colours, which represented Marlborough's share of the trophies of Blenheim, and which had been deposited in the Tower, were borne amid every circumstance of military pomp and popular enthusiasm to Westminster Hall.

On the 17th Marlborough himself received a wonderful ovation when, followed by a numerous company of distinguished guests, he rode in state to the City to dine with the Lord Mayor and the Court of Aldermen. But national gratitude was now to assume a more enduring form. By a unanimous vote the House of Commons resolved to address the Queen in favour of "some proper means to perpetuate the memory of the great services performed" by the Duke. Anne was delighted. A few days later she informed the Commons that she proposed "to grant the interest of the Crown in the Honour and Manor of Woodstock, and Hundred of Wootton to him and to his heirs";[35]

---

34. *Ibid.*, p. 471.
35. *Ibid.*, p. 474

and she requested the assistance of the House in clearing the property of all incumbrances.

The transaction was completed by Act of Parliament, "cheerfully and unanimously,"[36] as the preamble declared. The sole condition attached to the tenure was that of "rendering to the Queen, her heirs, and successors, on the second day of August, in every year, for ever, at the Castle of Windsor, one standard or colours, with three Flower de Luces painted thereon."[37]

But Anne herself went farther. The ancient palace of Woodstock, associated with memories of Rosamund, of Chaucer, and of Elizabeth was now no more. The Queen commanded that a new palace should be erected by the Board of Works at the royal expense. She desired that it be called Blenheim after the English distortion of the name of the little village on the Danube, which Marlborough had immortalised. Vanbrugh was appointed architect, and was instructed to submit a model of his design for Her Majesty's approval.

That the nation as a whole endorsed the policy of the war was palpable enough. But the voice of discord was by no means silenced. When Marlborough was marching to the Danube, Rochester and Seymour had threatened him with impeachment. In their capacity as military critics they had denounced the battle of the Schellenberg as a bloody and unprofitable holocaust. Stricken temporarily dumb by the news of Blenheim, they and their like speedily contrived to make themselves ridiculous by disparaging a victory which astonished all Europe. They sagaciously observed that "to the French king" the loss of 40,000 soldiers was "no more than to take a bucket of water out of a river."[38]

The malicious drivelling of this vindictive group was keenly resented by the Duke. "If," he remarked, "they will allow us to draw one or two such buckets more, I should think we might then let the river run quietly, and not much apprehend its overflowing and destroying its neighbours."[39] When Parliament met, the handiwork of these malcontents was exhibited in the Commons' address to the Queen, which eulogised Blenheim and Malaga in identical terms. This device was too puerile to affect public opinion. But it effectually advertised the silliness of its authors, and it ruined the career of the Tory admiral,

---

36. *Ibid.*, p. 478.
37. *Ibid.*
38. Coxe, vol. 1, p. 234: Mrs. Burnett to the Duchess, September 9, 1702.
39. *Ibid.*: The Duke to the Duchess, September 2, 1704.

Rooke.

The necessary supplies for the war were unanimously voted, and the Government were hopeful that the question of Occasional Conformity would not be raised. But under the terms of the Triennial Act a general election was now imminent. If the Tories had abandoned a measure so ardently desired by the mass of the parochial clergy, they would never have dared to face their constituents. For a third time, therefore, the bill was introduced. It was certain to pass the Lower House, and equally certain to be rejected in the Upper. To circumvent the opposition of the peers, the promoters decided in secret conclave to adopt the unconstitutional dodge of "tacking." The bill was to be combined with the bill for the land-tax, the rejection of which would render the prosecution of the war impossible.

But the Lords could not accept it in this form without forfeiting their place in the constitution; and the power of amending money-bills did not reside in them. A disagreeable dilemma would result. Harley himself, it is alleged, insidiously recommended this unpatriotic plan. Nothing could have better served the ministry to which he belonged: "the Tackers" played straight into Godolphin's hand. Marlborough, who had concluded his treaty with Prussia on the credit of the land-tax, was furious. The Tory soldier, Cutts, the Tory Secretary of State, Hedges, and the Tory Chancellor of the Exchequer, Boyle, denounced the proposal in the House. It meant, they protested, the ruin of Savoy and the disgrace of England in the eyes of all Europe.

More than a hundred Tories voted against "the tack," which was defeated by 251 to 134. The bill itself was subsequently passed by the Commons, and rejected by the Lords at the end of December by a majority of twenty-one, Marlborough and Godolphin both voting against it. "If the enemy give no quarter," said the Duke, "they should have none given to them."[40] The failure of "the tack," secured as it was by a coalition of Whigs and moderate Tories, was indeed a triumph for the policy of the "*Triumvirate*," and more particularly for the peculiar talents of Harley, to whose "prudent management and zeal for the public"[41] Marlborough unreservedly ascribed it.

But the price paid was a heavy one. From this time onward the parochial priesthood of the Church of England, by far the most influential body of organised opinion in the country, became profoundly and permanently hostile to the ministry of Godolphin. And in the end

---

40. *Ibid.*, p. 250: Marlborough to Godolphin, April 14, 1705.
41. *Ibid.*, p. 249: Marlborough to Harley, December 16, 1704.

they obtained their revenge.

Blenheim had saved the government. The nation had at last got something to show for its money. All men could see and count the banners of France suspended in Westminster Hall. All men were free to gaze upon the Maréchal Duc de Tallard, the Marquis de Montpeyrout, Monsieur de Hautefeuille, and the rest of the aristocratic captives with the unpronounceable names. The opposition of Rochester and Nottingham was discounted by the notorious fact that each of them aspired to Godolphin's place. They and their associates in Parliament, in so far as they criticised and obstructed the policy of the war, were an army of officers with very few men save known or suspected Jacobites. In so far as they represented the exasperated clergy, they were more dangerous.

But for the present nothing could stand against the torrent of enthusiasm which Marlborough's victories had unloosed. The majority of Englishmen, though devoted to the Church, and firmly persuaded of the justice of her case, saw clearly that the vigorous prosecution of the war must now take precedence of all else. They were not prepared, at the bidding of a handful of mortified place-hunters, to overthrow a government which could point to such dazzling results. They believed, moreover, that the crisis of the struggle was approaching, and that, as soon as an honourable peace had been secured, the Church's grievance would be remedied.

"All people," says Burnet, "looked on the affairs of France as reduced to such a state that the war could not run beyond the period of the next Parliament."[42]

Public opinion was admirably expressed by that butcher of Nottingham, who cried out, as Tallard's carriage rolled into the town, "Welcome to England, sir; I hope to see your master here next year."

Encouraged by the extraordinary popularity of the war, Marlborough and Godolphin determined to maintain their political system in its entirety. At the beginning of April, 1705, on the eve of the general election, they announced some changes which showed that the Cabinet was conscious of its power. By appointing Whigs to lord-lieutenancies, they redressed the balance of local administration which Nottingham had spoiled. By admitting others to subordinate offices and to the Privy Council, they broadened the basis of the government without impairing its essential Toryism. And by depriving Bucking-

---

42. Burnet, vol. 4, p. 84.

ham of the Privy Seal, they relieved themselves of an obstructive colleague, who, but for the Queen's friendship, would have been ejected a year before with Jersey, Nottingham, and Seymour. Nevertheless, although they transferred the Seal to the Duke of Newcastle, a prominent personality in Whig society, they steadily persisted in ignoring the recognised leaders of that party, Somers, Halifax, Wharton, Orford, and Sunderland.

"Caress the fools of them most," said Defoe to Harley, "there are enough among them. Buy them with here and there a place."[43] These tactics were intended to divide the Whigs, who were strongly suspected of a disposition to coalesce with the Tory malcontents.

The government hoped that the general election would result in such a deadlock of parties as would leave Godolphin at liberty to choose his own men and to pursue his own measures without regard to the dictates of organised faction. The Queen's speech at the close of the session referred to the excellent prospects of a glorious peace, "if we do not disappoint it by our own unreasonable humour and animosity," and recommended everybody, especially "such as are in public stations, to carry themselves with the greatest prudence and moderation"[44] in the forthcoming contest in the country. But these, as can well be imagined, were largely counsels of perfection. The clergy and the universities rushed furiously into the fray with the war-cry of "The Church in Danger." They denounced the latitudinarian bishops as faithless shepherds. And they flooded the kingdom with savage pamphlets, in which the Queen herself was not always spared. They were strongly supported by a class, very influential in rural England, the justices of the peace.

The Whigs responded with equal ardour. They summoned to their aid the most trenchant of their scribes, and they deluged the constituencies with black lists of "the Tackers," who were held up to popular execration as traitors, Jacobites, and hirelings of France. Ministers stood aloof, surveying the combat, as Burnet sorrowfully remarks, "like indifferent spectators."[45] But ministers soon realised that their calculations had been somewhat at fault. The Whigs, though still a minority, improved their position to a marked degree. It was obvious that no long time could elapse before Godolphin would be constrained to

---

43. Portland MSS.: Defoe to Harley, November 3, 1704 (Hist. MSS. Comm 15th Report, Appendix, part 4, p. 148).
44. Boyer, vol. 3, p. 224.
45. Burnet, vol. 4, p. 100.

admit still more of them to power.

The elections had not yet begun when Marlborough quitted England, and after a bad passage reached the Hague on April 13. The change in the European situation, since he crossed twelve months before, was indeed remarkable. What he had already achieved, and what he now purposed to achieve, the inscription on the obelisk at Woodstock, attributed to St. John, sets forth in language not unworthy of the theme:

"The arms of France, favoured by the defection of the Elector of Bavaria, had penetrated into the heart of the Empire. This mighty body lay exposed to immediate ruin. In that memorable crisis, the Duke of Marlborough led his troops with unexampled celerity, secrecy, order, from the ocean to the Danube. He saw, he attacked, nor stopped, but to conquer the enemy. He forced the Bavarians, sustained by the French, in their strong entrenchments at Schellenberg. He passed the Danube. A second royal army, composed of the best troops of France, was sent to reinforce the first. That of the Confederates was divided. With one part of it the siege of Ingolstadt was carried on: with the other, the Duke gave battle to the united strength of France and Bavaria.

On the second day of August, one thousand seven hundred and four, he gained a more glorious victory than the history of any age can boast. The heaps of slain were dreadful proofs of his valour: a marshal of France, whole legions of French, his prisoners, proclaimed his mercy. Bavaria was subdued, Ratisbon, Augsburg, Ulm, Memmingen, all the usurpations of the enemy were restored. From the Danube, the Duke turned his victorious arms toward the Rhine, and the Moselle. Landau, Trèves, Trarbach, were taken. In the course of one campaign the very nature of the war was changed. The invaders of other states were reduced to defend their own. The frontier of France was exposed in its weakest part to the efforts of the allies," etc.

CHAPTER 11

The Lines of Brabant

In the spring of 1705 Louis XIV and his advisers did not underestimate the magnitude of the peril which menaced France. The capture of Trarbach, the quartering of 10,000 of the allied troops along the Moselle, and the formation of immense magazines at Coblenz and Trèves, left little possibility of doubt as to the true intentions of the enemy. Invasion was imminent, and invasion by "the real road" (*le vrai chemin*),[1] as Marlborough himself described it.

The French government exerted itself to repair the losses of the last campaign, and to concentrate every available man, horse, and gun upon the frontiers. Marsin commanded in Alsace, and Villeroi and the Elector in Flanders. The intervening space, the line from Luxembourg to Saarlouis, was the post of danger. Here ran "the real road," and here with admirable discernment Louis entrusted the defence to Villars, the ablest of his generals.

Villars had served his country well when he prepared the offensive combination against Vienna. Since then he had done most valuable work in the Cevennes, where, despite the efforts of the Grand Alliance to encourage the rebels, he had partly pacified and partly crushed a movement, which was diverting large bodies of troops from the various theatres of the war. His qualities were peculiarly adapted to the present crisis. An excellent type of the French officer at his best, he blended discretion with dash, and a natural instinct for tactics with a scientific knowledge of the military art. A consistently fortunate commander in the field, he enjoyed immense popularity among the men, who knew by experience that, if he was severe in matters of discipline, he was invariably just.

---

1. Murray, vol. 2, p. 5: Marlborough to Wratislaw, April 17, 1705.

A certain facility in the use of boastful and mendacious rhetoric exposed him to no little ridicule, and tended, in the eyes of superficial observers, to diminish the solidity of his exploits. But in reality he owed his triumphs in no small measure to the judicious exercise of this amusing talent. Villars, like Napoleon, understood the psychology of the French soldier to a nicety. In no army in the world is the maintenance of moral so vital to success as in the army of France. And never was that fact more palpable than in the period of dejection which ensued upon the disasters of the Schellenberg and Blenheim.

On February 2 Villars arrived at Metz, where he found the enemy from Trèves raiding the country up to the very walls. He was hampered by the weakness of his cavalry, the disease, which had originated in Tallard's army, having carried off large numbers of trained horses. But he ordered five battalions of foot to Thionville, and established a chain of posts between that place and Saarlouis. In the depth of winter he traversed the rugged borderland committed to his care, inspecting the fortresses and examining the defensive positions. The state of the soldiers he discovered to be excellent; but he reported to his government that an excessive number of superior officers were absent from their duty. This abuse he firmly checked.

He also took steps to suppress the scandalous luxury of the commissioned ranks, and mindful of the infamy of Blenheim, he cautioned the governors of towns against premature capitulations. At the beginning of March he would have attacked the allies in their entrenched camp at Trèves, had not extraordinary rains rendered the movement of troops impossible. Thereupon he hastened to Paris to concert with Villeroi and Marsin the necessary arrangements for mutual aid in the forthcoming campaign. On March 21 he returned to Metz. To raise the spirit of his men, he planned a dash upon the enemy's cantonments.

The continuance of the rains, however, delayed the operation until April 19. On that day he passed three separate *corps* across the Saar. They met with some slight successes; but the difficulty of subsistence and the renewal of the rains compelled them to go back. All this while, barges laden with munitions and supplies were steadily ascending the Rhine and the Moselle and discharging at Trèves. Convinced that he would shortly be confronted by enormous forces, Villars returned to his study of the landscape. It was necessary to select a situation where, with an inferior army, he could bar the road into Champagne, and at the same time frustrate the investment of Saarlouis, Thionville, and

Luxembourg.

Villars did not exaggerate the ambitious character of Marlborough's designs. The Duke proposed to invade France with no fewer than 90,000 men. So large a concentration of troops was exceptional in that age; and the problem of feeding them in the barren region between the Moselle and the Saar would have led the majority of contemporary generals to condemn the project as impracticable. Marlborough believed that he had solved it. Not only had he induced the Dutch to accumulate vast magazines at Coblenz, Trarbach, and Trèves, but he had also arranged that the invading force should act as two distinct armies, subsisting on two separate lines of country.

He himself, with 60,000 soldiers in the pay of England and Holland, would advance from Trèves along the Moselle, while the Margrave of Baden, with 30,000 Austrians and Germans, would direct his march from Landau to the River Saar. The two armies were to act in support of one another, and to be ready to combine if necessity should arise. This simple but correct plan he had contrived with Eugène in the preceding autumn. In subsequent communications[2] with Vienna he had steadily rejected all suggestions involving a dissipation of force.

The Germans were afraid that, unless a considerable body of troops were retained upon the Rhine, Marsin would attack them from Alsace. But Marlborough pointed out that the movement which he contemplated would compel Marsin to retire, or to make such detachments as would incapacitate him from offensive action. Loyally supported as he was by Eugène, he succeeded in securing a promise from the Austrian government that an army of 30,000 men should be ready in good time to co-operate with him in the manner proposed.

But the Emperor, who was rapidly descending to the grave, was served by ministers deficient alike in insight and in energy. Entirely absorbed in unprofitable attempts to suppress the Hungarian rebellion, they seemed to consider that an inadequate provision for the maintenance of the war in Italy would cover their obligations to the Grand Alliance. In the opening months of 1705 Marlborough was concerned to observe the insufficiency of the Austrian preparations on the side of the Rhine. The regiments were not recruited; the magazines were empty; the supplies of ammunition were depleted; the artillery did not exist.

---

2. Murray, vol. 1, p. 574: Marlborough to Wratislaw, January 9, 1705,

The fortifications of Landau were in ruins, and unless they should be speedily repaired, the army of invasion must be weakened to furnish a very powerful garrison. Marlborough wrote repeatedly to Stepney, instructing him to remonstrate with the Emperor's ministers. He wrote also, and in the strongest terms, to Wratislaw, Sinzendorf, and Eugène. But neither he himself nor his friends at Vienna could awaken the government to the danger of delay. The peril, from which Marlborough had rescued the Empire at Blenheim, was now forgotten; the deference which was due to his judgement, was forgotten too.

To make matters worse, a coolness arose between the Duke and Wratislaw, who suspected Stepney of Hungarian sympathies and induced the Emperor to press for his recall. Not until Eugène had threatened that, unless proper measures were taken, he would refuse any longer to serve the state, did the government begin to redeem its pledges to the English general. But valuable time had been wasted. And time was an important factor in the execution of Marlborough's plan.

How important it was, became plain by the middle of March, when Marlborough learned that the States, which in December had sanctioned his project of a campaign upon the Moselle, no longer approved it. This result had been directly produced by the skilful strategy of France. By rapidly concentrating his finest and largest army under Villeroi and the Elector in Flanders, and by ordering his own Household regiments to that theatre of the war, Louis was playing on the Dutchmen's nerves. And the alarm in Holland was by no means groundless. If Marlborough's design were vigorously executed, Holland would have little to fear from Villeroi and the Elector. But if, as seemed possible, he received no proper support from the Empire, it would be loolish and dangerous to weaken the army on the Meuse for the sake of an ineffective operation on the Moselle. The truth of this proposition was manifest to nobody more than to Marlborough himself. He used it to incite the Court of Vienna to a more strenuous activity. But his faith in the feasibility of his own plan remained unshaken.

Immediately upon his arrival in Holland he exerted himself to combat the terrors of the Dutch. The difficulty which he experienced in persuading them to allow him a sufficient contingent for his purpose kept him three weeks at the Hague. But he got his way at last. On May 4 he set out for Maestricht, which he reached on the 8th. Maestricht was the rendezvous not only of the Dutch army, which under the command of Overkirk was to defend the Meuse during Marlborough's absence, but also of the English forces which were destined for the Moselle. This great concentration of troops, coupled with the presence of the Duke himself, perplexed the French. Villars received orders to hold himself in readiness to proceed to Flanders. But on the 15th the English took the road to Trèves, and all uncertainty was at an end.

On the same day Marlborough departed for Coblenz. Two obstacles he had surmounted, Austrian lethargy and Dutch timidity; he was now confronted by a third, the jealousy of the Margrave of Baden. This general had never forgiven either Marlborough or Eugène for the complete eclipse which his own reputation had suffered in the campaign of Blenheim. He had already exhibited so much reluctance to co-operate with Marlborough on the Moselle that the Duke had been constrained to appeal to Vienna.

Peremptory instructions had been sent to Rastatt; and the Margrave, affecting to obey, had suggested a conference with Marlborough at Kreuznach on the 20th. But at Coblenz, on the 18th, the Duke received a letter, cancelling the appointment and explaining that the wound Louis had received in his leg at the battle of the Schellenberg was too inflamed to permit of any serious exertion. The tone of this communication excited grave misgivings. Whether the excuse were true or false, it meant, at the best, delay.

"My dearest soul," wrote Marlborough to his wife at this moment, "till I come to live with you I shall have nothing but vexation."[3] But intelligence from Vienna gave him some encouragement.

The Emperor Leopold was dead; Joseph, the King of the Romans, had succeeded; and the influence of Eugène would now become supreme. Joseph had written to the Duke with his own hand, "if my affairs permitted me, I would do myself the pleasure of joining you at the army, to testify in person the sentiments of my esteem and friendship. I have, nevertheless, ordered the Prince of Baden to act in concert with you on the Moselle, and I wish you a campaign as glorious as that of last year."[4]

Marlborough determined that, if the Margrave would not come to

---

3. Coxe, vol. 1, p. 270: The Duke to the Duchess, May 6/17, 1705.
4. *Ibid.*, p. 271: Original letter of the Emperor Joseph, dated Vienna, May 9. 1705. and signed "Josephus."

him, he would go to the Margrave. Quitting Coblenz on the 19th, he arrived on the 21st at Rastatt, where Louis received him with every appearance of affection and respect. But the English officers remarked that the accounts of the Margrave's infirmity appeared to be exaggerated; and the Duke learned, to his dismay, that for the present, at any rate, not more than 9,000 men could be dispatched towards the Saar. The conception of two armies, acting in support of one another, must therefore be abandoned.

The failure of the Austrian government to redeem its promises had crippled the execution of Marlborough's grand design. This cruel disappointment justified the strong remonstrance which he now addressed to Vienna; but it did not deter him from his projected advance along the Moselle. Having extracted from the Margrave a promise to march on the 27th, and having ridden forty miles to view the lines of Stollhofen and the adjacent country, he departed for Trèves, which he reached on the 26th,

From Trèves he wrote to Godolphin, Harley, Hedges, and Sinzendorf, complaining bitterly that, instead of two armies, the dishonourable negligence of the Austrian government had reduced him to one. That one amounted at present to only 30,000 men. More than a month before he had been endeavouring through Lord Raby, the English minister at Berlin, to accelerate the march of the Prussian contingent, 12,000 strong. They had not arrived, and they were not expected for a fortnight, if then. Nor had the 7,000 Palatine troops in Dutch and English pay as yet come in. More serious still was the failure of the Elector on the Rhine to supply him with the 3,000 horses which he needed for the transport of his cannon and munitions. Reiterated letters elicited no practical response. But the crowning misfortune was the discovery that the superintendent of the magazines, who was either a traitor or a thief, had disappeared, and that there was "not near half the quantity in the stores that should have been."[5]

But the Duke refused to despair. To husband his stocks, he quartered the English troops on the western side of the Moselle; and he dispatched expresses to Cologne and Mainz to order up supplies of corn and flour sufficient for a month. At the same time, he endeavoured to calm the anxiety of the Dutch, who were alarmed by the motions of Villeroi. He explained his situation to the States, and promised to create a strong diversion as speedily as possible.

Never was a great undertaking more shamefully obstructed by

---

5. Coxe, vol. 1, p. 274.

those in whose interest it was conceived. "We shall lose the finest opportunity in the world"⁶ (*nous perdrons la plus belle occasion du monde*), wrote Marlborough in the bitterness of his soul, as the days slipped by, and neither men nor horses appeared at Trèves. Necessity at length compelled him either to abandon the enterprise altogether, or to advance beyond the Saar. The sterility of the country, the backwardness of the season, and the diligence which the French had very properly displayed in destroying all forage and burning the villages,⁷ rendered it impossible for his cavalry to subsist any longer in their present situation.

At 2 a.m. on June 3 the English crossed the Moselle; and the combined army, having passed the Saar in two columns, moved rapidly towards the south.

Villars had concentrated his forces on May 18. He had again examined the country for a position adapted to his needs, and he had found nothing suitable which was nearer to the enemy than Sierck. On the right bank of the Moselle the little town of Sierck, surmounted by the ruins of its mediæval castle, nestles at the foot of a massive mountain, the lower slopes of which are clothed with vineyards and with scrub, and the upper with impenetrable woods. This mountain, running southwards for the distance of a mile, presents towards an enemy advancing from the Saar a precipitous rampart, moated at its base by the stony bed of a rapid torrent. On the summit is an extensive plateau, an ideal site for an encampment. It was here that Villars decided to await the enemy. He had nothing to dread from a frontal attack.

Not only was the eastern face of this natural fortress well-nigh impregnable in itself, but the country before it consisted of a succession of lofty ridges and profound ravines peculiarly unfavourable to the passage and deployment of an army. His left flank was protected by a loop of the Moselle, while his cannon dominated the river road through Sierck to Thionville. The castle of Sierck, though obsolete as a fortress, was a solid post, which he occupied with a small garrison. His right was not equally secure. For here the southern face of the mountain, sloping less steeply than the eastern, did not prohibit an assault. But here the Marshal threw up entrenchments of a formidable kind.

Moreover, the extremity of this flank was shielded by a dense forest, and guarded by cavalry extending backwards to the river. In this position, barring the road to Thionville, and ready to move swiftly to

---

6. Murray, vol. 2, p. 61: Marlborough to M. Pesters, May 31, 1703.
7. *Ibid.*, p. 55: Marlborough to Harley, May 27, 1705.

the assistance of Saarlouis or of Luxembourg, he confidently awaited developments, while from Metz and from the fertile region behind him he drew an abundance of supplies. The French soldiers, high and healthy in their windswept camp, lived upon the fat of the land and drank to the prosperity of their astute commander.

Villars had done exactly what Marlborough, who knew the country well, had expected him to do. Before quitting the Hague, he had impressed upon Hompesch and Noyelles, the officers commanding at Trèves, the importance of the position at Sierck and the desirability of endeavouring to hinder any attempt to fortify it. But when the Duke advanced on the morning of the 3rd, he still hoped that his enemy might be tempted to resist his progress at a more advanced point. A battle, even with the numerical odds against him, he would have greatly welcomed. Villars, however, was not aware that the allied army consisted of but 30,000 men.

From intercepted dispatches he had learned the magnitude of the Duke's designs; and he seems to have imagined that the forces assembled at Trèves were as large as they ought to have been. At Marlborough's approach, therefore, he hastily called in an outlying corps, and permitted the allies to enter their camp without molestation. This camp, which was reached at 6 in the evening after a forced march of eighteen miles, ran along elevated ground from the Moselle on the west through Perl and Merschweiler to Eft and Hellendorf upon the east. The troops, though weary, were elated. They believed the French to be afraid.

Villars, who had been reinforced by a detachment from Marsin, could now dispose of 52,000 men. Yet he left the initiative to Marlborough with 30,000. The Duke was strengthened on the 5th by the arrival of 7,000 Palatines, and in spite of the disparity of numbers he proposed, by a movement of his left, to thrust himself between the French Marshal and Saarlouis, and to invest that place. Should a collision result, he asked for no better opportunity than a decisive battle. But nothing could be done without artillery. Far in the rear the great train lay idly at Trarbach, while the Electors talked about terms and promised none. The Duke was haunted also by the fear of famine. But on the whole his commissariat department served him well. Horses were the crying need; and horses, to the eternal shame of the German princes, came not.

Meanwhile, the Margrave was sending perpetual excuses for his own delay. At last he announced that he would be at Birkenfeld on the 13th. Cadogan went to meet him, and found on his arrival that Louis had delegated his command to a subordinate, and departed for Schlangenbad to drink the waters. "If we could have had what was absolutely necessary," said Marlborough, "I could have borne this disappointment."[8]

All this time the opposing armies remained passive in their camps. The monotony was broken by nothing more exciting than a skirmish or a reconnaissance. Marlborough maintained his high reputation among the French for chivalrous politeness by sending Villars a case of wine, cider, and English spirits (*liqueurs d'Angleterre*), and Villars replied in kind.[9] The Duke had begun by informing the Marshal that with such an antagonist he looked forward to a fine campaign. Very courteous communications passed in reference to the exchange of prisoners. But the English soldiers were spoiling for a fight; and the Marshal refused to budge.

"We cannot possibly come at him," wrote Major Cranstoun, "though we were six times his force."[10]

And the Duke was eating his heart out. The anxiety affected his health.

"I own to you," he wrote to his wife, "that my sickness comes from fretting; for I have been disappointed in everything that was promised me."[11]

On a bold and storm-beaten bluff, high above the deep ravine of Mandern which lay before the left centre of the allied lines, the sombre towers of the castle of Mensberg stand sternly up against the sky. "*Schloss Mensberg*" the Prussians call it, but to the peasantry of Lorraine it is and will for ever be the "*Château de Malbrook*." For here, according to the fixed tradition of the countryside, that almost legendary warrior established his headquarters.[12] And hither at least he must have often ridden, to sweep with his glass the approaches to Saarlouis and the

---

8. Coxe, vol. 1, p. 285: The Duke to the Duchess, June 7/18, 1705.
9. Pelet, t. 5., p. 451: *Lettre de Villars à Chamillart*, 13 *juin*, 1705.
10. Portland MSS.: Major Cranstoun to Robert Cunningham, May 29, 1705 (Hist MSS. Comm., 15th Report, Appendix, part 4. p. 187).
11. Coxe, vol. 1, p. 279: The Duke to the Duchess, June 1/12, 1705.
12. They seem, in fact, to have been situated farther to the rear, at Elft. A peasant told the writer that the *château* was the residence of "Malbrook." Perhaps he identified one of its towers with the famous tower in the ballad—
Madame à sa tour monte
Si haut qu'elle peut monter.

circuitous defiles that led to Villars' right.

This situation could not long endure. The dice were too heavily weighted against Holland. Villeroi had quitted his lines on May 21. On the 28th he had invested Huy. The army of Overkirk, outnumbered by more than two to one, was tied to its fortified camp under the cannon of Maestricht. Huy fell on June 13; and Villeroi, moving quickly upon Liège, captured the town and laid siege to the citadel. It was evident that Overkirk would speedily be confronted with a choice between annihilation or retreat. All Holland was in a state of panic.

On June 11 Marlborough had written to Eugène, advising him of the critical condition of affairs, "which must," he said, "be attributed to the delays in the arrival of the German troops. Had they joined me in time, the enemy must have made a considerable detachment from the Netherlands."[13] The Duke had done his best to create such a diversion by alarming Villars. He had announced the total of his forces to be 110,000 men; and all the prisoners, whom Villars took, repeated these figures with suspicious unanimity. But the artifice failed. Villars was delighted.

After making a generous deduction, he could still estimate his enemies at 80,000 as against the 52,000 under his own command; and he could tell his government and his army that this enormous advantage in numbers had been more than neutralised by the superior skill of a French general and the superior courage of French soldiers. When Marlborough wrote to Eugène, he was in daily expectation of recall to Flanders. On the 16th Hompesch arrived with a piteous appeal from Overkirk. On the same date came an express from the field-deputies at Maestricht, requiring him to send them thirty battalions forthwith. If he obeyed, it would be useless to continue with diminished forces in Lorraine. Indeed, it was useless to continue there in any case.

The advent of Württemberg with 4,000 horse in Dutch and English pay, and also of 12,000 Prussians, had at last raised his army to comparative equality with that of Villars. But the Margrave's men had not yet appeared, forage was almost unobtainable, and horses and carts "for the drawing of everything to the siege"[14] could not be expected within less than six weeks. Moreover, the Duke was justifiably afraid lest in his continued absence the feeble government of Holland should be terrified into some disastrous peace. He therefore resolved to return immediately to the Meuse. It was better to go where he was

---

13. Coxe, vol. 1, p. 280: Marlborough to Eugène, June 11 1705.
14. *Ibid.*, p. 282: Marlborough to Godolphin, June 16, 1705.

wanted than to remain where he was impotent.

At midnight on the 17th, he noiselessly decamped, and covered by a strong rearguard of cavalry, moved back in pouring rain towards the Saar. At Consaarbriick he halted, and endeavoured to communicate with the Margrave's general, who, however, successfully avoided an interview. On the 19th he resumed his march, which was in no way impeded by the French at Sierck. He had decided to retain the magazines at Trèves, in case it might subsequently be found possible to reopen operations on the Moselle. The protection of this post he assigned to the Palatine and Westphahan troops, sixteen battalions and fifteen squadrons in all. Württemberg's men and the Prussians he ordered to join the Margrave.

Thus terminated an enterprise, conceived in the spirit of the soundest strategy, and ruined in its execution by the jealousy, incapacity, and sloth of those who were bound by every motive of honour and expediency to be most forward in promoting it. The Duke, said Major Cranstoun, was "innocent and ill-used."[15] But how bitterly he felt the mortification of failure, his private correspondence clearly shows.

"If I had known beforehand," he wrote to the Duchess, "what I must have endured by relying on the people of this country, no reasons should have persuaded me to have undertaken this campaign.... My dearest soul, pity me and love me."[16]

To Godolphin he said:

"I think if it were possible to vex me so for a fortnight longer, it would make an end of me. In short, I am weary of my life."[17]

He was naturally concerned for his own reputation. To publish the whole truth to Europe would be highly injurious to the Grand Alliance. To endure in silence, would encourage his detractors to proclaim that he was no match for generals above the class of Tallard. Marlborough knew Villars, and respected him. He set so high a value on the good opinion of the Marshal that he actually sent him a letter, apologising for the poorness of the sport which he had provided, and ascribing the entire responsibility to the Margrave, whose contemptible jealousy was already notorious. More than that it would have been impolitic to say. But Villars of course contrived to give forth his

---

15. Portland MSS.: Major Cranstoun to Robert Cunningham, October 1 , 1705 (Hist. MSS. Comm., 15th Report, Appendix, part 4, p. 250).
16. Coxe, vol. 1, p. 282: The Duke to the Duchess, June 16, 1705.
17. *Ibid.*: Marlborough to Godolphin, June 16, 1705.

calculated rhodomontades. He had done well. No man could have done better. But nothing could have saved him, had Marlborough been properly supported. Sierck was an earlier Valmy, for at Sierck as at Valmy the invaders of France defeated themselves.

But the personal question was of comparatively minor importance. What mattered most, was the loss to the coalised powers of the fairest opportunity that they were ever to obtain of ending the war at one stroke. In 1705 Marlborough, at the best, might have marched to Paris itself; at the worst, he could have wintered in Lorraine, severed connections with Alsace, and raised contributions to the gates of the capital. "It is most certain," he wrote, "the Moselle is the place where we might have done the French most hurt."[18]

And again, "I see but too plainly that the jealousy of Prince Louis and the backwardness of the German princes, will always hinder us from succeeding here, which is the most sensible part."[19]

So "the real road" was closed. And what was the alternative? The road through the Spanish Netherlands, where the mighty fortresses, which he had hoped to turn, must be conquered one by one. That was a process peculiarly agreeable to the talents of the Dutch generals and ambitions of the Dutch people. But what would they say in England? Marlborough knew only too well what they would say. And he knew that to a large extent it would be justified. He knew also that he, who above all men detested the idea of transferring operations to Belgium, and who craved most ardently for an early retirement to the quietude of domestic life, would be accused at home of prolonging, in his own interest, a war, which from the very outset he had consistently striven to terminate by swift and paralysing blows.[20]

"I never knew the Duke of Marlborough," said Burnet, "go out so full of hopes."[21] Now all those hopes were levelled. The character of the war was completely altered. For three campaigns the whole strategy of the Grand Alliance, in so far as Marlborough had controlled it, had been directed towards the preparation of a strong offensive movement through Lorraine. And now that movement had ended in collapse almost before it was begun. It might indeed be resumed; and the Duke's letters to Vienna and elsewhere referred to the possibility of a

---

18. Coxe, vol. 1, p. 286: The Duke to the Duchess, June 18/29, 1705.
19. *Ibid.*, p. 285: The Duke to the Duchess, June 21, 1705.
20. See, for example, the line taken by Dalrymple in his *Memoirs of Great Britain and Ireland*, part 4, book 1.
21. Burnet, vol. 4, p. 89.

return to the Moselle after six weeks. But it is questionable whether he seriously contemplated such a return.

As a matter of history, he never ventured to risk a repetition of the fiasco of Sierck. The lesson had been too sharp. Nothing of all that he had suffered in the past and was yet to suffer at the hands of the Dutch, ever affected him so acutely as the shameful misconduct of the Austrian government, the Margrave of Baden, and the German princes of the Rhine.

The Duke resolved that at the conclusion of the campaign he would resign his command. This determination was the outcome, not of ill-temper, but of a very proper reluctance to accept continued responsibility for operations which he was not permitted to control. In informing the Duchess of his decision, he promised in the meantime to "take all occasion of doing service to the Queen and public."[22] He redeemed his promise in characteristic fashion. Having dispatched Colonel Durel to Vienna with a full account of all that had passed, he began the march to Maestricht on the 19th. Churchill, with the infantry, the artillery, and a few squadrons, moved off in two columns, and took the route through Steffeln and Auel. The main body of the horse, under the Duke himself, started on the 20th, and followed the road by Bitburg, Prum, and Dreiborn.

The general rendezvous was Düren in the territory of Jülich. Hompesch rode on before to apprise Overkirk of the movement, and to arrange, if possible, for a combined attack on Villeroi. The Dutch were in agonies of terror. Express after express came in with intelligence more and more alarming. Marlborough wasted no time. In miserable weather, and through the bleak hill-country of the Volcanic Eifel, which could barely sustain its own inhabitants, his columns pressed forward with surprising diligence. They had little inducement to tarry. Privation and desertion thinned their ranks; the unseasoned horses perished in great numbers; but in spite of all hardships the spirit of the army as a whole continued to be excellent.

Having learned that Villars was sending a strong detachment to the Meuse, Marlborough affected to delay, as though he would return to the Moselle; but he ordered Churchill on the 21st to send on all his squadrons together with a picked detachment of 10,000 foot under Lord Orkney. Then he himself again dashed forward. Orkney moved so fast that he reached Düren on the 25th, some hours before

---

22. Coxe, vol. 1, p. 286: The Duke to the Duchess, June 18/29, 1705.

the Duke, who in his last two marches covered sixty miles. At Düren they learned that the rapidity of their march had astonished and confounded Villeroi, that he had recalled a detachment which was on its way to Sierck, and that he was hurriedly preparing to retire from Liège. Marlborough rested on the 26th; but Orkney, the sturdy Scot, rushed on with his untiring marches. Churchill reached Düren on the same day. At noon on the 27th Marlborough and his cavalry arrived at Maestricht. Villeroi was already in full retreat to Tongres.

Marlborough and Overkirk decided that their first operation must be the recovery of Huy. But "the Lord knows," wrote the Duke, "what we shall do next."[23] A return to the Moselle seemed more than ever improbable, for on the 29th came the astounding news that Aubach, the Palatine general, scared by the motions of a small detachment which Villars had thrown across the Saar, had burned the magazines at Trèves and hastily abandoned that city. Villars, who had dispatched a part of his army to Flanders, and was himself conducting the remainder to Alsace, had no serious design on Trèves. The place remained without any garrison for four days, when a French force came down from Luxembourg and occupied it. Villars, continuing his march, easily outstripped the troops which Marlborough had ordered up the Rhine. He joined Marsin on July 3, and on the ensuing day drove the Imperialists from their lines at Weissenburg.

Midway between Maestricht and Liège Marlborough army passed the Meuse on July 2, and advanced to Haneffe, where it was joined by Overkirk's. Villeroi, who had already retired to Montenaeken, withdrew precipitately to the shelter of his lines. On the 4th the allies moved on to Lens-les-Beguines. A detachment was sent to recapture Huy; and Overkirk went to Vinaimont to cover the siege. Villeroi made no attempt to relieve the garrison, though the division of the allied forces into three parts invited an attack. He had 70,000 men, which was probably more, and certainly not much less than the combined armies of Overkirk and Marlborough. But the French government proposed to take no risks. They were informed that Marlborough's relations with the Dutch were strained; and they imagined that they could force the English general to endure once more his exasperating experiences of the campaign of 1703.

The Duke was still determined to resign at the end of the summer. On June 29, the very day on which he received the news of Aubach's

---

23. *Ibid.*: The Duke to the Duchess, July 1 1705.

retreat from Trèves, he wrote to Heinsius:

> I am so weary at all the follys and villanys I have met with whilest I was on the Moselle that I should be extreamly obliged to you, if you would find some proper person to be in my post when this campaign is end'd so that I might be quiet in England.[24]

In this resolution he was daily confirmed by the accounts which reached him from home of the indecent exultation of "the Tackers" at his miscarriage on the Moselle. It was actually suggested in England that victories like that of Blenheim were a menace to the liberty of the subject and that the constitution itself was in peril from the ambition of a too successful soldier.

To Godolphin the Duke had already written,

> As I have no other ambition but that of serving well Her Majesty, and being thought what I am, a good Englishman, this vile, enormous faction of theirs vexes me so much, that I hope the Queen will after this campaign give me leave to retire, and end my days in praying for her prosperity, and making my own peace with God.[25]

To the Queen herself he declared,

> I think this retirement of mine is not only necessary for me, but also good for you; for as my principle is, that I would not have your Majesty in either of the parties' hands, so I have them both my enemies, which must be a weight to your business.[26]

And this was his considered judgement. For no personal pique could have survived the expressions of sympathy and regard which were now reaching him by every post. From Vienna Durel brought him a dispatch, assuring him of the Emperor's undivided confidence, and promising that, if he would return to the Moselle at an early date, he should be zealously supported by the Imperial government. The Queen wrote to him at length, and in a strain of simple, unaffected familiarity very consoling to his wounded pride.

In a letter to the Duchess of Marlborough the King of Spain expressed his "great chagrin" that the Duke should be "deprived of the success which would always follow his enterprises if others had no

---

24. Von Noorden, part 1, vol. 2, ch. 3, p. 165: *Marlborough an Heinsius*, 29 *Juni*, 1705, *Heinsiusarchiv*.
25. Coxe, vol. 1, p. 285: Marlborough to Godolphin, June 13/24, 1705.
26. *Ibid.*, p. 287: Marlborough to the Queen, July 16/27, 1705.

share in them."[27] Those whose opinion he most valued, exhorted him not to abandon the public service. And the whole body of his friends and admirers on both sides of the North Sea set up an indignant clamour against the Prince of Baden, who was openly declared to have been corrupted by the gold of France.

Huy capitulated on the 12th. Marlborough, in the meantime, had not been idle. For he did not propose to remain with the army as a mere figurehead: he intended that the French should once more feel the sharpness of his sword before he sheathed it. And he had been pondering the ways and means. It was certain that Villeroi would never of his own free will come out into the open. It was no less certain that the Dutch would never consent to an assault in form upon the French army as it lay within its lines. But those lines were very long. Extending as they did from Namur to Antwerp, they could not be adequately guarded with equal forces at every point. They were therefore open to surprise, a manifestation of the art of war which invariably attracted the mind of Marlborough. A successful surprise, moreover, would obviate the necessity for a hard-fought battle. It might therefore be expected to appeal to the Dutch proclivity for bloodless victories.

As in the campaign of 1703, the Duke had now two enemies to fight, the French and the Dutch; and the French were the less dangerous of the two. He had learned by melancholy experience that to solicit the active assistance of the generals and deputies of Holland in any decisive operation of war, was mere waste of time and temper. On this occasion, therefore, he adopted a novel course. On July 1 he had dispatched Hompesch to the Hague with an outline of his proposals, and had obtained from the government an approval which he deemed sufficient for his purpose. That purpose was to surprise and penetrate the French lines with the English troops and the auxiliaries in English pay.

The Dutch generals and deputies were not to be consulted; the Dutch army was not to be employed. To facilitate this design, he permitted the forces under Overkirk's command to retain their organisation as a separate unit. The details of his plan he kept locked in his own breast. But in two councils of war he suggested the feasibility of surprising the lines, and invited a free expression of opinion on the subject. The idea was coldly received by most of the English officers; it was opposed by the Dutch with the exception of Overkirk.

---

27. Private Correspondence of the Duchess of Marlborough (1838), July 27, 1705, vol. 1, p. 10.

The Duke's mind was now made up. He knew that the English, whatever they might think of his orders, would obey them to the letter. He knew too that nothing which a majority of the Dutch generals condemned would ever be sanctioned by the field-deputies. To the army of the Moselle, therefore, must belong all the danger of the enterprise, and all the glory.

The French were posted by brigades along the lines, Villeroi's headquarters being at Merdorp over against those of Marlborough at Lens-les-Beguines. The point which the Duke had selected for attack was the Château of Wanghe on the Little Geete, ten good miles to the north. The defences in that locality were reckoned, by reason of the marshy river in their front, to be quite impregnable. But at the Chateau of Wanghe the river was traversed by a stone bridge, which the French, for their own convenience, had not destroyed. The peasantry reported that this post was normally guarded by a force of only thirty or forty men.

At Orsmael, nearly two miles to the north-east of it, lay three regiments of dragoons. Four miles to the south-west of it, the extremity of Villeroi's left wing rested upon Gossoncourt, where thirty-three squadrons of cavalry were encamped. At Racour, about the same distance to the south, were eleven battalions of foot. These supports were sufficiently remote from Wanghe to encourage the belief that the bridge might be carried by surprise, and the lines traversed by a considerable force before the French could concentrate in adequate numbers to frustrate the operation.

Marlborough proceeded to mature his plan with a patient thoroughness and attention to detail, which practically ensured its success. He began by creating "the fog of war." Villeroi and the Elector believed that the Duke was now a discredited person, that his relations with the States-General were seriously strained, and that in no event would he be permitted to make any attempt upon the Unes. To encourage them in these ideas, Marlborough circulated a rumour that he was returning to the Moselle. When Huy fell on the 12th, instead of calling in the besieging force, he left it on the Meuse, as though it were destined to form the advance-guard of a southward march.

On the other hand, deserters arrived in the French camp with circumstantial stories of an attack which the Duke was alleged to be meditating at Merdorp in the French centre, at Meeffe on the right, and at Heylissem on the left. Villeroi and the Elector were not convinced; but, as a measure of precaution, they concentrated more closely about Merdorp, and kept their troops continually under arms. To draw them still further to their right, which was considered the most vulnerable portion of the lines, Marlborough ordered Overkirk to quit Vinaimont, pass the Mehaigne, and advance to Ville-en-Hesbaye. Schlangenberg and others protested that this movement would dangerously expose the Dutch army.

Schlangenberg indeed addressed a formal complaint on the subject to the States-General, But the brave and experienced veteran, Overkirk, to whom the Duke by now had partially opened his mind, executed the order at 3 a.m. on the morning of the 17th. Thereupon Marlborough made a slight motion with his own left, and threw bridges across the Mehaigne, as if he would support a Dutch attack. Villeroi and the Elector were puzzled. They were still unconvinced that the allies intended to give battle. But this massing of forces in close proximity to their centre and right compelled them to make corresponding dispositions. In and about Merdorp they concentrated almost all their foot. But they sent the four battalions of the *Regiment du Roi*, which had just arrived from the Moselle, to the extreme right. To the same point also they sent three regiments of dragoons which had hitherto acted as a reserve.

Meantime, the allied detachment at Huy returned to Lens-les-Beguines. Apparently, therefore, it was not the advance-guard of a march to the Moselle. But that a march of some sort was in contemplation, could not be doubted. All reports agreed that the Duke was moving that night. Some captured letters were brought to Villeroi. They declared that the English general intended to go north, as if he would attack the lines in that quarter, but that his real destination was St. Trond. The Marshal was disposed to believe it. A quiet promenade to St. Trond, where the surrounding country would afford good subsistence to an idle army, was exactly the operation which, in Marlborough's place, Villeroi himself would have proposed.

By the afternoon of the 17th this process of mystification had prepared the minds of the Duke's antagonists for everything except the actual truth. A march to the Moselle, a march to St. Trond, a grand attack upon the lines in separate places at the same time, all these were regarded by Villeroi and the Elector as possible solutions of the puzzle. The conception of a sudden swoop in, overwhelming force upon a remote and isolated point was the one factor which they omitted from their calculations. They considered that the most likely contingency was a march to St. Trond.

But the road to St. Trond was, for two-thirds of the way at least, the road to Wanghe. Consequently, Marlborough could arrive within striking distance of his objective without arousing any particular suspicion. They considered, on the other hand, that a triple assault was highly improbable. But the necessity of preparing for it had induced them to concentrate the bulk of their army, and particularly their infantry and guns, in such a position that it could render no effective succour until long after the decisive blow had fallen. Marlborough was employing, on a small scale, the very strategy which in 1704 had carried him to the Danube.

Nevertheless, Villeroi and the Elector can hardly be accused of negligence or want of caution. The orders for the night were strict and comprehensive. The infantry were to remain under arms, the cavalry were to keep their horses saddled, the general officers were to sleep at the head of their troops. Patrols were to be out the whole length of the lines, and they were specially instructed to follow by ear the direction of the enemy's march in the darkness.

By 4 in the afternoon Marlborough had completed his preparations. The attack upon the lines was to be delivered by a detachment of twenty battalions and thirty-eight squadrons under the command of Noyelles, a general in whose knowledge of the country and natural daring the Duke reposed the utmost confidence. Officers, who had proved their worth, Lumley, Hompesch, Wood, Palmes, Meredith, and Lord John Hay, were selected for the service. The soldiers received orders to assemble on the right at 8 in the evening, but their destination was not revealed to them. They were to march at 9. The rest of the army of the Moselle was to hold itself in readiness to follow them at 10. At 11 the army of Overkirk was to abandon its position on the extreme left, and recrossing the Mehaigne by the twelve bridges which had just been constructed, was to take the same road.

And now the Duke disclosed the details of his project to the Dutch commander, requesting him to show his cavalry towards Merdorp and Meeffe before sunset, and at the moment of departure to send a strong body of dragoons along the Namur road to alarm the extreme right of the enemy's lines. At 6 the heavy baggage moved off towards Liège. When all was ready, Marlborough sat down to supper. His secret had been well kept, and he was not a little astonished to find that the field-deputies had obtained some inkling of it.[28] He persuaded them, how-

---

28. Hare MSS.: Letter of July 18, 1705 (Hist. MSS. Comm., 14th Report, Appendix, part 9., p. 202).

ever, that he intended nothing more than a reconnaissance in force.

Twilight was fading into night, when Noyelles and his men set off, taking with them 600 labourers, besides timber and tools. Colonel Chanclos, an officer who was thoroughly acquainted with the country, led the way with five squadrons.[29] Competent guides had been furnished by a local gentleman of property, who disliked the French troops as neighbours. Fascines, which would have revealed too much, were not provided; but every trooper carried on his horse a small truss of hay, as if for a considerable journey.

An hour later, Marlborough himself with the remainder of the army of the Moselle, took the same road. Villeroi and the Elector were speedily in possession of the news. Report after report announced that the enemy was marching to St. Trond. It was almost certain now that Overkirk's advance was only a feint, intended to cover a retirement or to facilitate an attack at some other point. But the movements which Overkirk's cavalry had made that evening, and the fact that the Dutch army had not yet decamped, created a doubt as to the real intentions of the allies. A new rumour, to the effect that Marlborough was sending off a detachment of 15,000 men towards the Rhine, suggested that no attack of any sort was in contemplation.

Even when Overkirk himself began to withdraw, the advance of his dragoons along the Namur road was distinctly perplexing. Villeroi and the Elector redoubled their precautions. Repeatedly that night they sent word along the lines that the enemy was moving, that he was supposed to be making for St. Trond, but that the utmost vigilance must be exercised until the truth was known. In particular, they warned the officers commanding the left wing, Biron, d'Alègre, and Roquelaure, that the country on their front must be thoroughly patrolled, and that the dragoons at Orsmael must be exceptionally alert.

All through the summer night the silent columns of the allies filed on towards the north. So intense was the darkness that the guides themselves became confused. Some disorder resulted, and considerable delay; and at certain points the leading horsemen let fall their trusses of forage on the road to serve as signposts to the troops behind. Three o'clock had sounded from the village steeples, when Noyelles' detachment drew near to the famous battle-ground of Landen. Hitherto, the French patrols, who dogged with straining ears the direction of this unseen march, had correctly reported that the enemy was following the route to St. Trond. But at Landen, where the traveller to

---

29. Lediard, vol. 1, p. 493.

St. Trond turns off towards the right, Noyelles bore swiftly to his left, which was the way to Tirlemont. It was also the way to the Château of Wanghe and the bridge across the Little Geete.

And now there was no dearth of competent guides, for many a man in the English regiments had stood up to Luxembourg at Landen, and even the youngest recruit had been taught in the tales of bivouac and barrack-room the topography of the bloodiest field which the preceding century had ever known. Very grey and ghostlike in the waning darkness, they stole across the haunted earth where 20,000 warriors lay sleeping. From time to time men and horses started uneasily, as hoof or heel struck sharply on the bleaching bones of the still unburied dead.

Right in the centre of Wilham's old encampment they halted, less than two-thirds of a mile from the enemy's lines. Before them the ground sloped downwards to the Little Geete, that steep-banked stream which, twelve years before, had been choked with corpses, when the tameless King and his handful of English cavalry turned furiously at bay. At last the purpose of their march was plain to all. As the crowding memories of the place rose round them, they realised with grim delight that the wheel had turned full circle, and that their wondrous commander had planned for them and for England a startling revenge.

But they were nearly two hours late, and behind them the day was already breaking. Happily a thick, white, morning mist crept upwards from the river, and hid them as they made their final dispositions. The Duke's orders had been simple. Noyelles was to surprise the French if he could; but if he found them prepared, he was to storm the lines. He therefore split his detachment into three columns. General Schultz, with ten battalions and twelve squadrons was to march to the right, and attempt to effect a crossing at the villages of Overhespen and Neerhespen, half-way between Wanghe and Orsmael. Three battalions were directed to the left, where, at Elixem, a quarter of a mile above Wanghe, the existence of a stone bridge invited an attack. Both these posts, if the stories of the peasants could be credited, were no more strongly held than Wanghe itself.

Noyelles, with the residue of his forces, remained in the centre, immediately in front of the *château*. It was broad daylight when he gave the word, and the column stepped briskly down towards the river. Before it went sixty chosen grenadiers. Looming gigantic through the mist, they dashed upon the bridge and scaled the barrier. The Frenchmen there were instantly cut down. The Frenchmen in the *château* fled back into the lines, with the grenadiers close at their heels. A few volleys were fired; but the resistance offered was of the feeblest. The casualties of the allies did not exceed half a dozen. An advance-guard, also of grenadiers, pressed hard after their comrades. The bridge, the chateau, and the entrance to the lines, were swiftly seized. The signal was given to lay pontoons.

But the soldiers refused to wait. They broke their ranks. With ringing cheers they plunged into the river, and scrambled up the steep bank beyond. They waded through a belt of ooze. They tore open the hedges. They leapt down into the slimy fosse. They scaled the massive mounds, showed for a moment exultant on the parapets, and then dropped within the works. As fast as they arrived, their officers formed them at right angles to the lines with their faces to the south-west. Meantime the pontoons were laid. The cavalry came pouring on. And grenadiers and labourers alike fell to enlarging the entrance and creating new apertures to facilitate the passage of the horsemen.

The shots fired by the defenders of Wanghe alarmed the posts at Elixem and Overhespen, The tumult of cheering and the spectacle of scarlet coats upon the summit of the rampart struck them with panic. They did not wait to be attacked. The three battalions on the left immediately occupied Elixem, while Schultz's men, pressing forward to the rising ground which intervenes between Wanghe and Tirlemont, formed fast upon the right of those that had already crossed at the chateau. Schultz had no trouble with the three dragoon regiments at Orsmael. They neither fired a shot, nor attempted to give the alarm to the French left at Gossoncourt. They simply bolted to Léau. The completeness of the surprise was in the highest degree discreditable to the work of Roquelaure's patrols.

No mounted fugitive could have carried the tidings to Gossoncourt, for it was 6 o'clock before they reached Roquelaure, the general officer commanding on the extremity of Villeroi's left. Roquelaure sped it back to Merdorp, and then with d'Alègre and Horn got instantly to horse. The trumpets pealed; and the Life Guards of Bavaria mounted, and the Life Guards of Cologne; and the Spaniards mounted, the Black Troop, the White, and the Bay, and the Walloons, and the French, and they all rode on at the gallop, five and thirty squadrons of them, and their steel *cuirasses* shone like silver in the rising sun.

And after them came Caraman with two brigades of foot, and after them two more. And a battery of triple-barrelled cannon of marvellous design, that fired three balls at once, rushed without orders to the front, the gunners burning to display the prowess of their new machine. Four squadrons that drew first into the field perceived with amazement that within those vaunted works, which they had grown accustomed to regard as inexpugnable, a hostile army was rapidly deploying. Low down beside the Geete, the village of Elixem was swarming with the allied foot, and all the hedges to Wanghe were alive with marksmen.

Across the water-meadows, and up the long rise that stretched away to where, above the horizon, grew the towers of Tirlemont, the allied cavalry sat motionless in double ranks, which like some magical serpent continually lengthened as troop after troop cantered up from the riverside, and wheeled into the line. Behind them, the infantry, two deep, were forming fast. All Noyelle's men were there. And Marlborough's were close at hand.

The first rank of the allied horse was entirely British. Their officers marked the sparkle of Roquelaure's breastplates in the south-west, and counted his squadrons as they galloped up. The word was passed back to Wanghe that the enemy's *cuirassiers* were at hand. Marlborough's advance-guard had already reached the Geete, and the news was immediately brought to the Duke. Pressing on to the head of the column, he passed the river with his leading squadrons, and dashed forward to the front.

The enemy were forming rapidly. They had thirty-five squadrons; but those of Bavaria, which numbered three-fourths of the total, had been poorly recruited, and had fallen in some cases to only sixty men. It was obvious to Roquelaure that, unless he extended them in a single line, his left would be outflanked. It would probably be outflanked in any event, for Marlborough's horse were pouring fast across the Geete. His strongest chance was to impose upon the allies, and to hold them till his infantry arrived. The head of Caraman's column was already visible. Roquelaure decided to play for time.

Though the country as a whole was open and undulating, the ground which intervened between the hostile forces was by no means favourable to cavalry, because it was traversed by the hollow road running up from Elixem to Tirlemont. This hollow road was a deep, steep-sided cutting; indeed, for the first half-mile of its course, it was a veritable chasm. Judging that with so serious an obstacle before them, his guns would be secure against a sudden dash, Roquelaure posted them between his squadrons and opened fire at very close range upon the English horse. Marlborough, who had quickly taken in the situation, determined to attack at once. He immediately occupied the hollow road with five battalions, whose first volley compelled the enemy to recede. Then he ordered his cavalry to pass the precipitous ravine. Protected by the fire of the foot, they executed this difficult movement with a degree of success that bespoke a high standard of horsemanship.

On the extreme right, where the passage was simpler, they were no sooner over than the Scots Greys were seen to be outflanking the enemy. The trumpets sounded, and in close array the long line of British men and British horses swung in upon the foe. Roquelaure's cavalry, it would seem, did not spring forward to meet shock with shock; or if they moved at all, they moved too late. All who waited for the impact went down before it. But the great majority fled without striking a blow. The Duke himself rode in the charge. He instantly rallied his men, re-formed them, and, supported by his second line and by the infantry, again advanced.

Galloping headlong over another hollow road, much shallower than the first, the mob of fugitives drew rein before Caraman's two brigades of foot, which had already deployed across the plain, resting their right upon the river at the village of Esemael. Marlborough came on at a smart pace, and overtaking the guns and ammunition wagons, which had narrowly escaped in the first charge, captured them all. They had not fired more than thirty rounds, and had scarcely justified that pathetic confidence which the French soldier is too apt to repose in mechanical inventions. But now the English on the left began to suffer from the fire of some of Caraman's infantry who had occupied the hedges of Esemael.

Marlborough halted, ordered his squadrons to take ground to the right, and brought up six battalions to clear the village. This manoeuvre, while it threatened to deprive the right of the enemy's cavalry of the support which they had obtained from the troops in Esemael, tended still more to outflank their left. Nevertheless, reinforced by five squadrons, and encouraged by their officers as well as by the proximity of Caraman's two brigades, they seem to have attempted a charge. But the British line, which was already once more in motion, struck them with a weight and an impetuosity superior to their own. In the brief struggle that ensued, a squadron which Marlborough himself was leading gave back a little.

A Bavarian officer dashed forward to cut him down, but overbalancing in the very act, tumbled from his saddle, and was secured by the Duke's trumpeter. "I asked my Lord if it was so," says Orkney;" he said it was absolutely so. See what a happy man he is."[30]

The British drove their opponents through the intervals of Caraman's foot, and again rallied. Caraman's own position was now becoming critical. No other infantry had yet joined him. From the cavalry he could expect nothing. The handful of Spaniards had done their duty, and two French squadrons are said to have behaved well. But the great mass of Bavarian horsemen displayed conspicuous cowardice. Caraman's left was therefore wholly in the air. He very properly decided to retire.

Ordering his two brigades to form into a hollow square, he summoned the defenders of Esemael, which seemed to be threatened with the fate of Blindheim, to rejoin at once. They obeyed, but they were severely punished in the process. Then Caraman commenced to retreat towards Noduwez. His two brigades amounted to eleven battalions in all; but they were confronted in an open plain by an equal number of exultant horsemen. The circumstances were highly discouraging. Before them they saw the lost artillery, and behind them the wreckage of those brilliant squadrons whose double disgrace they had just witnessed. In this emergency Caraman kept his head.

Contemporary tacticians held that no cavalry on earth could get the better of a hollow square which had sufficient discipline and nerve to retain its formation. Inspired by the coolness of their general, the Alsatians and Spaniards, who composed the bulk of the two brigades, presented Marlborough with an excellent opportunity of testing the correctness of this opinion. Firing by platoons as they steadily drew off, they held their pursuers at a respectful distance with rolling volleys. The British, both officers and men, were eager to charge home. Their blood was up. The passage of the lines, the capture of the guns, and the two defeats which they had inflicted on the enemy's horse, had given them entire confidence in themselves and their commander. They were precisely in that mood which has always begotten the greatest exploits of cavalry.

But Marlborough would take no risks. He continued to follow the retreating enemy, but he kept his impatient squadrons well in hand, and absolutely refused to bring on a close engagement. Though he was subsequently censured in certain quarters for excess of prudence,

---

30. *English Historical Review*. April. 1004: Letters of the first Lord Orkney during Marlborough's Campaigns. Letter 2: An Account of the Forcing the French Lines.

there can be little doubt that he was right. No general ever believed more firmly than he in the capabilities of cavalry, and of British cavalry in particular. But he knew, by the firm demeanour of Caraman's men, that he might easily incur a sanguinary repulse, which would only tarnish the laurels he had already won. Had his own infantry been available, the position would have been different. But weary with their long night's march, the allied foot could not hope to overtake the rapidly retreating square.

The dominant consideration, however, was the Duke's ignorance of the whereabouts of the rest of the French army. The lines had been entered at 4 o'clock. It was now past 7. Marlborough's view was obstructed by rising ground. He did not, and he could not, know what was passing "behind the hill." But he was amply justified in assuming that, after the lapse of more than three hours, Villeroi and the Elector must be rapidly approaching. Overkirk, on the other hand, had not yet reached the Geete. Having no desire to be involved in a battle against superior numbers, Marlborough refused to sanction a charge upon the square; and he ought rather to be commended than criticised for his restraint.

In reality the danger was less than he supposed. Roquelaure's message had only just arrived at Merdorp. Snatching up all the cavalry at hand, Villeroi and the Elector sent orders to the rest of the army to follow, and set off at the gallop. Beyond Noduwez they overtook two brigades of foot, which had started somewhat later than Caraman's and from quarters more remote. Soon they beheld the fields covered with a beaten rabble that had once been forty squadrons. Behind these demoralised fugitives they saw the great square, firing and retiring with a beautiful precision which excited the enthusiastic admiration of friend and foe alike.[31] They saw the fifty squadrons of Marlborough, dogging and enveloping its line of march. And in the far distance they saw an army in position, stretching like a ribbon of blue and scarlet from the Little Geete well-nigh to Tirlemont.

They did not hesitate. Not wishing to be beaten in detail, they fell back on Noduwez, whence they directed an immediate retreat of the whole army on Louvain. This movement was executed with such precipitation that it resembled a flight. But speed was essential, if Brussels

---

31. See Kane's *Campaigns*, p. 63. General Kane, who was an eyewitness, observes: "This shows what resolution and keeping good order can do." And in his manual of *Discipline for a Regiment of Foot upon Action* he cites the exploit of Caraman as an example of the perfect use of the hollow square (p. 123).

and Antwerp were to be saved.

"God forgive those," wrote the Elector, "who suffered themselves to be surprised."[32]

Roquelaure was protected by the friendship of Villeroi; but his military career was ruined. Caraman received an unprecedented honour. The King created him a Knight of St. Louis, although no vacancy existed in the Order.

Marlborough remained in possession of the field. His casualties did not exceed 200. According to Villeroi, the French dead amounted to no more than 80; but according to English accounts, their killed and wounded numbered 1,000. According to English accounts also, nearly 1,000 prisoners were captured, whereas Villeroi fixes the total at 200.[33] But certain trophies, neither equivocal nor disputable, remained in Marlborough's hands. The British cavalry had taken no fewer than 79 officers of various grades, including the Marquis d'Alègre and the Comte de Horn, both lieutenant-generals, 1 major-general, 2 brigadier-generals, 4 colonels, and 5 lieutenant-colonels. They had taken 10 pieces of cannon,[34] 8 of them being triple-bored.

They had taken also "nine standards of blue satin, richly embroidered with the Bavarian arms," and adorned with vainglorious devices,"[35] besides a colour which had been wrested from Caraman's foot. Of these nine standards, four were captured by a single regiment, Cadogan's (now the 5th Dragoon Guards), which particularly distinguished itself.

The Scots Greys did not lose a man in either charge. Yet their colonel took d'Alègre with his own hand. Ross's regiment had broken the squadrons with which d'Alègre was riding, and had killed his charger. Several pistols were fired at him as he lay on the ground, and a dozen dragoons were "using him very ruffly,"[36] when the Greys came in upon the flank, and Lord John Hay promptly rescued the Marquis

---

32. Lediard. vol. 1, ch. 10, p. 501: The Elector to Baron de Malknecht.
33. See *Millner's Journal*, July 6, 1705. Maffei says that Villeroi lost in killed, wounded, and prisoners, 1,000 (*Mémoires de Maffei*, t. 2., p. 133).—Coxe, vol. 1, p. 295: Marlborough to Godolphin, July 7/18, 1705: "The French made such haste to get over this river yesterday that I took above 1,000 prisoners."
34. Maffei says seven. Lamberty, and Overkirk's report, say eighteen. Possibly this figure includes artillery found in Tirlemont (Lamberty, *Mémoires pour servir à l'histoire du XVIII. siècle*, t. 3., p. 473).
35. E.g., "*Per ardua laurus*," "*Obstantia firmant*," "*Ex duris gloria*," etc. Pelet, t. 5., p. 586: *Lettre de M. D'Overkirke aux États-Généraux*, 14 juillet 1705.
36. *English Historical Review*, April, 1904.

from his tormentors.

This action, which has been somewhat inadequately termed "a skirmish," formed a brilliant sequel to the passage of the lines. For several reasons it is deserving of close attention. While it exhibits Marlborough in the character of an accomplished cavalry tactician, it also illustrates the precise stage of efficiency to which he had developed his favourite arm. Although there is no explicit evidence that the British delivered their two charges at the utmost speed of their horses, the almost instantaneous collapse of the mail-clad enemy could hardly have been produced without a high degree of cohesion and of pace. Another essential of a good cavalry, the faculty of rapid rallying, these squadrons obviously possessed.

That fact, as well as the ease with which they crossed the hollow road, maintaining their formation under the fire of the cannon, would seem to presuppose in them an admirable discipline as well as a perfect mastery of their mounts. Of their spirit there was never any question. Eugène had correctly gauged it at Gross Heppach, On the plain of Tirlemont, as a century later on the plain of Waterloo, these historic regiments cared nothing for the advantage which the possession of armour conferred upon their foes. The behaviour of their antagonists is also worthy of remark. It is true that Marlborough, as usual, had secured for his men the moral superiority which attaches to surprise. It is also true that his chargers were fresher than Roquelaure's, which had galloped a distance of from three to five miles. But these circumstances alone do not explain misconduct.

The real cause lay deeper. Most of the enemy's cavalry, and all the most pusillanimous, belonged to the Elector. They had fought bravely at Blenheim; but at Blenheim they had not been confronted by the scarlet coats. Now, for the first time since the battle of the Schellenberg, Bavarians and English met. That the Bavarians were not only beaten, but disgraced, is a signal proof of the value of prestige in war. Conspicuous in the British ranks were those tall dragoons on the grey horses, of whom every survivor of d'Arco's army had had something to tell.

Marlborough was reaping now one of the fruits of that victory which the wiseacres had most fatuously disparaged. He was also preparing for a greater triumph. The Dutch troopers had done so well at Blenheim that they had already lost that old sense of inferiority, which dated from the days of Leuze and of Fleurus. By this example of their British comrades their growing confidence was strengthened and confirmed. In the next campaign they furnished convincing proofs of their regeneration.

The French affected to regard the loss of the lines, which they had been at such pains to construct and to maintain, as a trivial episode of no strategical importance whatsoever. But they deceived nobody, not even themselves. It is true that that excellent critic, Feuquières, utterly ridicules and condemns the use of fortifications of this description, and emphasises the fact that Condé, Turenne, and Luxembourg never condescended to employ them. But Feuquières' view was not accepted by the majority of contemporary soldiers, French, German, or Dutch.

Marlborough's achievement was regarded by the mass of opinion, both civil and military, with astonishment and admiration.[37] That fact alone gave it a moral value that counted for much. In any event, it was not a little absurd for Villeroi and his government to pretend that nothing had been done. If the lines were really worthless, only the insane would have spent so much money on their construction, and taken such elaborate precautions for their defence.

The truth of this matter is very simple. Those who designed the lines of Brabant intended them to prevent an invading army from subsisting on the soil of Brabant and Flanders. They intended them also to be used as a screen, behind which an army could mobilise within striking distance of Maestricht and the Meuse. And finally they intended them to serve as a species of outwork to that barrier of fortresses which guarded the road to Picardy and Artois. These three objects they had successfully fulfilled for more than three years. Against a government so timorous as that of Holland, and against generals so hide-bound as those whom it ordinarily employed, the lines had played a long and useful part in Louis' system of defensive strategy. Had Marlborough been permitted a free hand, he would have forced or turned them in his first campaign. But Marlborough was probably the only officer in either army who thoroughly despised them.

The fortresses behind them, however, he did not despise. Sieges meant delay; and to the Grand Alhance delay meant danger. For this reason alone, the French government had always desired nothing better than to fix the war in the Spanish Netherlands.

"Our army is in great heart," wrote Marlborough, shortly after the capture of the lines, "but you know this country is such

---

37. Alison, vol. 1., p. 216.

that it is very hard to force an enemy to fight when he has no mind to it."[38]

And Louis certainly had no mind to it. He was playing still for time. By the mere efflux of time he believed that the coalition was certain to dissolve. To evacuate the country inch by inch, to surrender after a protracted defence one fortress, or two at the most, in each campaign, to watch the growth of popular discontents and mutual jealousies among the members of the coalition, and then, at the proper moment, by the judicious offer of attractive terms to one of them, to cast among his enemies the apple of discord—such was the sagacious policy of Louis. Marlborough saw through it from the very beginning. His answer to it was the invasion of France herself by the valley of the Moselle.

But this project had collapsed. The Germans and the Austrians had ruined it. The Dutch themselves had adopted it with considerable reluctance, for all that the Dutch desired out of the war was the acquisition of a barrier of French and Spanish fortresses. Marlborough knew well that the piecemeal conquest of this barrier could be effected only by the expenditure of a wholly disproportionate quantity of blood and money. He knew too that every acre of earth wrested from the French in the Spanish Netherlands, would become a fertile source of dissension between the people of Holland and the House of Hapsburg. On military and political grounds alike, the cheapest, the swiftest, and the safest policy for the Grand Alliance was to march their armies through Champagne to Paris, and to dictate terms at Versailles. When the booty had been won, there would be time enough to quarrel over the division of it.

The campaign of 1705, in which the coalition definitely showed itself unable or unwilling to adopt the strategy of Marlborough, and deliberately, and with open eyes, played into the hands of Louis, is the most critical epoch in the whole struggle. Wars such as that of the Spanish Succession can be waged in two ways. Each of the allies may proceed upon his own account to attack that portion of the common enemy's territory, which lies nearest to his own frontier, and to hold all that he can conquer, for his own benefit. This method is congenial to selfish and narrow-minded governments and to military systems of the more slow than sure variety. Strategically, it is so vicious and

---

38. Portland MSS.: Letter from the Duke of Marlborough to Lord [Portland], July 27, 1705 (Hist. MSS. Comm., 15th Report, Appendix, part 5., p. 212).

unsound that, as against an opponent who is guided by the true principles of defensive warfare, it is bound to fail.

As against all others, it possesses some advantages. Each member of the confederacy has his whole heart in the work; and each is likely to secure something which he will be able to barter or to retain, when the ultimate settlement arrives. On the other hand, the allies may agree to treat their forces as a homogeneous whole, to be arranged and applied according to the judgement of the best commanders and with the sole object of procuring as quickly as possible a decisive result. This is the most efficient, the most humane, and the most economical method of procedure. It is thus that all great soldiers in the service of coalitions have desired to act.

It was on this principle that Marlborough, and the English government, inspired by Marlborough, endeavoured from the outset to conduct the war. England had rejected Rochester's policy of grabbing what she could for herself by land and sea, and had concentrated all her resources, both military and naval, on the single object of breaking the French power in Europe. She chose the better part; but the rest of the coalition refused to follow her example. The English people have a right to congratulate themselves on the action of those English statesmen, who, disregarding the easy and the popular course, insisted that England at any rate should 'play the game' for the common good and not for her own hand. It is also a matter for legitimate pride that a nation, not usually accepted on the continent as a leading authority upon military science, should, alone among the members of the Grand Alliance, have striven to conduct the war in accordance with the principles of an enhghtened strategy.

Chapter 12

Schlangenberg

Greeted upon every hand by the plaudits of the army, Marlborough rode straight from the field of battle to Tirlemont. The regiment of Monluc, 500 strong, which formed the garrison, immediately laid down its arms. Its commissioned officers, who numbered twenty-one, raised the total of the prisoners of that category to 100. In Tirlemont, today a 'dead' town, but at that time an important centre, the allies discovered a Bavarian magazine. The great church of Notre Dame was crowded with captives; and the resources of the hospital of St. John were soon overtaxed.

The heart of the Duke was very full. He had been profoundly touched by the unpolished, but sincere congratulations of the soldiery.

"It is impossible," he declared, when he wrote a few hours later to the Duchess, "to say too much good of the troops that were with me, for never men fought better."[1]

But it was to him, and not to themselves, that these men ascribed the glory. The British private has a long memory. In 1705 he had not forgotten the wasted opportunities of 1702, or the humiliating farce of 1703. Still less had he forgotten how, in 1704, freedom from Dutch interference had automatically resulted in splendid achievements. He noted that the lines had now been entered and the French well beaten without any assistance from Overkirk's army. And he contrived to season his eulogies with something of the resentment which he had long nourished against those whom he regarded as envious and incompetent meddlers.

The absence of the Dutch army, said Marlborough, "was not their

---
1. Coxe, vol. 1, p. 294: The Duke to the Duchess, July 7/18, 1705.

fault, for they could not come sooner; but this gave occasion to the troops with me to make me very kind expressions, even in the heat of the action, which I own to you gives me great pleasure, and makes me resolve to endure anything for their sake."[2]

But the common soldiers did not restrict themselves to compliments. The men who had fought at Landen and knew the whole country by heart, cried out to the Duke, as he rode towards the town, that there must be no delay at Tirlemont. The famous city of Louvain, with its immense magazines and its obsolete fortifications, was the natural perquisite of victory. An immediate march to Louvain would probably compel the enemy to retreat upon Namur. Mechlin, Brussels, even Antwerp itself would probably be lost to Louis. But if Villeroi and the Elector were permitted to pass the Dyle, they would assume some defensive position which would cover all those places, and which the Dutch would, of course, be frightened to assail. That the strategists in the ranks were right for once, none knew better than Marlborough himself. Exhausted and feverish though he was, he was eager to press on.

It was 10 o'clock. Overkirk had crossed the Little Geete, and the heads of his columns were approaching Tirlemont. In answer to a message from the Duke he reported that his infantry was extremely fatigued. The Dutch army had decamped from Vinaimont at 3 a.m. on the preceding day, and had marched ten miles to make their feint against the French right. At 11 p.m. they had again taken to the road, and had covered another seventeen miles before they reached Tirlemont.

The normal march at that period was from nine to twelve miles for a day of twenty-four hours. Overkirk's men had already done twenty-seven in thirty-one hours. From Tirlemont to Louvain was over eleven miles more. Could they do it? Overkirk was willing to ask them for the effort. But the rest of their generals, and more particularly Dopf, objected.[3]

In Tirlemont the British officers were congratulating the Duke, and Orkney and others were openly advocating an immediate advance, when Schlangenberg arrived. Having complimented Marlborough on his victory, he expressed the view that, unless they proceeded at once to Louvain, they would have accomplished nothing. Marlborough, who had already learned that the Dutch generals had pronounced

---

2. *Ibid.*, p. 296: The Duke to the Duchess, July 9/20, 1705.
3. See Schlangenberg's letter in Lamberty, August 27, 1705 (t. 3., p. 488).

against the march, was astonished.[4] "I am very glad, Sir," he replied, "to find you are of my opinion, for that is my judgement of it too; I think we should march on, and I entreat you go back and dispose your generals to it." Schlangenberg went, but he did not return. Out on the plain the Dutch soldiers were already pitching their tents.

Far in the south Max Emanuel was observing the motions of the allies through his glass. He was consumed with anxiety lest they should beat him in a race for Louvain, or should intercept him at Judoigne.[5] He too had fought by William's side at Landen, and he knew as well as Marlborough and his men the strategic importance of Louvain and the Dyle. If the allies marched, they would march by the chord of the semi-circle; and the French upon the arc could never outstrip them. But when from Tirlemont to the Little Geete he saw the long white lines of tents spring up, he "cried out three or four times in a rapture, '*Grace au Dieu, grace au ciel,*'" and dashed on towards Louvain.[6]

A British officer, who took part in these events, has left on record the opinion that the Dutch infantry could certainly have marched.

"Those," he observes in a very notable passage, "who know an army, and what soldiers are, know very well that upon occasions like this where even the common soldier is sensible of the reason of what he is to do, and especially in the joy of success and victory, soldiers with little entreaty will even outdo themselves, and march and fatigue double with cheerfulness what their officers would at another time compel them to do."[7]

He also maintains that, even if six hours had been granted for repose, the French would have been beaten in the race. But in that event a collision might have resulted. It is certain that the Dutch would never have consented to resume the advance at 4 o'clock in the afternoon with a prospect of ultimately committing the tired army to a disorderly action in the twilight.

No official explanation of the halt at Tirlemont has ever been published. Marlborough was always extremely loath to suggest on paper that his relations with the Dutch were other than harmonious. "One sees no forwardness in any of these men," wrote Orkney, "but we must not speak of what can't be helped, and, I do assure you, not of my

---

4. Portland MSS.: Major J. Cranstoun to Robert Cunningham, October 1, 1705 (Hist. MSS. Comm., 15th Report, Appendix, part 4, p. 252).
5. *Mémoires de Maffei,* t. 2., pp. 136, 137.
6. Cranstoun's letter, p. 253.
7. *Ibid.*

Lord's fault."⁸ In his politic anxiety to facilitate the smooth working of the coalition, and to conceal from the knowledge of the French those symptoms of dissension for which they were continually looking, the Duke preferred to hazard his own reputation by a patriotic silence. But sooner or later his soldiers and his friends always divined the truth. In the present instance the cause of the trouble was not far to seek. Just as in the preceding year Marlborough had tricked the States, when he carried his army from the Neckar to the Danube, so now he had tricked the deputies and generals of the States into the passage of the lines.

"I was forced," he wrote to Godolphin, "to cheat them into this action."⁹

In the words of his chaplain, he "perfectly bubbled them into it."¹⁰ The Dutch officers, with the exception of Overkirk, resented the somewhat ridiculous part which they had been obliged to play. Their tempers were not improved by the freedom of comment in which the English openly indulged. His melancholy experiences in the campaigns of 1703 and 1703 more than justified the artifice of Marlborough. But that was an argument which the Dutchmen naturally could not allow. They felt themselves humiliated in the sight of both armies and of all Europe. And they determined to gratify their spite by spoiling the victory.

When Schlangenberg declared that it was imperative to march forthwith to Louvain, he had no intention of translating his words into action. He said what he did, and said it publicly, in the hope that he might afterwards be enabled to manipulate the incident, to the detriment of the Duke. Schlangenberg was a brave man, who at Walcourt and at Eeckeren had exhibited under fire both resolution and resource. But he was deficient in that higher courage, which, in cold blood, accepts without shrinking the heaviest responsibilities. Moreover, he was a chronic sufferer from constitutional disinclination to obey superiors, a serious impediment to a military career.

Already, in the campaign of 1703, he had made no secret of his jealousy of Marlborough. His formal complaint on the subject of Overkirk's movement across the Mehaigne was even now upon its

8. *English Historical Review*, April, 1904: Letters of Lord Orkney during Marlborough's Campaigns, letter 2, July 20, 1705.
9. Coxe, vol. 1, p. 295: Marlborough to Godolphin, July 7/18, 1705.
10. Hare MSS.: Francis Hare to his cousin (George Naylor), July 18, 1705 (Hist. MSS. Comm., 14th Report, Appendix, part 9., p. 202).

way to the Hague. At Tirlemont, therefore, he must have felt not a little foolish. But his clumsy attempt to carry it off must have deceived nobody.

That Marlborough was disappointed, goes without saying. He particularly wanted Louvain, because Louvain would relieve him of the necessity of victualling his army from so remote a base as Liège. But it does not appear that he made any protest; or if he did, he abstained from pressing it. The wasted opportunity was not necessarily an irreparable loss. Marlborough believed, and rightly, that the enemy had little stomach for a fight; and he may well have anticipated that Villeroi would abandon the line of the Dyle exactly as in the last campaign he had abandoned the positions on the Lauter and the Queich. But if, on the contrary, the French stood firm, they could be given what the Duke was uniformly anxious and able to bestow upon them, a crushing overthrow.

To manoeuvre the enemy out of any number of square miles of valuable territory, was always, in Marlborough's judgement, a less desirable object than to pulverise their armed forces in the field. But in any event, he would require the cordial co-operation of the Dutch in the work which lay before him. He knew that the government at the Hague would be delighted at his latest exploit. As for the deputies, they came to him that afternoon at Tirlemont, and frankly told him that, if he had not rejoined the army, the lines would never have been forced.

It only remained to conciliate the generals. The Duke was a little apprehensive of the generals. He trusted, however, that in the universal jubilation over the success of his design, they would pardon him for the secrecy in which he had enveloped it. Friction, at such a moment, must be avoided at all costs. When therefore he ascertained that Overkirk's army had pitched its tents, he prudently determined to acquiesce in a decision, which, though it was opposed to his own judgement, did not, upon the face of it, compromise the prospects of a fine campaign. His patience surprised the English officers.

"To tell truth," wrote Orkney, "the Dutch are so untoward in everything, and my Lord so pestered with them that it is a wonder he doth not leave the army."[11]

On the morning of Sunday, the 19th, the allies resumed their advance. The main body of the enemy had passed the Dyle in the dark-

---

11. *English Historical Review*, April, 1904.

ness; but Marlborough's cavalry just struck their rear, and captured over 1,400 stragglers. The net loss to the French army, in killed, wounded, and prisoners, amounted therefore to at least 3,000 men, and possibly exceeded 4,000. Counting deserters, the total was fixed by some as high as 7,000 or 8,000.[12] The garrisons of Diest and Aerschot fell hastily back on Louvain. At Bierbeek, over against that city, Marlborough established his headquarters, and the allied army extended itself to right and left along the banks of the Dyle.

The troops were in the highest spirits. The enemy, on the other hand, had fallen into a state of consternation not far removed from panic. There were English officers in Marlborough's army who considered that, if, instead of encamping, he had instantly bridged the river, and hurled his men against the French position, he would have met with no serious resistance.[13] This opinion may well have been justified. It may well have been shared by Marlborough himself. But the Dutch generals and field-deputies would assuredly have denounced a frontal attack under such conditions as mere massacre. To propose it to them would have been a futile waste of time and temper.

The French in Louvain saluted Marlborough's quarters with round-shot. He immediately sent to warn them that, unless they desisted, he would lay the city in ashes. He was expecting a convoy of bread from Liège on the 21st, and he intended to attempt the passage of the river on the 22nd. Incredible as it appears, he had actually obtained the unanimous consent of the Dutch generals. But the luck was now against him. Heavy rains set in on the 20th, and continued with slight intermission for more than a week. The little streams, so numerous in that low country, overflowed their banks. The highways, which were poor at the best of times, became practically impassable. The Dyle, a "deep, still river,"[14] grew deeper and less still. The marshlands, bordering it on either side, expanded to lagoons. Writing to Godolphin on the 23rd, Marlborough reported that he was unable to move.

"The great rains," he said, "have drowned all the meadows by which we were to have marched."[15] This delay robbed him of much of the moral advantage on which he had relied. The ardour of his victorious troops began to cool, while the French had time to recover confidence and to complete their dispositions for defence. Such influ-

---

12. Lamberty, t. 3., p. 473.
13. Cranstoun's letter, p. 253.
14. Kane, p. 63.
15. Coxe, vol. 1, p. 300: Marlborough to Godolphin, July 12/23, 1705.

ence as the Duke, by his recent success, had acquired over the field-deputies, waned from day to day. For the vindictive generals, profiting by the disappointment and depression which prevailed on every hand, insinuated to their civilian colleagues that the Englishman was a muddler, who, by an excess of good fortune which he little merited, obtained opportunities which he was not competent to utilise.

Schlangenberg, in particular, though he knew that Marlborough was not to blame,[16] dilated on the text that, but for the neglect shown to the advice which he had disingenuously offered to the Duke at Tirlemont, Louvain and the Dyle would already have been theirs.

In these circumstances, it would not have been surprising, if Marlborough had decided to level the captured lines and return forthwith to Lorraine. Had he taken this course, he would have gratified the government at Vienna, and he would probably have received efficient support from the princes on the Rhine. But apart from his invincible mistrust of the Margrave, and his natural repugnance to risking his reputation a second time in that country, his true instinct for war prompted him to strike again where he had already struck. The Spanish Netherlands may not have been an ideal theatre of operations; but it was better to follow up a good blow in the Spanish Netherlands than to fritter away the all too brief campaigning season in marching backwards and forwards between the Meuse and the Moselle. He never doubted his own ability to make short work of Villeroi and the Elector, if only the Dutch government would strengthen his hands against their own field-deputies and generals.

Hompesch, whom he had dispatched to the Hague with the news of the capture of the lines, had been instructed to obtain, if possible, such enlarged powers as would facilitate the adoption of a vigorous offensive. Fresh from the perusal of Overkirk's report, in which "all the honour"[17] of the victory was frankly attributed to Marlborough, the States might have been expected, in their own most obvious interest, to augment the Duke's authority. Yet they conceded nothing. They did indeed express approval of his proposals, but always with the deadly and stultifying proviso that the consent of the field-deputies and generals must first be given on the spot.

Marlborough might well have despaired. Now, when his military reputation in Europe stood at least as high as Eugène's, he was no more trusted by this committee of merchants and money-lenders than

---

16. See his letter in Lamberty, August 27, 1705 (t. 3., p. 488).
17. Pelet, t. 5, p. 586: *Lettre de M. D'Overkirke aux États-Généraux, 18 juillet,* 1705.

when, as a comparatively unknown soldier, he had assumed the command of their armies more than three years before. Nevertheless, he still persevered. He submitted his plans to a council of war, and patiently endured whatever of criticism the malevolence and ineptitude of the Dutch generals could devise. Thanks to their loquacity, or as Marlborough himself suspected, their actual treachery, the enemy got wind of his designs. Certain movements, which he intended as feints against the left of the French position, were pointedly ignored by the enemy, who concentrated persistently on their centre and right. But the Duke declined to be discouraged. In the last resort, he relied, as in the passage of the lines, upon his own troops.

> "I think it is for the service to continue in two armies," he had written to Godolphin, "for mine, that is much the biggest, does whatever I will have them; and the others have got the ill custom of doing nothing but by council of war."[18]

When the weather improved, and the floods began to subside, he prepared for the attempt. It was fixed for the morning of the 29th. But at the last moment the field-deputies consulted the generals of Overkirk's army, who thereupon "unanimously retracted"[19] the favourable opinion which only a week before they had unanimously expressed. They now suggested an attack upon the French left.

> "But I know," wrote Marlborough, "they will let that fall also as soon as they shall see the ground; for that has much more difficulties in it than what I was desirous they should do. In short, these generals are so cautious that we shall be able to do nothing, unless an occasion offers, which must be put in execution before they can have a council of war. It is very mortifying to find much more obstructions from friends than from enemies; but that is now the case with me, and yet I dare not show my resentment for fear of too much alarming the Dutch, and indeed encouraging the enemy."[20]

But Marlborough would not acknowledge defeat. At length, by patience and persuasion, he carried his point. The field-deputies reluctantly consented, but only on the understanding that no risks were taken, a stipulation, which, in all the circumstances, was suggestive of congenital idiocy. The right of the French position was selected for

---

18. Coxe, vol. 1, p. 295: Marlborough to Godolphin, July 9/20, 1705.
19. *Ibid.*, p. 303: Marlborough to Godolphin, July 29, 1705.
20. *Ibid.*, pp. 303, 304: Marlborough to Godolphin, July 29, 1705.

attack. The precise points chosen were the villages of Corbeek and Neeryssche, which were separated from one another by a distance of a mile and a half. A detachment from Marlborough's army was to cross the Dyle at Corbeek, and a detachment from Ovcikirk's at Neeryssche. In each case, the main body was to follow, and support its own detachment. The appointed time was daybreak on the 30th.

On the afternoon of the 29th the two detachments assembled on the left of the line. Marlborough's consisted of twelve battalions and thirty-seven squadrons under Oxenstiern, and Overkirk's of five battalions and nine squadrons under Heukelom. They were accompanied by artillery and pontoons. At 5 o'clock they started, and the French observed their departure. Between 11 and midnight the two armies followed, the Dutch, who had been encamped on the left, leading the way. It was known at once in the enemy's camp that the allies were in motion; but the direction of their march, which was screened by the forest of Meerdael, and shrouded in the darkness of the night, remained uncertain.

As hour after hour went by, various and conflicting rumours arrived. The Elector, who declined to assume that the main body had followed the two detachments, was nervous for the safety of Louvain. But a little before dawn Villeroi, who had formed the opinion that his right was seriously threatened, ordered Guiscard with all the cavalry of that wing and some brigades of foot to proceed towards Neeryssche.

Meanwhile, the two detachments, which had arrived in the vicinity of Corbeek and Neeryssche at 10 o'clock, had continued all night under arms. At daybreak they advanced to the banks of the Dyle, and covered by the fire of their batteries, commenced to lay pontoons. The enemy's posts defended themselves well; but Heukelom crossed with the whole of his infantry, and driving the French from hedge to hedge, expelled two battalions and a regiment of dragoons from the village of Neeryssche. Oxenstiern, though he had the larger detachment, had by far the harder task; for Guiscard, attracted by the sound of the cannon, pushed rapidly forward to Corbeek, and deploying his foot along the river bank, opened fire upon the pontoons with a battery of ten triple-barrelled guns.

Nevertheless, at this point also, 500 grenadiers eventually got over and effected a lodgment. But the marshy nature of the ground did not encourage Oxenstiern to risk his squadrons. The Dutch army had now arrived. Instead, however, of supporting the two attacks with alacrity and vigour, the men remained idle spectators of the combat, while the generals discussed among themselves the probabilities of failure. Dopf, who had been largely responsible for the halt at Tirlemont, displayed conspicuous timidity at this juncture. The main body of the French had followed Guiscard. In comparison with the allies, they had a short road to travel, and the heads of their columns were already discernible in the far distance.

This terrifying apparition completed the paralysis of Dutch leadership. Marlborough's army, which had lost its way in the darkness, was not yet up, but it was approaching. The Duke himself was the first to reach Corbeek, where he ascertained the exact position of affairs both there and at Neeryssche. He instantly dispatched an *aide-de-camp* to the Dutch generals with instructions either to support Heukelom at once, or to recall him. Pausing for a moment to examine the situation at Corbeek, he was accosted by Brigadier Ferguson, a fine soldier, who impatiently enquired the reason of the delay. [21]

The Duke gripped his hand. "Hold your tongue," he said, "you know nothing. I have given my word to do nothing without consent." Then he spurred forward to Neeryssche. Galloping up to the group of palavering Dutchmen, he demanded to know whether they would push home the attack or not.

"For God's sake, my Lord Duke, don't" said Schlangenberg, taking him aside, and expatiating with excited gestures on the probability that, if the army crossed, it would be crushed before it could deploy. The others, who had been moved by Schlangenberg's arguments, remained silent. But Marlborough cut the matter short. He told them plainly that there was "no time to reason," that they must do one thing or the other, but that, whichever it was, it must be done immediately. They still hesitated. Thereupon the Duke sent orders of recall to both detachments. Oxenstiern's grenadiers returned at once.

Heukelom, who had not only carried all before him but had now establhshed himself in a strong, defensive position, which he was confident would cover the passage of the rest of the army, was indignant and incredulous, and flatly refused to retreat. His attitude was natural enough, for he, who was infinitely the best judge of the prospects of success, had not even been consulted by those vacillating commanders, who lacked the moral courage either to advance or to retire. All this time the French columns were drawing rapidly nearer.

Marlborough sent Heukelom a second message, so peremptory in

---

21. Cranstoun's letter, p. 254.

tone that the stubborn soldier, though he stormed like a madman, had no option but to obey. So little was he pressed that he brought off his entire force without the loss of a single man or pontoon. The two armies then withdrew to Meldert. Their casualties did not exceed fifty. But the French were alleged to have suffered severely from the fire of the batteries.[22]

It can well be imagined that the spirit of the allied troops was not exalted by this rebuff. The French, on the other hand, astonished to find that they had not been beaten, were ridiculously elated. These disagreeable results were viewed by Schlangenberg with equanimity. His object had been fully achieved. For the deception practised at the passage of the lines Marlborough had now been soundly punished. He had been driven to break his own project in the very moment of execution, and to countermand his own attacks in the face of an enemy whom he despised.

Marlborough was far too public-spirited to advertise to the whole world the combination of imbecility and spite by which he had been victimised. A plain statement of the facts would have irritated English opinion, embarrassed the Dutch government, and delighted Louis beyond measure. His official reports of the operation concluded, therefore, with such brief and unilluminating sentences as these:

> "It was thought fit to order our men to retire."[23] "It was not thought fit to pursue the attempt,"[24] and "It was not considered opportune to pursue the affair."[25]

How far he sacrificed his own reputation by the exercise of this patriotic restraint, may be judged from one very remarkable circumstance. His English biographers, of that and the succeeding generation, remained in complete ignorance of the truth.[26] Monotonously and often fulsomely eulogistic as they were, in their narratives of this particular episode they did grave injustice to their idol.

The fiasco on the Dyle should have convinced the Dutch government of the utter futility of their system of command. Hoping that what had been refused to argument might now be conceded to example, Marlborough again sent Hompesch to the Hague. Hompesch carried with him a private letter for the Pensionary, couched in the

---

22. *Mémoires de Maffei*, t. 2., p. 142. Maffei says that they had seventy killed.
23. Murray, vol. 2., p. 195: Marlborough to Hedges, July 30, 1705.
24. *Ibid.*: Marlborough to Harley, July 30, 1705.
25. *Ibid.*, p. 194: Marlborough to the States-General, July 30, 1705.
26. Boyer, *The History of Queen Anne* (1735), p. 198; Lediard, vol. 1 p. 502.

strongest language of admonition and remonstrance.

"I am very uneasy in my own mind," wrote Marlborough to his friend, "to see how everything here is like to go, notwithstanding the superiority, and goodness of our own troops, which ought to make us not doubt of success."

Inefficiency, he explained, was the necessary consequence of councils of war, which ruined all chances of secrecy and dispatch, while they favoured the growth of personal animosities and an insane spirit of partisanship.

"It is absolutely necessary," he declared, "that such power be lodged with the general as may enable him to act as he thinks proper, according to the best of his judgement, without being obliged ever to communicate what he intends further than he thinks convenient. The success of the last campaign, with the blessing of God, was owing to that power which I wish you would now give, for the good of the public and that of the States in particular. And if you think anybody can execute it better than myself I shall be willing to stay in any of the towns here, having a very good pretext, for I really am sick. I know this is a very nice point, but it is of the last importance, for without it no general can act offensively with advantage."

Hompesch, he added, would unfold the new plans which he had formed, and which, if properly carried out, might end the war. But he prophesied that, unless the incubus of the existing system were removed, nothing could be achieved beyond "the levelling of the lines and the taking of Léau." He concluded with a hint that he could say much more, and a request that, whatever resolution was taken should be taken quickly.[27]

On the day preceding the miscarriage on the Dyle Lord Sunderland arrived in the allied camp. The death of Leopold and the accession of Joseph had placed the Queen under the necessity of sending an Envoy Extraordinary to the Court of Vienna, "to make the compliments of condolence and congratulation."[28] Whoever was chosen, would also be required to undertake the delicate task of promoting an accommodation between the Emperor and the Hungarian rebels. The Whigs exerted all their influence to procure the post for Sunderland. The Duchess supported the claims of her son-in-law with her ac-

---

27. Murray, vol. 2., p. 197: Marlborough to the Pensioner, August 2, 1705.
28. Boyer, *The History of Queen Anne*, p. 180.

customed warmth, Godolphin, who considered that the result of the elections had rendered the policy of ostracising the *Junta* no longer safe, saw in the proposal an opportunity for gratifying the Whig leaders without admitting them to real power.

Marlborough knew well that a more inept appointment could hardly have been imagined. The friction between Wratislaw and Stepney, which still continued, showed how sensitive the Austrian government was to foreign interference in the Hungarian question. An extreme Republican in theory, and an acrimonious Whig in practice, Sunderland was of all men the most likely to aggravate the trouble which he would be expected to assuage. But the miserable exigencies of party politics compelled the Duke to acquiesce in a selection which his own judgement unhesitatingly condemned. To the huge delight of the Whigs, the Queen swallowed her natural prejudice against Sunderland, and accepted the advice of her Prime Minister. But when the Envoy Extraordinary turned out of his road to visit the army in Brabant, his father-in-law took every advantage of the opportunity to warn him against the diplomatic pitfalls that awaited him at Vienna.

Wratislaw, who knew Sunderland well, had already informed Marlborough of the very unfavourable impression which the appointment had created in that capital. "I entreat you," wrote the Austrian minister, "to soften by your influence the republican zeal of Lord Sunderland."[29] And again: "I frankly declare to you that I dread the republican principles of Lord Sunderland."[30] And again: "If he hopes to establish a republic in Hungary, he will not succeed."[31]

This anxiety was only too well founded. The Envoy Extraordinary had need of all the admirable counsel which an accomplished diplomatist could impart to a narrow doctrinaire. In the choice of his suite he had already exhibited his unfitness for his task. He brought with him, said Hare, "a parcel of notable Whigs—their company will not much advance the Hungarian mediation."[32] During the week that these visitors remained with the army, Marlborough showed them everything of interest, and personally conducted them along the front of the French position. In their many conversations upon Austrian politics Sunderland exhibited so much deference to the opinions

---

29. Coxe, vol. 1, p. 340: Wratislaw to Marlborough, July 19, 1705.
30. Postscript to the same.
31. *Ibid.*
32. Hare MSS., August 3, 1705 (Hist. MSS. Comm., 14th Report, Appendix, part 9, p. 204).

of his father-in-law that on August 6, when he departed for Vienna, the Duke felt justified in writing to Wratislaw that, despite his "humour and ardour," the Emperor's ministers would find him "very flexible."[33]

In their camp at Meldert the soldiers of Marlborough indignantly discussed the contemptible exhibition which the army had offered to the enemy on the banks of the Dyle. Bitterly as the Duke resented the treatment to which he had been subjected, his men resented it more bitterly than he. How high was the value which he set upon their affection, appears from a letter which he sent at this time to the Duchess, who had rebuked him for venturing his life at the passage of the lines.

"As I would deserve and keep the kindness of this army," he wrote, "I must let them see that, when I expose them, I would not exempt myself."[34] And never were troops more devoted to their commander or more eager to be led against the foe. Yet thanks to the imbecile policy of the Dutch government, all this magnificent fighting material was condemned to inactivity, or else to a grotesque parody of war, which St. John most truly described as a "jest to our enemies."[35]

On August 2, Hompesch returned from the Hague with a resolution of the States. For sheer silliness it could hardly have been excelled. The field-deputies were informed that Marlborough had conceived a design, the execution of which would necessitate two or three marches. These marches they must permit him to make without summoning a council of war. A council of war, they were told, was never to be summoned unless it should be absolutely necessary. The Duke, on the other hand, was warned that he must attempt nothing without the concurrence of Overkirk and the field-deputies.

But inasmuch as the field-deputies could form no opinion on military subjects without the advice of military men, it was certain that in practice they would always consult the officers of their own army. The whole resolution was consequently useless. Indeed, it was worse than useless, for it was so drawn as to increase the irritation of the Dutch generals, while it could be so worked as to leave their power for mischief unimpaired. The very men, who were known to be aggrieved because Marlborough had not confided to them his project for the passage of the lines, were now directed to assist him on the execution

---

33. Murray, vol. 2., p. 204: Marlborough to Wratislaw, August 6, 1705.
34. Coxe, vol. 1., p. 297: The Duke to the Duchess, August 6, 1705.
35. *Ibid.* 304: St. John to Marlborough, August 18, 1705.

of another mysterious enterprise, and were provided, at the same time, with an ample opportunity of ruining it at the last moment, if they so desired.

Nevertheless the Duke did not abandon hope. Now, as ever, his aim was to crush the enemy in battle. But as the enemy would never attack, and as the Dutch would not permit them to be attacked in existing circumstances, it became necessary to devise some means of provoking or compelling an encounter. The plan conceived by Marlborough exhibited both imagination and insight, and combined within itself a variety of chances of bringing the French to action. It involved, in the first place, a two days' march to Genappe, twenty-five miles to the south-west of Meldert. This movement, however it might be interpreted by Villeroi and the Elector, would certainly be condemned by them as a hazardous violation of the rules, because it would carry Marlborough clean past the front of the hostile position, and would leave his communications with Maestricht and Liège through Diest and Tirlemont entirely exposed.

The Duke, who always studied the psychology of his antagonists with the utmost care, was not without hope that the advantage, theoretically accruing to the French from this incorrect strategy, might tempt them to forsake the line of the Dyle and throw themselves upon his rear. If only he were once attacked, even the Dutch field-deputies could not refuse him permission to defend himself. Assuming, however, that the enemy declined to be drawn into the open, the advance of the allies to Genappe, while it would disclose no definite intention, could not fail to excite anxiety for at least five fortresses, Ath, Mons, Charleroi, Brussels, and Namur. Villeroi and the Elector would therefore be compelled to weaken their army by detaching reinforcements to the threatened garrisons.

As an alternative to this unpleasant process, they might reluctantly determine to offer battle. But if, after all, they adhered to their defensive system, and remained, though with diminished numbers, between Brussels and Louvain, Marlborough intended, by a third march to the north, to occupy the ridge of Mont St. Jean. This movement was calculated to excite so much alarm for the safety of Brussels, the fortifications of which were notoriously feeble, that the enemy might be expected to make yet another detachment for the protection of the capital. Then, when the numerical odds were palpably in his favour, when the obstacle of the Dyle no longer barred his progress, and when he stood between the aimy of France and the French frontier, wheeling swiftly to the right, he would fall upon the foe in circumstances so propitious that, for once, even the Dutch field-deputies and generals would cheerfully declare for battle.

It was obvious to Marlborough that, if Villeroi and the Elector could materially augment the numbers under their command, the calculations upon which his whole design reposed would be vitiated. He had already taken precautions to ensure that the French and Spanish garrisons of northern Flanders should be too busy to assist their army in the field. On August 3, Spaar, who led the handful of Dutch troops operating in that region, crossed the canal between Bruges and Ghent, and under cover of darkness attacked the lines. With little loss he captured four forts and over 300 prisoners, and marching day and night, levying contributions and arresting hostages as he went, spread panic far and wide.

Not until the 7th did he retire before a superior force, hastily collected from the garrisons of those parts. In this diversion, which had been concerted with Marlborough, Spaar exhibited so much activity and enterprise that it became unsafe for Villeroi and the Elector to call men southward, as long as this dashing raider continued within striking distance of the lines. But Marlborough had learned that a powerful contingent from Villars' army in Alsace was already on the way to Flanders. To anticipate its arrival, he proposed to march as soon as possible. He waited only for the huge convoy of provisions, which he had been accumulating at Liège, and without which he dared not cut himself adrift in the enemy's country.

On August 13 the convoy reached Meldert with biscuit and bread for ten days. The anniversary of Blenheim was duly celebrated in the allied camp, and the Dutch field-deputies and generals dined with the Duke. At Louvain the French spies reported that the waggons had not been unloaded. It was evident, therefore, that Marlborough was about to move. But whither? Since he withdrew to Meldert, many rumours had been afloat. Some said that he would march towards the Demer, others that he would make for Hal, others that he intended to besiege Namur, and others that he meditated a battle. Villeroi and the Elector, who had reinforced the garrisons of Mons and Cliarleroi, and warned the governors of Givet, Philippeville, and Maubeuge, patiently awaited developments. The Dutch generals were as much in the dark as they. One of them, Albemarle, William's old favourite, wrote at this time to Heinsius to complain that they were "treated like children."[36]

---

36. *Heinsius Archives (Rijks-Achief* [State Archives] at the Hague), August 13. 1705.

On Saturday, the 15th, Marlborough marched to Corbais, and Overkirk on a parallel line to Nil St. Martin. This movement disclosed nothing definite. Villeroi and the Elector were disinclined to believe that Namur was threatened, as the numerical superiority of the allies seemed insufficient to justify so serious a siege. They anticipated rather that the Duke would pass the Dyle at Wavre, and would either operate against their right wing, or make a dash on Brussels. They therefore dispatched Grimaldi with nine battalions and twelve squadrons to the capital, while they themselves with the main body stood ready to move round, as Marlborough moved, but not before, lest Louvain should be prematurely uncovered.

On Sunday, Marlborough and Overkirk crossed the Dyle at and about Ottignies (where Grouchy would have crossed it, a century later, had he marched to "the sound of the cannon"), and encamped together on the heights above Genappe (where Uxbridge's Life Guards rode down the lancers of Napoleon). Villeroi and the Elector were surprised and puzzled. They were totally at a loss to comprehend how any general could so far forget the book as to abandon his magazines and march across the enemy's front into the heart of a hostile country. Yet they displayed no eagerness to profit by the advantage which Marlborough's theoretically unsound movement was supposed to have conferred upon them. Instead of attempting to punish him for his blunder, they merely shifted their position a little further from Louvain and a little nearer to Brussels.

Pushing out their right to Overyssche, and bringing up their left to Neeryssche, they encamped between the forest of Soignies and the Dyle, with the little River Yssche upon their front. At the same time, they dispatched nine more battalions to Grimaldi, and sent Pasteur with six squadrons of dragoons to Waterloo, to hold the main road from Genappe to Brussels. In Louvain they left three battalions and three squadrons with orders to patrol the country unceasingly. Even so, they were not satisfied. Ath, Mons, and Charleroi, all lay within the zone of danger. Each of these garrisons, therefore, they reinforced with one battalion apiece. Marlborough was attaining his end. Though he had not succeeded in luring the enemy into the open, he had drawn them from the Dyle, and he was compelling them to make so many detachments in various directions that their numerical inferiority began to be very pronounced.

On Monday, the allied army, altering its direction from south-west to north, marched up to the ridge of Mont St. Jean, and encamped with its left at Braine l'Alleud and its right at La Hulpe, on the very ground which Wellington selected in 1815 for a different purpose. Marlborough's own headquarters were at Fischermont. Villeroi and the Elector, who had been joined on the 15th by Marsin, were virtually convinced that the Duke's real objective was the city of Brussels. But they wanted to be sure. They therefore reinforced Pasteur with a battalion of foot and 350 grenadiers.

If he was unable to maintain his ground, he was instructed to retire upon a prepared position which Grimaldi occupied at the junction of the roads from Waterloo and La Hulpe. All the intervening land being covered with impenetrable wood, these dispositions appeared adequate to delay the progress of the allied army, while the main body of the French fell back at the very last moment upon Brussels. But in case Grimaldi and Pasteur should prove unequal to their task, three brigades of foot were transferred to the extreme right of the French line, and posted on the eastern fringe of the forest of Soignies,

Marlborough, who had early intelligence of the enemy's movements, saw with satisfaction their growing anxiety for Brussels, On Monday afternoon, to confirm them in the erroneous opinion which they had evidently formed, he ordered a detachment from Overkirk's army to dislodge Pasteur from Waterloo. After a sharp engagement, Pasteur was driven from his entrenchments, and pursued for three miles towards Brussels. Meantime, the Duke was busily engaged in interrogating peasants familiar with the valley of the Yssche, and in selecting guides who had a thorough knowledge of the banks and fords. That evening he retired to bed at an early hour. But he was soon awakened by a report that the enemy were advancing in force. He hastily mounted, and rode out to Waterloo, only to discover that the alarm originated in nothing more important than the return of Pasteur to his former post.

Before daybreak on Tuesday Marlborough dispatched his heavy baggage to Wavre, and ordered Churchill with twenty battalions and twenty squadrons to take the road to Groenendael, which was also the straight road from La Hulpe to Brussels. It was Churchill's real function to act against the right flank of the French position, while Marlborough himself assailed the front. But the Duke anticipated that this powerful column, advancing in the direction of the capital, would be taken for the vanguard of the allied army. Meantime that army was marching by its right in three columns, between the Yssche and the Lasne.

Rumours of these movements came quickly to the French generals. They saw at once that, if Churchill pressed on, through Groenendael and Boitsfort, into the plain of Brussels, he would turn the strong position which Grimaldi had prepared on the Waterloo road. They therefore instructed that general to abandon a post, which no longer possessed any value, and to occupy a new one at Boitsfort, where Churchill presumably would debouch from the forest. They also sent Grimaldi a couple of brigades of foot, which could ill be spared from the already reduced forces available for the defence of the Yssche. A little before 7, they received an explicit report that the whole of the infantry of the allied army was moving upon Brussels, and that the columns in motion between the Yssche and the Lasne consisted only of mounted troops, intended to amuse the main body of the French.

This statement, coinciding as it did with their own presuppositions, they accepted as entirely true. It placed them in a terrible dilemma. If they stayed where they were, they would sacrifice Brussels; if they rushed to Brussels, they would abandon Louvain. It was necessary to choose, and to choose quickly. After a brief debate, they decided that, whatever else was lost, the capital must be preserved. But they postponed for a little the necessary orders, while they rode out in person to reconnoitre the advancing columns. Marlborough's leading squadrons were now distinctly visible. More and more cavalry followed. Suddenly from the dark masses of woodland the scarlet-coated infantry issued forth into the plain. It was enough. Realising at last that they had been completely fooled, the three generals galloped back to camp. They knew now that they must fight, and fight at a grave disadvantage. For now, as at Blenheim, Marlborough had surprised his enemy.

By 9 o'clock the allied army, having passed the forest and several defiles, which might easily have been held against them, obtained a fair view of the French position. From the bustle and excitement which prevailed among the enemy, it was evident that the contingency of a battle on the Yssche had not been seriously contemplated. The Elector and the Marshals were therefore compelled to make their dispositions and improvise their defences under the interested eye of Marlborough himself. The Duke dashed eagerly forward to examine the ground. He discovered no fewer than four points which seemed to him most suitable for assault. He rode so close to one of them that he attracted the fire of the French gunners.

When the round-shot came whistling across the stream, he remarked with a smile that these gentlemen did not choose to have that particular place too narrowly inspected. He could plainly see that, try as they would to extend themselves for effect, the French forces were insufficient in number for the position which they occupied. He also noted that the sun had hardened the marshy ground adjacent to the river. As he returned from Neeryssche, he encountered Overkirk and showed him the situation of the French right, which the Dutch army was destined to attack. The two rode back towards Huldenberg, when the Duke's eye detected a spot so feebly defended that he ordered the nearest troops to seize it forthwith. But on learning that his artillery had not yet arrived, he held his hand.

Thereupon, the enemy, who had perceived his intention, hastily brought cannon to the threatened point. The guns of the allies had marched in a separate column, and under strict injunctions to proceed with the utmost expedition. They had, however, been wantonly delayed by Schlangenberg, who, in spite of the Duke's express command that no baggage should mingle with the train, had insisted with his usual brutality and insolence that his own belongings should hamper the mobility of this important arm.

Shortly after noon the allied line was entirely formed. For the third time Marlborough rode along the front of the French position, and for the third time satisfied himself that the task which he had set his army was well within their powers. He was convinced that the enemy would be beaten in any event, and that if they seriously attempted to stand their ground they would be destroyed. Approaching the field-deputies, he congratulated them upon the prospect of a brilliant victory. They received him coolly; and when he suggested that they should sanction an immediate advance, they replied that it was necessary in the first place to consult their generals.

All superfluous delay reduced the advantages, both moral and material, which Marlborough's skill had secured. He submitted, however, with a good grace, and himself addressed the Dutch officers. He told them that he had carefully examined the ground, and made every preparation for immediate attack. He expressed the opinion that the allies were already too deeply committed to withdraw, except at the price of their reputation, and that the opportunity was too fair to be lightly thrown away. In particular, he drew attention to the hurry and confusion, manifest in all the motions of the French; and while he admitted that the day was already far spent, he urged that, if a night's respite were granted, the position would be fortified under cover of darkness and the price of victory indefinitely raised.

An ominous murmur ran round the group; but none made answer, till Schlangenberg at last cried out that, since he had been brought to Overyssche without having been previously consulted, it was his opinion that an assault at that point was impracticable. The conclusion in no way followed from the premises. But the Dutch generals, feeling as Albemarle had complained to Heinsius that they were "treated like children," had evidently resolved to behave as such. Schlangenberg having added that whatever orders he received, he was prepared to execute, Marlborough remarked that he was fortunate in possessing the services of so courageous and capable a subordinate. He requested the Dutchmen to raise no difficulties, when time was precious, and offered to entrust him with the command of the attack on Overyssche.

"Murder and massacre,"[37] growled Schlangenberg. Thereupon, the Duke suggested that, to spare the army of Holland, two English regiments should be employed to every Dutch one. Schlangenberg objected that he could not speak the English language. Then Marlborough promised him German troops. Schlangenberg merely reiterated his original statement that an assault at that point was impracticable.

The Duke, who had not hitherto abandoned his accustomed gentleness of tone, began to be angry. As he would not condescend, he said, to expose his soldiers to risks which he himself was unwilling to share, he would in person direct the assault at Overyssche. He then exhorted the field-deputies, in the most solemn language, not to fling away so splendid an opportunity. They remained unmoved. The discussion prolonged itself for two hours. A messenger arrived from Churchill with the news that he had occupied Groenendael at 10 o'clock, but that, the enemy having blocked the ways with timber, and concentrated a powerful force in the neighbourhood of Boitsfort, he could not debouch from the forest at that point. Marlborough sent him orders for a temporary retirement. Meanwhile the senseless controversy continued for yet another hour.

"That beast Schlangenberg," says Hare,[38] "was very noisy"; and according to Cranstoun, he "spoke frowardly and harshly to the Duke."[39] Overkirk, to his everlasting honour, advised the field-deputies to consent to the attempt, and alone among his compatriots maintained that

---

37. Coxe, vol. 1., p. 310.
38. Hare MSS.: Francis Hare to his cousin (George Naylor), August 20, 1705 (Hist. MSS. Comm., 14th Report, Appendix, part 9., p. 205).
39. Portland MSS.: Major J. Cranstoun to Robert Cunningham, October 1, 1705 (Hist. MSS. Comm., 15th Report, part 4, p. 254).

it was perfectly feasible.

Marlborough at one moment would stand a little way apart, wrestling with his indignation and his shame; at another, he would plunge into the discussion, using "sometimes fair words and sometimes hard ones."[40] Eventually he told the field-deputies that "if they neglected this opportunity, they could never answer to it to God or their masters, and that this should be the last time he would lead them to an enemy."[41]

But the generals, with the exception of Overkirk, were unanimous against him. And the field- deputies decided, like true republicans, by counting noses. What did it matter that Overkirk was their own field-marshal, a favourite soldier of William, and a veteran fighter who had seen more of war than any man in the Dutch service? What did it matter that Marlborough was commander-in-chief of both the allied armies, that he had virtually been appointed by William himself, that his last campaign had amazed Europe, that at the passage of the lines he had just exhibited afresh the superiority of his talents? In the Dutch army, besides Schlangenberg and Salisch, generals of infantry, there were seven lieutenant-generals, and nine major-generals, or eighteen in all. What were two against so many? Unless they were prepared to admit the fatal doctrine that majorities can err, the representatives of the Republic had really no option in the matter. But after all, their faith in the democratic principle was not very robust. It stopped short at general officers. Had they taken a poll of the rank and file, the result might have astonished them.

It was resolved that an assault at Overyssche was impracticable. In regard to the remaining points which Marlborough and Overkirk had selected for attack, the Dutch generals, who had not inspected them, declined to express any opinion. They proposed that, in the first instance, Schlangenberg, Salisch, and Tilly should examine the ground. Marlborough requested three of his own officers, Noyelles, Bothmar, and Stark, to accompany the Dutchmen. Noyelles, who could not trust himself to keep the peace with such an insufferable person as Schlangenberg, begged to be excused. The other five rode off towards Huldenberg, while Marlborough withdrew to his own quarters with a heart well-nigh broken. The opportunity was passing. Before this reconnaissance was finished, it would have passed.

Bothmar and Stark did not enjoy their promenade. Everything

---

40. Hare MSS.: *Ibid.*
41. *Ibid.*

which the Dutchmen saw was a text for adverse criticism. The infantry could never wade through the Yssche, because it was too deep, nor the cavalry manoeuvre on its banks, because they were too soft. The French position was studded with villages, which were natural fortresses, and seamed with hollow roads, which were natural entrenchments. Even if a column succeeded in fording the river, its head would be blown away before it could deploy. And even if any portion of the Duke's project had once been feasible, it was so no longer, for the French were now busily employed with pick and shovel.

The party did not proceed as far as Neeryssche. In the circumstances it was unnecessary. Enough had been seen for the purposes of argument, and enough time had been squandered to damn the whole enterprise. The sun was descending towards the forest of Soignies when they turned their faces to the west. As they rode towards Overyssche, they discussed the relative strength of the opposing forces, and Schlangenberg produced a document, which purported to demonstrate in black and white that, both in squadrons and battalions, the allies were vastly outnumbered. Salisch enquired of Bothmar, who had fought at Blenheim, whether the position on the Yssche was not stronger than the position on the Nebel.

According to Schlangenberg (who was not a respecter of the truth), Bothmar replied that it was thrice as strong. Thereupon Salisch triumphantly remarked that the battle of Blenheim itself was widely condemned as an example of inconsiderate temerity on the part of the allies. Bothmar and Stark, who were Marlborough's men, heard him in silence. And in silence they quitted the party, and went to make their report to the Duke.

The others rode on to Overkirk's quarters. On the way they encountered Marlborough, who passed them without speaking. They found the Field-Marshal asleep in his coach, a spectacle which Schlangenberg appears to have regarded as peculiarly diverting.[42] The time was August. Overkirk was sixty-four. He had had little rest on the preceding night, and he had been long in the saddle. Also he had assisted for three hours at a debate in which Schlangenberg had been the principal orator. If he was drowsy, he had every excuse. But Schlangenberg's sense of humour was as abnormal as his sense of duty.

When Bothmar had finished his tale, Marlborough did not attempt to conceal his feelings. "I am at this moment," he said, "ten years older

---

42. See Schlangenberg's letter, printed in Lamberty, August 27, 1705 (t. 3., p. 487).

than I was four days ago."[43]

The French generals were astounded at their escape. But they made good use of the respite, for they regarded it as nothing more. That night they recalled the greater part of Grimaldi's detachment from the neighbourhood of Brussels. They erected new batteries at dominating points. They posted thirteen squadrons of the Household at Neeryssche, where the ground was suitable for cavalry. And all through the hours of darkness they laboured to fortify their line from end to end.

On Wednesday morning Overkirk informed Marlborough that the report of the three generals was entirely adverse, and advised him of the transformation which the art of the French engineers had effected in the night. The Duke, having personally examined the works, which were still in progress, realised that it would be worse than waste of time to reason with the field-deputies, and ordered the army to prepare to march. The French, who were fully expecting to be attacked, watched with anxiety the commotion in the allied camp. Late in the afternoon they saw, to their amazement, the hostile columns retiring on Basse Wavre. They were more than satisfied with their good fortune. Having dispatched four squadrons to observe the retreat, they made no attempt to harass it. In the words of Hare, "thus fell this noble enterprise."[44]

From Basse Wavre Marlborough dispatched his report to the States-General.

> "I should have writ," he informed the Duchess, "in a very angry style, but I was afraid it might have given the French an advantage."[45]

The style which he adopted was certainly restrained. Yet it exceeded what was usual in his communications with the Dutch government.

"I flattered myself," he told them, after briefly describing the situation on the Yssche, "I flattered myself that I might soon have congratulated your High Mightinesses on a glorious victory." He did not condescend to elaborate the technical arguments, which had been used at the council of war. With obvious irony he left that task to "*Messieurs* the Deputies." But he emphasised the fact that, in thinking that "the opportunity was too fair to let slip," he had been support-

---

43. Coxe, vol. 1, p. 311.
44. Hare MSS.: Francis Hare to his cousin (George Naylor), August 20, 1705 (Hist. MSS. Comm., 14th Report, Appendix, part 9, p. 205).
45. Coxe, vol. 1, p. 312: The Duke to the Duchess, August 19, 1705.

ed by the judgement of Overkirk. "However," he said, "I submitted, though with much reluctancy." The bitterness of his disappointment was fully revealed only in the postscript, which ran as follows:

> My heart is so full, that I cannot forbear representing to your High Mightinesses on this occasion, that I find my authority here to be much less than when I had the honour to command your troops in Germany.[46]

The report of the field-deputies was twice as long as the Duke's. They declared that all the generals, with the exception of Overkirk, had considered the attempt most hazardous, and had dwelt upon the horrors to which defeat would have exposed the army, cut off as it was from its hospitals and magazines, and had urged that the affairs of Holland and the Grand Alliance were "not yet reduced to such a condition" as to justify "so desperate a work." It was a plausible dispatch; but those who framed it had not sufficiently mastered the art of reticence. Having referred at the end to the mysterious marches which they had been instructed to permit without summoning a council of war, they added these illuminating words: "And we cannot conceal from your High Mightinesses that all the generals of our army think it very strange that they should not have the least notice of the said marches."[47]

By this one sentence they condemned themselves. For in exposing the malice which actuated their advisers, they exposed their own incompetence in accepting advice, which they well knew to be derived from a polluted source.

In justice to the Dutch generals it should be said that a majority of the officers of Marlborough's own army considered that an attack would have been attended with the gravest risks. But similar views were taken on the eve of Blenheim. Marlborough himself was entirely confident of success. That fact alone is not far short of scientific proof that success would have been assured. In any case, it is impossible to believe in the peculiarly "desperate" character of an undertaking, which had been approved by so wary and experienced a veteran as Overkirk, and which the French generals themselves, most cautious and orthodox of soldiers, fully expected to be carried through, even after time had been allowed them to fortify their position.

---

46. Murray, vol. 2 pp. 223, 224: Marlborough to the States-General, August 19, 1705.
47. Pelet, t. 5, p. 592: *Lettre des députées des États-Généraux au pensionaire Heinsius*, 19 *août*, 1705.

Marlborough's opinion did not rest upon the configuration of the ground or the details of the landscape. It rested on his certain knowledge that the three great factors of surprise, numbers, and moral were all upon the side of the allied army. That the French were surprised was manifest from the dispositions which they had made for the defence of Brussels, and from those which they had neglected to make for the defence of the Yssche. That they were outnumbered was known beforehand from the many detachments which they had sent away, and was demonstrated now by the dangerous sparseness of their lines at several points.

"We were at least one-third stronger than they,"[48] wrote Marlborough to Godolphin. That the moral of the allies was infinitely superior, could be presumed from the fact that very many of them had fought at the Schellenberg and Blenheim, and that all of them had just participated in the passage of the lines. By infallible signs, which he detected in his daily contact with the army, Marlborough knew well the spirit of the men. It was a significant circumstance that the warmest advocates of battle were to be found among the officers of his cavalry, the very arm which was supposed to be least able to operate against the French position. But the cavalry since its triumph on the plain of Tirlemont, would stop at nothing. Now, of these three factors, surprise, numbers, and moral, any one, by itself, might have sufficed to turn the scale in favour of a tactician so accomplished as Marlborough. The three together made victory certain.

As for the dangers consequent upon defeat, they were at least as serious for the French as for the allies. So sensible were the enemy of the magnitude of their risk, that all the prisoners and deserters, who were subsequently brought into the allied camp, unanimously declared that the Elector and the Marshals would never have stood before a resolute attack, but would have retired forthwith to Brussels. If, on the other hand, they had offered a determined resistance, it was Marlborough's considered judgement that "the affair would have been somewhat serious, and would have cost us a good many men, but that, according to all appearances, and considering our superiority and the excellence of our troops, we should have gained one of the most complete of victories."[49]

The allied army fell back by easy stages through Corbais to Tirlemont. Marlborough's correspondence on the road sufficiently dis-

---
48. Coxe, vol. 1, p. 314: Marlborough to Godolphin, August 19, 1705.
49. Murray, vol. 2, p. 225: Marlborough to Wratislaw, August 20, 1705.

plays his feelings. "The people I am joined with," he told Godolphin, "will never do anything."[50] And again: "It is next to impossible to act offensively with this army, so governed as they are; for when their general and I agree, as we did in this, that it shall be in the power of subaltern generals to hinder the execution, is against all discipline. Nor can I ever serve with them without losing the little reputation I have; for in most countries they think I have power in this army to do what I please."[51]

To Eugène, who had complained of apathy at Vienna, he wrote that he would gladly transport himself and half the forces in the Netherlands to Italy.[52] To Shrewsbury, who was suffering from gout, he declared: "Our army is in a manner laid up too by a disease, for which I see no cure."[53] To the States, who were sending him more soldiers, he explained that he had already too many for the use which he was permitted to make of them.

From Tirlemont he sent Dedem to besiege Léau, a small place surrounded by marshes, which had served as a point for the lines of Brabant. Dedem having threatened that he would put the garrison to the sword if they prolonged their resistance, they surrendered within a week. Four hundred men were taken, with twenty cannon and abundance of ammunition and meal. The demolition of the lines, which had been begun before the march to Overyssche, was now completed from Léau to the Mehaigne. The fortifications of Tirlemont, also, were dismantled. Then Marlborough passed the Demer, and encamped on September 19 at Aerschot. The French immediately abandoned their old lines on this side, and retired to new ones which they had constructed farther to the west.

Meantime the news of the fiasco on the Yssche had become the common property of Europe. Stanhope, the British ambassador at the Hague, printed and published Marlborough's dispatch to the States before the States themselves had seen it. A wave of shame and indignation swept across the masses of the Dutch people, who cherished an instinctive faith in the genius of the Duke. The generals and the field-deputies defended themselves as best they could. But the publication of their letters failed entirely to allay the storm. Except among the professed partisans of peace, they found no friends. The citizens of the

---

50. Coxe, vol. 1, p. 312: Marlborough to Godolphin, August 24, 1705.
51. *Ibid.*, p. 314: Marlborough to Godolphin, August 19, 1705.
52. Murray, vol. 2, p. 230: Marlborough to the Prince of Savoy, August 23. 1705.
53. *Ibid.*, p. 237: Marlborough to the Duke of Shrewsbury, August 27, 1705.

Hague convened a meeting to denounce them; and the government was urged on all sides to remedy so monstrous a scandal.

In England, where the passage of the lines had excited the highest hopes, the resentment of Marlborough's countrymen took even more active forms. The English knew little or nothing of scientific warfare; but they could recognise foolery when they saw it, as well as other men. A pamphlet, which assailed the Dutch in unsparing language, was openly sold in the streets of London, and nobody was punished for it. Vryberg, the Dutch ambassador, who had endeavoured to explain away the failure on the Dyle, was now "struck dumb."[54]

The Queen insisted upon strong action. The Cabinet resolved to send Lord Pembroke to the Hague to remonstrate with the States.

"What shall one say?" wrote Harley to Marlborough. "Your Grace's superior talents prepared a glorious victory for them, and they dared not, or would not, take hold of it. I know not what name to call this by; I cannot trust myself to reason upon it."

And he spoke as a practical statesman when he added, "this sort of conduct will put vast difficulties upon the Queen in obtaining supplies for another year; and it is a very great hardship that those who set themselves at home to oppose the Queen's measures and everything she shall do for the public good, should be furnished with such plausible, fatal arguments by our friends in Holland."[55] It was only too true. On August 23 the Queen had attended a public thanksgiving at St. Paul's. On August 29 it was known in London that Marlborough had failed. Rochester and his set were jubilant.

This aspect of the matter was continually before the eyes of Marlborough. While the clamorous sympathy of two peoples could not fail to alleviate his personal vexation, he dreaded the encouragement which the enemy must derive from a public exposure of the inherent vices of the Grand Alliance. He dreaded also the possible consequences to the Alliance itself. A blow of a particularly insidious kind had just been directed by Louis against the fabric of the coalition. In August he had secretly proposed to the States a treaty of peace upon terms distinctly advantageous to Holland. At such a moment, anything tending to create friction between the allied powers was much to be deprecated. For this reason, Marlborough, who had thought of resigning the command, determined to continue at his post. And for this reason also, he induced the Cabinet to abandon the idea of sending

---

54. Coxe, vol. i., p. 315: Harley to Marlborough, August 18/29, 1705.
55. *Ibid.*

Pembroke to the Hague, though the Earl's instructions had actually been drafted by Harley, and signed by Anne.[56]

At the same time, the Duke made no endeavour to conceal from the Dutch his contempt for the system upon which they expected him to conduct the war. "I entirely approve of your printing my letter,"[57] he wrote to Stanhope, whose action had been criticised. To the States-General, who were so deficient in humour as to suggest the expediency of concluding the campaign with some startling exploit, he wrote:

> Your High Mightinesses will permit me to reply to them that I have always been of the same opinion; that the situation of affairs demands that we push the enemy to the uttermost, as I have repeated more than once to the deputies and the generals,[58]

He assured them, however, of his anxiety to seize the first opportunity that should offer. He had reason to believe that the deputies and generals would not again have thwarted him. But it was now too late. The French, though they had been reinforced from Alsace, wisely preferred to remain quiescent, and to boast of a superiority which they dared not expose to the proof.

Schlangenberg, whose evil temper had not been improved by the outcry in Holland, talked at large against the Duke. He also circulated some letters in Dutch, which were reported to be highly disrespectful to his commander. Thereupon General Churchill took up his brother's cause, and sent Brigadier Palmes to Schlangenberg with a challenge. Schlangenberg denied that the letters contained anything offensive; and the matter was arranged. His position, however, grew more and more unpleasant.

Although he retained the sympathy of certain of his colleagues, such as Albemarle, who protested to Heinsius that the Dutch generals could not have been treated worse had they been suspected of being French partisans, the populace raged furiously against him. The government was weary of his intrigues and his insolence. His suggestion that the unprofitable march to the Yssche had been contrived by Marlborough for the sole and subtle purpose of discrediting the Dutch generals was received with incredulity.

"Had he come to Amsterdam—after he hindered the battle," said

---

56. Portland MSS.: The Queen to [the Earl of Pembroke], August 30, 1705 (Hist. MSS. Comm., 15th Report, Appendix, part 4., p. 237).
57. Murray, vol. 2., p. 255; Marlborough to Stanhope, September 5, 1705.
58. Ibid., p. 260; Marlborough to the States-General, September 14, 1705.

Shrewsbury, "he would have been de Witted."[59] Yet Amsterdam was the headquarters of the peace party. Before the army left Tirlemont, Schlangenberg took himself off to Maestricht on a convenient plea of ill-health.

"It would have been happy for the common cause," said Marlborough, "had he been sick two months ago."[60] He never served under the Duke again. He never served in any capacity again.

Marlborough himself was far from well. Repeated disappointments had depressed his mind and lowered his vitality. At Tirlemont he drank the waters of Spa; but he soon discontinued them, as they caused his head to ache. At Turnhout, on September 21, he had an interview with Buys, the leader of the peace party, who told him that the constitution did not permit the government to deprive the field-deputies of their powers. But Buys explained that King William had solved the problem by exerting his authority to procure the appointment of such persons "as he was sure would nowise oppose or dispute what he thought for the service,"[61] and "as always agreed to whatever he had a mind to."[62]

Assurances were now given that this method should be adopted in future, and that Schlangenberg at any rate should never be employed where the Duke commanded. On these "fair promises," Marlborough's comment to Harley was laconic: "I wish we may find the effects of them."[63]

"By the whole," he wrote to Godolphin, "I find they would be very glad to content me."[64] But he did not fail to remark that they had an invincible dislike of fighting battles. He had always regarded the policy of waging offensive warfare in the Spanish Netherlands as unsound. He now regarded it as impossible.

Eugène summed up the situation in two sentences: "I speak to you as a sincere friend. You will never be able to perform anything considerable with your army, unless you are absolute."[65]

Having given orders for the fortification of Diest, Tongres, and Hasselt, posts which were intended to cover the winter-quarters of

---

59. Buccleuch MSS., vol. 2, part 2, p. 796; Journal of the Duke of Shrewsbury, December 5, 1705.
60. Coxe, vol. 1, p. 323: Marlborough to Godolphin, September 17, 1705.
61. Murray, vol. 2., p. 276: Marlborough to Harley, September 24, 1705.
62. Coxe, vol. 1, p. 323.
63. Murray, vol. 2, p. 271: Marlborough to Harley, September 22, 1705.
64. Coxe, vol. 1., p. 323.
65. *Ibid.*, p. 322: Eugène to Marlborough, September 13, 1705..

the troops, Marlborough moved from Aerschot, on the 28th, to Herenthals. A fortnight later he paid a brief visit to the Hague, where among other matters he discussed with Heinsius the French offer to Holland, and satisfied himself that it would not be accepted. He decamped from Herenthals on October 20, and marching by Oostmael and Brecht, arrived on the 23rd at Campthout. Noyelles was detached to besiege Santvliet, the garrison of which had annoyed the inhabitants of Zealand. Santvliet surrendered on the 29th. Marlborough had departed three days earlier for Düsseldorf. He was bound for Vienna, whither the Emperor had urgently summoned him.

While the allied army was at Campthout, d'Artaignan swooped suddenly on Diest, and captured four battalions and a regiment of dragoons. Diest had only the remnants of a Roman wall, a dry ditch, and some newly erected redoubts and palisades. Knowing the risk, Marlborough and the Dutch generals had resisted the proposal to remove the army so far away as Santvliet. But the States of Zealand had insisted. The French were absurdly uplifted by the recovery of this insignificant post, which they had abandoned with precipitation when the lines were forced. With this ludicrous anti-climax terminated a campaign which Marlborough had hoped to finish within striking distance of the gates of Paris.

Ever since the humiliating exhibition of the Yssche, Villeroi and Chamillart had been exchanging views derogatory to the English general.

> "I have formed," wrote the minister, whose name has long been forgotten in Europe, "I have formed a mediocre opinion of the capacity of the Duke of Marlborough."[66]

The Marshal, whose name, unhappily for himself, is still remembered, described his antagonist as a "mortified adventurer."[67] Conveniently overlooking the agonies of apprehension, which he and his colleagues had suffered when the allies marched up from Genappe to Mont St. Jean, he pretended that Marlborough's strategy on that occasion was fantastic and unprofitable. He represented the notorious obstruction of the Dutch generals as a figment, invented to cloke the incompetence of the commander-in-chief. He depicted the Duke as a desperate gambler, whose wonderful luck at Blenheim had turned

---

66. Pelet, t. 5, p. 608: *Lettre de M. de Chamillart à M. le Maréchal de Villeroy*, 6 *septembre*, 1705.

67. *Ibid.*, p. 90; *Lettre de M. le Maréchal de Villeroy à M. de Chamillart*, 30 *septembre*, 1705.

his head.

According to Villeroi, Marlborough spent September and October in soliciting the States for permission to hazard all upon a final throw. The Marshal sincerely believed what he said. On his theory of war, which resembled that of the Dutch generals, a commander who consistently set out to destroy the enemy in battle was a dangerous lunatic, who ought, in the interests of both sides, to be placed under restraint.

"Flanders," he declared, "has been saved by a miracle."[68] In a sense he was right, for Schlangenberg and the political and military system for which Schlangenberg stood might almost be said to have transcended human experience. But it is unsafe to presume upon miracles. Marlborough's next throw left Villeroi bankrupt.

---

68. *Ibid.*

Chapter 13

1705–1706

When Marlborough turned his gaze to Germany and Italy, he saw but little to compensate the Grand Alliance for the frustration of his projects in Lorraine and the Spanish Netherlands. Villars, after driving the Imperialists from the lines of Weissenburg, had been compelled to abandon the offensive, because the Margrave of Baden had concentrated an army which considerably outnumbered the French. But despite the remonstrances which reached him from Vienna, and the insulting criticisms which assailed him on all hands, the Margrave was painfully slow to act. In September, however, he suddenly threw off his lethargy, surprised Drusenheim, forced the lines of Hagenau, and blockaded Fort Louis, when the lateness of the season brought his progress to an end.

In Italy, where the fall of Ivrea, after a defence which lasted from October, 1704, to April, 1705, had left the Duke of Savoy with no other fortress than his capital of Turin, Eugène had made a desperate effort to break through to the rescue of that indomitable prince. But even with the assistance of the 8,000 Prussians, the ragged and half-starved army which the government of Vienna had placed at his disposal was unequal to the task. By sheer audacity and skill he did indeed advance as far as Cassano on the Adda. But here, on August 16, after a bloody and indecisive battle with Vendôme, he was compelled to relinquish the attempt. He had done enough, however, to turn the French from their design of besieging Turin; and when in November both armies retired to winter-quarters. Savoy still stood, resolute and unconquered, at the gates of Italy.

The French government, which was admittedly playing for time, had reason to congratulate itself on these results. But its satisfaction was rudely broken by events in Spain, where Marlborough's Mediterranean policy bore substantial fruit. Gibraltar, which had been skilfully relieved by Leake, held out until the last week of April, when Tessé abandoned the siege. It had cost the Bourbons 12,000 soldiers, 1,700 seamen, and 5 line-of-battle ships, besides frigates and other vessels.[1] The defenders' losses did not exceed 1,500 men.

On April 24 Galway took the field with 17,000 men, of whom 12,000 were Portuguese and the remainder Dutch and English. He had wished to besiege Badajos; but the Portuguese obliged him to begin with Valencia and Albuquerque. Both places fell before the end of May. The allied army then advanced towards Badajos, and encamped within four miles of the town. Tessé, who had returned from Gibraltar with 5,000 men, made ready to dislodge them; but before the middle of June the Portuguese government recalled the troops, and dispersed them in their summer-quarters.

Encouraged by the success at Gibraltar, the English Cabinet had resolved once more to employ its naval strength in the Mediterranean, and to attempt, if possible, a diversion in Catalonia, where the inhabitants were credibly reported to be ripe for revolt. On June 20 the fleet, under Shovel, arrived at Lisbon. It consisted, with Leake's squadron, of fifty-two sail of the line. A Dutch squadron of fourteen sail of the line was already awaiting it. The land forces on board numbered 6,500, British and Dutch. Indisputably the fittest person to command the troops of Queen Anne was Hesse-Darmstadt, who knew Catalonia well, and was popular among the inhabitants, and whose military reputation had been firmly established long before he illustrated it at Gibraltar.

But the Prince's religion disqualified him for service under the English Crown. It was necessary to select a Protestant. The choice had fallen upon Charles Mordaunt, Earl of Peterborough and Monmouth, one of the most eccentric and unintelligible characters in history. That Peterborough had talents of the highest order is hardly to be gainsaid. But he was very deficient in that power of concentration which is essential to solid achievement.

"His desire to do too much, and all things at once," said Methuen, "often hinders the success of any."[2]

He alternately dazzled his contemporaries by his brilliance, and disgusted them by his affectation and his inveterate self-advertisement.

"I question not," said Newcastle, "our Condé de Peterborough will

---

1. Colonel Arthur Parnell, *The Way of the Succession in Spain*, p 96.
2. Murray, vol. 2., p. 573.

not be out rhodomontado'd by any Don of 'em all."³

While his fascinating manners conquered the hearts of both sexes, his inordinate vanity forbade him to contemplate greatness in others without a malicious desire to humiliate or ruin them. His conduct in the affair of Sir John Fenwick was a shameful example of this unpleasing trait. But even the disgrace which this incurred had attractions for Peterborough, for disgrace brought with it notoriety. The Marlboroughs apparently bore him no grudge for the part which he had played on that occasion. The Duchess indeed had been captivated by his charm, no less than by his uncompromising Whiggery. She supported his candidature for the Spanish command, and her husband did not oppose it. It was true that the Earl possessed no practical knowledge of the art of war. But Marlborough had perfect confidence in the Prince of Hesse-Darmstadt, and he may well have hoped that the authority of the Prince would derive additional strength from the inexperience of the English general. As for the government, they were doubtless pleased at this juncture to exercise their patronage in favour of a known Whig.

At Lisbon on July 12 a council of war was held under the presidency of King Charles. Darmstadt, who had been summoned from Gibraltar, described the favourable disposition of the Catalans and moved that the expedition proceed forthwith to Barcelona. Some of those present advocated an attack on Cadiz. But Darmstadt's resolution, which followed the known preference of the English government, was carried by a great majority, which included Galway, Peterborough, and the King himself. On July 24 Charles embarked with two regiments of Galway's dragoons, and the fleet set sail. At Gibraltar eight seasoned battalions were taken on board in exchange for English recruits.

On August 11 Shovel cast anchor in Altea Bay on the coast of Valencia. Charles was well received by the inhabitants, with whose assistance he seized the fortress of Denia, and converted it into a centre of insurrection. At this stage Peterborough, who seems to have had some sort of secret understanding with the Duke of Savoy, proposed to abandon the attempt on Barcelona and to sail for Italy. But knowing by a letter from Mr. Hill, the English envoy at Turin, that Victor Amadeus was in no immediate peril, Charles declined to modify his plans. On the 16th Darmstadt sailed on before to Mataro, where he arranged with the leaders of the Catalans for an armed rising.

---

3. Portland MSS.: The Duke of Newcastle to R. Harley, August 1, 1705 Hist. MSS. Comm., 15th Report, Appendix, part 4., p. 215).

On the 22nd the fleet dropped anchor three miles east of Barcelona. The troops and marines disembarked, and encamped within a mile of the city. Here they were joined by an ever-increasing swarm of Catalans. But although Barcelona was an obsolete fortress with an untrustworthy garrison and a disloyal populace, and although the allied troops and the insurgent Catalans were eager to be led to the assault, a delay of three weeks ensued. For this waste of valuable time Peterborough was entirely responsible. He summoned no fewer than six councils of war, at which he represented the project as a hopeless one, and urged the necessity of proceeding to the assistance of Savoy.

He was supported by his generals; but Darmstadt, Shovel, and the Admirals opposed him, and Charles refused flatly to desert the Catalans. In these discussions Peterborough displayed both obstinacy and inconsistency. His conduct disgusted the regular forces, and alarmed the irregular ones. At last he was induced by Darmstadt to consent to a proposal to surprise Montjuich, an outlying fort situated on a hill, 1,100 yards to the south-west of the town, and garrisoned by no more than 200 men.

On the evening of September 13 the troops selected for the operation marched off into the country. Darmstadt and Peterborough accompanied them. They followed a circuitous route of twelve miles, and owing to the darkness of the night and the badness of the roads, did not arrive before Montjuich until the day had broken. Nevertheless Darmstadt delivered the assault. The ladders were found to be too short, the stormers were repulsed, and the governor of Barcelona threw into the fort 100 dragoons, each with a grenadier upon his crupper.

Dashing off with 400 men to intercept communications with the town, Darmstadt received a mortal wound in the thigh. He expired almost immediately, and with him "the very life and soul of the Austrian cause in Spain."[4] A panic ensued. At this crisis Peterborough, who was nothing if not theatrical, drew his sword and threw away the scabbard. But he exhibited a great deal of gallantry, successfully rallied the runaways, and with the help of Stanhope brought up the reserves and restored order. Montjuich was isolated. It was then bombarded. On the 17th it surrendered. The siege of Barcelona itself was now undertaken.

Shovel landed the heavy artillery and a serviceable detachment of seamen. A breach was effected. On October 4 the governor began to

---

4. Colonel Arthur Parnell, *The War of the Succession in Spain*, p. 132.

negotiate. On the 14th the populace rose and admitted the Catalans. The allies entered the city, and Peterborough exerted himself to restrain disorder and to protect both life and property. Two thousand five hundred soldiers, or two-thirds of the garrison, enlisted under Charles.

Meantime the Catalans in the west had seized Lerida and other places, and were threatening the frontiers of Aragon. In the south they took Tortosa and invested Tarragona, which being cannonaded by some vessels from Shovel's fleet, surrendered on October 27. Valencia, too, was seething with disaffection. All Catalonia declared outright for Charles. At last he was king in fact of one Spanish province, and of one that was exceptionally fertile in fighting men. This was a powerful diversion; it was also a distinct step towards the conquest of the kingdom. Darmstadt, Marlborough, and the English government were more than justified.

The enemy had been unable to relieve Barcelona, because in the beginning of October the army of Portugal had again taken the field, and had appeared before Badajos with 21,000 men. Tessé was therefore fully occupied in endeavouring to raise the siege of this important fortress. Galway having lost an arm, the command of the allies devolved upon Fagel. Tessé by a skilful movement threw 1,000 foot into Badajos. Thereupon Fagel, who had little heart in the enterprise, abandoned it, and retired to Lisbon.

In the autumn of 1705 all men could see that the Grand Alliance had more to fear from its own vices than from the power of France. Dissipated energies and divided counsels were hurrying the coalition to the brink of ruin. Marlborough's misfortunes in Lorraine and the Netherlands have already been described. The Emperor was urging him to resume operations on the Moselle, while Sunderland was urging the Emperor to dismiss the Margrave in the first instance. French diplomacy was tampering with Holland. Austria was protesting against the duplicity of the Dutch, and questioning the integrity of England. The King of Prussia, who had various complaints against the States-General, the Emperor, and the Margrave, was threatening to withdraw his troops from Italy and the Rhine.

As if the interminable rebellion in Hungary were not a sufficient drain upon Austrian resources, the Bavarian peasantry, provoked by maladministration and French intrigue, had openly revolted. Eugène was representing that, without large reinforcements and larger subsidies, the army of Italy must be recalled. Godolphin was grumbling that England had already done enough and more than enough for the House of Austria. And Charles was employing in Catalonia troops which Peterborough desired to divert to Italy, and which Eugène himself desired to see in Naples or Piedmont.

Sensible that unity of purpose and concentration of force could alone ensure success, the Emperor was anxious to take counsel with Marlborough in person at Vienna. After the fatigues of the last campaign, the Duke regarded the prospect of so long a journey on the eve of winter without enthusiasm.

"I am worn to nothing," he wrote to Godolphin, ". . . I am so extremely lean that it is uneasy to me when I am in bed."[5]

But Sunderland reported that the presence of his father-in-law at Vienna was "absolutely necessary," and "that if he does come, there is nothing in the power of this court that he will not persuade them to."[6] The King of Prussia desired that Marlborough should visit the Emperor, the Emperor desired that he should visit the King of Prussia, and the States-General desired that he should visit them both. The English ministers, though they wanted him in London, decided in the interest of the common cause, that he should proceed to Vienna and return by way of Berlin and Hanover. They gave him ample powers of negotiation. During his short visit to the Hague he procured from the Dutch government authority sufficient for his purpose. On all hands it seemed to be accepted that the Duke was the only man in Europe who could hold the coalition together, and utilise its resources to any real advantage.

Marlborough arrived at Düsseldorf on October 28. On the 29th he was magnificently entertained by the Elector Palatine, with whom he provisionally arranged for the increase of the Palatine forces and for the dispatch of a strong contingent to Italy. On the 31st he reached Frankfurt, where he was visited by the Margrave of Baden. Marlborough listened attentively to the Margrave's projects for the next campaign; but he attached no value to the promises of a prince who could sacrifice the interest of Europe to a private grudge. Their public intercourse, however, revealed nothing to the closest observers but cordiality and confidence. The Duke continued his journey on the 3rd, and came on the 6th to Ratisbon. At every stage, he encountered fresh evidences of his popularity in Germany. Everywhere he was re-

---

5. Coxe, vol. 1, p. 342: Marlborough to Godolpliin.
6. *Ibid.*: Lord Sunderland to Godolphin, September 26/October 7, 1705.

ceived as the victor of Blenheim and the liberator of the Empire.

At Ratisbon he embarked upon a yacht, and after a six days' voyage on the Danube, reached Vienna on the 12th. He was met by Sunderland and Stepney, whom he accompanied to the British embassy. Joseph had offered to defray his expenses, and had prepared a princely palace for his use. But both these favours he declined. After a gratifying reception by the Emperor and the ladies of the Imperial family, Marlborough engaged in a series of important conferences with the Austrian ministers. He formed the opinion that they were sincerely desirous of pushing the war with vigour; but he recognised that their resources were unequal to their zeal.

Having settled the terms of a new treaty with the maritime powers in place of the old one which had lapsed at Leopold's death, he urged that the Empire would neither attain its own ends nor fulfil its obligations to its allies, so long as the Hungarian insurrection diverted its armies from their true objective. This was a delicate topic; but Joseph lent a willing ear to the Duke's representations, and promised that, if reasonable concessions would pacify the rebels, no mistaken notions of imperial dignity should stand in the way. He also exhibited a similar inclination to satisfy and to concihate the King of Prussia, who had actually recalled three regiments from the Rhine. Neither he nor his advisers, however, were so easily persuaded of the loyalty of the Dutch to the Grand Alliance.

But Marlborough was in a position to prove that the French proposals were not regarded seriously at the Hague; and he succeeded at length in allaying, if not in entirely removing, the suspicions which not unnaturally existed at the Austrian Court. In discussing the prospects of the next campaign, it was generally agreed that the Margrave of Baden should be bidden to Vienna to explain his views. And Marlborough wrote him a friendly letter, urging him in the public interest, no less than in his own, to accept the invitation.

But the question which at this time overshadowed all others was the question of the war in Italy.

"My army," wrote Eugène to Marlborough, "is ruined, the horses worn out with past fatigues, no sure footing in the country, and the enemy reassembling their forces in my front,"[7]

In these circumstances, much as he had desired to meet the Duke at Vienna, he did not venture to abandon his command. His immediate

---

7. Coxe, vol. 1, p. 356: Eugène to Marlborough, October, 1705.

need was money. To keep the field at all, he required 300,000 crowns. Marlborough did not hesitate. He pledged the maritime powers to advance this amount, England guaranteeing to find two-thirds of it. His own credit and the credit of his country stood high at Vienna. The bankers and merchants of that city readily consented to pay over to Eugène a first instalment of 100,000 crowns on behalf of the English government. But Marlborough had no intention of feeding a merely defensive war in Italy. He knew that the French were resolved to treat the Duke of Savoy as the allies had treated the Elector of Bavaria, and that they would spare neither men nor money in the attainment of their purpose. They must be met with equal spirit, Eugène must be enabled to march to Turin, and to expel the armies of Louis from Italian soil.

"If we could once be in a condition to act offensively in Italy," he wrote to Hill, "we should soon feel the good effects of it everywhere else."[8]

It was estimated that with £250,000 the offensive could be assumed. Marlborough undertook to raise that sum. It was possible, though hardly probable, that the Dutch might be willing to assist him. But in the event of their refusal, the Duke proposed to ask the people of England to subscribe the entire loan.

The Austrian ministers were satisfied. The Emperor's gratitude took a tangible form. He presented Sunderland with his portrait set in diamonds, and Marlborough with a diamond ring. And he took the opportunity of creating the Duke a Prince of the Holy Roman Empire. More than twelve months before, Leopold had desired to bestow this mark of imperial favour on the victor of Blenheim. But Marlborough having objected that a title without a territory was a barren honour, the offer had remained unaccepted, while the Court of Vienna was making various inadequate proposals which the Duke declined.

A suitable fief had now been discovered in the lordship of Mindelheim in Bavaria. Joseph created Mindelheim into a principality, and by a patent of November 14, 1705, he conferred the title of Prince upon the English general, as also upon his heirs and descendants both male and female. Marlborough had no time to make the acquaintance of his new subjects or to receive their homage. Formal and ceremonial matters arising out of the grant he entrusted to the management of Stepney.

---

8. Murray, vol. 2, p. 327: Marlborough to Hill, November 8, 1705.

An attack of the gout confined the Duke to his room for three days. During that time he was visited by everybody of distinction at the Imperial Court. Nowhere indeed did his amiable personality stand him in better stead than at Vienna. The Emperor treated him as an intimate friend; and Sinzendorf, Wratislaw, and the Prince of Salm did not disdain to imitate the example of their master. Wratislaw in particular he won completely by a secret promise to remove Stepney to some other capital at an early date.

On November 23 Marlborough and Sunderland set off for Berlin. With a considerate prevision, very grateful to travellers in late November, the Emperor had ordered elaborate and expensive preparations for their comfort on the way. They made the journey with three coaches and two waggons; but at every stage relays of six horses for each vehicle were awaiting them. The route lay through Ölmutz, Breslau, and Frankfurt on the Oder. In all the towns enthusiastic multitudes assembled to gaze upon the deliverer of the Empire. The nobility and the magistrates vied with one another in magnificent hospitahty. It was a hard season. The distance to be traversed was 532 miles. But thanks to the excellence of the arrangements, Marlborough and Sunderland accomplished the journey in eight days, and arrived at Berlin on the 30th.

Marlborough received a cordial welcome at the Prussian capital, where he was saluted by the Imperial Resident as Prince of Mindelheim. The King, who had a peculiar regard for him, poured into his ears a catalogue of grievances both imaginary and real. That the Margrave of Baden was an indifferent commander, Marlborough of all men was in no position to dispute. That the Dutch were in arrear with their payments to the Prussian troops, was also undeniable. But the demands upon their exchequer had been very heavy. Marlborough excused them as best he could, and promised on their behalf a prompt settlement of outstanding claims. He also laboured to remove such misunderstanding as had arisen with the Austrian government. His task was no easy one, for he found the monarch, as he reported to Harley, "very much exasperated both against the court of Vienna and the States."[9] The King's ill-humour was so pronounced, that Marlborough did not venture to raise the question of the regiments that had been recalled from the Rhine. But he spoke plainly to the ministers on the subject.

And he succeeded in renewing for another year the treaty which

---

9. *Ibid.*, p. 333: Marlborough to Harley, December 1, 1705.

secured the presence of 8,000 Prussian troops in Italy, though Frederick consented to sign it only "as a mark of respect to the Queen, and of particular friendship to the Duke."[10] In view of the continued troubles in the north, it included a secret article guaranteeing in the name of England the safety of the Prussian dominions. At parting, the King presented Marlborough with a diamond-mounted sword, while to Sunderland he gave a diamond ring.

On December 3 the Duke and his son-in-law set off for Hanover, which they reached on the 6th. Letters from England were awaiting him there. They contained intelligence which closely concerned the affairs of that court, and which imposed on him a task of extreme delicacy.

It was not without reason that the Cabinet had desired his presence in London in the autumn. The new Parliament had met in October; and although Harley was confident of a working majority in the House of Commons, which had proceeded with alacrity to the business of supply, the opposition was known to be powerful and vindictive.[11] In pursuance of the policy which had sent Lord Sunderland to Vienna, the Whigs had been gratified by the dismissal of Sir Nathan Wright, the incompetent Lord Keeper, and the appointment in his stead of William Cowper, who was one of the *Junta's* most prominent and able supporters.

The Queen's consent to this departure, which placed ecclesiastical patronage under the control of those whom she regarded as the enemies of the Church, had not been easily obtained. The influence of the Duchess had been exerted in vain. The methods of Sarah, which were peremptory rather than persuasive, had irritated Anne beyond endurance, and had caused the first unkindness between the two friends. Eventually the Queen had appealed to Marlborough himself for support. The Duke in his reply, while he manifested his personal sympathy with her views, had convinced her of the necessity of sacrificing them to the public good. Cowper was appointed only a fortnight before the meeting of Parliament. The Whigs were delighted. In the voting for a new Speaker of the House of Commons, Bromley, "the Tackers'" candidate, was beaten by forty-three votes.

But Tories like St. John regretted that circumstances should have compelled them to support his opponent, Smith, who was a deter-

---

10. Coxe, vol. 1, p. 360.
11. MSS. of the Earl of Mar and Kellie: The Earl of Loudoun to the Earl of Mar, October 12. 1705 (Hist. MSS. Comm., p. 237).

mined Whig. The bitterness of the vanquished was not concealed. In the debates on the disputed elections, the Duchess of Marlborough, who had exerted her influence in the borough of St. Albans, was denounced by Bromley as an Alice Perrers.

But the opposition had something more in their arsenal than common abuse. They put up Lord Haversham in the House of Lords to move that the Protestant succession could never be secure unless the Queen's heir, the old Electress of Hanover, came to reside in England. This was a stone judiciously calculated to slay several birds at the same time. In the first place, a proposal so essentially Whiggish in character, was expected by the Tories who promoted it to kill the electioneering slander that every Tory was a concealed Jacobite. Secondly, it was intended to secure for the Tory party the favour of the Queen's successor. And thirdly, it was designed to place the government in a dilemma. The project of inviting the Electress to England was, obviously, a prudent and sensible one. Nor was it new. Already the Duchess of Marlborough had frequently suggested it to the Queen. No subject of the Crown, unless he were a Jacobite, could honestly find fault with it. But the Crown itself both could and did.

The Queen detested the idea, "it being," as she declared, "a thing I cannot bear, to have any successor here, though but for a week."[12] When the Duchess "pressed her that she would at least invite hither the young Prince of Hanover, who was not to be her immediate successor, and that she would let him live here as her son,"[13] Anne most emphatically declined.

"She would listen," says Sarah, "to no proposal of this kind in any shape whatsoever." Rochester and Nottingham knew well "how insuperably averse"[14] the Queen had shown herself to any such measure. But they had nothing to lose. They could not forfeit a favour which had already been withdrawn from them. The ministry on the other hand must choose between two risks. If they supported Lord Haversham's motion, their relations with the Queen would become intolerably strained. If they opposed it, their loyalty to the Protestant succession could be questioned in the country. Godolphin's decision was soon made.

Supported by the lords of the *Junta*, he resisted the motion and

---

13. Conduct of the Duchess of Marlborough, p. 144: The Queen to Marlborough, July 22, 1708.
14. *Ibid* p. 142.
15. *Ibid* p. 143.

defeated it. There were those among the Whigs who considered that an error had been committed, and that advantage should have been taken of so fair an opportunity of ensuring the succession. These critics, however, could have known little or nothing of the Queen's mind. Anne was extremely irritated. She was fully capable of dismissing Godolphin, had he attempted any other course.

Suspecting that "the disagreeable proposal," as she termed it, was secretly encouraged by the Court of Hanover, she wrote to Marlborough that she depended on his "kindness and friendship to set them right in notions of things here."[16] It was more easily said than done. The old Electress, whose sympathies were already Tory, and who would gladly have fixed her residence in England, was highly indignant that Godolphin's ministry should have combined with the Whigs to defeat Lord Haversham's resolution.

Marlborough himself, as a member of that ministry and a personal friend of the Queen, was in a somewhat false position. Fortunately the Cabinet had decided to spoil the Tory game by introducing bills to naturalise the House of Hanover, and to provide for a commission of regency in the event of the Queen's death. The Duke was able to communicate this intelligence to the Electress and her son. They received it with genuine satisfaction. The Elector, who was inclined to Whiggery, gave little trouble.

"He has commanded me," wrote Marlborough to Godolphin, "to assure Her Majesty that he will never have any thoughts but what may be agreeable to hers."[17]

His mother was charmed by the Duke's manners, and persuaded by his arguments of the futility of antagonism to Anne. All misunderstanding had been completely removed when Marlborough and Sunderland departed on the 9th for the Hague. The Elector gave the Duke a coach and six, and the Earl a set of horses. The Duchess of Marlborough and the Electress subsequently exchanged presents.

On December 14 the Duke arrived at the Hague, where a letter from Eugène informed him that the French were sparing no effort to maintain and to augment their forces in Italy. The Prince insisted that the allied army must do one of two things, either take the offensive in superior strength, or abandon that theatre of the war altogether. "No consideration," he declared, "shall induce me to make another cam-

---

16. Coxe, vol. 1, p. 361: The Queen to Marlborough, November 13/24, 1705.
17. *Ibid.*, p. 362: Marlborough to Godolphin, December 8, 1705.

paign like the last, in which I wanted everything."[18] He urged that the maritime powers should furnish him with 10,000 men and a quarter of a million of money, that the Emperor should recruit and remount the Austrian troops, and that the fleet should effect a diversion on the Itahan coast. Marlborough had virtually arranged with the Elector Palatine and the Duke of Saxe-Gotha for the dispatch of 10,000 men to Eugène, on the understanding that the Dutch provided one-third of the cost, and the English the remaining two.

But the government of the Hague was so pressed for money that it was not until December 25 that they could be induced to pay their share of the loan of 300,000 crowns, and not until the 30th that they assented to the bargain with the Elector Palatine. When Marlborough hinted at the project of a second loan of a quarter of a milhon pounds sterling, the suggestion was so coldly received that, rather than hazard a rebuff, he determined to reserve for his own countrymen the entire honour of rendering this signal service to the common cause. Meantime the English Parliament was cheerfully voting both men and money to be employed in every theatre of the war. Marlborough had ascertained that the French were diverting troops from Alsace to Catalonia, and that with the exception of Italy, they regarded Spain as the most important field of action in the coming campaign.

Nevertheless he had experienced no little difficulty in persuading the Dutch to contribute their share of support to the operations in the Peninsula. "They pretend," he informed Godolphin, "to want everything."[19] At this time also he was much annoyed by the objections of the Princes on the Rhine to the quartering of troops in their territories during the winter; and he was eventually compelled to invoke the imperial authority in settlement of the dispute. But his principal vexation came from Vienna. An accidental delay having occurred in the payment of the first instalment of 100,000 crowns,

Wratislaw, who knew only too well that the army of Eugène was reduced to the most miserable straits, wrote to the Duke on December 12 in terms so bitter that a smaller man might have deemed them deliberately insulting. "We require realities and not merely hopes," he said. He spoke of "the cruel fate to which our own inability, and the negligence of our friends condemn us." In particular he complained of the insidious methods of French diplomacy. "I cannot sufficiently express our concern and surprise," he said, "in observing that the em-

18. *Ibid.*, p. 364: Eugène to Marlborough, December 2, 1705.
19. Coxe, vol. 1, p. 369: Marlborough to Godolphin, December 25, 1705.

issaries of France are freely permitted to appear at the Hague. Your Highness will recollect that you assured us they would be dismissed, and we gave full credit to your assertion, on which account we have not made any pressing remonstrances."

He went on to suggest that the negotiation was already far advanced, and that England, notwithstanding her high professions, was hypocritically promoting it. "We are already acquainted," he remarked, "with various intrigues of the German princes, who have followed the example of the Dutch."

In a postscript he inserted these words:

> A prompt succour in men and money is necessary for Italy, or at least we must entreat you to be so kind as to tell us plainly that it cannot be granted.[20]

Marlborough replied on December 27. He wrote with dignity, and with that gentleness which he invariably manifested under extreme provocation. Wratislaw's zeal for the House of Hapsburg had carried him too far. Marlborough told him as much. He stated precisely what he had done, what he was doing, and what he intended to do. He declared that the negotiations at the Hague were dead, and that those Dutchmen who had favoured them had already admitted their mistake. He referred to the sacrifices which England was making for the common cause, and which, as he justly observed, should have protected her from the stigma of Austrian suspicion. For himself, he protested that, if he had believed that his countrymen were contemplating a treachery, he should have held himself in honour bound to tell the Emperor.

The Duke continued at the Hague till January 7. Having procured the acceptance of all his proposals and arranged for the immediate departure of 4,000 Palatines, who would be useful in suppressing the disturbances in Bavaria, he sailed for home. He was accompanied by several of the captured officers, and also by Buys, whom the Dutch government had selected as a special envoy to the Court of St. James.

Marlborough received the thanks of the House of Commons for "his great services."[21] In his reply he expressed his indifference to all attacks originating in "private malice."[22] He had recently been libelled by one Stephens, a Whig clergyman, who was subsequently sentenced

---

20. *Ibid.*, pp. 366, 367: Wratislaw to Marlborough, December 12, 1705.
21. *Ibid.*, p. 374.
22. *Ibid.*

to be fined and pilloried for the offence. Stephens confessed his fault, and for the sake of his wife and children piteously appealed to the Duchess of Marlborough for a remission of the degrading part of his punishment.

The Duchess begged the Queen to exercise the royal prerogative. Anne consented, though reluctantly. "Nothing but your desire," she wrote, "could have inclined me to it."[23]

Marlborough was pleased with this result. "I should be very uneasy," he said, "if the law had not found him guilty, but much more uneasy if he suffered the punishment on my account."[24] Marlborough had all the English gentleman's loathing of publicity. "I do not love to see my name in print," he said, when the Duchess sent him an eulogistic pamphlet, "for I am persuaded that an honest man must be justified by his own actions and not by the pen of a writer, though he should be a zealous friend."[25]

Immediately upon his arrival in England, the Duke proceeded to negotiate the loan of a quarter of a million for the army of Italy. A quarter of a million had a much higher purchasing power then than now; and the population of England at that period did not exceed 6,000,000. The moment seemed hardly propitious, seeing that the Treasury was borrowing two and a half millions for its own uses. Nevertheless, the merchants and bankers of the City of London entered heartily into the project. The Emperor's credit was good; the security offered, "his lands, rents, and revenues whatsoever within the province of Silesia," was deemed satisfactory; but the rate of interest was fixed at 8 *per cent.*, though the Austrian government had suggested 7.

The capital was to be repaid in eight years. To encourage the public, Marlborough collected over £160,000 before the lists were open. Prince George subscribed £20,000. The Duke himself contributed £10,000, Portland £10,000, and Godolphin and Boyle £5,000 apiece. But no encouragement was needed. Eugène, as a fighting general and a loyal colleague, was immensely popular with all classes of the nation. The lists, which were opened on a Thursday, were complete on the following Tuesday, when money was refused.

This transaction was regarded by contemporary opinion as a remarkable proof of the country's wealth, and also as a vote of confidence in the foreign policy of the Cabinet. Marlborough announced

---

23. *Ibid.*, p. 375: The Queen to the Duchess.
24. *Ibid.*, p. 376: The Duke to the Duchess, May 20, 1706. 25. Ibid., p. 375: The Duke to the Duchess, May 9/20, 1706.

his success to the Austrian government with pardonable pride. He informed Wratislaw that the English people had taken a step without precedent in their history.[26]

And he congratulated Eugène on their evident belief that their money would not be wasted.

Marlborough found his colleagues of the government tolerably well satisfied with the progress of the first session of the new Parliament. Although the party system had not yet reached its full development, the fact that, unless ministers could collect and retain a majority of some sort in the House of Commons, they must sooner or later resign office, was broadly recognised. Godolphin and Harley flattered themselves that in the freshly elected House they were safe from defeat. There is in existence a document, which was addressed by Godolphin to Harley at the conclusion of the session, and which contains an analysis of the voting in the division on the Speakership. Out of 450 members who took part in it, no fewer than 100 are described as "the Queen's Servants."[27]

These were the men who held offices or seats or both by favour of the Crown, and who were expected to vote, and almost always did vote in obedience to the directions of the government of the day. They were for the most part Tories of the type of Harley and St. John. Of the remaining 350, 190 are described as Tories, and 160 as Whigs. More than two-thirds of the Tories had been "Tackers"; and Godolphin remarks that "their behaviour in this session has shown as much inveteracy and as little sense as was possible." Nevertheless with the steady support of the Whigs, who were well drilled and could generally be trusted to act together, the government had commanded a clear majority. Godolphin proposes to carry on upon the same basis. He has no objection to receiving Tory votes, but not at the expense of Whig ones. "I take it," he says, "our business is, to get as many as we can from the 190, without doing anything to lose one of the 160."

The alternative policy of playing entirely to the Tory party he regards as dangerous, because, as he argues, for every Tory vote that was captured, two if not three Whig ones would be lost. If those of the Whigs who were alienated should coalesce with those of the Tories who were not conciliatory, ministers might find themselves in a minority. In this conclusion Harley would appear, for the time being at

---

26. Murray, vol. 2., p. 404: Marlborough to Wratislaw, January 18, 1706.
27. Portland MSS.: Godolphin to Harley, March 22, 1705/6 (Hist. MSS. Comm., 15th Report, Appendix, part 4., p. 291).

any rate, to have concurred. But it constituted a distinct departure from the principle upon which the Commons had been "managed" in the preceding Parliament. Then it had been the aim of ministers, calling themselves Tories, to attract the less fanatical of both parties; now they were determined to rely upon a coalition of "the Queen's Servants" with the whole body of the Whigs.

It may be that Godolphin had really no option in the matter. It may be that the temper of politicians was now so embittered that the course which he and Marlborough had mapped out in 1702 could no longer be pursued. He at any rate was responsible for this altered policy. The Duke had neither taste nor time for the mysteries of wire-pulling. It was physically impossible that a man no longer young, and so immersed in military and diplomatic affairs as Marlborough was in 1705 and 1706, could give more than the most cursory attention to domestic politics.

When Godolphin represented to him the advantages of a change of front, he acquiesced with an almost suspicious readiness. "You shall govern me entirely as to my behaviour," he wrote, "for I shall with all my heart live friendly with those that have shown so much service to you and friendship to the Queen."[28] These words were written at the Hague on December 25, 1705, at a moment when the Duke's energies were wholly absorbed in the multitude of complex details, strategical, financial, and diplomatic, which composed the internal machinery of the Grand Alliance.

When Marlborough returned to England, he consented to join Godolphin and St. John at a dinner at Harley's, to which Halifax, Sunderland, Cowper, and Boyle were invited. The affair was an unqualified success; but when Harley, in giving the toast of "love and friendship," expressed regret that the supply of Tokay had run out, Cowper remarked that the "white Lisbon was best to drink it in, being very clear."[29] The Whigs, in short, suspected Harley of duplicity. And doubtless he had grave misgivings. Godolphin considered it "more reasonable and more easy "to use the Whigs than to woo the Tories. More easy it certainly was.

But the new system had perils of its own. Harley, who combined with the duties of a Secretary of State the responsibilities of a government Whip, was perhaps the first Englishman to make a scientific study of public opinion and the forces which modified and controlled

---

28. Coxe, vol. 1, p. 376.
29. Lord Cowper's Diary; Hardwicke Papers; Miscellaneous State Papers, 1501-1726

it. He had taken Defoe into his own service, and had employed that acute journalist to investigate the political conditions of parishes and boroughs in various parts of the country. He knew from the reports which Defoe sent him that the Toryism which everywhere rallied round the manor-house and the parish church was indisputably the greatest power in the country.

Despite the popularity of the war, the Whigs, with all the influence of their territorial magnates and their big financiers, were thirty votes to the bad as against the independent Tories alone, after an election in which Whiggery was considered to have done extremely well. Moreover, the Toryism of "the Queen's Servants" was not abjectly servile. It was not without reluctance that St. John had voted for the new Speaker. On that occasion the majority had fallen to 43, some 15 or 16 of the 100 having actually revolted. One of the mutineers, Dr. Clark,[30] member for a Cornish borough and secretary to the Prince of Denmark, was dismissed from the Royal Household 'to encourage the others.' If this tendency should develop, the position of the government might become precarious. In any case the moral authority of a Tory ministry which existed by the votes of placemen and of Whigs alone, could not fail to suffer diminution in the country at large.

The Queen herself was another source of anxiety. It was true that she had deeply resented the Tory proposal to invite the old Electress to England, and that she had admitted to "dear Mrs. Freeman "that she was not only grateful to the Whigs for their protection, but "thoroughly convinced of the malice and ignorance of others that you have been always speaking against."[31] But Haversham's motion had been an affair of tactics, not of principles.

On the other hand it was a principle with Anne that she should not be at the mercy of either party, and more particularly of the Whigs. Cowper's appointment had mortified her extremely. She would certainly resist the introduction of members of the *Junta* into the Cabinet. But how long could ministers who profited in Parliament by the votes of the obedient battalion of 160, ignore the claims of its distinguished leaders?

It was also a principle with Anne that the foes of the Church of England were her foes. The loss of the Occasional Conformity Bill, which she had always regarded as a just and necessary measure, had

---

30. Portland MSS.; News Letter, October 27, 1705 (Hist. MSS. Comm. 15th Report, Appendix, part 4, p. 268).

31. Coxe, vol. 1, p. 376: The Queen to the Duchess.

turned the mass of the parochial clergy into determined opponents of the existing administration. The Whig peers, after a set debate, had solemnly voted that the Church of England was "in a most safe and flourishing condition,"[32] and that whoever suggested that it was in danger was a public enemy. But the indignant clergy declined to accommodate their views to the votes of the Whig peers. They continued assiduously to undermine the popularity of the government in nine-tenths of the parishes of the kingdom.

Godolphin imagined that whoever controlled ecclesiastical patronage controlled the consciences of the Anglican priesthood. He was not the only English statesman who has made the mistake of doubting the sincerity of the Church and miscalculating her power. In an eyewitness of the Revolution the error was a gross one. He must at any rate have perceived that the profound discontent of the clergy was a cause of chronic uneasiness to so good a Churchwoman as the Queen. If a remedy were not forthcoming, the fact that the Sovereign could dismiss a ministry at will was not to be overlooked.

Even the greatest of Godolphin's achievements, the Union with Scotland, was at this time at any rate a source of embarrassment. William III, who was far too good a soldier not to realise that an impoverished, discontented, and separated Scotland was a grievous impediment to English strategy, almost with his dying breath recommended a Parliamentary union between the two countries. The idea was very unpopular beyond the Tweed. It could hardly be otherwise. A small but haughty people cannot be expected to contemplate with pleasure the partial sacrifice of nationality which incorporation in a larger state necessarily involves. The religion of the majority, moreover, was Presbyterian; and the Kirk was alarmed at the prospect of subjection to a legislature in which bishops and laity of the Church of England would overwhelmingly predominate.

Yet every intelligent Scot was sullenly conscious of the fact that, if his country was ever to be raised from a condition of squalid misery and chronic impecuniosity, she must get access to the markets of England and the English colonies. Parliamentary union was the price demanded. In the first year of her reign Anne appointed commissioners from both kingdoms to discuss the articles. Marlborough was one of them. His view of the question, which was also William's, plainly appeared in the Queen's expression of the hope that the result of the Commons' deliberations would be to "render this island more formi-

---

32. Boyer, vol. 5, p. 210.

dable than it has been in ages past,"³³ Unfortunately, commercial interests in England were too strong for the government, and the project speedily collapsed. Thereupon the Scottish Parliament assumed a defiant attitude.

In 1703 they declined to accept the Hanoverian Succession; and they carried a measure commonly known as the Act of Security, which declared that at the Queen's death, they should select a Protestant monarch, who should not be the monarch who succeeded to the Crown of England, unless in the meantime they had obtained a treaty guaranteeing "the honour and sovereignty of this crown and kingdom; the freedom, frequency, and power of Parliaments, the religion, liberty, and trade of the nation from English or any foreign influence."³⁴

To this disintegrating proposal the royal assent was refused. The Scots only hardened their hearts. They declined to vote a subsidy and gave orders to arm the nation. In July, 1704, the Queen regretfully informed them that "dissensions have proceeded to such a height as to prove matter of encouragement to our enemies beyond sea."³⁵ Yet they carried the Act of Security a second time, and "tacked "it to the subsidy for the army. Godolphin was now in a dilemma. The war had reached a most critical stage.

Marlborough was marching to the Danube, and no man knew if he would ever return. At any moment France might attempt a descent upon the Scottish coast. Setting the immediate safety of the realm above all other considerations, the Lord Treasurer advised the Queen to assent to a measure, which apparently might relegate the two countries to the position of antagonism which they had occupied in Tudor times. When Wharton heard that the Act of Security had become law, he remarked that "they now had the Lord Treasurer's head safe in the bag."³⁶ This elegant observation is illustrative of the patriotism of the Whig *Junta*. It meant that, if Godolphin were impeached, he could only be saved by Whig votes; and Whig votes would only be given in exchange for ofhce. There was much talk of impeachment that summer. According to Rochester and Nottingham, Marlborough himself was to be sent to the block for his march to the Danube. Blenheim shut these silly mouths.

But the union was now become a question of extreme urgency.

---

33. *Ibid.*, vol. 1, p. 158.
34. Ibid., vol. 2, p. 52.
35. *Ibid.*, vol. 3, p. 10.
36. *Ibid.*, *The History of Queen Anne*, p. 177.

According to Dalrymple, the Earl of Stair had warned Godolphin, on the passing of the Act of Security, "that he was on the brink of a precipice and the two countries on that of a civil war. From that instant the union was resolved upon in the Cabinet of England." [37] In 1705 the Queen was empowered to appoint commissioners. In England, however, the opposition of the commercial interests was strongly reinforced by the opposition of the Church.

The clergy contended that the Queen could not decently be asked to set up two religions in a single realm. They contended also that, so long as the Kirk refused even bare toleration to the Scottish Episcopalians and denounced it as "the establishment of iniquity by law,"[38] no English Churchman could vote for the Union. A government which had permitted the Occasional Conformity Bill to be lost, might recommend these things; but such a government deserved and would receive the inveterate hostility of every sincere member of the Anglican community.

It was abundantly evident that the government must stand or fall by the results of its foreign policy. The war was certainly popular; but its popularity could not be trusted to survive another campaign conducted on the peculiar methods of the Margrave of Baden and General Schlangenberg. The speech in which Lord Haversham proposed the invitation to the old Electress, had dealt very faithfully with the miscarriages on the Moselle and the Yssche. Haversham did not commit the blunder of attacking Marlborough. He rendered full justice to the generalship that had contrived both enterprises. But for that very reason the indictment which he drew against the allies was the more damning.

"Those who command your army," he said, "are men of that bravery, and every common soldier hath so much courage, that no equal number of men in the world, I think, can stand before them, but let our supplies be never so full and speedy, let our management be never so great and frugal, yet if it be our misfortune to have allies that are as slow and backward as we are zealous and forward, that hold our hands, and suffer us not to take any opportunity that offers, that are coming into the field when we are going into winter quarters, I cannot see what it is we are reasonably to expect."[39]

Haversham is contemptuously dubbed by the Duchess "a great

---

37. *Dalrymple's Memoirs*, p. 346, Appendix No. 7.
38. Lang, *History of Scotland*, vol. 4, p. 91.
39. Boyer, vol. 4, p. 193.

speech-maker and publisher of his speeches,"[40] But he was no mere hack of the Tory party. He had generally been regarded as a Whig; and he was conspicuous among the opponents of the Occasional Conformity Bill. He created a great reputation by a happy facility in the expression of ideas that were uppermost in the public mind. But the government, fearful of offending the allies, and especially the Dutch, deprecated all discussion on the miscarriages of the last campaign. Their majority in the Upper House rejected an embarrassing motion for enquiry which Haversham moved, and their press denounced this unseasonable orator in immoderate language.

He did not conceal his resentment that he should be scurrilously attacked for saying in a free assembly what every Englishman knew in his heart to be the truth, and what ministers themselves had only a few weeks before instructed Lord Pembroke to say in the Queen's name to the government at the Hague. It was distinctly to the interest of the Grand Alliance that the Germans and the Dutch should learn from some respectable source that English patience had limits. The popular indignation to which Haversham gave inconvenient utterance was strongly founded on deplorable facts. It menaced the very existence of the ministry, for those who were most ardent in their country's cause were precisely those who, in their hearts at any rate, were most disgusted by the misconduct of the allies.

None knew the reality of the danger better than Marlborough. He saw plainly that, unless decisive results could be obtained in the forthcoming campaign, the English people would in all human probability desert the coalition. For those results he looked to Italy and Spain. Much had already been done to establish the war in Italy on a proper footing. In Spain the success in Catalonia had been followed by the reduction of the province of Valencia. But Louis was making immense preparations to recover the lost ground. Tessé's army was to abandon the Portuguese frontier, and in conjunction with a second force that was assembling in Roussillon and with a fleet that was fitting out at Toulon, to form the siege of Barcelona by land and sea. To break this project the maritime powers were equipping fresh squadrons and were dispatching 5,000 troops to Catalonia.

They were also sending out that competent officer, Noyelles, who though in the Dutch service was a Spaniard by birth. Marlborough had persuaded him to assume command of the Spanish contingent in the army of Charles. At the same time, Galway, if the Portuguese

---

40. Conduct of the Duchess of Marlborough, p. 143.

would consent, was to take advantage of the departure of Tessé and march upon Madrid. Marlborough attached extreme importance to a vigorous movement in the direction of the capital.[41] To add to the accumulated anxieties of the French government, the Duke was planning a descent upon the coast of Guienne. This project had been suggested by Guiscard, a French nobleman who for private reasons had attached himself to the enemies of France. Seeing how dispersed and how remote from the centre of the kingdom the armies of Louis must necessarily be, Marlborough anticipated excellent results from this diversion, especially if it could be combined, as Guiscard hoped, with an insurrection in the Cevennes.

> "We may conclude," he wrote to Heinsius, "that this is the time that we ought to do something that they do not expect; . . . if they are surprised, they will find it very difficult to oppose us."[42]

Marlborough was in fact the organiser of victory in every theatre of the war. From October, 1705, to May, 1706, no soldier or statesman of the Grand Alliance laboured more indefatigably than he. The prompt arrival of the English recruits in Holland surprised and delighted Heinsius, who displayed what Marlborough regarded as unwarrantable nervousness of French intentions in the Netherlands. The Duke believed that both there and on the Rhine the enemy would remain upon the defensive. But he entertained no hope of beating them in either quarter.

The permanent obstacle to decisive action was the Margrave of Baden. The Margrave had steadily refused the Emperor's invitations to Vienna. His plans, if he had any, remained unrevealed until the last week in March,[43] when he transmitted to Marlborough a lengthy dissertation in German which he had promised to prepare five months before. The Austrian government had set its heart upon that strategy which Marlborough had always known to be the best, and which involved a great concentration of forces on the Moselle and the Saar. They actually formulated a plan by which Marlborough alone was to undertake the invasion of France at this point, while the Margrave was to be kept in ignorance of everything until the last moment, when he was to be left behind with a diminished army on the Upper Rhine.

---

41. Murray, vol. 2., pp. 407-416: January 28 to February 5, 1706.
42. Vreede, *Correspondance diplomatique et miilitaire*, p. 17: *Marlborough au Grand-Pensionnaire*, March 26, 1706.
43. Murray, vol. 2, p. 460: Marlborough to the King of Prussia, March 26, 1706.

Marlborough doubted the feasibility of deceiving Baden. Nor could he conquer the intense repugnance which, thanks to his experiences of the preceding campaign, he entertained towards a design that was in theory irreproachable.

But the Dutch government relieved him of all responsibility in the matter. They had satisfied themselves that the Margrave's army was inefficient, that his magazines were empty, and that he himself was incompetent and impracticable. They were fully determined that no army of theirs should again be committed to operations in which anything, great or little, depended upon his co-operation. Marlborough was aware of their sentiments. But they themselves, for all military purposes, were only one degree less incapable than the Margrave. Despite the assurances which he had received at the conclusion of the last campaign, the Duke expected that the new field-deputies would be little better than the old ones, and that another summer would be wasted in marking time in Brabant. In these circumstances he conceived the idea of leading 20,000 men from Flanders to Lombardy. Liberated from Dutch interference and once more united with Eugène, he hoped to chase the French from Italy as he had chased them from Bavaria.

From Italy he would pass into Provence, and with the assistance of the Mediterranean fleet accomplish the destruction of the naval arsenal of Toulon. To this brilliant and perfectly practicable design he obtained the immediate assent of the English Cabinet. That the government of the Hague would permit their soldiers to follow him so far, was more than he dared promise himself. On March 29 he wrote to Wratislaw from London that the States were unlikely to agree to anything in which Baden was concerned.

> "These uncertainties," he continued, "have made me turn my views on another project, which will be equally for the Emperor's interests." The nature of this project he abstained from revealing until, as he said, "I have sounded the humour of the States thereon."[44]

But it was evident from his letter that he was meditating something on a grand scale, "*quelque chose d'éclatant*,"[45] as he himself subsequently termed it. It was evident also that he regarded the general prospects

---

44. Murray, vol. 2., p. 462: Marlborough to Wratislaw, March 29, 1706.
45. *Ibid.*, p. 49G: Marlborough to the King of Prussia, May 9, 1706.

of the coalition with a pessimistic eye. "I pass the sea with sufficiently sad reflections,"[46] he said. The hardest and most sanguine workers have their moments of reaction.

When Marlborough embarked for Holland on April 21 he was accompanied by Buys, whose mission to England had been a complete success, and by Halifax, who, though a member of the Junta, had been selected to convey the Garter to the Electoral Prince of Hanover. The Duke arrived at the Hague on the 24th.

---

46. *Ibid.*, p. 462: Marlborough to Wratislaw, March 29, 1706.

CHAPTER 14

Ramillies

The Duke had every reason to be pleased with his reception at the Hague. The Dutch government, conscious that the military situation of the Grand Alliance was now extremely critical, and warned by the imperfectly muzzled growlings from across the Channel that even English patience had limits, seemed specially anxious to make itself agreeable to the Cabinet of Queen Anne. The report of Buys, which, in Marlborough's words, was characterised by "all the zeal and respect to Her Majesty and friendship to us imaginable, even beyond what I could have expected,"[1] completed the good understanding between the maritime powers. The States being in this accommodating temper, Marlborough presented them with a memorandum, in which the English government requested them to consider the expediency of guaranteeing by treaty the Protestant succession to the Crown of England. The deputies received the suggestion with favour, and according to Halifax, warmly expressed "their inclinations to comply with everything that the Queen desires of them."[2]

They showed themselves equally reasonable when he touched upon strategic questions. To one proposition, however, they were obdurately hostile. They would have nothing to do with any combinations whatsoever which depended in any way on the concurrence of the Margrave of Baden. Marlborough represented, as he had represented before, that an army of invasion on the Moselle and the Saar would threaten the French frontier in its most sensitive part.[3] This opinion he had always held; but the experiences of the campaign of 1705 had

---
1. Murray, vol. 2., p. 485: Marlborough to Harley, May 4, 1706.
2. Halifax to Harley, May 1/11, 1706. Record Office, State Papers, Holland, 225.
3. Murray, vol. 2., p. 473: Marlborough to Wratislaw, April 26, 1706: p. 495: Marlborough to the Emperor, May 9, 1706.

killed his desire to act upon it. He urged it now out of deference to the Emperor's wishes, though he knew beforehand that, as long as the Margrave commanded on the Rhine, it would never be admitted by the Dutch except as a counsel of perfection and an abstract truth.

He then unfolded to a few his Italian project. He was agreeably surprised to find that it was not immediately condemned.

"They are very positive," he wrote to Godolphin, "that they dare not consent to the letting their own countrymen go."[4]

But they were willing to entertain the suggestion, so long as it involved the use of no troops save the English and the auxiliaries. The merits of the design were rendered more apparent by the receipt of alarming news from Italy. On April 19, when Eugène had not yet arrived from Vienna, Vendôme had suddenly attacked the Imperialists with superior forces and beaten them at Calcinato in a battle which cost the allies 3,000 men.

But nothing could be done either in Lombardy, Germany, or the Netherlands without soldiers. And soldiers in sufficient numbers were not forthcoming. The King of Denmark presented a claim for arrears of pay, and refused to allow his troops to leave their winter-quarters until it was settled. The Elector of Hanover and the Landgrave of Hesse would not consent to the employment of their forces in Italy. The Elector indeed had adopted so peculiar a tone that Anne was provoked into sending him a remonstrance couched in no gentle terms. But Marlborough, who had already dispatched Cadogan to the Court of Hanover, wisely took upon himself to intercept the Queen's letter.

More serious still was the attitude of the King of Prussia, who had recently renewed his complaints against Vienna and the Hague. He embodied his demands in eleven articles, which Marlborough described as "very unseasonable at this time of day."[5] Pending a settlement, the King's "extreme ill-humour"[6] led him to retain his troops at Wesel when they ought to have been at Mainz. Marlborough wrote to him on April 26, and plainly warned him that his selfish policy was exposing the allies to the risk of a reverse, which might ruin the entire campaign. Unfortunately, the enemies of Wartenberg, the Prussian prime minister, had persuaded the King that Prussian interests were being sacrificed. They had even undermined the position of Lord Raby by insinuating that Wartenberg was governed by his wife,

---

4. Coxe, vol. 1, p. 402: Marlborough to Godolphin, April 19/30, 1706.
5. Murray, vol. 2, p. 476: Marlborough to Harley, April 27, 1706.
6. *Ibid.*, p. 478: Marlborough to Lord Raby, April 30, 1706.

and that his wife was the mistress of the English ambassador.

"Everybody must own you have a very difficult task," wrote Marlborough to Raby, "to struggle with so ticklish a court as yours is."[7]

It was also one of Frederick's grievances that he was not admitted to the counsels of the Grand Alliance. Marlborough assured him that he was mistaken, and that it was impossible to communicate plans before they had been formed. But the Duke suspected that Prussia was in reality preparing to abandon the coalition, and he reported his suspicions to London and Vienna. He informed Harley that he had received a letter from Frederick, written "in a very odd style."[8]

To Godolphin he said:

The little zeal that the King of Prussia, the King of Denmark, and almost all the other princes show, gives me so dismal thoughts that I almost despair of good success.[9]

What the Duke had anticipated came quickly to pass. On May 1 the Margrave, who was holding the line of the Motter with no more than 7,000 ill-found troops, was attacked in front by Villars, who commanded in Alsace. At the same moment, Marsin, who had been demonstrating against Trarbach and Coblenz with the army of the Moselle, swooped suddenly down upon his flank. The Germans were compelled to relinquish the blockade of Fort Louis, to abandon their valuable magazines, and to retire beyond the Rhine. This disaster, though not unexpected, made a deep impression on the Dutch. Marlborough reported to Salm that, while it was perfectly true that nothing could be "more advantageous for the allies, or could touch the enemy more closely"[10] than an offensive movement on the Moselle, the States, having refused to participate in any such design hitherto, would certainly never consent to it now.

Very regretfully also the Duke was compelled to announce to the Emperor and to Eugène that he had formed a plan of marching from the Meuse to the Po with 20,000 men, and that the States had virtually accepted it and were on the point of passing the necessary resolutions, when the deplorable news from the Rhine destroyed it absolutely. But he still cherished the hope of one day exhibiting on

---

7. *Ibid.*, p. 514: Marlborough to Lord Raby, May 18, 1706.
8. *Ibid.*, p. 481: Marlborough to Harley, April 30, 1706.
9. Coxe, vol. 1, p. 402: Marlborough to Godolphin, May 4, 1706.
10. Murray, vol. 2, p. 505: Marlborough to the Prince of Salm, May 10, 1706.

Hannibal's battle-ground talents which bore a particular resemblance to Hannibal's own. The dream was never realised. Exactly one hundred years were to elapse before the British army went into action on Italian soil. The eight regiments of the line, which in July, 1806, achieved the right to inscribe the name of "Maida" on their banners, so bore themselves that, if Marlborough was an unseen witness of that day, he had no cause to be ashamed.

The Duke's disappointment was not shared by Godolphin, who rejoiced that his friend was not to undertake so difficult and dangerous an expedition. It was not shared by the Dutch, who assured him that if he "would continue at the head of the army on their frontier," there was nothing he "could think reasonable to propose, but they would readily comply withal."[11] In proof of their good faith they appointed as field-deputies men who could be trusted not to make themselves ridiculous.

The situation now was simple, if unsatisfactory. As Marlborough saw it, Italy and Spain were the only theatres of decisive war. The army of the Netherlands he regarded as almost certainly doomed to inactivity. He therefore exerted himself, at the expense of his own prospects of accomplishing anything that "shall make a noise,"[12] to procure another contingent of 10,000 Hessians for Eugène, and to augment with Dutch and English regiments the forces destined for the diversion in Guienne.

Accompanied by Overkirk, he quitted the Hague on May 9, and reached Maestricht on the 12th. He found the Dutch troops encamped in the neighbourhood of Tongres. The British, under Churchill, were still marching from their cantonments. As soon as they arrived, he proposed to advance towards Louvain, where Villeroi and the Elector had concentrated their forces.

"God knows," he wrote to Godolphin on the 15th, "I go with a heavy heart."[13]

Despite their numerical superiority, he did not believe that the enemy would face him in the open. But Marsin, who had quitted Villars, was hastening to join the army of the Netherlands. He was now at Metz, and his advance-guard of twenty squadrons was approaching Namur. It was possible that, when a junction had been effected, Vil-

---

11. Coxe, vol. 1, p. 403: Marlborough to Godolphin, April 28/May 9, 1706.
12. *Ibid.*, p. 405: The Duke to the Duchess, May 4/15, 1706.
13. *Ibid.*, p. 405: Marlborough to Godolphin, May 4/15, 1706.

leroi and the Elector might be tempted to march out.

"If they do," wrote Marlborough, "I will most certainly attack them, not doubting, with the blessing of God, to beat them."[14] As late as the 18th, however, he expressed the opinion that, not even when Marsin came, would they venture to give battle.[15]

His pessimism was natural enough. All his labours of the last six months had so far resulted in nothing but failure. Both in Italy and on the Rhine France had proved herself swifter and stronger than the Grand Alliance. In Spain, for aught that he knew to the contrary, it was the same story. On April 1 Toulouse had anchored in Barcelona Roads; on the 2nd Legal had arrived from Roussillon; and on the 3rd Phihp and Tessé had completed the blockade. The siege was vigorously pushed. Peterborough was too weak to raise it; and despite the gallant defence of the garrison, who were animated by the presence of King Charles, the place would assuredly have fallen, had not Leake arrived on May 9 with the combined fleets of England and Holland. Thereupon Toulouse fled to Toulon without firing a shot, and Tessé and Legal retreated, leaving behind them 129 cannon and immense stores. They had lost 6,000 men, and the garrison not more than 1,000. But this consolatory intelligence had not yet arrived at Tongres.

Nevertheless, the Duke's judgement for once had played him false. Ever since January he had presupposed that the enemy would not assume the offensive in every theatre of the war at the same time. But he was not aware that Chamillart had conceived "a mediocre opinion" of his capacity, that Villeroi regarded him as "a mortified adventurer," and that both of them believed him to be still helplessly fettered by the control of the field-deputies. He was not aware that, even without Marsin, the enemy's army was estimated both at Louvain and Versailles to be overwhelmingly superior in numbers to any that he could bring against it. He was not aware that both the rulers and the soldiers of France were unduly elated by the initial successes which had rewarded their resolute strategy in Italy, Germany, and Spain, and that Villeroi and the Elector were burning to signalise their own command by some similar exploit.

Above all, he was not aware that on May 6 Louis had dispatched instructions to the Marshal to besiege Léau, and to fight, if he were attacked, and that the Marshal in. his reply had laid special emphasis

---
14. *Ibid.*
15. Murray, vol. 2, p. 515: Marlborough to Gueldermalsen, May 18, 1706.

on the numbers, the quality, and the confident spirit of his troops, and on the expediency of giving battle, not merely for the sake of Léau, but upon general grounds. All these things were hidden from Marlborough. In the hope of compelling the enemy to action he had formed a project, with the connivance of an agent in Namur, for the surprise of that valuable fortress. But as late as the 18th he despaired of the chances of a decisive encounter. To his amazement he learned on the 19th that Villeroi had crossed the Dyle and advanced almost to Tirlemont.

There are some miscalculations that do not matter. Marlborough's was one of them. Upon what hypothesis, or with what design the enemy was acting, he neither knew nor cared. He only knew that they were out at last, and that the rest, "with the blessing of God,"[16] would be easy. He instantly dispatched an express to the Duke of Württemberg, who commanded the Danes, with urgent orders to bring up the horse of that nation by forced marches, and the infantry as rapidly as should be possible without exhausting them. He solemnly pledged himself, in conjunction with the field-deputies, that all arrears of pay should be discharged. Württemberg, keen soldier that he was, obeyed upon his own responsibility and without reference to Copenhagen. On the 20th Marlborough advanced to Borchloen.

He was joined that day by the British. On the 21st he rested his men, and waited for the Danes. Villeroi, to show the perfection of his confidence in himself, passed the Great Geete and moved out to Gossoncourt. He reported to Versailles that he was certainly superior in numbers, that he had never commanded a finer army, and that he believed his march to have made a great impression on the foe. This style is reminiscent of the Duke of Burgundy's "audacious marches2 in 1702.

On Saturday, the 22nd, Marlborough pushed forward as far as Montenaeken and Corswaren, where he learned that the Danish cavalry was only a league behind. Villeroi, who knew nothing of the Danish cavalry, was surprised. He decided, however, that it was necessary to terminate summarily a movement which threatened Namur and Louvain, besides his own communications and his eventual junction with Marsin. One march to the south would place him athwart the line of his antagonist's advance. He determined to take it on the morrow. The Elector, who fully concurred with the Marshal, posted from Brussels to Tirlemont forthwith.

---

16. Coxe, vol. 1, p. 407: Marlborough to Godolphin, May 9/20, 1706.

Villeroi's concern for the strategic possibilities of the situation was altogether misplaced. Marlborough cared nothing for its strategic possibilities. His object was a simple one. He wished to make a circuit round the sources of the Little Geete that he might come at the enemy in the open field. He was informed that they were about to move to Judoigne. Determined to attack them there, he ordered the army to be ready to march before dawn. He proposed to encamp on the plateau of Mont St. André. But the plateau of Mont St. André was the very position which Villeroi had selected for himself. Each general was ignorant of the other's intention; and a collision was inevitable.

Before he retired to rest that evening, Marlborough found time to compose a letter,[17] which, seeing that it might well have been his last, possesses a peculiar charm. It was written on behalf of an officer's widow, who was soliciting a pension from the King of Prussia.

At 3 o'clock on the morning of Whitsunday, May 23, the allies marched in eight columns. A heavy fall of rain had made the ways laborious, and thick fog obscured the view. Cadogan, pushing forward with 600 horse, passed the recently levelled lines at Merdorp at 8 o'clock. Here a surprise awaited him. Though the mist had not yet lifted, it was possible to descry upon the distant plateau of Mont St. André dark, moving specks, which to his experienced eye could be none other than the hussars of Villeroi. He instantly sent back the news to Marlborough.

At 10 o'clock the Duke arrived. He was accompanied by Overkirk and other officers, and by Goslinga, one of the new field-deputies. The whole party rode on with Cadogan to reconnoitre. Uncertain as to the precise significance of the enemy's motions, the Duke ordered his cavalry to go forward and establish contact. But now the fog dispersed, and revealed the startling yet welcome truth. The entire French army, resplendent in new and untarnished uniforms, was already in possession of the plateau, and was evidently preparing to dispute the further progress of the allied forces.

Feuquières,[18] who does not condemn Villeroi for quitting his lines, censures him severely for fighting a battle. The argument is a little difficult to follow. When Villeroi marched over the Dyle, a battle became certain, because, if he did not go to Marlborough, Marlborough would assuredly go to him. This was a fact which Villeroi did not know at the time, and which Feuquières appears to have overlooked. Villeroi,

---
17. Murray, vol. 2, p. 521: Marlborough to Lord Raby, May 22, 1706.
18. *Mémoires de Feuquières*, t. 4, p. 16.

moreover, cannot very well be proved to have contravened the spirit of his instructions. The King had ordered him to invest Léau, and to fight if he were attacked. But he could not invest Léau if Marlborough were free to wander at will between the French army and its base.

It is true that the letter in which the King instructed him to fight, if the siege of Léau were interrupted, assumed that a junction with Marsin would be first effected. But a junction with Marsin might never be effected at all, if Marlborough were permitted to thrust himself between. And as Louis contemplated that Marsin would be detached to make the siege, while Villeroi covered it, the numbers available for combat would not, in that case, have been materially greater than they already were.

On the other hand, every day's delay increased the possibility that the allied army might be reinforced. Feuquières contended that the French in Flanders ought not to have taken the offensive. It may be that he was right. Marlborough certainly assumed that they would remain quiescent. But the blame, if blame was merited, belonged to the government which ordered the recovery of Léau, a distinctly offensive opening, and not to the Marshal, who, in circumstances which the government did not foresee, appears to have acted in accordance with the spirit of the instructions which they had given him.

If Marlborough was surprised, so also was Villeroi. In his own eagerness to fight, the Frenchman had never considered that his antagonist might exhibit an equal alacrity. He had planned to spend Whitsunday at Mont St. André, and to advance on Monday against an enemy, who, as he imagined, must either retire before him or suffer annihilation at his hands. The boldness with which that enemy was now himself advancing, caused the Marshal a momentary uneasiness. But he quickly made up his mind. Setting aside the unthinkable humiliation of a retreat to Tirlemont, he had two alternatives before him.

He could either press on to the attack or stand still to be attacked. If he pressed on, he would reap the full advantage of that national genius for the offensive, which is the strength of all French armies. He would also, according to Goslinga, have caught the allied forces in a situation of some embarrassment. But he chose the second alternative. Seduced by the exaggerated importance which the military science of his epoch attached to ground, he proceeded at once to occupy that famous position of Ramillies, the mere existence of which had been used by the Dutch generals in the campaign of 1703 as an argument

---

19. See Chapter 6, "1703."

against Marlborough's proposal to assail the lines of Brabant.[19]

His right flank was protected by the Mehaigne and the marshes bordering it. From the village of Tavières beside that river the open country rolled upwards to the north in gentle undulations as far as the village of Ramillies, which stood boldly out before his right centre. Northward of Ramillies, and somewhat in advance of his left centre, was the village of Offus, while his extreme left rested on the village of Autréglise, which had a steep and broken declivity before it. The front of both Offus and Autréglise was covered by bog-land, through which the Little Geete, descending from its spring by Ramillies, pursued a sluggish course towards the north. The whole position was about four miles in length.

The strength of such a situation was obvious. It could not easily be turned on either flank. The left and left centre were difficult of access. The right afforded excellent opportunities to cavalry, an arm in which the French imagined themselves to excel. The four villages stood out before the lines like four strong bastions. But certain weaknesses were equally apparent. Beyond the Little Geete and opposite to Autréglise rose the high ground of Foulz, where the assailants' right would be at least as safe as the defenders' left. The approach to Ramillies was an easy slope, presenting no natural obstacles to a frontal attack. Ramillies and Tavières were so far apart that the intervening ground could not be entirely swept by crossfire. That ground itself, ideal as it appeared to the French horsemen, would appear equally ideal to any others that were not afraid to try conclusions with them. And worst of all, the line of battle was decidedly concave in shape. The assailants, manoeuvring upon the chord of the arc, could concentrate superior forces upon a decisive point before the defenders would have time to effect a corresponding movement.

That the position had grave defects[20] was well known to the French engineers, who, in constructing the lines of Brabant, had refused to utilise it. And Villeroi himself had seen so good a judge as Luxembourg reject it as a fighting-ground. But believing his army, which had now been joined by Marsin's twenty squadrons, to be very superior in numbers, and reposing, as all Frenchmen did, an almost childish faith in the invincibility of the "*Maison du Roi*," he prepared for action with the utmost confidence. Having occupied Tavières with five battalions, he drew up seventy-eight squadrons (60 *per cent*, of his mounted men)

---

20. For a favourable opinion see *Wars in the Low Countries*, by Colonel Sir James Carmichael-Smyth, p. 158.

in three lines upon the open fields between Ramillies and the marshes of the Mehaigne. Into Ramillies itself, as also into Offus and Autréglise, he threw detachments of foot. In rear of these three villages, and in support of them, he placed the main body of his infantry in two lines. The residue of his horse, fifty squadrons in all, he stationed behind the left wing. His total force amounted to 62,000 men.

Meanwhile, the eight columns of the allied army, as fast as they arrived, deployed across the plain from Foulz to Boneffe. The movement was attended by some confusion,[21] for the ground was so narrow that the usual extension in two lines proved to be impracticable, and at certain points it became necessary to adopt a deeper formation. This circumstance alone must have suggested to Villeroi that the disparity of numbers was less than he had thought it, though even now he may not have realised that he had 60,000 men before him.

The Marshal watched the deployment of Marlborough's army with the keenest interest. The letter, in which Louis had instructed him to undertake the siege of Léau, contained directions for a day of battle.

> "It would be very important," wrote the King, "to have particular attention to that part of the line which will endure the first shock of the English troops."[22]

The British soldier could desire no higher testimonial. He, at any rate, was not included in the "mediocre opinion" entertained at Versailles of the capacity of his commander.

It was therefore with considerable satisfaction that Villeroi perceived the English regiments, both horse and foot, defiling to the right, and forming over against his left and left centre, where the nature of the ground gave great advantages to the defence. The King had also directed that the Elector's troops should not go into action as a single unit. It was recognised at Versailles that the *moral* of the Bavarians had been thoroughly shaken. They were therefore distributed at different points in the line of battle.

Marlborough, in the meantime, had carefully scrutinised the French position, and had matured his plan. Officers, who had served in the Spanish army and who knew the country well, told him that there were so many hedges, ditches, and marshes on his right that cavalry was useless there.[23] They suggested that the whole strength of the

---

21. *English Historical Review*, April, 1904: The Earl of Orkney's account of the Battle of Ramillies, letter 3., May 24, 1706.
22. Pelet, t. 6, p. 19: *Lettre du Roi à Villeroi*, 6 mai, 1706.
23. *Mémoires de Sicco van Goslinga*, p. 4.

mounted arm should be concentrated on the opposite wing. He heard them with respect, but without adopting their advice. Nevertheless he selected for his real attack the great body of horsemen which he saw between Ramillies and Tavières. He was not in the least afraid to match his Dutch troopers against the Household Cavalry of France, who rode conspicuous here in the foremost line. For he knew that Blenheim and the lines of Brabant had broken the evil tradition of Fleurus and Leuze and Neerwinden. In Overkirk, moreover, he had a leader who could be trusted to lead. But to puzzle the Marshal, and to induce him, if possible, to weaken the threatened point, the Duke determined to begin with a vigorous feint against Autréglise and Offus.

It was nearly 3, and the cannon upon both sides had been booming for an hour and a half before all was ready. The spectacle was now superb. All eyewitnesses agreed that the appearance of the French army was magnificent in the extreme. Marlborough told Burnet that "it looked the best of any he had ever seen."[24] At the last moment, the Elector, who, like Villeroi, had not believed in the possibility of a conflict before Monday, arrived at full gallop from Tirlemont, where he had been celebrating the festival of Pentecost as became a good Catholic. He fully approved of the dispositions which the Marshal had made.

Rain had fallen in the night, and the marshy meadows before Autréglise and Offus were reported to be impracticable. But the British infantry, sustained by the cavalry of the right wing, strode cheerfully down into the swamp.

When Villeroi and the Elector saw the scarlet lines in motion, they ordered the detachments in the two villages to be reinforced, and hastily transferred battalions from the right of their line to the centre and left. Those choice troops of the Household, the French Guards and the Swiss, were specially selected "to endure the first shock of the English.[25] Slowly and heavily the redcoats struggled through the morass under a galling fire from the enemy's batteries. Already a dozen battalions were over when an *aide-de-camp* dashed up with the unwelcome order of recall.

Orkney, who commanded there, ignored it. He assumed that it was based upon the supposition that the ground was impassable. That supposition he had now proved to be erroneous. On his own responsibility he formed his line, and amid a tempest of fire led it swiftly upon

---

24. Burnet, vol. 4, p. 129.
25. Pelet, t. 6., p. 19.

Offus, while Lumley, by extraordinary efforts, floundered through with a handful of British squadrons, and made shift to cover the right flank.

But horseman after horseman arrived with peremptory instructions to halt. Orkney still went forward. "Indeed, I think," he afterwards declared, "I never had more shot about my ears."[26] His blood was up. He saw the French line wavering, and he would not be balked, though no fewer than ten *aides-de-camp* were sent to call him off. The English had actually reached the village, when Cadogan himself appeared. He told the Earl that it was impossible to attack simultaneously at all points, and that, if the foot went forward now, the horse could not be spared to sustain them.

In profound disgust officers and men turned reluctantly about, and with many bitter mutterings retraced their steps. There were those who complained that the quartermaster, ignorant of the country and relying upon maps, had ruined a decisive movement. "I confess it vexed me to retire," said Orkney. "However we did it very well and in good order, and when the French pressed upon us, with the battalion of Guards and my own I was always able to make them stand and retire."[27] He does not appear to be aggrieved that Marlborough had not taken him into confidence beforehand. He probably realised that a feint, which is known to be a feint by those who are engaged in it, is apt to degenerate into an idle demonstration that imposes upon nobody.

As soon as the English regained the upland from which they had descended, the line which was nearest to the enemy wheeled round, and halted with sulky faces to the French. But the other continued to retreat till it was covered by a fold in the ground, when it turned sharply to the right and hastened away to the rear of the left centre. At the same time, eighteen squadrons of foreign cavalry passed over from the right wing to the left. This manoeuvre, suggestive of the arts of Hannibal, was partially observed by some and strongly suspected by others in the French army. But Villeroi obstinately declined to reply to it. He had seen that the wet land before his left was by no means impassable. He had been instructed "to have particular attention to that part of the line which will endure the first shock of the English troops."[28]

---

26. *English Historical Review*, April, 1904.
27. *Ibid.*
28. Pelet. t. 6., p. 19.

And he refused to believe that the redcoats, who still continued motionless upon the heights of Foulz, were there for nothing. And indeed they were not. Fiercely as those high-spirited regiments resented the part which they had been chosen to play, and which as yet they wholly failed to understand, it was in reality a part intensely flattering to them, and vital to the success of their great commander's plan.

Before these movements were completed, the true attack had already begun to develop. While French bayonets that would soon be needed on the right were defiling uselessly towards the left, four Dutch battalions with two guns marched forward upon Tavières, and the Dutch cavalry of Marlborough's left, forty-eight squadrons in all, moved slowly on in careful unison with this advance. They were supported by the Danes, who numbered twenty-one squadrons. The four battalions, driving in the enemy's sharpshooters, who from the outlying hamlet of Franquée had galled the extreme left of the allied horse, waded through the marsh and stormed into Tavières on front and flank.

Thereupon Guiscard, who commanded the French cavalry of the right wing, ordered fourteen squadrons of dragoons, which formed his third line, to dismount, and with two battalions of Swiss to proceed to the assistance of the detachment in the village. But the Dutch, already masters of Tavières, met this movement with a crushing fusillade. Overkirk saw the opportunity which the ill-timed march of these reinforcements presented to a cavalry leader. He instantly brought up the Danes, and flung them forward in column between Tavières and his left. The Danes were worthy of their hire. Splendidly handled by the Duke of Württemberg, they crashed into the wavering ranks of the dragoons and Swiss, shivered them to fragments, and hunted many of the survivors into the marshes of the Mehaigne. The horses of the dragoons bolted in panic. Guiscard's third line of cavalry no longer existed.

When Württemberg charged out upon the left, Overkirk, still keeping his Dutchmen well in hand, moved steadily on against the main body of Guiscard's horse, which even after the destruction of its third line still numbered sixty-four squadrons to his forty-eight. At the proper distance he broke into a trot. The enemy, who had been forbidden to move until the allied cavalry could be enfiladed by the cannon of Ramillies, saw that they must gather pace, if they would not be taken at a disadvantage. At once their foremost line, where rode the gorgeous regiments of the King's Household, rolled proudly forward on a foe whom they affected to despise.

It was remarked by the spectators that, whereas the French preserved the usual intervals between their squadrons, the Dutch came on like an unbroken wall. But whether this innovation in mounted tactics[29] was deliberately introduced as such by Marlborough or Overkirk, or whether it resulted from the wings closing towards the centre to avoid the fire of Ramillies and Tavières, is not recorded. The collision was severe. The Dutchmen, riding knee to knee, penetrated the intervals between the French squadrons, and attacked them from behind. But at several points the French drove clean through Overkirk's first line, and on into his second. Ten Dutch squadrons were dispersed or overthrown. This was the crisis of the battle.

Marlborough had selected General Schultz with twelve battalions to carry Ramillies. In preparation for the assault the place was vigorously shelled; but the defenders were too well covered to suffer much from the bombardment. As soon as Overkirk engaged the enemy's horse, the twelve battalions, supported by the whole line, marched up the gentle slope towards the village. They immediately drew upon themselves the attention of every gunner in Ramillies, and thus brought a welcome relief to Overkirk's right. But as long as the issue of the cavalry combat remained doubtful, Schultz's own left was insecure. Already the Bavarian *cuirassiers*, who formed the left of Guiscard's first line, were pressing forward under cover of the fire from Ramillies. This movement threatened to outflank both Schultz and Overkirk, and to split the allied army at a vital point.

Marlborough, who, at the head of the eighteen squadrons which had now arrived from the opposite wing, was watching the confused combat on the plain, saw the peril. He instantly dispatched an order to the extreme right for every remaining squadron, except the English, to join him at full speed. Then he himself led on the eighteen against the left of the enemy's horse. At the same time, Württemberg, who had promptly rallied his Danes on the edge of the marsh, wheeled them up into line and flung them upon the right flank of the French. The conflict was renewed with desperate ardour.

But the balance of numbers had now been turned. Marlborough had brought eighty-seven squadrons to bear upon Guiscard's sixty-four. Fired by the courageous example of their general, and reassured by the calm confidence with which he issued his command, the Dutch began to recover the advantage. He himself ran serious risks.

---

29. See Vol. 2, Appendix 1. (a): Marlborough's Cavalry at Ramillies.

He was recognised and assailed; but he fought his way through. His horse, which had saved him by its speed and strength, threw him at a ditch. He was ridden over; but he scrambled to his feet, and ran to take refuge with the infantry attacking Ramillies. With admirable presence of mind Major-General Murray wheeled a couple of Swiss battalions to the left and rescued his commander. So close were the pursuers that some of them, unable to check their horses, were impaled upon the bayonets of the Swiss. Then the Duke, bruised and shaken but imperturbable as ever, mounted the charger of his *aide-de-camp*. Captain Molesworth. Before he was well in the saddle, a cannon-ball took off the head of Colonel Bingfield, his equerry, who was holding the stirrup.

At this fateful moment, when fortune, though still dubious, was bending to the side of the allies, the cavalry which Marlborough had summoned from the right came racing to the scene. They were twenty-one squadrons in all; and the rhythmic thunder of their hoofs, audible even above the roar of the conflict, drew all eyes upon them. Their very appearance made victory certain, so profoundly did it cheer the allies and dismay the enemy. But before they could breathe their horses and press forward to the charge, the tactical skill of Württemberg had determined the result. The Danes were sweeping all before them. The greater part of Guiscard's second line bolted in panic. Musketeers, Light Horsemen, and *Gendarmes* of the Household, refusing to fly, were driven pell-mell into the marsh. And from Ramillies to the Tomb of Ottamond, a lofty tumulus which crowned the plateau far to the rear of Villeroi's right, the allied horse swung proudly round in two long, rolling waves, that threatened to engulf the whole French army from end to end.

Schultz in the meantime had carried Ramillies with the bayonet. The village was defended on its right by five battalions of Bavarian and Cologne Guards, and on its left by eight of French and Swiss. Their artillery was inferior to that of the allies, and was badly served. Nevertheless they repulsed two frontal assaults. When the third was delivered, a column under Spaar was thrown forward on the right to take the place in flank. Thereupon two Swiss battalions shamefully deserted their posts. Spaar pressed on into the village; and the Bavarians, fearing to be caught between two fires, wavered for a time, and then began to run. The Cologne Guards showed more steadiness; and Maffei withdrew them in tolerable order, as the main body of Schultz's men burst in like a torrent. Conspicuous in the assault were the Scottish regiments in the service of the States. The Duke of Argyle, claymore in hand, was the second or third man to enter the village. When Maffei emerged upon the plateau, he halted, not knowing that the right of the army had been completely turned, and that it was hopeless to attempt to stand in that situation, much less to recover the post. He soon learned the truth. Mistaking the Dutch cavalry for French, he was ignominiously made prisoner. His men dispersed.

The routed horse, regardless of the efforts of Villeroi and the Elector to restore order, was flying headlong across the rear of the French position. A brief pause ensued, while Overkirk's squadrons were breathing their chargers and re-forming for the final advance. Profiting by the respite, Villeroi, with the assistance of some of the cavalry which had hitherto continued idle on his left wing, endeavoured to form a new front from Geest-à-Gerompont to Offus and Autréglise. This manoeuvre, sufficiently hazardous in the face of an unbeaten enemy, was impeded by the presence of the baggage-train. It was still unfinished when Marlborough gave the word for the whole line to advance. The trumpets sounded, and once more the solid squadrons of Overkirk resumed their menacing career. The infantry of the right centre, supported by the regiments of Wood and Wyndham (the 3rd and 6th Dragoon Guards), moved swiftly forward upon Offus, while the battalions which had carried Ramillies wheeled to the right to co-operate in this new attack.

The English, nursing their grievance on the heights of Foulz, waited not for orders. Horse and foot, they dashed impetuously down into the marsh and up the steep ascent beyond to Autréglise. Awed by the spectacle of this combined onset, the whole of Villeroi's centre and left gave way. Between Offus and Ramillies French Guards and Swiss stood their ground right manfully at first; but they were not supported. Nowhere else was any serious resistance offered. This splendid-looking army, not half of which had been actually engaged, crumbled into ruin at the touch of Marlborough's master hand. In the moment of stress the recollection of the Schellenberg and Blenheim and the lines of Brabant was upon them, transmuting the easy confidence of the morning to demorahsation and despair.

It was 6 o'clock. Three hours of daylight still remained. But for a time the retreat of the centre and left towards Judoigne and Louvain was orderly and good. The centre was pursued by the regiments of Wood and Wyndham, which mustered no more than a couple of squadrons apiece. From the summit of a rise the English troopers presently sighted the long column of the enemy's artillery, retiring under the protection of seven squadrons of those Spanish and Bavarian Horse Guards, whom they had broken with ease upon the plains of Tirlemont. The recognition was mutual, but not equally agreeable. Like hunters that view the quarry, the redcoats put in the spur. Numbers counted for nothing now. On the right, Lieutenant-General Wood, at the head of his own regiment, crashed into the Bavarians at the gallop[30] and shattered them in an instant.

On the left, the two squadrons of the 6th Dragoon Guards charged home with equal speed and resolution on the Spaniards. Many were killed; and many, including two lieutenant-colonels, gave up their swords. The rout was complete. Wood himself came within ten yards of Villeroi and the Elector, "which had I been so fortunate to have known," he wrote, "I had strained Coriolanus (on whom I rode all the day of battle) to have made them prisoners."[31]

This feat of British cavalry was matched, if indeed it was not excelled, by another on the right, where the regiments of Lumley, Ross, and Lord John Hay pursued the enemy's left. Hay with his three squadrons overtook two battalions of the *Régiment du Roi*. Three other battalions, which had lined some adjacent hedges, fired with effect upon his flank and rear as he advanced. But, "sword in hand and at a gallop,"[32] he drove furiously upon the two, and killed or captured them all. Some, who, after laying down their arms, attempted to take them up again, were deservedly butchered.

It was on this occasion, if tradition may be credited, that the Scots Greys earned the honour of assuming the tall head-gear which they have carried ever since. It must not be forgotten that they were dragoons. At the Schellenberg they had dismounted to take their share with the infantry. But in their case at any rate, the difficult problem of preserving the cavalry spirit in the breast of a soldier who is also trained to fight on foot, was demonstrated to be not insoluble.

The spectacle of these disasters destroyed all firmness in the retreating columns. Maddened with terror, they abandoned every pretence of discipline, and flinging away their weapons fled fast towards Judoigne. The English cavalry followed hard upon their tracks. Lumley, with the King's Dragoon Guards, was foremost in the chase. The

---

30. See Vol 2. Appendix 1 (b): Marlborough's Cavalry at Ramillies.
31. Boyer, vol. 5., p. 82: Letter from Lieutenant-General Wood.
32. Portland MSS.: Lieutenant-Colonel Cranstoun to R. Cunningham, June 10, 1706 (Hist. MSS. Comm., 15th Report, Appendix, part 4, p. 311).

fugitives found every defile choked with a welter of baggage-wagons. Appalling sights were witnessed in the narrow ways. It is said that the allies, provoked by the vapourings of the French Household before the battle, gave little quarter to the terrified mob. Darkness brought them no relief. All through the twilight and the night Lumley and his handful of horsemen hung grimly on their heels. And after Lumley marched Orkney with the British foot. And to the left of Orkney, but further to the rear, came Marlborough and Overkirk with the rest of the allied army. Neither column had any exact knowledge of the other's whereabouts; but both pressed on with confidence towards the north. Lumley sent word to Orkney that, with the assistance of some foot, he could capture eight or nine battalions.

Marching "as fast as it was possible for men to march,"[33] the British infantry came just too late, to the intense disappointment of their ardent leader, who had galloped on before. Many distinguished prisoners were carried of necessity with the pursuing columns. With Orkney were Tallard's only son and a nephew of the great Luxembourg. A Bavarian officer, to whom Overkirk had courteously returned his sword, attempted to assassinate his gallant captor, and paid for his infamy with his life. At midnight Marlborough, having lost his guide, halted to await the dawn in the vicinity of Meldert, more than twelve miles from the field of battle. Spreading his cloak upon the ground, the Duke lay down to rest, and invited the field-deputy, Goslinga, to share his couch. Two hours later he was again in the saddle and moving to Beauvchain, where he encamped. But Lumley and Orkney held on towards the Dyle. Not until they came within range of the cannon of Louvain did the English troopers pause.

In the market-place of that ancient city, Villeroi and the Elector held a nocturnal and "tumultuous council of war."[34] As the yellow light of the smoking flamboys played fitfully upon smirched uniforms and reeking steeds and faces haggard with terror and fatigue, the scene must have been worthy of the brush of Rembrandt. It was quickly decided to abandon Louvain and the line of the Dyle, and to retreat forthwith behind the canal of Brussels. The Elector sent forward an express to the capital, announcing his defeat, and ordering pontoons and bread to be instantly prepared. Max Emanuel was a hardened soldier, who had witnessed many well-fought fields. But when he

---

33. *English Historical Review*, April, 1904: Letters of the first Lord Orkney during Marlborough's Campaigns. Letter 3; Battle of Ramillies.
34. Boyer, vol. 5, p. 85.

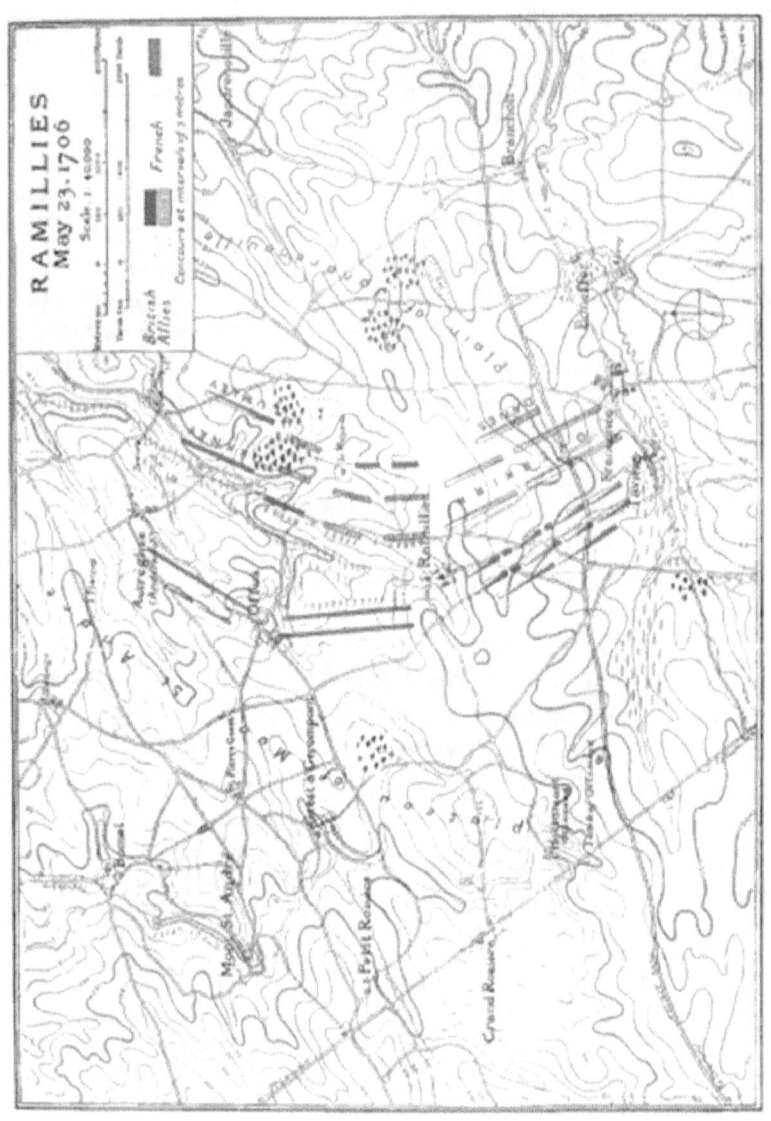

rode from Ramillies, he was seen to weep. Not even the catastrophe of Blenheim affected him so profoundly as the events of the last few hours.

"We were wonderfully well posted," he declared; "we had the finest army in the world. . . . But the defeat is so great, and the terror among the troops so horrible, that I know not what the morrow will bring forth."[35] What further witness is needed to the splendour of the victory and the vigour of the pursuit? The pursuit indeed almost challenges comparison with the classic examples of Jena and of Waterloo. In that epoch there was no parallel for a chase so merciless and keen.

The battle cost the allies 1,066 killed and 2,567 wounded. The casualties of the enemy were variously computed. But in killed, wounded, and prisoners they lost not fewer than 13,000 men. Immediate desertion swelled the total to over 15,000, or one-fourth of their entire army; and a remarkable wastage from this cause continued for many weeks. [36] All their cannon and baggage and eighty standards remained in the hands of the victors. The French, whose facility of self-deception is in part the secret of their recuperative power, endeavoured to minimise the effect of the disaster by publishing accounts of it which for ingenious puerility would have done credit to Napoleon himself. But the magnitude of the calamity could not be hidden from Europe, and not for ever from the Parisians, who presently produced a biting pasquinade on Villeroi.

Ramillies was in truth what Villars called it, "the most shameful, the most humiliating, the most deadly of defeats."[37] For more than half the army had fled without striking a blow; and the actual fighting, as Marlborough told Burnet, "lasted not above two hours."[38] The Elector wrote to Louis that the disaster was "as fatal as that of Höchstädt."[39] To Louis, the fact that Villeroi was his particular favourite, rendered the misfortune doubly bitter. He bore it like a gentleman.

"We have not been fortunate in Flanders," he wrote to Philip; and he added, "One must submit to the judgements of God."[40]

---

35. Vogüé, *Villars d'après sa correspondance*, t. 2, p. 424, *Appendice* 135.: *L'Electeur de Bavière au Comte de Bergeyck*, 23 *mai*, 1706.
36. By June 10 the deserters numbered between ten and twelve thousand. Murray, vol. 2., p. 575: Marlborough to the Duke of Savoy, June 10, 1706.
37. *Vie de Villars*, t. 1., p. 403.
38. Burnet, vol. 4., p. 129.
39. Lediard, vol. 2, ch. 1, p. 39: The Elector of Bavaria to the French King.
40. *Mémoires de Noailles* (1777), t. 3., p. 357.

But Feuquières expressed more accurately the disgust of his countrymen, when he concluded his narrative of the battle with the single observation that he was surprised that His Majesty should have taken so long to discover what all France had always known.[41]

The judgement is a harsh one. Following his usual custom, Feuquières is very precise and dogmatic at the expense of the loser. The battalions which the Marshal posted in Tavières were too weak in numbers, and those which he posted in Ramillies too poor in quality, for the work which was required of them. By neglecting to level the hedges in the rear of Ramillies he rendered it difficult to reinforce that village with celerity. By permitting his baggage to remain between his lines he ensured confusion in the event of a retreat or even of a change of front. These criticisms were probably true. But Feuquières, intent as always upon professional details, misses entirely the root of the matter. The battle was not lost, as he asserts, through errors of this character. Nor was it out of sheer stupidity, as he seems to suggest, that Villeroi declined under any circumstances to weaken his left. The determining factor was the moral one. On the one hand, the government and the Marshal were both obsessed with an exaggerated terror of the English, wliich led to the paralysis of half the army.

On the other, they altogether failed to realise that by Marlborough's magic influence the Dutch and the auxiliaries had been lifted far above themselves. It was expected in the French army that the King's Household would scatter the horsemen of Holland to the winds. It was confidently assumed that, in no case, could the Household be beaten. Time was when these suppositions would have been justified. But five years of Marlborough's leadership had wrought a miraculous change in the hearts of the Dutch troopers. Surprise was one of the secrets of his art. And, of all the many surprises which the Duke prepared for the armies and the generals of France, there was none greater than the transformation of the runaways of Neerwinden into disciplined and stubborn squadrons which refused to flinch from the most renowned cavalry in Europe.[42]

On the morning of the 24th Marlborough dispatched two letters to England, one for Godolphin and the other for the Duchess. To the Duchess he wrote as follows:

Monday, May 24. 11 o'clock.—I did not tell my dearest soul in my last the design I had of engaging the enemy if possible

---

41. Feuquières, t. 4., p. 30.
42. See Vol. 2 Appendix 1 (b): Marlborough's Cavalry at Ramillies.

to a battle, fearing the concern she had for me might make her uneasy; but I can now give her the satisfaction of letting her know that, on Sunday last we fought, and that God Almighty has been pleased to give us a victory. I must leave the particulars to this bearer, Colonel Richards, for having been on horseback all Sunday, and after the battle marching all night, my head aches to that degree that it is very uneasy to me to write.

Poor Bingfield, holding my stirrup for me, and helping me on horseback, was killed. I am told that he leaves his wife and mother in a poor condition. I can't write to any of my children, so that you will let them know I am well, and that I desire they will thank God for preserving me. And pray give my duty to the Queen, and let her know the truth of my heart, that the greatest pleasure I have in this success is, that it may be a great service to her affairs; for I am sincerely sensible of all her goodness to me and mine. Pray believe me when I assure you that I love you more than I can express.[43]

Nothing more characteristic of the man exists. His tender and considerate passion for his wife, his devotion to the Queen, his affection for his children, his simple piety, his care for the distressed, his modesty amounting almost to self-effacement—all these are to be found in the letter of Ramillies.

Richards arrived on Thursday night.

On Friday, says a diarist,[44] "the Duchess of Marlborough went and condoled Colonel Bingfield's widow upon the loss of her husband, and assured her from Her Majesty a pension for life."

And once again all England rang with joy. The Queen spoke from her heart, and from the heart of her people, when she wrote to the general,

"I want words to express my true sense of the great service you have done to your country."[45]

The pride of the nation was deeply stirred. It was true that the Dutch had endured the brunt of the fighting, and that the praises of the Danes were on every lip. But it was equally true that the pursuit, as conducted by the English, constituted a revolution in military science. The critics, who had professed to see in the popular hero no more

---

43. Coxe, vol. 1, p. 418: The Duke to the Duchess, May 24, 1706.
44. Luttrell, State Affairs from 1678-1714, vol. 6, p. 49.
45. Coxe, vol. 1, p. 419.

than a fortunate blunderer, were effectually silenced now. No longer could it be said that Marlborough did not know how to improve his own victories. For Ramillies from first to last was a masterpiece.

A deluge of congratulations poured in upon the throne. A general thanksgiving was ordered for a day in July. And then once more, amid the reverberation of cannon and the clash of bells and all the exultant clamour of a multitudinous concourse, the Queen and the Duchess rode side by side past tapestried houses and long lines of steel and scarlet to the shadow of the glorious dome. There "with vocal and instrumental music, after the composition of the late famous Mr. Henry Purcel,"[46] the great *Te Deum* was sung. The sermon was preached by the Dean of Canterbury from the text, "*Happy art thou, O Israel: Who is like unto thee, O people saved by the Lord, the shield of thy help?*"

That night the streets of London blazed with illumination, and bonfires roared aloft. For every Briton knew that one of the world's grand battles had been fought and won, and that for the second time the disturber of Europe was reeling from a stupendous blow, dealt him by the hand of England's incomparable soldier.

Today the fame of it is more than half forgotten. Yet even oblivion has compensations. Over the plain of Waterloo, deformed for ever and desecrated by ignoble vulgarities, complacent droves of tourists roam unintelligently. They know not, or if they know, they fortunately do not care, that only fifteen miles away the tomb of Ottamond and the village steeples of Ramillies and Offus look down upon a landscape yet unspoiled by modern imbecility and greed, and almost unchanged since it came under the discerning eye of Marlborough. The lonely field of Ramillies is still its own best monument.

---

46. Boyer, vol. 5, p. 154.

CHAPTER 15

The Dutch Barrier

After a halt of two hours, Marlborough again advanced, and pitched his camp at Beauvchain. Here he was rejoined by the stragglers, and by the various detachments which had separated from the main body in the course of the pursuit. Filthy, exhausted, and famishing, the triumphant soldiery marched in. No provisions arrived until the evening. "We look like a beaten army," said Orkney, who had neither eaten nor drunk for forty-eight hours, save "once or twice a glass of wine and a bit of bread."[1]

Marlborough himself, with the exception of his brief rest at Meldert, had been in the saddle from before dawn on Sunday to nearly noon on Monday, and his head was aching intolerably. But he was preparing to march towards the Dyle that night, when he received intelligence that the enemy had partially destroyed their magazines, and retired behind the canal of Brussels. Thereupon he dispatched 500 men to Louvain, whither the whole army followed on the morning of the 25th. Louvain, as the Duke informed the States with an irony which all the world appreciated, was the place, "where, for the good of the common cause, I had long wished to be."[2]

On the 26th he advanced to Dieghem; and the enemy, after ordering the garrisons of Lierre and Malines to take refuge at Antwerp, abandoned the capital, and passed the Dendre at Alost. Thence they continued their retreat to Ghent, which they entered with much of the confusion and terror that had characterised the flight from Ramillies.

At Dieghem Marlborough received the submission of the magistracy of Brussels, and of the Sovereign Council and the States of

1. *English Historical Review*, April, 1904.
2. Murray, vol. 2, p. 523: Marlborough to the States-General, May 25, 1706.

Brabant. He informed these bodies by letter that the allied army was come for no other purpose than "to uphold the just interests" of King Charles III; and he assured them, on the faith of the maritime powers, that His Catholic Majesty would respect their "ancient rights and privileges, as well ecclesiastical as secular," would make not "the least innovation in what concerns religion," and would "cause those concessions to be renewed which are termed 'The Joyful Entry of Brabant.'"[3] At the same time, the Duke gave warning to the troops in an order, which was read at the head of every squadron and every battalion in the army, that the inhabitants of the Spanish Netherlands must be treated with the utmost consideration.

"If any soldier," ran this seasonable document, "shall be taken plundering or doing any other damage to the said inhabitants, their houses, cattle, moveables, or other goods, he shall immediately be punished with death."

Moreover, the regiments, to which the offenders belonged, were required:
"to make good to the said inhabitants all the loss and damage they may have sustained, without any other form or process than the apprehending such soldiers in the fact, who (as is above said) shall suffer death without mercy."[4]

These reassuring pronouncements produced an excellent effect. So long as their churches, their purses, and their portly wives were safe, the Flemings were more than satisfied to be quit of the exactions of the French, who had centralised the administration of the country on the model of one of their own provinces.

The towns of Malines and Alost having followed the example of Brussels, the army passed the canal on the 27th, and encamped at Grimberghen. Here the Duke allowed his men a couple of days for repose. They had "marched six days together, without any rest," he wrote to Harley. "Nothing," he said, "could excuse the giving them so great a fatigue, especially after a battle, but the necessity of pursuing the enemy."[5] He himself was, in his own words, "half dead." On the 28th, however, he paid an official visit to the capital, which received him "with all possible demonstrations of joy and respect." On the 29th he sent Württemberg forward with 3,000 men and six guns to Alost.

---

3. Lediard, vol. 2., p. 44.
4. *Ibid.*, vol. 2, p. 56.
5. Murray, vol. 2, p. 538: Marlborough to Harley, May 28, 1706.

The army followed on the 30th.

At Ghent, Villeroi and the Elector, protected by the Schelde and the Lys, had been seeking to persuade themselves that they were covering that city, as well as Antwerp, Bruges, and Ostend. The numbers under their command had been augmented by the troops from the country of Waes, by the arrival of Marsin in the Netherlands, and by the return of large bodies of fugitives to the colours. They had conceived the idea of holding the line of the Schelde, when they learned on the 30th that Württemberg was moving with pontoons upon Gavre. This threat against their communications with France was sufficient.

Early on the 31st they decamped to Courtrai. The same day Marlborough advanced to Meirelbeke in the neighbourhood of Ghent. The *burghers* saluted his cavalry with shouts of welcome, and the Spanish garrison in the citadel surrendered. Bruges, Damme, and even the strong fortress of Audenarde, declared for King Charles. On June 4, the army passed both the Schelde and the Lys. On the 5th it reached Aerseele; and on the same day, Antwerp itself capitulated to Cadogan. Half the garrison were Spaniards, who all enlisted in the service of the Hapsburg sovereign.

"The hand of God appears visibly,"[6] wrote Marlborough to the States.

All Brabant and most of Spanish Flanders were already lost to France. The magnitude of the catastrophe astounded Louis. Nobody at Versailles could understand it. The comparatively trivial casualties at Ramillies did not explain it. To investigate the mystery, Chamillart himself took post to Courtrai, where he saw with his own eyes the unspeakable demoralisation of the French army. Of the best of the infantry, one-third had ceased to exist. Regiments of two, and even of three, battalions were reduced to one. The cavalry was completely disorganised. The Bavarians were deserting. Half the Spanish troops had gone over to the enemy, and the other half seemed hkely to follow their example.

But infinitely worse than any material losses was the pitiful dejection of all arms, without distinction of rank. Saint-Simon and Feuquières pretend that, if only Villeroi had kept his head, Flanders need never have been abandoned. But Saint-Simon and Feuquières are contradicted by both witnesses and facts. The army was incapable of fighting. Yet fight it must, if it proposed to keep the field. For Marl-

---

6. Murray, vol. 2, p. 558: Marlborough to the States-General, June 3, 1706.

borough, that insatiable gambler in battles, persisted in advancing. The problem was temporarily solved by distributing the bulk of the French infantry among the garrisons of the frontier, while the rest of the army took refuge behind this barrier of fortresses. Marsin commanded from Namur to Tournai, and Villeroi from Tournai to the sea. The Electors of Bavaria and Cologne established themselves at Mons. Vendôme was summoned from Italy to supersede Villeroi; thirty battalions and twenty-six squadrons were detached from Alsace to the Netherlands; and more of the troops of the Household were ordered to the front. The popular ear was regaled, in the meantime, with rumours that France would shortly resume the offensive with 80,000 men.

Marlborough was interested, but not deceived. He had drawn detachments from every Dutch garrison. He had sent for the Hanoverians; and with permission from Berlin, where the news of Ramillies had produced a good effect, the Prussians were marching to join him. He knew that the French could obtain a superiority of numbers in the Netherlands only by reducing their armies in Italy and Alsace to a weak defensive.

"I wish they may endeavour it," he wrote to Godolphin, "for the men they have here will very unwillingly be brought to fight again this campaign."[7]

His own immediate interest was to take Ostend, a nest of privateers, very deleterious to the commerce of the maritime powers. The possession of that harbour would shorten his communications with England.

The capture of Ostend, moreover, was an essential preliminary to the capture of Dunkirk. But the army having quite outmarched its heavy artillery, Marlborough had a few days to spare. He devoted them to a brief visit to the Hague. He left Aerseele on June 8, and returned on the 13th. He found the Dutch government ready and williing to concur in everything that he proposed. He persuaded them to draw more troops from their garrisons, and to fix their quotas of men and money for the descent on Guienne. At Antwerp he received a hearty welcome from the populace. He was attended by the bishop, the clergy, and the magistrates, and also by the Spanish governor, Terracina, who had entered the service of Charles III. The keys of the city were presented to him, together with the flattering intimation that "they had never been delivered up to any person since the great Duke of

---

7. Coxe, vol. 1, p. 432: Marlborough to Godolphin, June 7, 1706.

Parma, and that after a siege of twelve months."[8]

On the 18th, Overkirk appeared before both Nieuport and Ostend, while Marlborough advanced with the covering army to Rousselaere. Nieuport was found to be so difficult of access, that Overkirk abandoned his original idea of storming it, and directed his attention solely to Ostend. He was assisted by Sir Stafford Fairborne, with a squadron of nine of the line, besides bomb-vessels. At this time, also, Terracina and Meredith blockaded Dendermonde, a fortress, which, by reason of artificial inundations, was almost inapproachable. The allied forces were therefore fully occupied. But Louis was so nervous for the safety of his coast-towns that he directed Vauban with twenty-four battalions to guard the line through Dunkirk, Gravelines, and Calais.

As soon as the siege of Ostend had been formed, Churchill, who commanded the garrison of Brussels, was startled by rumours that the Elector intended to make a sudden dash upon the capital. Terracina got wind of a similar story in regard to Antwerp. To calm their fears, and to provide against eventualities, Marlborough sent six squadrons under Cadogan to Audenarde, with orders to repair the roads as far as Ninove. If the enemy came out into the open with anything resembling an army, the Duke was resolved to fall upon them without a moment's hesitation. But in his own mind he attached no credence to these stories, which were far too good to be true. The Elector, however, was not entirely paralysed. On the 21st, a detachment of 3,000 horse and 2,000 foot, rushing up from Mons, threw 500 men with munitions and four guns into Dender monde. Cadogan rode from Audenarde to intercept them at the bridge of Alost, but he came an hour too late. The operation was an expensive one for France, for 600 or 700 soldiers of the detachment deserted on the road.

Marlborough was now committed to a type of war which he detested, a war of sieges. The road to Paris through the Spanish Netherlands was never the road which he had desired to follow. Circumstances, which it was not within his power to control, having obliged him to open the campaign of 1706 in Brabant, the surprising victory of Ramillies, and the still more surprising collapse of French power which followed it, left him no option in the matter.

> "So many towns," he wrote to the Duchess, "have submitted since the battle, that it really looks more like a dream than truth."[9]

---

8. Lediard, vol. 2, p. 83.
9. Coxe, vol. 1, p. 426: Marlborough to the Duchess, May 20/31, 1706.

The capitulation of such fortresses as Antwerp and Audenarde, either of which would have been deemed by soldiers of the school of William a sufficient reward for a whole campaign, had essentially modified the nature of the problem. None knew better than Marlborough that the coalition ought long since to have struck at France across Lorraine. But the coalition itself had decided otherwise. "To loosen the hold"[10] which he had now taken on the Spanish Netherlands, simply because the Spanish Netherlands were not an ideal theatre of war, as Marlborough understood the art, would have been pedantic folly. This view he expressed in letters to both Salm and Sinzendorf.[11] If he was right upon military grounds, he was no less right upon political ones.

At the first symptom of retreat, or even of relaxation of effort, Flanders and Brabant would have reverted to Philip as easily as they had declared for Charles. It was necessary to consolidate these conquests, and to augment them. In the Duke's own words to Godolphin:

> as God has blessed the beginning of this campaign beyond what the thoughts of man could reasonably suppose, so it must be our duty to improve it as far as occasion shall offer.[12]

It is abundantly clear that Marlborough at this time believed the war to be approaching its end. The catastrophe in the Spanish Netherlands and the humiliating failure at Barcelona seemed sufficient by themselves to reduce the enemy to reason. If the allies continued to press their advantages, it was difficult to see how France could maintain the contest. Under the nose of Berwick and a Spanish army, Galway and the Portuguese had taken Alcantara in April and Ciudad Rodrigo in May, and were marching on Madrid, where Charles might be expected to join them from Barcelona at an early date. In Italy, Turin was indeed besieged; but Eugène was completing his preparations, and Eugène could be trusted to show the people of England a good return for their money.

Meantime, the menace of the projected descent, the destination of which the French could not discover, "put all the maritime counties of France to a vast charge and under dismal apprehensions."[13] Only on the Rhine, where Villars, weakened by detachments for Flanders,

---

10. "*Lâcher prise*." Murray, vol. 2, p. 588: Marlborough to the Prince of Salm, June 16, 1706.
11. *Ibid.*: also p. 595: Marlborough to Sinzendorf, June 17, 1706.
12. Coxe, vol. 1, p. 431: Marlborough to Godolphin, June 24, 1706.
13. Burnet, vol. 4, p. 131.

seemed particularly open to attack, the allied forces displayed no sign of life. In Hare's opinion, more could have been done in the Spanish Netherlands than actually was done, "if they had made any diversion on the Rhine."[14] Marlborough sent vigorous and reiterated protests to Vienna against the criminal *inertia* of the Margrave, but without result. The Austrian government, by diverting some of that general's best regiments to the war in Hungary, supplied him with the semblance of an excuse for misconduct that was inexcusable. But on the whole, the outlook was extremely propitious. And Marlborough did not conceal his conviction that France must speedily be forced to accept the necessary conditions of "a good and solid peace."[15]

The siege of Ostend was strenuously pushed. On July 4, when Marlborough paid a flying visit to the scene, the town endured a bombardment by land and sea which ruined its defences and threatened to reduce it to a heap of rubbish. The same night an assault, headed by fifty English grenadiers, gave the allies a lodgment on the counterscarp. On the 5th, the garrison made a sortie, which was repulsed. The Spanish regiments were hardly to be trusted, and the inhabitants were clamorous to preserve their homes from total destruction. La Motte, the French commander, having vainly appealed to Vauban for assistance, capitulated on the 6th. Most of his troops took service under King Charles. The losses of the allies did not exceed 500. A century before Spinola expended three years and 80,000 lives on the conquest of Ostend.

While Marlborough lay at Rousselaere, he received from Vienna a communication, which affected profoundly both his own career and the fortunes of the Grand Alliance. Charles, on his departure for Spain, had left behind him a blank patent, for use in a case of emergency. The Emperor converted it into a commission of governor for the Spanish Netherlands, and inserted the name of Marlborough, The emoluments were £60,000 a year. The honour was one which sovereign princes did not disdain to covet. Coxe avers that the Emperor acted "in a transport of joy and gratitude"[16] for the news of Barcelona and Ramillies. But it is seldom that the decisions of statesmen are dictated by the simple and pleasing emotions alone.

Marlborough and the field-deputies had taken possession of Flan-

---

14. Hare MSS.: Francis Hare to his cousin (George Naylor), June 3, 1706 (Hist. MSS. Comm., 14th Report, Appendix, part 9).
15. Murray, vol. 2, p. 576: Letter to Eugène of June 10, 1706.
16. Coxe, vol. 1, p. 437.

ders and Brabant in the name of the rightful monarch, Charles III. But in spite of modern misrepresentation, which is sometimes ignorant and sometimes deliberate, England and Holland were not fighting to gratify an academic preference for the pedigree of the House of Hapsburg. The 5th Article of the Grand Alliance had provided that the allies should "use their utmost endeavours to recover the Spanish Netherlands," not in the interest of a particular claimant, but "to the end that they may serve as a fence, rampart, and barrier to keep France at a distance from the United Provinces."[17] It was common ground among the members of the coalition that, if Holland was to retain her independence, an artificial obstacle of some kind must be interposed between her frontier and the frontier of the strongest military power in Europe. But the precise nature of that obstacle had not been determined.

Time was when the mere presence of the Spanish armies in the Netherlands amply secured the United Provinces against French aggression. But Spain, if she was not effete, had long ceased to be efficient. She had long ceased, as William III observed, to contribute anything to the common cause save rhodomontades. Before the question of the Spanish succession arose, Louis had absorbed Artois, and valuable portions of Flanders and Hainault. The government of the Hague, which watched with anxiety the gradual sapping of Holland's bulwark against France, had stipulated at the peace of Ryswick for the right to garrison certain fortresses of the Spanish Netherlands with Dutch troops.

But in February, 1701, these troops, serving under the command of Spanish governors, had all been surprised and captured by Louis in a single night. It was evident, therefore, that to furnish the United Provinces with an effective barrier some new method must be devised. What that method should be, was not defined by the terms of the Grand Alliance. But the 9th Article declared that, "at a treaty of peace," the allies should agree upon "what are the proper ways to secure the States-General, by the aforesaid barrier."[18]

Language, so ambiguous and vague, resulted not from choice, but from necessity. To Holland the acquisition of a sufficient barrier was a matter of life and death. But the House of Hapsburg was naturally suspicious of a claim which might conceivably enable the Dutch Re-

---

17. Legrelle, *La diplomatie Française et la Succession d'Espagne*, t. 4, p. 522, Appendice No. 34.
18. *Ibid.*.

public to alienate the revenues, or even the territories, of the Spanish Monarchy. England, while she treated the independence of the United Provinces as a British interest, and regarded the Spanish fortresses, in Macaulay's phrase, as "the outworks of London," would have looked with a jealous eye on the territorial expansion of her chief competitor for the commerce of the world. In particular, she would have resented any attempt to place the harbours of Nieuport and Ostend under Dutch control. When the Grand Alliance was negotiated, there was no time to reconcile these conflicting views. But the conquest of Flanders and Brabant raised the question of the barrier in an acute and urgent form.

While the Dutch did not deny that the lawful sovereignty of the Spanish Netherlands was vested in Charles III, they were not prepared to yield him actual possession until their claim to a sufficient barrier had been fully met. In the meantime, therefore, some kind of temporary administration must be established in the recovered provinces. In the days that followed Ramillies, Marlborough and the field-deputies had promised, on the faith of the maritime powers, that the ancient privileges of the country, which had not been respected by the French, should now be restored. This timely stroke had resulted in wholesale defection, both civil and military.

Meanwhile, Goes, the Austrian ambassador, who was also the Spanish commissioner for Guelderland, which had been conquered in 1702, proposed to receive the homage of all captured towns on behalf of Charles III. He appealed for support to the English government and to Marlborough. Marlborough, who dreaded the effect of Austrian interference on the good work that had been so well begun, wrote to the Pensionary that the Court of Vienna must be prevented from "troubling this country."[19]

During his brief visit to the Hague, he discussed the situation at separate interviews with Heinsius and Goes. To the Dutchman he declared that England coveted neither Ostend nor Dunkirk nor any place upon the mainland, that she recognised the right of Holland to a sufficient barrier, and that, pending the settlement of that difficult question, she favoured the formation of a provisional government by the combined maritime powers.

To the Austrian he explained that it was neither politic nor possible to press the claims of Charles in the teeth of Dutch opposition, that

---

19. Vreede, *Correspondance diplomatique et militaire*, p. 33: Marlborough to Heinsius, June 5, 1706.

England would never permit the Republic to despoil the inheritance of the House of Hapsburg, and that, for the present at any rate, the measures taken were the best that could be devised in the interest of the coalition as a whole. When Goes sent in his report to Vienna, the Austrian ministers perceived at once that England alone could protect King Charles against Dutch cupidity. Wratislaw suggested to the Emperor that the appointment of governor should be conferred on Marlborough. It that proposal were accepted by all parties, the Hapsburg cause would be in trusty hands. But if it were rejected through the hostility of the Dutch, English suspicion of Holland would be aroused, and Marlborough himself would be deeply offended.

It was a skilful move; but Joseph was at first unwilling to take it. He considered that his relative, the Elector Palatine, had a prior claim to the appointment. His "transport of joy and gratitude" was wholly imagined by Archdeacon Coxe. But overwhelming necessity compelled him to adopt the only plan which promised to safeguard the Spanish Netherlands against the ambition of the Dutch. Marlborough's name was inserted in the patent. To mollify the Elector Palatine, the title of "Representative" was substituted for that of governor. Goes was to act as deputy in the Duke's absence, and always in matters of religion. The Elector was informed that the arrangement was unlikely to be of long duration, and that it was imperatively demanded by the circumstances of the time. On June 27, Marlborough received the patent. That he was surprised, can hardly be affirmed with certainty.

For it is at least probable that, on his recent visit to Vienna, Wratislaw had promised him the post, if opportunity should offer. That he was gratified, is clear. But his gratification was not merely selfish. From the public standpoint no more admirable solution of the problem could have been devised. As the subject of a power, which was claiming nothing in the Spanish Netherlands, Marlborough was entitled to the confidence of both the contending parties. As commander-in-chief of the armies of the Republic, and as a Prince of the Holy Roman Empire, he was attached to both but monopolised by neither.

As the saviour of Vienna, he had earned the gratitude of the one; as the conqueror of a potential barrier, he merited the gratitude of the other. But his principal qualification for the post was his own attitude towards the question of the administration of the Spanish Netherlands. Marlborough was, before all else, the strategist of the coalition. In that capacity, he did not regard the recovered provinces as so much loot; he regarded them as man-power and money-power to be added to the effective force of the Grand Alliance. If they were to be utilised to the best advantage, they must be brought to see that their own interests were identified with the success of the common cause. Marlborough believed that he could accomplish this result. For excellent reasons, and without vanity, he believed that nobody else could.

Immediately upon receipt of the Emperor's offer, he wrote to England for permission to accept it. At the same time, he communicated the news to Heinsius in strictest confidence. His letter to the Pensionary contained these words:

> I will do nothing in this matter, but what you shall think is best for the public good.... Your thoughts are what shall govern me; for I do assure you, if they would give me this country for my life, I would not take it, if it were not liked by the States.[20]

This language was more prudent than the Duke intended it to be. It was meant to disarm suspicion; in the event, it averted a catastrophe.

Marlborough did not anticipate that any serious difficulties would be raised at the Hague. But for his own satisfaction, he invited the Dutch statesman. Hop, who was now at Brussels, to visit him in the camp at Rousselaere. Hop arrived on July 1. The Duke told him the news, and asked for his advice. Hop, after making him "great compliments,"[21] replied that it was "a very delicate business,"[22] and one that might easily produce misunderstanding. He recalled how, when the Grand Alliance was formed, Anne had expressly disclaimed any design upon the territory of the Spanish Netherlands. And he observed that Marlborough himself had made that treaty, and that not many days had elapsed since Marlborough himself had reiterated the Queen's disclaimer. The danger was lest the Dutch should infer that they were to be excluded from the recovered provinces, while England acted as caretaker for the House of Hapsburg.[23]

This interview opened the Duke's eyes. He wrote to Godolphin that, if Heinsius agreed with Hop, the patent must be refused, since nothing could compensate for "a jealousy between the two nations."[24]

---

20. Vreede, *Correspondance diplomatique et militaire*, p. 45: Marlborough to the Pensionary, June 28, 1706.
21. Coxe, vol. 1, p. 439: Marlborough to Godolphin, July 1, 1706.
22. *Revue Historique*, 1876, 2., p. 508: Gisbert Cuypert, *Journal inédit d'un savant Hollandais*.
23. *Revue Historique*, 1876, 2, p. 507.
24. Coxe, vol. 1, p. 439: Marlborough to Godolphin, July 1, 1706.

Heinsius, who, in the meantime, had been apprised by Goes of the Emperor's offer, informed Marlborough, in friendly, but unmistakable style, that it was settled doctrine in Holland that Charles could have no possession until the question of the barrier had been determined.

On July 2 the States met. They had been summoned at the instigation of Goes, who had neglected to warn the Pensionary beforehand. They received the Emperor's message in "astonishment and silence." Then the storm broke. The Pensionary, wholly unprepared, could not reply to the interrogations which rained upon him. The assembly was convulsed with rage. Speaker after speaker denounced in passionate accents this conspiracy to filch from the Republic the fruits of her valour and self-sacrifice.

The Grand Alliance had been violated. Holland had recovered the Spanish provinces; and Holland would permit neither Charles nor Joseph to dispose of them behind her back. Even the Pensionary did not escape the invectives of the exasperated orators. They would have fallen at last upon Marlborough himself; but in the very crisis of the debate Heinsius produced the Duke's letter. At once the tempest was allayed. It was resolved that Hop should be sent to Marlborough to thank him for his words, to show him the objections to the Emperor's offer, and to tell him that refusal would be more glorious than acceptance.

On July 3, the Duke, knowing nothing of this explosion, again wrote to Heinsius. He promised that he would "take no step in this matter, but what shall be by the advice of the States." "I prefer infinitely their friendship," he declared, "before any particular interest to myself; for I thank God and the Queen I have no need nor desire of being richer, but I have a very great ambition of doing everything that can be for the public good; and as for the frontier, which is absolutely necessary for your security, you know my opinion of it."[25]

On the 6th, he informed the governments of London and Vienna that he must decline the patent. On the 8th Hop arrived. Marlborough told him that the affair was at an end. It was true, he said, that the Queen had not yet written. But that fact made no difference. If it should prove to be her wish that he should accept the Emperor's offer, he would ask her permission to disobey her. He had no son. His present riches and reputation sufficed for all his needs. It should be his one ambition to maintain confidence between the maritime powers. Taken in conjunction with his written declarations, this language was

---
25. *Ibid.*, p. 440: Marlborough to the Pensionary, July 3, 1706.

deemed by the States entirely satisfactory.

Marlborough's behaviour had been irreproachable. It merits the attention of those who assert that his whole life was dominated by the love of gold. Not many men would have relinquished so tempting a reward with so graceful an air. The sacrifice was a bitter one. It seemed more bitter still when he received Godolphin's reply to his first letter on the subject.

> "The Queen," wrote Godolphin, "likes the thing very well, and leaves it to you to do as you shall judge best for her service, and the good of the common cause."[26] He added that Somers and Sunderland were "both much pleased with it, as what they think is like to keep everything in those countries upon a right foot," and that "they seemed to think there was no reason for the Dutch not to like it as well as we do." Both the Lord Treasurer and the Whig peers were agreed that "it was one of the rightest thoughts that ever came from the Emperor's counsel."

The event astonished the English Cabinet.

> "It both surprised and troubled me very much," wrote Godolphin. "It is amazing," he exclaimed, "that after so much done for their advantage, and even for their safety, the States can have been capable of such a behaviour."

Such "folly and perverseness"[27] he could only ascribe to the machinations of the French faction at the Hague.

Wratislaw's object was certainly attained. In England, even the warmest friends of the Dutch looked with suspicion on a policy which appeared to subordinate the common cause to selfish ambition. Marlborough had been found to represent the question of the patent as a merely personal one; but none knew better than he the international importance of humouring the recovered provinces. The Republic was detested in the Spanish Netherlands.

"These great towns," said Marlborough, "had rather be under any nation than the Dutch."[28] Yet the States had already prepared an instrument of government, which they termed a "decret organique," and which was certain to prove highly obnoxious to the people of Flanders and Brabant. While it formally recognised the sovereignty of Charles III, it purported to establish a provincial administration by

---

26. *Ibid.*, p. 438: Godolphin to Marlborough, June 24/ July 5, 1706.
27. *Ibid.*, p. 441: Godolphin to Marlborough, July 4/15, 1706.
28. Coxe, vol. 1., p. 442: Marlborough to Godolphin, July 12, 1706.

the act of the Republic. England was indeed mentioned, but only as an inferior power.

When Hop presented this document to Marlborough, the Duke did not conceal his indignation. He resented the underlying assumption that Ramillies was a purely Dutch victory. He resented the arrogance of the States in proceeding thus far without the concurrence of the Queen. He told Hop that, if he were to affix his signature to such a paper, he would not dare to set foot in England again. He dispatched a strong remonstrance to Heinsius; and he reported to Godolphin that the proposals of the Dutch "would certainly set this whole country against them."[29]

"I hope," he said, "you will find some way of not letting them play the fool." He was obliged to have recourse to Godolphin, because the affair of the patent had rendered his own position invidious . He dared not write with his accustomed freedom to the Hague, lest his opinions should be attributed there to self-interest or pique.

But he warned Godolphin that, if the "*décret organique*" were not modified, it would be interpreted throughout the Spanish Netherlands as "the absolute government of the Dutch." He prophesied, moreover, that the French would be speedily apprised of the whole affair, and would endeavour to turn it to their own advantage.

After an unsuccessful effort to shake the Duke's resolution, Hop gave way. Marlborough agreed to draw up an "*acte*," regulating the administration of the recovered provinces. This "*acte*" corrected the vices of the "*décret organique*," and established a "*condominium*" of the maritime powers. But in practice, at any rate in Marlborough's absence, it left the Dutch supreme. It was, however, the only possible solution of an embarrassing problem. Marlborough explained the situation as best he could to the Austrian government. Wratislaw answered drily that "knowing on what principles of avarice and parsimony"[30] the Dutch proceeded, he was not surprised.

The Emperor was furious. Relations between Vienna and the Hague grew dangerously strained. "Both nations," said Stepney, "are equally incapable of bearing prosperity with moderation."[31] But Marlborough advised the Austrian ministers that a rupture in the middle of the campaign would be fatal. Patience, he declared, was the only rem-

---

29. *Ibid.*
30. Blenheim Archives, Wratislaw to Marlborough, July 14, 1706.
31. Stepney Papers, vol. 2: Stepney to Harley, October 24, 1706 (Brit. Mus. Add. MSS., 7059).

edy. Meantime, he promised to spare no efforts to protect the interests of the House of Hapsburg. Realising that expostulation was worse than useless, the Emperor submitted to the inevitable.

Notwithstanding the distraction of this unpleasant controversy, Marlborough continued to press the enemy with unabated vigour. On July 6, the day of the capitulation of Ostend, he advanced to the vicinity of Courtrai, which he had occupied the day before with a detachment. Three of his battalions he now dispatched to England to take part in the descent; but the arrival of the Prussians and Hanoverians more than made good the deficiency. On the 11th, he moved south to Helchin, and threw four bridges across the Schelde. In this position he threatened Tournai, Ypres, Menin, and Lille. The Elector of Bavaria, feeling himself unsafe at Mons, withdrew towards Valenciennes. On the 16th, the Prince Royal of Prussia arrived. Marlborough entertained him with a review, and a reconnaissance in the direction of Tournai.

On the 17th, Overkirk came down from Ostend, and encamped in the neighbourhood of Courtrai. Marlborough's real object was to capture Menin. Godolphin would have preferred, that chronic nuisance to the shipping of the maritime powers, Dunkirk. But Dunkirk had once been an English possession; and Marlborough at this moment was particularly fearful of arousing the suspicious temper of the Dutch. Menin, moreover, was on French soil; it served as an outwork to Lille; and it marked a stage upon the direct road from Ostend to Paris. The same sound strategy, which in 1702 had induced Marlborough to reject the insular and ineffective system of warfare advocated by Rochester, induced him in 1706 to prefer Menin to Dunkirk.

Constructed by Vauban, and "esteemed the best finished fortification in all those parts,"[32] Menin was defended by a garrison of nearly 6,000 men under that skilful and valiant commander, Caraman. It was partially protected by an inundation, which had so reduced the waters of the Lys and Schelde that the siege-train had to be conveyed overland from Ghent. General Salisch invested the place on July 23; but owing to the late arrival of the artillery, the trenches were not opened until August 4.

On the same day Vendôme arrived at Valenciennes. He was succeeded in Italy by Marsin and the Duke of Orléans, Villars having respectfully declined the post. At Versailles Vendôme had been welcomed as a deliverer; but when he reached the frontier, he realised at

---
32. Burnet, vol. 4, p. 129.

once that the task of restoring confidence would tax his powers to the utmost. He reported that the Spaniards were totally unreliable, and that the French officers were demoralised.

"Everybody here," he wrote, "is ready to take off his hat when one names the name of Marlborough."[33]

Menin could never be saved by such an army. But something might be attempted to encourage the men and to annoy the enemy. On August 16, Marlborough's foragers were successfully attacked.

"Poor Cadogan is taken prisoner or killed,"[34] wrote the Duke to Sarah, "which gives me a great deal of uneasiness, for he loved me, and I could rely on him."

But on the 18th Vendôme sent back the invaluable quartermaster safe and sound. He did it as a mark of gratitude for the exceptional kindness which Marlborough invariably showed to all his captives. The Duke released the Baron de Pallavicini in exchange.

On the evening of the 18th, the counterscarp of Menin was assaulted at two points, in Marlborough's presence. After a bloody and obstinate encounter, in which the regiment of Ingoldsby alone had fifteen officers killed and wounded, a lodgment was effected. On the 22nd the place surrendered upon honourable terms. Among the trophies were four cannon, stamped with the arms of England. They had been lost at Landen. By Marlborough's orders they were now sent home. The army remained at Helchin, while the fortifications were repaired. At this time, the Scots Greys lost their gallant colonel. Lord John Hay, who died at Courtrai of a lingering fever.

Meanwhile, Churchill was detached with nine battalions and six squadrons, to convert the blockade of Dendermonde into a regular siege. Dendermonde was so protected by inundations that it had "always been thought unattackable."[35]

"The garrison," wrote Hare, "is inconsiderable, sickly, and half-starved, and the fortifications in very ill condition—but its strength is water, which, though lessened by the extremely dry season we have had, we are afraid is still too much to be mastered."[36]

---

33. Pelet, t. 6, p. 94: *Vendôme à Chamillart*, 5 août, 1706.
34. Coxe, vol. 1, p. 452: Marlborough to the Duchess, August 16, 1706.
35. *Ibid.*, p. 453: Marlborough to Godolphin, August 26, 1706.
36. Hare MSS.: Francis Hare to his cousin (George Naylor), July 1, 1706 (Hist. MSS. Comm., 14th Report, Appendix, part 9, p. 212).

Louis himself had besieged the place for six weeks and failed. "They must have an army of ducks to take it,"[37] he exclaimed, when he was informed of the enterprise.

"In truth," wrote Marlborough, "we should not have thought of it, but the extraordinary drought makes us venture."[38]

That there might be no delay, he:

"had secretly taken care to have ammunition ready at Ghent—under the notion of supplies for the siege of Menin, by which means the siege of this place was begun in three days after the other was over."[39]

Vendôme endeavoured to break the sluices of Alost, Ghent, and Ninove; but he found them securely guarded.

On September 1, Marlborough, who was growing uneasy at the duration of the defence, went in person to the siege, "to try if his presence could put an end to it."[40] On the morning of Sunday, the 5th, he surprised a redoubt, and easily captured it. Some of his men getting into the town with the flying enemy, the governor was so alarmed that he requested permission to treat. Marlborough demanded that the garrison should yield themselves up as prisoners of war, and gave them two hours to decide.

At the end of that time the governor answered that he was in need of nothing, and that he "would sooner be cut into a thousand pieces than surrender on such terms."[41] But Marlborough was too old and too resolute a soldier to be deceived. He immediately returned the hostages, and ordered the attack to be resumed. Thereupon the governor asked for one hour more, in which to call a council. Marlborough consented, but warned him that if he delayed until another gun was fired, the conditions offered would be worse. Thirty minutes later Dendermonde and its garrison were in the hands of the allies. The officers were permitted to retain their baggage and their swords. In less than twenty-four hours the weather broke.

"It has rained every day since Dendermonde capitulated," wrote Hare on the 9th, "and the wet season seems to be set in, a week of which would have made that enterprise impracticable."[42]

---

37. *Ibid.*, p. 215, September 9, 1706.
38. Coxe, vol. 1, p. 453: Marlborough to Godolphin, August 26, 1706.
39. Hare MSS., p. 214, September 9, 1706.
40. Hare MSS., p. 214, September 9, 1706.
41. *Ibid.*
42. *Ibid.*, p. 215, September 9, 1706.

And the Duke wrote to Godolphin on the same date that the place "could never have been taken but by the hand of God, which gave us seven weeks without rain. The rain began the next day after we had possession, and continued till this evening."⁴³ Marlborough had always a simple faith in the divine favour; but his chaplain spoke no more than truth when he said:

> Next to Providence, who has given us so dry a season that the like has not been known here in the memory of man, the success is entirely owing to His Grace. ⁴⁴

The fortress of Ath was now selected for attack. Its fall would secure Brussels and open the road to Mons. Overkirk invested it on the 16th, while Marlborough, encamping in the vicinity of Leuze, covered the siege. His health, which had been bad when he went to Dendermonde, was now completely restored by success. Vendôme, alarmed for both Mons and Charleroi, strengthened the garrisons of these places, and wrote to Versailles for permission to fight a battle in defence of the line of the Sambre. The answer was an emphatic refusal.

> "You know," wrote Louis, "that the Duke of Marlborough is only seeking an opportunity for a battle; he attacks places in the hope of enticing you thither."⁴⁵

Vendôme's enormous army was therefore reduced to the inglorious business of cutting off foragers. But Marlborough's parties penetrated into French territory, and levied contributions in Cambresis. On October 2 Ath fell.

During the siege, persistent rumours that Turin had been relieved came over the French frontier. They proved to be well founded. Eugène had joined his army on the morrow of the defeat of Calcinato, and by his mere presence had restored its spirits. But more than two months elapsed before the arrival of recruits and reinforcements enabled him to move. Meantime, La Feuillade, Chamillart's son-in-law, invested Turin on May 14 with 40,000 men and an immense siege-train. But the investment was not complete; and on June 17, the Duke of Savoy escaped with his cavalry. The operations of the French were badly directed; the garrison defended themselves with vigour; and La Feuillade wasted both time and energy on ineffectual endeavours to capture the Duke. Nevertheless, the fall of Turin was assured, unless

---

43. Coxe, vol. 1, p. 454: Marlborough to Godolphin, September 9, 1706.
44. Hare MSS., p. 214, September 9, 1706.
45. Pelet, t. 6, p. 125: *Le Roi à Vendôme*, 24 *septembre*, 1706.

Eugène relieved it, and Eugène was apparently blockaded in the Tyrol by the superior army of Vendôme, who had fortified the line of the Upper Adige.

If material factors were supreme in war, nothing could have saved the capital of Piedmont. But the news of Barcelona, and still more the news of Ramillies, inspired the Imperialist troops with extraordinary confidence, and correspondingly depressed the French. Early in July, Eugène, having altogether outwitted Vendôme, easily passed the Lower Adige and the Canal Bianco, the resistance offered being of the feeblest. On the 17th, to the astonishment of the French, who were expecting him in prepared positions on the Mincio and Oglio, he crossed the Po. He pressed on to Ferrara and reached Finale on the 24th. In the midst of these disconcerting movements, Vendôme, at a lucky moment for his own reputation, departed for Versailles and Flanders.

The Duke of Orléans, who joined the army on the 18th, was surprised to find that the soldiers were already disheartened, and that the defensive system, which Vendôme had represented as impregnable, had already broken down. He resolved for the present to avoid a battle, and from the northern bank of the Po to observe the progress of Eugène. The Imperialists, having no magazines, supported themselves with difficulty; they were tortured by a scarcity of water; and they suffered so cruelly from the intolerable heat that they were forced to conduct their marches by the light of the moon. Passing the Sacchia, which the enemy made no attempt to defend, they captured Carpi on August 5, and Reggio on the 14th. These places served as hospitals for their numerous sick. On the 19th, they advanced to Piacenza.

Meantime, the Duke of Orléans found himself greatly embarrassed by the arrival of the contingent under the Prince of Hesse at Verona, where it joined a force of 6,000 men, whom Eugène had left behind. The Prince of Hesse passed the Mincio, and on August 19 captured Goito. Orléans was compelled to make a strong detachment under Medavi to watch this second army. Encouraged by so useful a diversion, the soldiers of Eugène pressed on towards their goal. They traversed the pass of Stradella without opposition, and marching by Tortona and Alessandria, crossed the Tanaro at Isola on the 29th, and entered Piedmont.

The day before, Orléans, who had vainly tried to induce Marsin to defend the Tanaro, effected a junction with La Feuillade at Turin. Desperate assaults were now delivered, but without avail. Hitherto, the

French commanders had cherished the hope that Eugène intended nothing more than a diversion. They were speedily undeceived. Leaving his baggage and his invalids at Alba, he marched straight on Turin. At Villastellone, on September 1, he joined hands with the Duke of Savoy. Their combined forces fell short of 36,000 men. The French were approximately 60,000.

At a council of war, held on the 5th, Orléans proposed to march against the enemy forthwith. Marsin, La Feuillade, and almost all the other generals, preferred to remain on the defensive within the lines, which they had drawn round Turin. Marsin, who was possessed by a fatalistic belief that he would not survive the battle, had entirely lost his nerve. Very reluctantly the Duke gave way; but his judgement was vindicated by the sequel. Eugène, who despite the numerical odds regarded the French as already "half-beaten," crossed the Po on the 4th. On the 5th, he captured a large convoy, passed the Dora, and seized Pianezza. That night he pitched his camp three miles to the north of Turin. At sunrise, on the 7th, he moved against the lines. From 8.30 to 11, he endured a cannonade, to which he could offer no effective reply.

Then the attack was delivered. The steadiness and resolution, with which the allies advanced under a terrific fire from the sheltered foe, were beyond all praise. On the left, the Prussians, after an initial check, returned under Eugène in person, and were the first to enter the works. On the right, where the contingent of Saxe-Gotha fought and was twice repulsed, the French cavalry essayed a counterstroke, only to be caught in flank by a brilliant charge under Baron Kirchbaum. In the centre, the Duke of Savoy was opposed to Marsin and Orléans; and here the Palatine troops succeeded only at the fourth assault. Orléans received two wounds, and Marsin a mortal one. By 1 o'clock the lines were carried, the French retiring in confusion. They left behind them 6,000 prisoners, and enormous quantities of material of every description.

Their casualties did not exceed 3,000; but "consternation," as Voltaire observed, "effects more than carnage." Contrary to the wishes of Orléans, who was eager to effect a junction with Medavi, the retreat was directed upon Pignerole, and thence towards Dauphiné. Two days later, Medavi inflicted a sharp reverse upon the Prince of Hesse at Castiglione. But this incident, unduly magnified by the French, had little importance now. Isolated as he was, Medavi could not hope to accomplish anything decisive. The victory of Eugène had not only saved Piedmont; it had made the Milanese the certain prey of the Grand Alliance.

The relief of Turin ranks among the grandest exploits in the history of war. Marlborough was delighted at the triumph of his friend. "It is impossible for me to express the joy it has given me," he wrote to the Duchess, "for I do not only esteem but I really love that prince."[46] He himself had contributed not a little to the result. It was he who had procured the men and money, without which the campaign could never have been undertaken. And it was his victory of Ramillies, which had ensured to the Imperialist troops the advantage of superior *moral*, while it deprived the French in Italy of the services of Vendôme, and prevented the dispatch of reinforcements to Piedmont.

But the Duke was disappointed to learn that, instead of pursuing the panic-stricken host of Orléans and La Feuillade with the utmost of his strength, Eugène had turned back to complete the reduction of the Milanese, a simple task, which might safely have been left to accomplish itself, while the Imperialist army invaded Dauphiné. The government of Vienna, like the government of the Hague, preferred the slow and short-sighted method of annexing the enemy's territory piecemeal to the swifter, cheaper, and more certain one of annihilating his armed forces in the field. How fair an opportunity they missed may be judged by the following quotation from the letter of a French officer:

> I am sorry to tell you that I no longer know our men. They are so changed from what they were at the battles of Seneff, Mont Cassel, and Landen, that one can hardly think them to be of the same nation. I will not give you a detail of the disorder in which they fought at Turin, and of the confusion which prevailed among us, when we turned our backs on an army, that even after the battle was much inferior to ours. I will draw a curtain over this disagreeable scene. But I cannot help telling you that our troops hardly think themselves safe here, divided as they are by the Alps from the enemy.

In Spain, the great expectations raised by the successful defence of Barcelona had not been realised. As soon as he learned at Ciudad Rodrigo of the retreat of Philip and Tessé, Galway marched straight upon Madrid. Berwick did not venture to oppose him; the government withdrew to Burgos; and Galway, with 14,000 men, reached

---

46. Coxe, vol. 1, p. 460: The Duke to the Duchess, September 26, 1706.

the capital on June 27. He had hoped to find Charles already there. The Castilians, who accorded but a cold reception to an army of Portuguese, commanded by a French heretic in the service of England, might conceivably have recognised the Hapsburg claimant, had he come amongst them. Galway sent several expresses to both Charles and Peterborough; but although seven weeks had elapsed since the relief of Barcelona, no advance from the east had even begun. It may be that this delay cost Charles his kingdom. The causes of it are somewhat obscure.

On May 18, Charles and his advisers had decided that the quickest and safest road to Madrid lay through Valencia, where Peterborough declared that he had already made every preparation for the march. Accordingly, the fleet conveyed the English general with 2,800 foot to the mouth of the Grao, while 900 horse proceeded thither by land. On June 23, Charles set out to join them; but on receipt of a dispatch from Peterborough, announcing that neither transport, nor money, nor supplies, sufficient for a march to Madrid, had been accumulated in Valencia, he stopped.

Meantime, the province of Aragon had recognised his title. Noyelles and Prince Henry of Hesse-Darmstadt, the brother of Prince George, had occupied Zaragoza with 3,000 men. The citizens offered to pay the expenses of the King's journey to his capital, on condition that he selected the route through Zaragoza. Contrary to the advice of the English envoy, Stanhope, Charles, who sorely needed money, accepted the invitation. He reached Zaragoza on July 15.

On the same day, Galway, deeming it advisable to occupy a position in advance of Madrid, encamped at Guadalajara, thirty-five miles north-east of that city. The King's delay was now producing most injurious consequences. The Castilians, who had shown but little zeal for Philip in the hour of his prosperity, were rising everywhere against his enemies. Reports were disseminated, and widely believed, that the Austrian claimant was dead.

On July 28, Berwick was joined by Legal; and Galway, whose army had wasted to 12,000 men, found himself confronted by a force of more than 25,000, nearly half of whom were French. But Charles was advancing now from Zaragoza with 2,000 men. He had expressly summoned Peterborough from Valencia; and on August 5, the Earl rode in with 400 dragoons. They reached Guadalajara on the ensuing day. On the 8th, 800 Spaniards from Valencia arrived. But even so, the allies were outnumbered by Berwick's army in the proportion of five to three. Berwick's cavalry had already occupied Alcala, and entered Madrid, where the inhabitants received them with enthusiasm.

On the 10th, Peterborough at his own request was permitted to depart for Genoa. Ostensibly he went to raise a loan of £100,000 for the allied troops; in reality, he desired to amuse himself on the Riviera, and to intrigue with the Duke of Savoy. Nobody at Guadalajara regretted his disappearance. The same day the army moved to Chinchon, where Berwick, despite a growing superiority of numbers, allowed it to remain for twenty-six days. Seeing that it was impossible to recover Madrid, and that communications with Portugal were now entirely severed, Charles began, on September 9, to retire upon Valencia. The distance was 200 miles. It was necessary to cross the Tagus, the Xucar, and the Gabriel. And Berwick was close behind. Yet Galway accomplished the march without mishap.

In the meantime, the fleet under Leake had captured Cartagena and Alicante. Berwick, turning off into Murcia, recovered Cartagena. But he could not recover the islands of Majorca and Ivica, which Leake, in accordance with Marlborough's Mediterranean policy, had seized in September in the name of Charles. Peterborough, judging that Leake's squadron was insufficient for the task, had declined to accompany this expedition. His absence was not regretted; for Leake and the seamen detested him.

Marlborough in Flanders and Godolphin in London were overwhelmed and perplexed by long and contradictory versions of events in the Peninsula. The dispatches of Charles, Peterborough, Stanhope, Noyelles, Galway, Methuen, Crowe, Wratislaw, and others were packed with explanations, recriminations, and abuse.

It is possible that neither Marlborough nor Godolphin had realised that, as Macaulay truly said, "there is no country in Europe which it is so easy to overrun as Spain; there is no country in Europe which is more difficult to conquer."[47]

But one thing was clear. Charles ought to have been at Madrid by the end of June at the latest. "I have not been able," said Godolphin, "to forbear complaining of his inexcusable delays."[48]

Had he made use of the time," said Marlborough, "and marched to Madrid, everything must have gone well."[49] For the rest, it was evident that Peterborough could never co-operate with the German advisers

---

47. *Macaulay's Essays*, vol. 1., *War of the Succession in Spain.*
48. Coxe, vol. 1, p. 471: Godolphin to Marlborough, September 2/13, 1706.
49. *Ibid.*, p. 470: Marlborough to Godolphin, August 5, 1706.

of the King of Spain. Their conduct appeared to Godolphin "worthless and contemptible to the last degree."[50]

"Nothing," he declared, "ever was so weak, so shameful, and so unaccountable."

"I agree with you," said Marlborough, "that the Germans that are with King Charles are good for nothing."[51]

But their judgement upon Peterborough himself was not less severe.

"Lord Peterborough," wrote Godolphin on August 24, "has written a volume to Mr. Secretary Hedges. It is a sort of remonstrance against the King of Spain, in the first place; and secondly, a complaint against all the orders and directions sent from hence, and as if he had not authority enough given him, either at land or sea. In a word, he is both useless and grievous there, and is preparing to be as troublesome here, whenever he is called home."[52]

On the 26th, he added that the Earl's attack on Charles was couched "in terms as unmanly as unjust."[53] Referring to Peterborough's departure from Guadalajara, Godolphin said:

The whole council agreed to it, by which we may conclude they were as well content to be rid of him, as he was to go.[54]

Godolphin also suggested that Marlborough should endeavour to ascertain what passed between Peterborough and the Duke of Savoy.

"My opinion is," he said, "it fully deserves your curiosity."[55] The Earl was in fact suspected of a design to transfer the Spanish monarchy from the House of Hapsburg to the House of Savoy. Marlborough considered that he personally was compromised by the misconduct of an officer whom he himself had recommended for command. Whatever were Peterborough's military talents (and even if they were as extraordinary as he and his admirers represent them to have been), a general who quarrelled with all his colleagues and superiors was worse than useless in an allied army.

"I do not think much ceremony ought to be used," wrote Marlborough to the Duchess, "in removing him from a place where he has

50. *Ibid.*, p. 469: Godolphin to Marlborough, June 11/22, 1706.
51. *Ibid.*, p. 470: Marlborough to Godolphin, August 16, 1706.
52. *Ibid.*, p. 471: Godolphin to Marlborough, August 13/24, 1706.
53. *Ibid.*, August 15/26, 1706.
54. *Ibid.*, September 30/October 11, 1706.
55. Coxe, vol. 1, p. 472: Godolphin to Marlborough, Sept. 30/Oct. 11, 1706.

hazarded the loss of the whole country."[56]

The Duchess had a liking for Peterborough, who possessed some key of his own to the feminine heart. He wrote to her from Spain in a style of extravagant flattery. But by her husband's advice she dropped the correspondence as soon as it appeared that Peterborough was preparing to attack the government.

> "I have observed, since I have been in the world," wrote Marlborough, "that the next misfortune to that of having friendship with such people, is that of having any dispute with them."[57]

The anti-climax in Spain was not the only disappointment which the Duke experienced that autumn. The expedition to Guienne, which sailed from Portsmouth on August 10, was driven by adverse winds to take refuge in Torbay on the 15th. While it lingered there, the government received information which conflicted with the optimistic anticipations of Guiscard. They eventually decided to abandon the descent, and to send the troops to Lisbon. Marlborough had desired to finish his campaign with the capture of Mons. But this project was not encouraged by the Dutch, who even during the siege of Ath had begun to manifest a curious apathy towards the conduct of the war.

> "Our friends," wrote Hare, "think they have done enough."[58]
> It was considered at the Hague that the expense of four sieges in a single summer was more than could be recovered from the conquered towns at a time when the war was "drawing to an end."[59]

The chaplain complained that the Dutch, with their false ideas of economy, had delayed the fall of Ostend, and that, but for the firmness of Marlborough, they would have played the same trick at Dendermonde, "fear and an ill-placed parsimony to save a little powder when the throwing it away is of most consequence, being never-failing qualities of those genius's that haunt a general in this country, I mean Dutch deputies."[60]

In any event, the siege of Mons was rendered "in a manner impracticable"[61] by three weeks of continuous rain, which ruined all

---

56. *Ibid.* p. 471: The Duke to the Duchess, September 13/24, 1706.
57. *Ibid.*, p. 473: The Duke to the Duchess.
58. Hare MSS.: Francis Hare to his cousin (George Naylor), September 2, 1706 (Hist. MSS. Comm., 14th Report, Appendix, part 9, p. 213).
59. Ibid.
60. *Ibid.*, p. 214, September 9, 1706.
61. Murray, vol. 3, p. 160: Marlborough to Harley, October 4, 1706.

the roads. On October 12, the Duke decamped from Grametz, passed the Dendre, and pitched his tents on the plain of Cambron. Vendôme was publicly threatening "to make him a visit" before the end of the season.

"I believe," said Marlborough, "he has neither will nor power to do it, which we shall see very quickly; for we are now camped in so open a country that, if he marches to us, we cannot refuse fighting."[62] On the 18th and 20th, Vendôme rode up with a large body of horse; but on each occasion he retired without striking a blow. In justice to him it must be remembered that his instructions prohibited a battle. On the 26th, the allied army withdrew towards Grammont. On the 27th, Marlborough went to Brussels.

> "At Brussels," he wrote to the Duchess, "I shall be torn to pieces, there being twenty pretenders to every place that must be given; for I have not been able to prevail with the deputies to declare them before my arrival."

He was accompanied by Stepney, who had newly arrived from Vienna, and who was destined to relieve him of the task of representing England in the "*condominium*" of the recovered provinces. The Duke had found this work to be more than he could properly perform in addition to his military duties. His correspondence during the summer and autumn shows how numerous and diverse were the questions referred to him. The distribution of patronage, the taxation of imports, the levying of native regiments, the postal communications with England, the settlement of disputes about precedence, the revival of the opera, which, to the great indignation of the ladies of the capital, had been suppressed upon political grounds—these were some among the multifarious problems of administration which engaged his attention at this time.

In August, therefore, the Duke had requested Godolphin to remove Stepney from Vienna, where he was hardly a success, and to transfer him to Brussels with full powers "to sign and act in conjunction with the deputies of the States." [63]

At Brussels all classes of the population combined to offer a magnificent welcome to their English liberator. "The same honours," says Lediard, "were paid to His Grace, as were, in former times, wont to be

---

62. Coxe, vol. 1, p. 456: Marlborough to Godolphin, October 14, 1706.
63. Coxe Papers, vol. 19, *Correspondence of the Duke of Marlborough*: Marlborough to Godolphin, August 15, 1706 (Brit. Mus. Add. MSS., 9096).

paid to the Duke of Burgundy."

The magistrates, wrote Marlborough, "could not be dissuaded from receiving me with great ceremony."[64] They presented him "with what they call the Wine of Honour, which was brought in a tun, gilded, and painted with His Grace's arms, upon a carriage, with streamers, drawn by six horses, preceded by trumpets and kettle-drums, and attended by a cavalcade of young students, on horseback, finely cloath'd, with devices in their hands, in honour to His Grace, and in particular representing the great actions of this campaign."[65] Among these jovial Flemings Marlborough, no doubt, successfully counterfeited a gaiety which he did not feel.

"I have never been so uneasy," he wrote to Godolphin on the 24th, "I have never been so uneasy as I am at this time since Her Majesty's coming to the Crown."[66]

At the termination of one of the most brilliant campaigns in history this utterance appears remarkable. It was, however, no exaggeration of the truth. Marlborough was profoundly troubled, and not without good reason. For he was now discovering that the most marvellous of military victories may also be the most pernicious of diplomatic defeats. He was now beginning to realise that, on the field of Ramillies, the Grand Alliance had recovered the Spanish Netherlands and had destroyed itself. When Flanders and Brabant were wrested from the grasp of Louis, one of the three principal members of the coalition ceased to be interested in the continuance of the struggle. In the very moment of success, when sustained energy could not fail of an enduring reward, the government of the Republic showed little anxiety to press the campaign, and none to prepare for the next.

"The Dutch," wrote Marlborough, on September 26, "are at this time unaccountable."[67]

But if they were indifferent to the common cause, they were almost openly hostile to the House of Hapsburg. Relations between Vienna and the Hague had long been bad; they tended now to become impossible. The Dutch considered that the Emperor was unjustly excluding them from the enjoyment of that barrier which they

---

64. Murray, vol. 3, p. 196: Marlborough to Harley, October 28, 1706.
65. Lediard, vol. 2, p. 119.
66. Coxe, vol. 1, p. 492: Marlborough to Godolphin, October 24, 1706.
67. Coxe Papers, *Correspondence of the Duke of Marlborough*: Marlborough to the Duchess, September 26, 1706 (Brit. Mus. Add. MSS., 9097.)

had made such immense sacrifices to win back.

"I am afraid," wrote Marlborough on August 23, "in a very little time we shall find that the court of Vienna and the Dutch are more desirous of quarrelling with each other than with France."[68]

Even England herself was now an object of suspicion and jealousy at the Hague. For England was playing consistently for all Europe, and not for her own hand alone; and England was sufficiently strong, and sufficiently resolute, to prevent a violation of the undoubted rights of the House of Hapsburg. The vices of all coalitions had come at last to the assistance of France. When Villars was almost at the gates of Vienna, the Grand Alliance had stood firm. But apathy and dissension, the unholy children of prosperity, were mightier than the sword of Villars.

When Marlborough was offered the government of the Spanish Netherlands, the Dutch showed their hand at once. They showed it even more plainly, when they were pressed by England to guarantee the Protestant succession. Before the battle of Ramillies, they had cordially received the memorial which Marlborough presented them on this subject. But when Halifax drafted a treaty, giving effect to a principle which was the common interest of the maritime powers, he found himself confronted by unexpected obstacles. The Dutch objected to a provision requiring Louis to recognise the Queen's title; they complained that Hanover was not a party to the agreement; they protested that the Elector did not do enough for the common cause; and finally, they proposed to make the Guarantee Treaty the basis of a Treaty of Peace with France on terms which, would be onerous for all the allies except themselves.

Halifax was not deceived by this attempt to clog the negotiations with frivolous and extraneous matter. Marlborough was highly indignant at it. In the midst of the discussions occurred the affair of the patent. Angry and alarmed, the Dutch determined that the treaty should extend to their cherished barrier. If Holland guaranteed the Protestant succession, England must guarantee the Dutch barrier. England was not unwilling, for she regarded it as her own interest, and as the common interest of Europe, that Holland should be adequately safeguarded against French aggression. But what did the Dutch understand by their barrier? Nobody knew; and the government of the Hague

---

68. Coxe, vol. 1, p. 482: Marlborough to Godolphin, August 23, 1706.

seemed reluctant to evolve a definition.

"They cannot agree among themselves concerning their barrier," said Marlborough, "but the most reasonable are extravagant."[69] This reluctance was not so mysterious as it at first appeared. On July 23, Louis, who was well aware of the friction that had arisen over the question of the patent, clandestinely proposed to the Dutch a treaty of peace upon terms most tempting to the Republic. Philip was to abandon his claim to Spain and the Indies, and to receive as compensation the Milanese, Naples, and Sicily, while the entire Spanish Netherlands were to become the absolute property of Holland. It was no wonder, therefore, that the Dutch should be loath to commit themselves to a purely military occupation of specified fortresses, when they were secretly flattered by Louis with the offer of the whole country.

On August 18, they presented Halifax with their views on the guarantee, in the form of a resolution. Holland would "make all efforts imaginable to induce the King of France—to recognise the Hanoverian succession."[70] In return, England was to assist her to recover the Spanish fortresses and to capture as many French ones as possible. As fast as the places were taken, the Dutch were to garrison as many as they chose, at the expense of the Spanish Netherlands. Anne was to procure the acquiescence of the Emperor; and no treaty of peace was to be concluded, if the substance of this resolution were not embodied in it.

To Halifax it seemed that these proposals were "extravagant," and that those who made them had acted "altogether like merchants."[71] "They know very well," he said, "that their demands are exorbitant."

The English government regarded the resolution as far too vague and comprehensive. But before replying to it, they waited a month for tidings of Eugène. This judicious delay was ended by the wonderful news from Turin, which spoiled the Dutch intrigue for a selfish and dishonourable peace. At Turin the French cause in Italy was irretrievably ruined. The project of compensating Philip with Italian territory became impracticable. And Halifax was authorised to inform the Dutch that, while the necessity of an effective barrier was fully recognised in England, the specific towns must be designated, the numbers

---

69. Coxe, vol. 1., p. 485: Marlborough to Godolphin, September 26 (N.S.), 1706.
70. Hanover State Papers, vol. 1.: *Extrait des résolutions des Seigneurs Etats*, August 17, 1706 (Brit. Mus. Stowe MSS., 222).
71. J. Macpherson, *Original Papers* (1776), vol. 2, p. 61: Lord Halifax to the Elector, August 23, 1706.

of the garrisons must be settled, and the contributions to upkeep must be fixed.

Meantime, Heinsius had endeavoured to persuade Marlborough to accept the proposal of Louis as a basis for negotiation. Marlborough referred him to Godolphin. A lengthy correspondence ensued between the Lord Treasurer and Buys, wherein the Dutchman urged that it was the mutual interest of the maritime powers to make their peace with France, and leave the other allies to look after themselves. But Godolphin, with the full concurrence of Marlborough, declined to be convinced. Louis' proposal, he contended, was bad in itself, both because it would make the French "entire masters of the Mediterranean," and because it was nothing more than a revival of the Treaty of Partition, which was formerly so unpopular in England.

The maritime powers at any rate were under no necessity to entertain it, as long as they could borrow money at 4 and 5 *per cent.*, while France could not borrow it at less than 20 or 25. The maritime powers, he argued, should embody their own ideas of a satisfactory settlement in a preliminary treaty between themselves before entering upon any negotiations with the enemy.

> "I am very much of your opinion," wrote Marlborough on September 20, "that before any step be made towards peace, we ought to have a treaty with Holland for the guarantee of any treaty of peace we may hereafter make with France; and that there be room left for the allies to come into it."[72]

Such views were wholly incompatible with those prevailing at the Hague; and the Dutch were compelled to recognise that England would not connive at a betrayal of the common cause. England, in fact, was demanding security for the good behaviour of Holland. If the Dutch refused to guarantee the Hanoverian succession without a promise of their barrier, the English refused to guarantee the barrier without an undertaking that the essential preliminaries of any peace should first be agreed between the maritime powers. No other attitude was possible.

"The inclinations of the Dutch," said Godolphin on October 24, "are so violent and plain, that I am of opinion nothing will be able to prevent their taking effect but our being as plain with them upon the same subject, and threatening them to publish and expose to the

---

72. Coxe, vol. 1, p. 483: Marlborough to Godolphin, September 20, 1706.
73. *Ibid.*, p. 490: Godolphin to Marlborough, October 13/24, 1706.

whole world the terms for which they solicit."[73]

And Marlborough described them as "so flattered from France, that whatever is easy to themselves, they think both just and reasonable."[74]

Fortified by the victory of Turin, Godolphin and Marlborough had trumped the French King's card. The defection of the Dutch from the Grand Alliance could not now be purchased by clandestine barter or bribery. But Louis was not at the end of his resources. On October 21, the Elector of Bavaria informed Marlborough that, the recent overtures having been misrepresented "by ill-designing persons," Louis had "resolved to show the sincerity of his intentions by renouncing all secret negotiations and openly proposing conferences, in which means may be found for re-establishing the tranquillity of Europe."[75]

A similar notification was sent to the field-deputies. Marlborough had little faith in Max Emanuel. In 1704, he had discovered the Elector's talent for time-wasting correspondence. He had encountered it again in the winter of 1705, when d'Alègre had presented a memorial to the States in favour of a peace, and yet again after the battle of Ramillies, when the Elector had pretended to be disgusted with his treatment by the French Court. The present suggestion came therefore from a tainted source. The Duke regarded it as a peculiarly insidious move. He believed that it was designed "to make the Dutch less zealous in their preparations for the next campaign,"[76] and to entrap the English Cabinet into some pronouncement which could be construed at the Hague as evidence of "a backwardness to a good peace." It was on this occasion that he wrote that he had "never been so uneasy—since Her Majesty's coming to the Crown."

Marlborough had arranged that, before returning to England, he would visit the Hague to settle, if possible, the treaty as to the preliminaries of peace, and to urge the Dutch to define their barrier. He contemplated the prospect with grave misgiving. "I see," he said, "they are preparing a great deal of business for me—but I hope the Queen will allow me to speak my mind freely."

"My inclinations," he confessed, "will lead me to make as little stay as possible, though the Pensionary tells me I must stay to finish the Treaty of Succession and their barrier, which, should I stay the whole

---

74. *Ibid.*, p. 491: Marlborough to Godolphin, October 21, 1706.
75. Lediard, vol. 2, ch. 3, p. 122: The Elector of Bavaria to the Duke of Marlborough, October 21, 1706.
76. Coxe, vol. 1, p. 492: Marlborough to Godolphin, October 24, 1706.

winter, I am very confident would not be brought to perfection. For they are of so many minds and all so very extravagant concerning their barrier, that I despair of doing any good till they are more reasonable, which they will not be, till they see that they have it not in their power to dispose of the Low Countries at their will and pleasure, in which the French flatter them."[77]

The extreme unpopularity of Holland in the Spanish Netherlands was also a matter of serious concern.

"Nothing but the Queen's authority," said Marlborough, kept the recovered provinces "in any tolerable measures with the Dutch." [78] But he promised to do his utmost at the Hague "to let the honest men see that the project of France is to make them fall out with their best friends, which is the only method they have left for disturbing of the confederacy."[79]

On October 31, Marlborough returned to the army, and gave the necessary directions for the winter-quarters. On November 5, he started for the Hague. He was accompanied by Stepney, whose appointment had been regarded by the Dutch with unnecessary suspicion. "To try, if possible, to cure these jealousies," the Duke intended to introduce him to the Dutch statesmen. Sinzendorf, whom the Emperor had selected to assist at the forthcoming discussions, was also of the party. They arrived at the Hague on the 9th.

Important interviews ensued. It was essential that the maritime powers should settle their reply to the Elector of Bavaria's letter. On the general question of a peace, the Dutch were already aware of Marlborough's own attitude. On October 10 he had written to Slingelandt that France, in his judgement, was "not yet reduced to her just bounds."

"Nothing," he had said, "can be more hurtful to us on this occasion than seeming over-forward to clap up a hasty peace." He had urged the importance of unanimity, and the danger of listening to "proposals which France may make in the dark on purpose to amuse and disunite us in our opinions."[80]

In regard to the public conferences, suggested by the Elector's letter, the Duke was now advised by Godolphin that they "could not fail of giving an immediate ease and support to all France, which lies

---

77. Coxe, vol. 1, p. 492: Marlborough to Godolphin, October 29, 1706.
78. Murray, vol. 3, p. 183: Marlborough to Harley, October 21, 1706.
79. Coxe, vol. 1, p. 491: Marlborough to Godolphin, October 21, 1706.
80. Murray, vol. 3, p. 166: Marlborough to Slingelandt, October 10, 1706.

almost gasping at this time, under an excessive want both of money and credit."[81] And he was armed with instructions from Hedges to the effect that, in the Queen's opinion, "the first proper step would be for herself and the States-General to concert and agree, between themselves, upon such a scheme of a peace as may be honourable and safe both for themselves and for the rest of the allies."

> "Her Majesty," said this document, "cannot but look upon this method as more honourable for the allies and more effectual for the end desired, than the conferences proposed by the Elector of Bavaria in the name of France, for the foundation of a treaty, without so much as knowing what particulars are to be considered in that treaty. Of which conferences, therefore. Her Majesty cannot see any other use than to distract the allies with jealousy, and to divert them from making in time the necessary preparations for continuing the war."[82]

The Duke was directed to reply to the Elector in terms identical with those employed by the States, "that so England and Holland may appear to France to be uniform and of one mind." The Dutch, who had already accepted the diplomatic defeat from the English government, made no difficulties now. On the 10th, a letter from the deputies to the Elector, couched in a style agreeable to the views of the Cabinet of Queen Anne, was sanctioned by the States. Marlborough's own letter was in similar language.

It expressed the pleasure of the Queen, his mistress, at "this notice of the King's inclination to agree to making a solid and lasting peace with all the allies," and her desire "to conclude it, in concert with all her allies, on such conditions as may secure them from all apprehensions of being forced to take up arms again after a short interval, as has so lately happened. Her Majesty is also willing I should declare, that she is ready to enter, jointly with all the high allies, into just necessary measures for attaining such a peace, her Majesty being resolved not to enter upon any negotiation without the participation of her said allies."[83]

On November 21, all the envoys of the allied powers were invited to a public congress, at which the history of the negotiations was laid before them, and emphatic assurances of Holland's loyalty to the coalition were given by the deputies.

---

81. Coxe, vol. 1, p. 493: Hedges to Marlborough, October 21, 1706.
82. *Ibid.*, p. 494: Hedges to Marlborough, October 21/November 1, 1706.
83. *Ibid.*, p. 496: Marlborough to the Elector, November 10, 1706.

This "deplorable result," as the Elector called it,[84] enraged the French. They endeavoured to console themselves with the reflection that the private interest of Marlborough, Eugène, and Heinsius, was the sole obstacle to the peace of Europe. Seeing that Heinsius had been anxious to treat upon the basis of the French proposal, and that the Emperor did not require the assistance of Eugène or anybody else to show him that that proposal was very injurious to the House of Hapsburg, the theory of a wicked *triumvirate*, fomenting strife for its own selfish gratification, was transparently absurd. Yet some such theory was widely held among the pacific party in Holland, and in Tory quarters at home.

"There is but too good reason to think," said Dr. George Clarke, who visited the Hague and Brussels in the summer of 1706, "that great art and industry were used by those who got immensely by the war to keep off a peace, to which both Dutch and French were inclined, and might have been had upon very advantageous terms to the confederacy. But England was to be sacrificed to private gain."[85]

And six years later, Swift complained of the refusal of "very advantageous offers of a peace after the battle of Ramillies."[86]

These were the utterances of partisans. But Lecky's assertion, that the terms offered "would have abundantly fulfilled every legitimate end of the war,"[87] is on a different footing. In the mouth of that sober and judicial historian it is tantamount to a grave indictment of the statesmanship of Marlborough and Godolphin. It rests, however, on the assumption that Louis was sincere, an assumption, which Marlborough and Godolphin, who knew much more than Lecky about the methods of French diplomacy, declined to make. But even granting, for the sake of argument, that they were wrong, even granting that Louis' object was not merely "to amuse and disunite" his enemies, it is still very difficult to understand how Lecky arrived at his positive and confident conclusion.

The war had only one end, legitimate or otherwise, the reduction of "the exorbitant power of France" to a proper level. But "the exorbitant power of France" did not begin with the seizure of the Span-

---

84. Legrelle, *La Diplomatie Française*, t. 5, p. 293: *Max Emmanuel au Roi*, November 24, 1706.
85. Leyborne-Popham MSS.: Autobiography of Dr. George Clarke, May, 1706 (Hist. MSS. Comm., Report on the MSS. of F.W. Leyborne-Popham, 1899, p. 284).
86. Swift, *Conduct of the Allies* (1712).
87. Lecky. *History of England in the Eighteenth Century*, vol. 1., p. 51.

ish monarchy. It would not have been terminated by erecting a new French dominion on Italian soil and tightening the grip of France on the Mediterranean Sea. It would not have been terminated by depriving Spain, already far too weak, of her possessions in Italy and the Netherlands. Moreover, the plan proposed by Louis was impracticable; or if it was not impracticable, it was hardly calculated to secure the peace of Europe.

The inhabitants of the Spanish Netherlands would have resisted to the uttermost any attempt to place them under the yoke of Holland. They would have appealed, and perhaps not vainly, to the people of England, who would have been little disposed to tolerate the occupation of Antwerp and Ostend by the strongest naval power upon the continent. And the Emperor, who after the battle of Turin was virtually master of Italy, would certainly have refused to abandon his ground to Philip without a long and sanguinary struggle.

It was obvious to the English government that Louis' diplomacy would be far less formidable to the Grand Alliance, if the maritime powers could agree between themselves upon the essential conditions of any treaty of peace with France. Marlborough was instructed to pursue this question. Buys prepared a set of preliminaries; Heinsius approved them; and Marlborough, after making certain modifications, transmitted them to London.

This document laid down that the whole Spanish monarchy must be surrendered to Charles, that to the Spanish Netherlands, as defined at Ryswick, the fortresses of Furnes, Ypres, Lille, Tournai, Valenciennes, Condé, Maubeuge, and Menin, must now be added, that an adequate barrier (which was still left undetermined) must be provided for Holland, that Louis should recognise Anne and the Hanoverian Succession, and should expel the Pretender from French soil, that favourable treaties of commerce should be made between France and the maritime powers, that the position of the Empire should be settled on the basis of the peace of Westphalia, that the King of Prussia should be acknowledged at Versailles, and that the full effect of their compacts with the Grand Alliance should be secured to Portugal and Savoy. These preliminaries were accepted by the English Cabinet, on the understanding that every article was strictly kept. But they were never presented to the States for ratification.

It was solely for the sake of their barrier that the Dutch, at England's bidding, had simulated a zeal for war and had rejected the tempting overtures of France.

But the barrier itself had still to be defined. The Pensionary recognised that this question could not be shirked indefinitely. Having first consulted the field-deputies, he now presented Marlborough and Sinzendorf with a state ment of the Republic's claim. Starting from the principle that a barrier was necessary for the safety of Holland, and incidentally also of the Spanish Netherlands, which the Spanish government had proved itself unable to defend, the Dutch arrived at three conclusions. A strong and connected line of fortresses on the French frontier must be garrisoned by Dutch troops; the absolute command of these troops must belong to Dutch generals; and the King of Spain, being benefited by the arrangement, must contribute to its cost.

The fortresses specified fell into three groups:

(1) Thionville, Luxembourg, Namur, Charleroi, and Mons;
(2) Maubeuge, Valenciennes, Condé, Tournai, Lille, Menin, Ypres, and Furnes;
(3) Nieuport, Ostend, and Dendermonde.

Taken together, these three groups composed a scientific curve, joined by Dendermonde to the United Provinces. The maintenance of forty, or at least thirty, battalions was to be defrayed by the Spanish Netherlands.

To this scheme the views of the House of Hapsburg, as enunciated by Sinzendorf, were diametrically opposed. Starting from the principle that the King of Spain must himself defend the Spanish Netherlands with his own forces, and that no other barrier was necessary, Sinzendorf, like the Dutch, arrived at three conclusions. If Holland insisted on an additional barrier, it must be carved out of French territory, and, to prevent usurpations, the towns selected must be isolated, and not contiguous; the garrisons, whether Dutch or Spanish, must be commanded by Spaniards; and Spain would furnish the upkeep of no troops other than her own.

The fortresses named were Gravelines, St. Omer, Aire, Arras, Cambrai, Bouchain, Valenciennes, Condé, Maubeuge, Charlemont, and Givet, an odd collection, devoid of military significance. If Spain provided twenty battalions for these places, the Dutch must pay them.

These proposals were absurd. The Republic could not be expected, after years of sacrifice, to restore, at her own expense, that Spanish system of control, the rottenness of which had been demonstrated in February, 1701. Yet Sinzendorf endeavoured to enlist the sympathy of Marlborough by arguing that what had happened in February, 1701, could never happen again, and that the military and financial powers which the Dutch demanded would be equivalent to sovereignty. These were arguable contentions; but that the Austrian plan was an impossible one, admitted of no argument whatsoever. In these circumstances, Marlborough, though pressed by Sinzendorf to use his gifts of persuasion on the Dutch, appears to have taken refuge in generalities. He promised that Anne would do nothing contrary to the interests of Charles, he thanked the Emperor for the assistance of Sinzendorf, who, as he said, had been "a great solace"[88] to him, and on November 24, he departed for England.

On the question of the barrier the Dutch and Austrian standpoints were hopelessly irreconcilable. Mr. Geikie complains that Marlborough made no attempt to reconcile them. But when compromise is clearly seen to be impossible, discussion serves only to accentuate differences, to aggravate tempers, and to waste time. Marlborough was the friend of both parties. His personality was the one reliable check upon the forces tending to disintegrate the Grand Alliance. In the existing temper of the disputants, the less he intervened in so delicate a business as the definition of the Dutch barrier, the more he was like to preserve the unique influence which he exercised at Vienna and the Hague.

At the Hague, indeed, his position was already somewhat impaired. The offer of the patent was never forgotten or forgiven in Holland. Never again were the Duke's relations with the Dutch statesmen, and even with Heinsius himself, so entirely frank and cordial as they had been down to July, 1706. The field-deputy, Goslinga, considered that a grievous blunder had been committed. He had advised his government that Marlborough was fully entitled to the patent, and that the interests of Holland were in no way concerned.

But the great majority of Goslinga's countrymen took a different view. In the field-deputy's opinion, their conduct kindled in the breast of Marlborough a secret but enduring resentment, which led him to prolong the war at their expense. The Duke was innocent of any such villainy. But he was quick to detect the shadow of suspicion, which from this time onward darkened his every transaction with the Dutch. He felt the change most keenly. "If a governor were necessary for the Low Countries," he observed two years later, "I do not know why I should be less agreeable to the Republic than another."[89] And he did

---

88. Murray, vol. 3, p. 237: Marlborough to the Emperor, November 24, 1706.
89. See Vol. 2., Chapter 24: "The Misery of France,"

not entirely abandon the hope that one day he would be permitted to accept an honour, which he richly-merited, and which it was to the interest of the coalition as a whole, though not perhaps to the selfish advantage of Holland, that he, above all men, should enjoy.

Chapter 16
1706-1707

Marlborough landed at Margate on November 27, and reached London on the 29th. By Godolphin, who was to meet Parliament on December 14, his coming had long been eagerly desired.

It is abundantly clear from the facts narrated in the foregoing chapter that the summer and autumn of 1706 were a time of crisis for the Grand Alliance. They were also a time of crisis for Godolphin's ministry. The government, which in the preceding session had regularly availed itself of the 160 Whig votes[1] in the House of Commons, was now presented with the bill. The Whig Junta, like the German Princes, expected to be subsidised for the services of their disciplined battalions. These were the men who in the crisis of 1704 had gleefully remarked that the Lord Treasurer's head was "safe in the bag."

The price which they now demanded was the removal of Hedges from the Secretaryship of State and the appointment of Sunderland in his stead. And Godolphin, anxious before all else to carry on the war, was prepared to pay it. But he was confronted at once by the opposition of his colleagues, Harley and St. John, and of the Queen herself. Harley and St. John considered that, if Godolphin yielded, he would be breaking for ever with the principles upon which the ministry had originally been formed. Anne took a similar view. Moreover, she objected strongly to personal association with a peer who prided himself on his Republican sympathies and his uncompromising plainness of speech.

The *Junta* imagined that, in pressing the claims of Marlborough's son-in-law, they were, as they told their friend the Duchess, "driving the nail that would go." But they were very much astonished at the

---

[1] See Chapter 13, "1705-1706,"

tenacity of the Queen's resistance. Excessively provoked by opposition from one whose intellect she despised, Sarah espoused the cause of Sunderland with such indecent violence that she seriously offended the Queen. The careless writing of a word produced an actual rupture.

In one of her letters the Duchess prayed that Mr. and Mrs. Morley might "see their errors as to this notion,"[2] by which she meant the notion that the government could be conducted on other than a Whig basis. Anne read the word "notion" as "nation." She complained to Godolphin, who experienced no little difficulty in repairing the breach. The Whig historian Hallam declares that the Queen's "understanding and fitness for government were below mediocrity,"[3] which merely means that she refused to recognise the Whig creed.

"The Whig creed," says Lord Rosebery, who was never a Tory, "lay in a triple divine right: the divine right of the Whig families to govern the Empire, to be maintained by the Empire, to prove their superiority by humbling and bullying the sovereign of the Empire." Like her predecessor William, the Queen was too good a Stuart to admit such claims. On the other hand she had no love for "the Lackers," whom she described to Godolphin as "those violent persons, that have behaved themselves so ill towards me."[4]

Her position was simple.

"All I desire," she told the Lord Treasurer, "is my liberty in encouraging and employing all those that concur faithfully in my service, whether they are called Whigs or Tories, not to be tied to one nor the other; for if I should be so unfortunate as to fall into the hands of either, I shall not imagine myself, though I have the name of Queen, to be in reality but their slave, which as it will be my personal ruin, so it will be the destroying all government; for instead of putting an end to faction, it will lay a lasting foundation for it. You press the bringing Lord Sunderland into business ... and you think, if this is not complied with, they will not be hearty in pursuing my service in the parliament. But is it not very hard that men of sense and honour will not promote the good of their country, because everything in the world is not done that they desire?"[5]

---

2. Coxe, vol. 2, p. 13: The Duchess to the Queen.
3. Hallam, vol. 2, p. 745.
4. Coxe, vol. 2, p. 3: The Queen to Godolphin, August 30/September 10.
5. *Ibid.*

Theoretically at any rate this language was unanswerable. What Anne said to Godolphin innumerable thinking persons are saying in the twentieth century, after 200 years of that government by faction which she clearly foresaw. But Godolphin was a practical administrator. It was his business to find the sinews of war. Without a reliable majority in the Commons, he had no guarantee that supplies would be voted. He therefore offered to resign.

Anne would not hear of it. "Never leave my service, for Jesus Christ's sake," she had already said to him, . . . "this is a blow I cannot bear."[6] She suggested as a compromise that Sunderland should be made a privy councillor, and should receive a more remunerative appointment than the Secretaryship of State. But the *Junta* were obdurate. On September 28, in a letter from Sunderland to the Duchess, they delivered their ultimatum.

"Lord Somers, Lord Halifax, and I," it ran, "have talked very fully over all this matter, and we are come to our last resolution in it, that this and what other things have been promised, must be done, or we and the Lord Treasurer must have nothing more to do together about business; and that we must let all our friends know just how the matter stands between us and the Lord Treasurer, whatever is the consequence of it."[7]

These words had only one meaning. Unless they were admitted to office on their own terms, the Whig leaders proposed to wreck the ministry.

It is questionable whether any body of men, who in time of war undertake to embarrass or to overthrow their country's government, can ever be right. It is certain that their motives should be such as can at least endure inspection. If they consider that the war is unjustifiable, or is grossly mismanaged, they are entitled to be heard with respect. Some such excuse may be pleaded on behalf of Rochester, who heartily believed that England was doing too much and was doing it in the wrong way. Or if like the clergy and "the Tackers" they consider that the government has gratuitously betrayed some vital principle, it may be said that they are deficient in their sense of proportion, but not in their sense of honour. The Whigs, however, could not find language to express their enthusiasm for the war and for the triumphant manner in which it had hitherto been conducted.

---

6. *Ibid.*
7. *Ibid.*, p. 4: Sunderland to the Duchess, September 17/28, 1706.

They recognised with delight that Godolphin and Marlborough had adopted William's policy, and had pursued it with more success than William ever dreamed of. They could not but acknowledge that in the matter of the Occasional Conformity Bill the Cabinet, at its own risk, had dealt very tenderly with their allies, the Dissenters. Members of their party had not been excluded from office and patronage. Nevertheless, from the very men who were diligently practising the dearest of Whig principles they demanded to be paid their own price for Whig votes. Otherwise "we must let all our friends know just how the matter stands between us and the Lord Treasurer, whatever is the consequence of it." For this proceeding there is only one word in the English language. It is 'blackmail.'

At various stages in the ignoble controversy everybody turned, as usual, to Marlborough, whose military and diplomatic duties were already more than one man could thoroughly discharge. The Duchess and Godolphin urged him to use his influence with Anne on behalf of Sunderland. Harley and St. John appealed to him to adhere to the basis on which the government had originally been constituted. The persecuted Queen implored him to save her from the machinations of the Whigs. The Duke was sincerely devoted to Anne; he considered Sunderland an unsuitable person for the Secretaryship of State; and he cordially detested the party system.

On the other hand, he regarded Godolphin's financial ability as indispensable to the Cabinet, and he trusted implicitly to Godolphin's judgement on political affairs. While, therefore, he differed strongly from his wife in regard to the appointment of Sunderland, and plainly told her that "when it is too late, you will be of my opinion, that it would have been much happier if he had been employed in any other place of profit and honour,"[8] he did his best to persuade the Queen to accept the advice of the Lord Treasurer. But Anne remained unconvinced.

When Godolphin spoke of retiring, Marlborough was alarmed:

"You could not justify yourself to God or man," he wrote, "for without flattery, as England is divided, there is nobody that can execute your place but yourself."[9]

When the Whigs delivered their ultimatum, he was furious.

"Since the resolution is taken," he wrote to the Duchess, "to

---

8. Coxe, vol. 2, p. 2: The Duke to the Duchess, August 9, 1706.
9. *Ibid.*, vol. 2, p. 6: Marlborough to Godolphin, September 9, 1706.

vex and ruin the Lord Treasurer, because the Queen has not complied with what was desired for Lord Sunderland, I shall from henceforth despise all mankind, and think there is no such thing as virtue; for I know with what zeal the Lord Treasurer has pressed the Queen in that matter. I do pity him, and shall love him as long as I live, and will never be a friend to any that can be his enemy."[10]

And to Godolphin himself he wrote,

"As I know you to be a sincere, honest man, may God bless me as I shall be careful that whatever man is your enemy shall never be my friend."[11]

He also declared to the Duchess that:

"if my Lord Treasurer be obliged to retire, I cannot serve in the ministry."[12]

It is evident that the Duke did not enjoy being blackmailed. Nevertheless, believing as he did that the war would be finished in another campaign, he continued to press the Queen to accept the *Junta's* terms.

"The Lord Treasurer," he told her, "assures me that any other measures but those he has proposed must ruin your business, and oblige him to quit his staff.... It is true that your reign has been so manifestly blessed by God, that one might reasonably think you might govern without making use of the heads of either party, but as it might be easy to yourself. This might be practicable, if both parties sought your favour, as in reason and duty they ought. But, Madam, the truth is that the heads of one party have declared against you and your government, as far as it is possible, without going into open rebellion. Now, should your Majesty disoblige the others, how is it possible to obtain near five millions for carrying on the war with vigour, without which all is undone? Your Majesty has had so much knowledge and experience ... of the Lord Treasurer, that you cannot but know you may safely rely upon his advice."[13]

The Duchess had already said the same thing.

"'Tis certain," she had written, "that your government can't be

---

10. *Ibid.*, pp. 8, 9: The Duke to the Duchess.
11. *Ibid.*, p. 9: Marlborough to Godolphin.
12. *Ibid.*, p. 16; The Duke to the Duchess, October 18, 1706.
13. *Ibid.*, p. 17: Marlborough to the Queen, October 2, 1706.

carried on with a part of the Tories, and the Whigs disobliged, *who when that happens, will join with any people to torment you, and those that are your true servants.*"[14]

The Duchess cherished no illusions as to the blackmailing propensities of her Whig associates. Anne, however, still stood firm. Sarah and the *Junta* believed, and not without reason, that the Queen was supported and encouraged in her resistance by Harley. They therefore denounced him to Godolphin and Marlborough; but neither Godolphin nor Marlborough would believe any ill of their trusted colleague. Coxe, like Sarah and the *Junta*, would insinuate that Harley acted with peculiar baseness. But the Queen was fully entitled to console herself with the sympathy of the moderate Tories. And the moderate Tories were fully entitled to contend for the maintenance of the government on the original footing on which they had entered it.

Harley wrote freely to Godolphin on the subject.

"I know no difference between a mad Whig and a mad Tory," he exclaimed. He utterly condemned "the Tackers"; "but, my lord," he said, "this is now carrying further. Not only the 134 are to be persecuted, but all the rest."

Of the Whigs he wrote:

"there is no need of going back two years, nor scarce four months, to hear the most inveterate, malicious things said by their leaders against the Queen, my lord duke, and your lordship, that tongue could utter; . . . this is so notorious, that it is very common to match one malicious story from a Tory with another from a Whig."

He added that:

"another election will show that the party, as a party, are very far from being a majority, though clothed with all manner of authority that can be given it."[15]

Presumably he meant that, if Godolphin resigned and the *Junta* were called to power, they would not be able to carry the country. On that point he was better informed than any man in public life.

To Marlborough he wrote in a similar strain.

"I heartily wish your grace a prosperous voyage and a speedy arrival here," he said, "I doubt not but your grace has had all the

---

14. Coxe, vol. 2, p. 13: The Duchess to the Queen.
15. *Ibid.*, p. 20: Harley to Godolphin, November 16, 1706.

requisite powers sent to you during my absence, and I am sure your grace will manage and improve everything for the glory of the Queen, and the common benefit of the nation."[16]

St. John took the same line.

"There are some restless spirits," he said, "who are foolishly imagined to be heads of a party, who make much noise and have no real strength, that expect the Queen, crowned with success abroad, and governing without blemish at home, should court them at the expense of her own authority, and support her administration by the same shifts that a vile and profligate one can only be kept up with. Nothing but unnecessary compliance can give these people strength; and their having that, is the great terror of those who are trusty servants to the Queen, and who are entirely attached to your grace, and to my Lord Treasurer."[17]

St. John at any rate knew how to deal with blackmailers. "Nothing but unnecessary compliance can give these people strength," was the language of a man of honour.

The crisis was terminated by the arrival of Marlborough. In a personal interview with the Queen he persuaded her to give way. Sunderland's appointment was announced on the very day of the opening of Parliament. Peerages were conferred upon Cowper and other Whigs. Wharton became a viscount. Halifax's brother was made Solicitor-General. Minor appointments were bestowed upon other members of the party. The Tories, Rochester, Nottingham, Jersey, Gower, and Rooke, were removed from the Privy Council. Godolphin himself received an earldom.

The *Junta* had triumphed. The supplies were now secure. Another campaign was certain. But the price paid was far too high. Anne brooded over her defeat. She never forgave the Duchess; and her confidence in Marlborough and Godolphin was severely shaken. When Marlborough and Godolphin yielded to the Whigs in the matter of the Occasional Conformity Bill, they lost the clergy; when they yielded again in the matter of Sunderland's appointment, they lost the Queen.

But for the time all went well. The thanks of both Houses were accorded to the Duke. And the Speaker announced to the Queen:—

---

16. *Ibid.*, p. 21: Harley to Marlborough, November 12/23, 1706.
17. *Ibid.*, p. 21: St. John to Marlborough.

that as the glorious victory obtained by the Duke of Marlborough at Ramillies was so surprising, that the battle was fought, before it could be thought the armies were in the field; so it was no less surprising that the Commons had granted supplies to Her Majesty before her enemies could well know that her Parliament was sitting.[18]

Even the contentious and complicated measure for the Parliamentary union of England and Scotland was carried in this session with astonishing ease. In the summer of 1706 the Lords Commissioners of both kingdoms, appointed to adjust the articles, had held no fewer than forty-five meetings at "the Cockpit," near Whitehall, the Queen herself being often present. Somers was prominent in this discussion. In October the result of their labours was laid before the Parliament of Scotland. Bitter opposition was encountered there. Though England had acted with great moderation and generosity, a combination of Jacobites and Cameronians endeavoured to destroy the scheme.

The mob rose in Edinburgh and other towns. In November insurrection seemed probable. The debates were "long and fierce." But before the end of January, 1707, the Act was approved by no voices to 69. It was approved, because as Defoe, who was present as Harley's spy and pamphleteer, clearly saw, it was in "the nature of things."[19] There is no evidence that it was carried by corruption. In England much less difficulty was encountered. The extreme Tories opposed the measure; but they were somewhat embarrassed by the form in which Harcourt had drawn it.

All the articles, as already approved by the Scottish Parliament, appeared in the preamble, while the body of the Bill consisted of a single enacting clause. Harley and St. John supported it in the Commons. Haversham spoke against it in the Upper House, and contrived to introduce into his oration an insulting reference to the "she-favourite." Haversham as usual represented a large body of opinion; England was grumbling, just as Scotland was rioting. But neither grumbling nor rioting can alter "the nature of things."

The royal assent was given on March 17. "Neither of the contracting parties," says Lecky, "entered into it with any enthusiasm, but each of them gained by the treaty an end of the utmost importance. England, at the expense of commercial concessions, at which her manufacturers were deeply indignant, obtained a strength in every contest

18. Lediard, vol. 2, p. 150.
19. Lang, *History of Scotland*, vol. 4, p. no.

with her enemies such as she had never before enjoyed. Scotland, at the price of the partial sacrifice of a nationality to which she was most passionately and most legitimately attached, acquired the possibility of industrial fife, and raised her people from the condition of the most abject wretchedness."[20]

To England in her struggle with France the Union was a strategical gain of the first importance. To the Pretender's hopes it was a serious blow. Those who regard Godolphin and Marlborough as concealed Jacobites must allow that in this critical test, they were disagreeably successful in "dissembling their love."

The nation's gratitude for Ramillies did not stop short at votes of thanks. By acts unanimously carried, Marlborough's dukedom, together with the estate of Woodstock and the house of Blenheim, were settled at his death upon his daughters and their posterity, and the Queen's grant of £5,000 a year was entailed in perpetuity, first upon his Duchess and afterwards upon his children. At the request of the Corporation the colours taken in the battle were entrusted to the keeping of the City of London. And with every circumstance of military splendour and popular enthusiasm, they were borne in triumph through St. James' Park, Pall Mall, and the Strand, and ultimately suspended in the Guildhall "to remain there as trophies of that signal victory."[21]

The Queen witnessed the procession from the windows of the palace. Marlborough himself followed in a royal coach. He was accompanied by the Dukes of Somerset and Ormond, and attended by a lengthy train of officers, nobles, and ambassadors. He was ceremoniously received at Temple Bar, and magnificently entertained at Vintners' Hall. But the bravest welcome that he got that day was the welcome of the street.

The Acts of Parliament relating to the dukedom and to Woodstock were peculiarly gratifying, because, as Marlborough informed Sinzendorf and Wratislaw, they were "without precedent among us."[22] He hinted to his Austrian friends that he would be well pleased if a similar course could be adopted in regard to the principality of Mindelheim. But the natural pleasure which he felt in the recognition accorded to his services by his own countrymen was partially spoiled by the renewal of the outcry in Holland on the subject of the patent.

---

20. Lecky, vol. 2, p. 300.
21. Lediard, vol. 2., p. 149.
22. Murray, vol. 3 p. 305: Marlborough to Wratislaw, January 28, 1707.

Charles' confirmation of the Emperor's offer did not arrive till December 20. Though Marlborough had long since promised that he would not accept this honour, the suspicions of the Dutch took fire at once. The Duke did not conceal his indignation.

"I am not conscious," he wrote to Slingelandt, "to have at any time deserved the imputation of breaking my word."[23]

"I think I may venture to say," he wrote to Gueldermalsen, "without much vanity, that I have deserved better usage."[24]

"I am so perfectly satisfied," he wrote to Stepney, "with Her Majesty's bounty and goodness to me that I desire nothing more than to enjoy it quietly at home, without coveting any such thing abroad, but rather to spend the remainder of my life with those who have a more grateful sense of the services I have done to the common cause."[25]

To the Pensionary he repeated the pledge which he had given six months before.

"And you will do me the honour to believe," he added, "if you please, that I would never be false to my word, even to have this whole country in possession."[26]

Cardonnel wrote to Stepney of "the obstinacy and ingratitude of the Dutch, whom I take for the most part of them to be the mere scum of the earth."[27]

Something of a scene occurred between Stepney and Heinsius; and the Englishman roundly declared that "this unreasonable jealousy was hardly to be conceived." Stepney's position at this time was not a pleasant one. The Dutch definition of the barrier being irreconcilable with the Austrian one, the last hope of Holland was to secure the support of England and to exert the combined pressure of the maritime powers at Vienna. Before his departure Marlborough told Sinzendorf that of the fortresses named in the Dutch list, Dendermonde was unnecessary, and Ostend impossible; and he warned Stepney that in regard to these two places there must be no yielding. After several interviews with Heinsius, who contended that England's objections were

---

23. *Ibid.*, p. 271: Marlborough to Slingelandt, December 27, 1706.
24. *Ibid.*, p. 271: Marlborough to Gueldermalsen, December 27, 1706.
25. *Ibid.*, p. 270: Marlborough to Stepney, December 27, 1706.
26. *Ibid.*, p. 272: Marlborough to the Pensioner, December 27, 1706.
27. Stepney Papers, vol. 6.: Cardonnel to Stepney, December 27, 1706 (Brit. Mus. Add. MSS., 7063).

unreasonable, Stepney wrote to Marlborough suggesting a surrender.

Marlborough replied on December 17 that "the ministry and everybody here" were "very positive not to allow these two places."[28] Considerable bitterness ensued, the Dutch maintaining that whether they had or had not a right to ask, the English had no right to refuse.

"There we stick,"[29] wrote Stepney to Harley. After the explosion which ensued upon the receipt of the King of Spain's letter, Marlborough requested Stepney to correspond in future with the Secretary of State. The dispute dragged on for some months. But the deadlock remained unbroken.

During the first quarter of the new year, Marlborough as usual was busy with the collection and dispatch of horses, clothing, and recruits to the army in Belgium. An important detail of equipment also engaged his attention at this period. He induced the Dutch to strengthen their cavalry by the addition of eight men to every troop. As an equivalent for this expense, the British government promised to equip and arm troops at the cost of £50,000. In the recent combats with the enemy's *cuirassiers*, the brilliant successes of the allied cavalry had been won in despite of the fact that it carried no defensive armour. Marlborough determined to relieve it of this disadvantage. He therefore supplied the English horse with breastplates; with the true instinct of a fighting general he omitted the back plates. He also suggested to the Dutch and Hanoverian governments that they should follow his example. Overkirk supported him strongly.

Writing on March 11, Marlborough thanked him for his assistance, and added,

> "There is nothing at this hour which we may not reasonably expect from your people, who without that advantage have already rendered themselves so formidable to the enemy."[30]

But these were trivial matters in comparison with the vital question of the strategy to be adopted by the Grand Alliance in the forthcoming campaign. The plan which Marlborough, had he possessed unfettered control of the forces of the coalition, would have pursued from the outset of the war, the plan of marching through Champagne to Paris, and of extorting at Versailles the surrender of the entire Spanish monarchy, had been steadily thwarted by Dutch selfishness and

---

28. Murray, vol. 3, p. 245: Marlborough to Stepney, December 6, 1706.
29. Stepney Papers, vol. 2: Stepney to Harley, December 28, 1706 (Brit. Mus. Add. MSB., 7059).
30. Murray, vol. 3, p. 335: Marlborough to Overkirk, March 11, 1707.

German apathy. Instead, the tedious, uncertain, and expensive method of recovering piecemeal those territories which the Bourbons had acquired under the will of Charles II had been everywhere followed.

And, thanks to the genius of Marlborough and Eugène, it had met with more success than it deserved. The Spanish Netherlands were conquered; the Milanese, save for a few French garrisons, were conquered too; and Naples, though still occupied by Philip's troops, lay wholly at the mercy of the Grand Alliance. Only Spain itself held out; and even in Spain the armies of Charles had marched from end to end of the country and had entered the capital itself. Marlborough never shut his eyes to facts. He recognised that the strategy of the coalition, inferior as it was to his own, had achieved results. He recognised that he had now only to accept it and to make the most of it. If the Spanish Netherlands were won, if Italy was as good as won, the ejection of Philip and the armies of France from the Spanish Peninsula must, as it seemed to him, terminate the war.

To this end it was essential that Charles should make a supreme effort. The expedition, originally intended for Guienne, was ordered from Lisbon to Alicante, where on February 8, 1707, Lord Rivers landed with 7,500 men. With this reinforcement, which should raise the army of Charles to 30,000, and with the assistance of the Portuguese, who were to be stiffened on their own frontier with four British regiments, Marlborough conceived that the Imperialists would be in a position to resume the offensive. But realising that the issue would entirely depend upon the degree of support which Berwick might receive from France, he formulated a plan which would not only prevent the French government from sending fresh troops to Spain, but would probably oblige them to draw upon those which were already there.

This plan was the climax of that Mediterranean policy to which the Duke had steadily adhered. It was to begin with the invasion of Provence by Eugène and Savoy, supported by the navies of the maritime powers, and to terminate with the siege and capture of Toulon with all her dockyards, arsenals, merchantmen, and men-of-war. The mere menace of so appalling a catastrophe was bound to absorb the energies of the French government to the uttermost, and might even of itself compel them to abandon the Peninsula. Marlborough never doubted its efficacy for a single moment. As early as December, 1706, he was urging its adoption upon the Court of Vienna, And he used the prospect of this "powerful diversion" as an inducement to Charles and his bickering generals to forget their miserable intrigues and jealousies and prepare for an early and a decisive campaign.

The Duke knew well that, if this grand strategy succeeded, France must sue for terms. He was therefore entirely reconciled to that passive part which he anticipated that he himself would be constrained to play in Belgium where the troops would probably remain behind their lines and fortresses, and where the Dutch, having conquered their potential barrier, would assuredly refuse to take new risks. But he was nervous for the safety of Germany. On January 4, 1707, the Margrave of Baden died, "little esteemed and little lamented,"[31] according to the judgement of Burnet. He had treated Marlborough ill; but as orthodox soldiers went, he was a good one, and his dying lamentation that "the greatest misfortune that could befall a man of honour was to command an Imperial Army"[32] had some foundation in fact.

He was succeeded by the Margrave of Bayreuth, an incompetent officer, incapable of raising the German forces from the deplorable condition in which he found them. Marlborough was not ignorant that so enterprising a general as Villars could be trusted to make the most of this opportunity. Nevertheless he had strongly resisted a proposal to send Eugène to the Rhine. The genius of Eugène was necessary to the success of the design on Toulon. The Duke suggested that Starhemberg should serve under Bayreuth. But Starhemberg was ordered to Hungary. Germany therefore had everything to fear from Villars. Yet nothing that Villars could accomplish would really matter, if Marlborough's strategy were vigorously pushed to a triumphant issue.

At any other time the Austrian government, counselled as it was by so great a soldier as Eugène, would naturally have entered into Marlborough's project with enthusiasm. But the events which immediately ensued upon the battle of Ramillies had not been forgotten at Vienna. The refusal of the patent, the erection of the "*condominium*," and the maladministration of the Spanish Netherlands, which was alienating the inhabitants from the common cause, had made a deep and unpleasant impression on the Emperor and his advisers, who considered that the Dutch, with the acquiescence if not the connivance of England, were playing a shameless game of grab. Everything which was now proposed by the maritime powers was seen by the Austrians with jaundiced eyes. It was natural that those powers should desire by the

---

31. Burnet, vol. 4, p. 153.
32. Boyer, vol. 5, p. 316.

capture of Toulon to cripple a naval and mercantile competitor; it was natural that Savoy should desire to annex some portion of Provence.

But Vienna did not propose to go out of the way to assist in the gratification of these very human ambitions. If the war was to be conducted as a game of grab, others besides the Dutch could take a hand. The Emperor was resolved to seize what he could, and while he could. Already he had quarrelled with the Duke of Savoy over the fulfilment of the treaty under which that Prince had joined the coalition, and over the question of Charles' sovereignty in the Milanese. In particular he would make it his first business to secure Naples, which impudent peacemongers in France and Holland had coolly proposed to bargain away to Philip as compensation for the loss of Spain.

Between Marlborough, who was thinking solely of the advantage of the common cause, and the Austrian ministers, who were now altogether dominated by their bitter resentment against the Dutch, a somewhat acrimonious correspondence occurred in the opening months of 1707. Although it was obvious that the pressure of the overwhelming sea-power of the coalition ought to be applied to the enemy wherever possible, the Austrians affected to consider that the invasion of Dauphiné would be preferable to the invasion of Provence. And although the success of Marlborough's strategy must largely depend upon its prompt and vigorous execution, they insisted that Naples and Sicily must be subjugated before any offensive movement whatsoever was undertaken on the French frontier.

They suggested that the Duke of Savoy, whose daughter was the wife of Philip, was anxious to facilitate the cession of those territories to his son-in-law. They insinuated that the favour of England had been transferred from the Court of Vienna to the Court of Turin, and that once the destruction of the naval power of France in the Mediterranean had been accomplished at Toulon, the English would be as eager as the Dutch to conclude a peace detrimental to the interests of the House of Hapsburg. They also complained of the slowness of Lord Rivers' voyage to Alicante; and they made it a grievance that the English fleet had not wintered in the Mediterranean and made a descent upon Naples.

Marlborough was indignant. Conscious that the policy of England had been distinguished by its rectitude and even by its generosity, he wrote strongly to Wratislaw.

"Permit me to tell you frankly," he said, "that I fail to see with what particle of reason the Queen and her ministers can be accused of partiality for the Duke of Savoy, seeing that no monarchy has ever made such efforts or laboured more disinterestedly than that of England throughout the whole course of this war; it is a truth which everybody recognizes. It is certain that Her Majesty seeks only the good of the common cause."[33]

33. Murray, vol. 3, p. 330: Marlborough to Wratislaw, March 7, 1707.

A few weeks later he wrote again in the following terms:

Neither have I, if I may mention myself, nor has England, ever shown more partiality for any prince or ally than she has always done and continues to do for the Emperor.... The reproaches which you make against us in this respect have no justification whatever. I could give you proof; but I will content myself by offering you one only, which ought to suffice to protect us from such reproaches: it is the expense and the maintenance of the 20,000 men for Italy, the greater part of which burden is borne by England, under no treaty obligations, but solely at the instance of the Emperor, made to me during the siege of Landau.

It is very certain that the Queen could not give a greater mark of her friendship for His Imperial Majesty; so that you will permit me to tell you, as a friend, that considering the heavy expenditure we incur for that body of troops that it seems to me a little hard that you should be puzzled at Vienna just because we insist on the invasion of France on that side in preference to every other project. If we were asking the smallest acquisition for ourselves, and if all Her Majesty's views did not tend solely to the safety and aggrandisement of the august House, than which nothing could be clearer, I should not say so much to you upon the subject. Permit me, if you please, to add that it appears to me that the jealousies entertained among you in regard to the Treaty of Partition are equally ill founded.

You who know the bottom of my heart as well as the sentiments of the entire nation, touching that treaty, should be able, as it seems to me, to tranquillise opinion somewhat upon that score. I have already told you several times, and I reiterate the assurance, that provided the Emperor and the allies stand fast and do their duty everywhere, the Queen will never consent to leave any part of the Spanish monarchy, no matter how small, to the House of Bourbon. Thus, it depends on yourselves to get what you want; but to attain that end, I am bound to remind you that it is convenient to take generous views for the common good, and not to allow oneself to be wholly bounded by particular interests.[34]

The correspondence in the course of which these just rebukes occur, proves beyond all question how thorough was the English soldier's comprehension of the meaning and the uses of sea-power. He promised Eugène that the fleet should remain throughout the summer in the Mediterranean "to lend a hand to the operations." "It could even winter there," he added, "if we were masters of Port Mahon, or some other good port, where the ships and stores could be safe; that would be much more convenient for us and serviceable to the common cause, as holding the enemy continually in check."[35]

He promised Wratislaw that the strength of the fleet should be raised from thirty ships of the line to forty. "You may rely upon it," he said, "that we shall be careful to maintain our superiority in these waters throughout the year, so that the enemy will not be able, without excessive risk, to transport troops by sea to Naples or Spain."[36]

After the expedition to Provence," he told Eugène, "which it is hoped will have succeeded before the end of August, Your Highness can count on the Queen giving all the orders you may then desire for the fleet to act in concert with the troops that shall be employed in the reduction of Naples."[37]

To Wratislaw again he wrote in these terms:

> As regards the expedition to Naples ... permit me to add that it is King Charles' interest alone which makes us prefer the invasion of France, since unless it takes place, and that at an early date, Spain may be regarded as lost for ever to that Prince, notwithstanding the Lord Rivers' reinforcements, and the 3,000 men whom the Queen is embarking for Portugal. We are entirely persuaded of this truth, so you cannot find it strange that one should insist on postponing for a little while a project which jeopardises everything, and which, if successful, is of no

---

34. Murray, vol. 3, p. 340: Marlborough to Wratislaw, April 18, 1707.
35. *Ibid.*, p. 268: Marlborough to the Prince of Savoy, December 27, 1706.
36. *Ibid.*, p. 279: Marlborough to Wratislaw, January 10, 1707.
37. *Ibid.*, p. 326: Marlborough to the Prince of Savoy, March 7, 1707.

consequence at all, in order to follow another on which everything depends. The latter will oblige the enemy to hasten with all his forces to the rescue, and will leave the field open to His Christian Majesty to pursue his end; and when he has happily attained it by driving the enemy out of Spain, Naples and Sicily will yield of their own accord.

But if there should be any difficulty about that, the success which we have reason to anticipate in Provence will greatly facilitate the means of leaving the fleet for the whole winter in the Mediterranean. We have no objection at all to that; on the contrary, I have told you we should be very glad to do it, provided the fleet could remain in security. But after all, if there should be too many difficulties in the way, I do not see that that prevents the execution of the other project, since we hope that the expedition to Provence will produce its effect before August, and then there will be time enough left for the fleet to act in concert with the troops which will be destined for Naples.[38]

On April 18 he wrote again to Wratislaw:

Nothing that you can say will ever persuade England and Holland that the invasion of France is not the essential thing, and that in case of success, for which we may reasonably hope, it will not involve all the rest. Why then make so much difficulty about it? For my own part, I should be delighted if the kingdoms of Naples and Sicily were already conquered, but you must agree that we cannot undertake it now without going back, and perhaps ruining the other project, the consequences of which would be fatal to King Charles, since France would then be in a position to send such powerful reinforcements into Spain that His Christian Majesty would be indubitably obliged to retire.

We should run the risk of seeing our entire army in that country scattered, and consequently of losing the fruit which is reasonably to be expected for the immense sums which have been used to establish that Prince on his throne. On the other hand, if we could successfully penetrate into France, the enemy will be obliged to withdraw the greater part of his troops to come to the rescue, the King will march without opposition to Ma-

---

38. Murray, vol. 3, p. 329: Marlborough to Wratislaw, March 7, 1707.

drid, and all the rest will follow without difficulty."³⁹

The argument was unanswerable. But the sullen and vindictive Austrians persisted in their own course. They certainly conceded that an attack upon Toulon by land and sea should be a feature of the campaign of 1707; but they refused to recognise that unless this attack were speedily and strongly delivered, it must fail of its principal purpose—the relief of the allied forces in Spain. Justly indignant that the Dutch should have consistently subordinated the common cause to the acquisition of the "barrier fortresses," should have refused to hand over the Spanish Netherlands to Charles, and should now apparently have lost all further interest in the prosecution of the war, the Emperor was resolved to pay their High Mightinesses in their own coin. He was determined that if Holland and France were eager to arrange a bargain, Naples at any rate should not be used as the medium of exchange.

Accordingly, on March 13 he took a very serious step. Under the terms of a so-called capitulation, which was in fact a treaty of neutrality for Northern Italy, Milan, Cremona, Mirandola, and the other fortresses of Lombardy were surrendered to Eugène, and the French and Spanish garrisons were permitted to evacuate the country. Technically, perhaps, this document did not exceed the Emperor's powers; but in effect it violated the spirit of the Grand Alliance, the members of which were not even consulted. Moreover, it presented the French government with 20,000 excellent soldiers who must in the ordinary course have become prisoners of war.

On the other hand, it liberated the whole of the allied forces in those parts for immediate service elsewhere. Had they been concentrated forthwith for the invasion of Provence, no great harm would have been done . But a large detachment of them was destined to be diverted to Naples; and the conquest of that kingdom was given the priority over the capture of Toulon. In short, Marlborough's strategy was accepted, but only in conditions that were fatal to its efficacy.

The Duke was justifiably aggrieved that the Court of Vienna should deliberately obstruct a design well calculated to terminate the war in a single summer. He was also alarmed lest something worse than a mere prolongation of the struggle should result. All the news from Spain was disquieting in the extreme. In January Charles had convened a council of war at Valencia. All the generals (who were

---

39. *Ibid.*, p. 340: Marlborough to Wratislaw, April 18, 1707.

far too many) assisted. Peterborough himself, having returned from Genoa, was present. Galway and Stanhope, who knew the wishes of Marlborough and the English government, urged the King to make a dash upon Madrid with the entire army. They were supported by a majority.

Peterborough, however, advocated a defensive policy in Catalonia and Valencia. Noyelles and the German ministers agreed with Peterborough. Their influence prevailed with Charles. Thereupon Stanhope told him that the Queen of England did not spend money and raise soldiers for the defence of towns in Catalonia and Valencia, but to make him master of the Spanish monarchy. A violent quarrel between Stanhope and Peterborough ensued. Whichever of the two was right, the course ultimately adopted by Charles was undoubtedly wrong. Pretending that Catalonia was menaced by a French army assembled under Noailles in Roussillon, he quitted Valencia in the middle of March, and with two regiments of foot and five squadrons of horse proceeded to Barcelona. He was advised and accompanied by Noyelles, who had been anxious from the outset to secure an independent command where he was free from the control of English generals.

Rivers, who desired in his own interest to discredit both Peterborough and Galway, had supported Noyelles. Stanhope, in his capacity of envoy, was obliged to follow Charles. Galway, whose resignation had been offered to Godolphin but not accepted, continued at Valencia, while Rivers and Peterborough were recalled by the English government. Their departure cleared the air. But the dangerous separation of the forces still remained. It excited in the breast of Marlborough the gravest apprehensions, and rendered the postponement of a "powerful diversion" in Provence extremely perilous to the allied cause in Spain.

It was during this critical phase of the great contest, when a favourable decision lay well within the reach of the coalised powers, that their attention was distracted and their preparations embarrassed by the appearance of Charles XII of Sweden at the head of 50,000 victorious soldiers upon German soil. Charles had ascended the throne in 1697, at the age of fifteen. Three years later, Peter the Great of Russia, Augustus the Strong, Elector of Saxony and King of Poland, and Frederick IV of Denmark, imagining that the accession of a boy king was their opportunity, had combined together to rob Sweden of her possessions on the mainland.

A terrible surprise awaited them. Charles was a military genius of a rare kind. Assisted by the fleets of England and Holland, he had Denmark at his mercy in three months. She was saved only by the intervention of the maritime powers. Turning next upon the Russians, he inflicted upon their vastly superior forces the astonishing defeat of Narwa. In the following year he routed the Saxons on the Düna. Not content with the overthrow of his three antagonists, he thirsted for revenge. In 1702 he invaded Poland, occupied Warsaw, and destroyed the army of Augustus at Klissow.

Success continued to attend his every action. In 1704 he compelled the Poles to depose Augustus, and to elect Stanislaus in his stead. In 1705 he drove the Russians from Lithuania. In 1706 his field-marshal, Renschild, defeated the combined army of Russians, Poles, and Saxons at Frauenstädt. In September of the same year he entered Saxony itself, laid the hereditary dominions of Augustus under contribution, and imposed upon the prince the humiliating treaty of Alt-Ranstädt. To ensure the execution of the terms of the treaty, he remained in the country, quartering his army on the inhabitants, and seemingly content to linger for an indefinite period on German soil.

Although it was necessary that the Swedes should winter somewhere, and natural enough that they should winter in Saxony, their presence alarmed the neighbouring princes and seriously perturbed the Grand Alliance. Charles, however, made no declaration of his ultimate intentions sufficiently explicit to tranquilise the fears of Europe. Apparently he was gratified by the apprehensions which he created and regarded it as a tribute to his military prowess. The general uncertainty gave birth to various conjectures. It was rumoured that he contemplated an alliance with the Hungarian insurgents, that he was projecting the restoration of the Elector of Bavaria, and that he had actually signed a compact with the King of France. It was known that he took pleasure in posing as heir to the tradition of Gustavus, "the Lion of the North."

But the tradition of Gustavus was an ambiguous phrase, which at that time of day might mean much or little. It might mean no more than a sympathetic attitude towards Protestant States and Protestant congregations in Germany and elsewhere. Or it might mean active intervention in the religious and political differences of the Empire, coupled with a war to the death against the House of Hapsburg. It might conceivably embrace an offensive alliance with that nation which, in the days of Gustavus, had been guided by the genius of

Richelieu. Nobody could foretell with certainty what line of action might attract a young and triumphant monarch, who was adored by his soldiery, and who hungered insatiably for martial fame.

The statesmen of England and Holland were disinclined to believe in the possibility of a quarrel between Sweden and the maritime powers. But fearful lest the disquietude of Austria and the German princes should paralyse the preparations of the Grand Alliance for the next campaign, they endeavoured to penetrate the plans of Charles. They received assurances that he wished them no ill, and that his invasion of Saxony must not be regarded as anything more than a strategical necessity of his conflict with Augustus. But the prevailing uneasiness was only partially allayed by correct generalities, the value of which was largely discounted by known facts. Charles, for example, was recruiting far and wide on German soil. He was listening to the complaints of Silesian Protestants; he was listening also to the complaints of the Electors of Bavaria and Cologne. And in March, 1707, he gave audience to an envoy from Versailles.

From the outbreak of the Scandinavian war Louis XIV had plainly seen that, if the Swedes should enter Germany, France would be the gainer. He therefore exerted himself to reconcile Charles with both Denmark and Russia, and to isolate Saxony. Unsuccessful in these attempts, he watched with pleasure the amazing progress of the Swedish arms. The appearance of Charles at Alt-Ranstädt, at the very moment when the Bourbon cause had reached its lowest ebb, excited new hopes at Versailles. Louis determined to send a representative to the Swedish camp. He selected Besenval[40] an able and energetic soldier of Swiss extraction, who had fought at Ramillies.

The instructions which Torcy handed to Besenval were skilfully drawn. Louis had no illusions. He knew that an offensive alliance was out of the question, because "the tradition of Gustavus" could not easily be stretched to cover an attack upon such recognised champions of Protestantism as England and Holland in the interest of the persecutors of the Huguenots. Besenval therefore was to confine himself to congratulations, to agreeable reminiscences, and to the practical suggestion that Charles, as a Prince of the Empire, and one of the guarantors of the peace of Westphalia, should assume the honourable part of mediator between France and the coalition. He was to press the argument that the monarch who had pacified the north by his arms had now a glorious opportunity of pacifying the west by his authority.

---

40. Coxe is mistaken in saying Ricoux. Ricoux was first chosen, but he fell ill.

Disguised as the valet of a Swedish gentleman, Besenval traversed 100 leagues of hostile country, and reached Leipzig on March 5. Sinzendorf, Robinson, and Kranenberg, the representatives of Austria, England, and Holland, did not attempt to conceal their disgust at his arrival. But the manner of his reception went far to reassure them. The ambassador of France experienced the utmost difficulty in procuring lodgings, servants, and ready money. Neither from the first minister, Piper, nor from the second, Hermelin, could he extract anything material.

He was invited to dine with Piper's countess, who talked continually but never of the business in hand. Her husband, however, did go so far as to observe that mediation would be very difficult in view of the unwillingness of the maritime powers to accept it. He also spoke of Russia; and when Besenval declared that a lieutenant could deal with such barbarians as Peter's subjects, but that Charles should reserve himself for European politics, the Count changed the subject. Charles, who only received the ambassador of France because he was beset by the representatives of all the powers and he found it impossible to make an exception, treated Besenval with a studied coldness and indifference that were almost insulting. But the Swiss refused to be discouraged.

At length, having bestowed a bribe on Hermelin, he succeeded in discovering that Charles intended to gratify his revenge by an immediate attack on Russia, but that after two years he would return and settle the affairs of the Empire. Hermelin explained that at present his master had no quarrel with the Emperor, who, though he had at first refused to recognise Stanislaus, had recently given way on this important point. From Hermelin's conversation and also from Piper's, Besenval gathered that the Swedes believed in the essential moderation of the Grand Alliance no less than in the ability of France to hold her own for at least two years more.

Having failed in an attempt to bribe Piper, he concluded that the first minister had already been bought by England and Holland. And before he had been three weeks at Leipzig he was fully satisfied that the maritime powers were masters of the Swedish court, and that Charles would never accept the proffered post of mediator in opposition to their wishes. In short, he realised that his mission was a hopeless one. But he still remained at Leipzig as an observer and a spy. And he still hoped that the execution of the details of the treaty of Alt-Ranstädt might detain Charles in Saxony. He was disappointed.

With the help of the representatives of the Grand Alliance everything was arranged between Charles and Augustus. By April the Swedish army was ready to march. And Besenval was forbidden to accompany it even as a volunteer.

Correct as Besenval's deductions were, they were known only to himself and to his employers. The fact that he was at Leipzig, even though he appeared to make but little progress there, gave colour to the terrifying tales with which Europe had been flooded. And now, as was usual upon all occasions of anxiety and doubt, everybody turned to Marlborough. In England, in Holland, and above all in Austria, the opinion grew that only by personal contact between Marlborough and Charles could the riddle be satisfactorily solved.

The Duke was in no hurry to accept the task. Having much more than one man's work upon his hands already, he found this flattering confidence in his diplomatic skill a huge embarrassment. Moreover, all the information which he had been able to collect from the numerous and admirable sources of intelligence which he constantly employed, led him to regard the current talk of Europe as unjustifiably alarmist, if not demonstrably false. He knew that it was the palpable interest of France to fabricate and to disseminate rumours, which would produce a panic in Germany, and compel the princes of the Empire to retain their troops within their own borders. Having actually obtained a copy of the instructions handed to Besenval, he was aware of the precise game which Louis was playing, and he did not regard it as a serious menace to the Grand Alliance.

In common with the statesmen of England and Holland he was confident that Charles would never attempt to force his good offices upon the maritime powers, which were bound to Sweden not only by a common Protestantism, but also by the gratitude which they had earned when they kept the Baltic open for the passage of Charles' army. The official reports from Leipzig of the little headway made by Besenval only confirmed this view. As to the future destination of the formidable forces assembled in Saxony, Marlborough was assured by the Elector of Hanover, who had excellent information, that the Grand Alliance had nothing to fear. He was also advised by the Prussian general, Grumbkow, a keen observer, who was at Alt-Ranstädt in January on behalf of the Court of Berlin, that everything pointed to Russia as the next objective of the Swedish army. In these circumstances the Duke was naturally anxious to spare himself the fatigue of a superfluous mission to Saxony, though he was willing enough to undertake the business, if real necessity could be shown for it.

In this undecided mood he quitted London on April 1. Contrary winds detaining him at Margate, he did not arrive at the Hague until the 16th. The loss of so much valuable time on the very eve of the new campaign, rendered him more than ever disinclined to visit Leipzig. Yet three days later he wrote to Wratislaw that he had the Queen's orders to set out forthwith.

Events had suddenly taken a more serious turn. Relations between Charles and the Emperor had become dangerously strained. The trouble, which was trivial enough in its origin, had been vastly magnified by the arrogant fashion in which Charles approached it. Certain unfortunate incidents had occurred. Count Zobor, a Hungarian noble, had insulted the King of Sweden in the presence of the Swedish ambassador. The ambassador had given him "a box o' the ear"; the Emperor had imprisoned him in the castle of Gratz; yet Charles insisted that he should be handed over to the Swedish government. Some Swedish officers, who were enlisting men at Breslau, had been attacked by the mob; their recruits had been taken from them, and a corporal had been killed in the scuffle.

The Emperor had promised to investigate the affair; but Charles imperatively demanded immediate satisfaction. In the previous year 1,200 Russian soldiers had escaped from Poland into Germany, where they were entertained by the Imperial forces on the Upper Rhine. Charles considered that they were his lawful prisoners and that the Emperor should surrender them to him forthwith. On March 30 Piper presented to Sinzendorf a strong complaint upon this subject. The tone of the document was peremptory, and even threatening. It angered Sinzendorf and frightened Robinson and Kranenberg.

Negotiations, conducted in this style with so proud a Court as that of Vienna, might easily provoke a rupture. None realised the danger more clearly than the statesmen of England and Holland. At length they were seriously alarmed, and not without a cause. They did not believe in Swedish intervention or Swedish mediation in the War of the Spanish Succession. But they fully believed in the possibility of a breach of the peace between the House of Vasa and the House of Hapsburg. To Marlborough in particular the prospect was a gloomy one. It had always been difficult to induce Austria to shoulder her fair share of the burdens of the Grand Alliance. Hitherto the Hungarian rebellion had been a constant drain upon her powers. This new peril might paralyse them entirely. In that event, his Mediterranean strategy, which was to finish the war in one campaign, must be relegated to the land of dreams.

On April 19 the Duke wrote to Robinson to announce his coming. "I must pray you will be so kind," he said, "as to procure me leave to set up my own field-bed in some farmhouse at Alt-Ranstädt so near as may be to the King's quarters."[41] Having obtained permission from the Dutch government to make the journey, and having instructed Overkirk to assemble the army and to watch the movements of the French, he set off for Leipzig on the 20th. He reached Hanover on the 24th, paid his compliments to the Elector, and departed at 4 o'clock next morning. On the 26th he reached Halle, where he was met by Robinson, Kranenberg, and Sinzendorf. They dined together, and afterwards proceeded to Alt-Ranstädt, where they arrived at 9 in the evening.

Marlborough immediately visited Count Piper, with whom he remained in conference for an hour. He then retired to the quarters assigned to him by Charles' orders. That same night he saw Sinzendorf. Early on the morning of the 27th he was visited by the general-officers and foreign envoys. Ciederholm came to tell him that the King would receive him at 10 o'clock. The Duke drove to Count Piper's quarters, and they went on together in Piper's carriage to the audience. So vast a concourse of curious spectators had assembled on the ground that three regiments of horse were detailed to keep order. Marlborough was met by the high officials of the Court, and immediately introduced into the King's presence. Charles was surrounded by his councillors and men of war. He advanced with a gracious air to meet the Duke.

Marlborough, who was accompanied by Robinson, presented his credentials, and speaking in English, which Robinson interpreted, addressed the King as follows:

> "I present to your Majesty a letter, not from the chancery, but from the heart of the Queen, my mistress, and written with her own hand. Had not her sex prevented it, she would have crossed the sea to see a prince admired by the whole universe. I am in this particular more happy than the Queen, and I wish I could serve some campaigns under so great a general as your Majesty, that I might learn what I yet want to know in the art of war."[42]

---

41. Murray. vol. 3, p. 343: Marlborough to Robinson April 19, 1707.
42. Coxe, vol. 2, p. 45.

It has been questioned whether flattery so crude could ever have been uttered. But the authenticity of the speech is well supported. The Duke knew his man. It must always be remembered that Charles XII was only twenty-five, that he had been inconceivably successful, that he deemed himself a second Alexander, and that in several of his attributes he was no better than a semi-savage. Moreover, it was expedient to gratify his adoring soldiery.

The King did not conceal his pleasure. His reply, which was interpreted by Piper, was happily framed. The conversation then became general, and lasted for nearly two hours. Marlborough talked in French, a language which Charles understood, though he never made use of it. At noon dinner was announced. The King invited the Duke to remain. At table, Piper sat upon Charles' left, and Marlborough on his right. Everybody remarked the contrast between the unpolished manners of the young monarch and the easy and elegant bearing of the Englishman.

The Swedes declared that Marlborough looked more like a courtier than a soldier, and that they could well understand how a fortune, completed with the sword, had been founded originally upon love. At the same time, they could not but admire a warrior who was also the finest of fine gentlemen. The meal was prolonged by half an hour in honour of the guest. At its conclusion, Piper signed to the company to retire. He himself, with Hermelin and Robinson, remained alone with the King and Marlborough. In the conversation which ensued and which lasted more than an hour, every question of immediate interest both to Sweden and the Grand Alliance, was examined and discussed.

Marlborough was struck by the extreme friendliness of the King's tone towards England, and by his evident conviction that "the exorbitant power of France" must be reduced. But Charles did not confine himself to generalities. He declared that, unless and until the Queen of England desired it, he would never undertake the business of mediation. He expressed his sympathy with the English view that the fortifications of Dunkirk should be demolished.

And he even proposed a secret alliance with England for the promotion of the cause of Protestantism. This very inconvenient suggestion was adroitly turned by Marlborough, who showed that its adoption might render Charles unacceptable as a future mediator between Catholic powers. As the Duke no doubt anticipated, the least satisfactory part of the interview related to the dispute with Austria. Charles exhibited "a great deal of coolness towards the court of Vienna,"[43] and an obstinate determination to insist upon whatever he deemed to be his rights, however trifling.[44]

He also manifested an inclination to champion the cause of the Silesian Protestants, whose churches had been suppressed. Marlborough pointed out that it was impossible for Sweden to intervene in the religious quarrels of Germany without embarrassing the Grand Alliance. He suggested that the settlement of all such questions should be deferred until the negotiations for a general peace. And while he endeavoured to persuade the King that the Austrian government would assuredly concede to Sweden whatever was reasonable and just, he plainly indicated that, if Sweden would be the friend of the maritime powers, Sweden must not lay hands on their ally, because, in the existing fortune of affairs, to injure one was to injure all.

At the termination of the audience Marlborough returned to his quarters, and wrote a short report to Harley.

"I have good reason to hope," he said, "my journey may have all the success Her Majesty and the public expect from it."[45]

Augustus invited him to Leipzig. Marlborough accepted for the following day. He spent the afternoon in visiting "the ministers, general officers, and other persons of distinction" at the Swedish Court. He paid his respects to the Countess Piper; and he was about to take supper with Marshal Renschild and his wife when three couriers summoned him away, and he was seen no more.

On the morning of the 28th he was received by Augustus at Leipzig. Augustus expressed the warmest sympathy with the Grand Alliance, and complained bitterly of his treatment at the hands of Charles. Marlborough advised him to raise no question "that might give the least handle to the King of Sweden to delay his march out of Saxony."[46] Augustus, whose army was a heavy drain on his depleted purse, had been already approached by the English government, which was anxious to hire 4,500 Saxon troops.

Marlborough took the opportunity of completing this negotiation; and at the King's request, he promised to press the Emperor to engage 3,000 or 4,000 more. Charles, who was uneasy lest Augustus

---

43. Murray, vol. 3, p. 358: Marlborough to Harley, May 10, 1707.
44. *Ibid.*, p. 348: Marlborough to the Prince of Salm, May 1, 1707; p. 350: Marlborough to Sinzendorf, May 1, 1707.
45. *Ibid.*, p. 347: Marlborough to Harley, April 27, 1707.
46. Coxe, vol. 2, p. 49.

should get the ear of the maritime powers, managed to arrive during the interview. Marlborough then went to dinner at the Pipers' with Sinzendorf and Robinson. Subsequently he discussed with Piper and Count Goertz a dispute which had arisen between Sweden and Denmark about the bishopric of Lübeck. Supper was taken with Marshal Renschild and his wife and a distinguished company.

On the 29th he was visited in his quarters by Piper and Ciederholm, whose mission it was "to recapitulate in the King's name the essential of all that had passed before."[47] Charles was the friend, and the grateful friend, of the Queen of England; he recognised the necessity of restoring the balance of power; and he considered that, when peace was made, the German Protestants should be amply secured against the persecuting policy of Rome.

"This point of religion," said Marlborough, "was what the King seemed most warmly bent upon; and it was not without difficulty that I convinced him and Count Piper of the necessity of deferring everything of this nature till we come to that of a general peace, for fear of weakening the alliance, by creating unreasonable jealousy among such of the allies as are of the Romish religion."[48]

Marlborough suggested that if a clandestine correspondence were maintained between the two Courts, it would be advantageous to both, and offered to act as intermediary, "and that with all the secrecy and faithfulness the matter did require."[49] The offer was accepted. Having received the visits of other personages of importance, the Duke dined with Goertz. His audience of leave was for 3 o'clock. The King's manner left nothing to be desired. But at the very moment of departure Stanislaus arrived.

Stanislaus had not yet been acknowledged by England or Holland. Charles, who had planned the whole affair, enquired whether Marlborough would meet the King of Poland. The position was a delicate one. It was necessary to please Charles without offending Augustus. Marlborough consented to the introduction. He told Stanislaus that he himself brought no message from Queen Anne, but that doubtless an envoy would be sent from England with letters of congratulation. Charles was delighted. Thereupon the Duke took his leave. Before departing, he had a final interview with Kranenberg. At the moment of farewell, Sinzendorf was seen to have tears in his eyes. The Aus-

---

47. *Ibid*, p. 50.
48. *Ibid*.
49. *Ibid*.

trian had followed the Duke everywhere, "paying court to him as to a king."[50]

Such was the celebrated embassy of Marlborough to Alt-Ranstädt, in regard to which Voltaire and others disseminated what Coxe has justly described as "idle and improbable narratives." The Duke accomplished as much as he anticipated; but he did not anticipate, and he did not accomplish as much as his panegyrists have given the world to believe. He had entirely satisfied himself that Charles had "no manner of engagement with the French,"[51] and that he was "not inclined to take any measures with them that may occasion the least disturbance to the allies in the prosecution of the war."

But on these points Marlborough at any rate had never entertained any serious doubts. He had obtained a promise that the religious question in Silesia should not be raised until the termination of hostihties. But the religious question in Silesia was not the real danger. The real danger was the existing dispute between Sweden and Austria in reference to the three affairs of Breslau, Zobor, and the 1,200 Muscovites. And here the Duke had secured no positive assurances of a pacific settlement.

Doubtless it was something to the good that he should have plainly told Charles that to attack Austria at the moment would be in effect to attack the maritime powers. But it was obvious that a monarch of Charles' impulsive temperament could never be trusted to abstain from actions inconsistent with his own principles and policy. Consequently the Duke took every possible precaution to ensure a speedy accommodation with Austria He impressed upon Sinzendorf the necessity of moderation. He wrote to Vienna to urge the adoption of a conciliatory attitude. He recommended that the 1,200 Muscovites should be surrendered to Stanislaus and that, in exchange for an equal number of Swedish prisoners, they should then be returned to their own country. He persuaded both Hermelin and Ciederholm to become the pensioners of England; and with the assistance of the Countess, he persuaded Piper also. And finally, having once established personal relations with the King and his Cabinet, he cleverly arranged to maintain them in the future by a secret correspondence.

In a case of this sort it is necessarily difficult to estimate how far the personal touch counts. Charles, says Burnet, "looked on foreign ministers as spies by their charter, and treated them accordingly."[52] Writing

---

50. Gabriel Syveton, *Louis XIV et Charles XII*, p. 97.
51. Murray, vol. 3, 357: Marlborough to Harley, May 10, 1707.

to the Prince of Salm, Marlborough declared that it was impossible to negotiate with the Court of Sweden, "as one would elsewhere."[53] In his dealings with the representatives of foreign powers, the King was habitually secretive, and loath to descend from the general to the particular. Lediard, who was specially well informed upon this topic, declares that he had "refused to open his mind to anyone but to the Duke of Marlborough."[54] He did not open it to the Duke as fully as could have been desired. But it is certain that he derived an almost childish pleasure from the visit of a soldier so renowned, and that he was fascinated by that personality which had subdued many more sophisticated hearts than his. Nor was the attraction entirely on one side.

> "This journey," wrote Marlborough to his wife, "has given me the advantage of seeing four kings, three of whom I had never seen. . . . If I was obliged to make a choice, it should be the youngest, which is the King of Sweden."[55]

This mutual liking gave sincerity to an intercourse which otherwise would have been merely official. That Charles honestly desired to continue the relations so happily begun, he proved in a practical fashion, when, contrary to his own most strict regulations, he permitted Robinson's secretary, Jefferies, to accompany his army on the march, nominally as a volunteer, but really as correspondent between Marlborough and the Swedish government.

The Duke considered that his journey had not been wasted.

> "Now that it is over," he wrote to his wife, "I am entirely well pleased to have made it, since I am persuaded it will be of some use to the public, and a good deal to the Queen."[56]

To Wratislaw he wrote:

> "I flatter myself that it has succeeded so well for the advantage of the common cause that I should have no reason to repent of the trouble it has cost me."[57]

The statesmen of the Grand Alliance took the same view. They had acted wisely. In playing against a power which used the weapons

---

52. Burnet, vol. 4, p. 155.
53. Murray, vol. 3., p. 348: Marlborough to the Prince of Salm, May 1, 1707.
54. Lediard, vol. 2, p. 139.
55. Coxe, vol. 2, p. 54: The Duke to the Duchess, April 29/May 10, 1707.
56. *Ibid.*
57. Murray, vol. 3, p. 349: Marlborough to Wratislaw, May 1, 1707.

of diplomacy as often and as skilfully as the weapons of war, they had produced their trump card when they sent the first diplomatist of the age to Alt-Ranstädt. Intercepted dispatches from Besenval to Versailles showed that Louis' representative regarded his master's game as lost.

In obedience to a pressing invitation from the King of Prussia, Marlborough proceeded from Alt-Ranstädt to Berlin, where he arrived on the 30th. Here he exerted himself to soften the dislike which the King entertained for Lord Raby, an ambassador whom Marlborough regarded as by no means satisfactory, but whom he did not see his way to have replaced. Having been presented by his host, who was not famed for generosity, with "a diamond ring valued at £1,000,"[58] the Duke set off on May 2 for Hanover, which he reached on the 3rd. He apprised the Elector of the result of his mission, and continuing his journey on the 4th, came on the evening of Sunday the 8th to the Hague.

---

58. Coxe, vol. 2., p. 53.

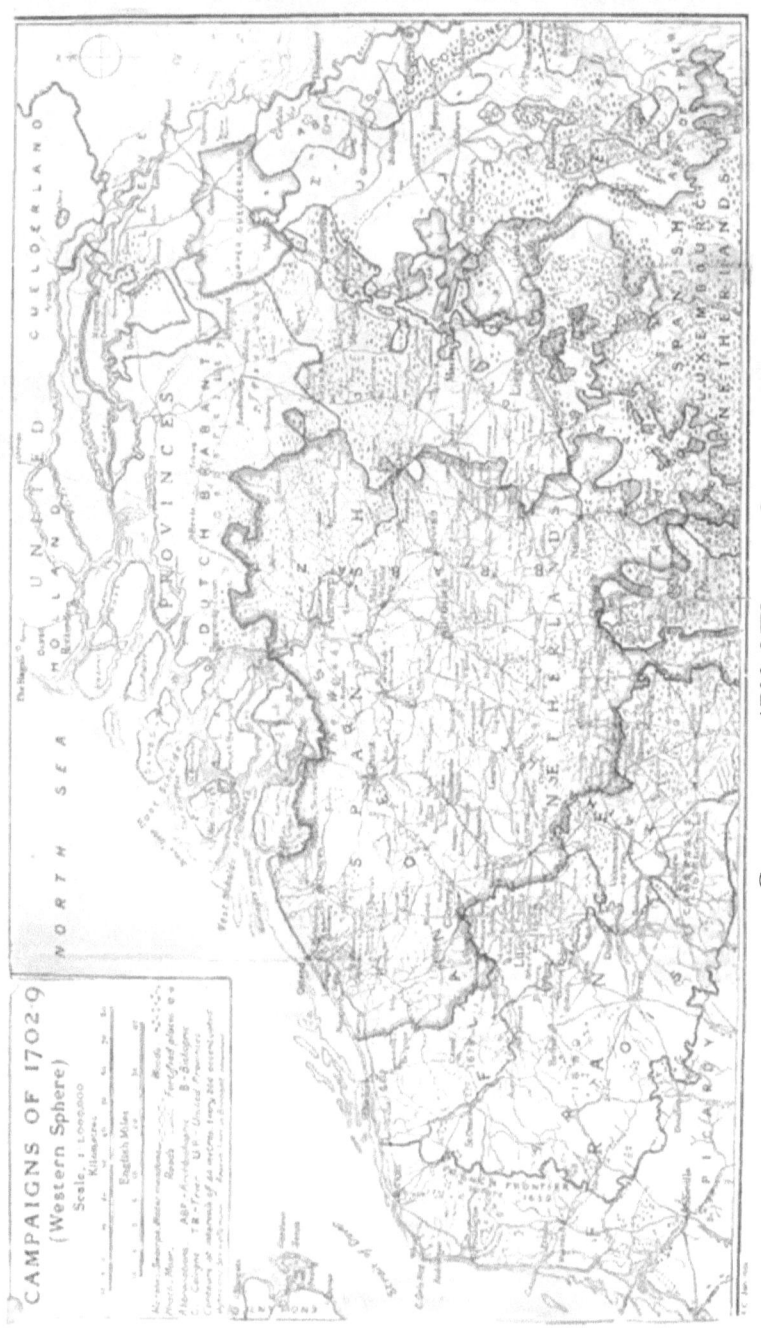

Campaigns of 1702-9 Western Sphere

CAMPAIGNS OF 1702-9

EASTERN SPHERE

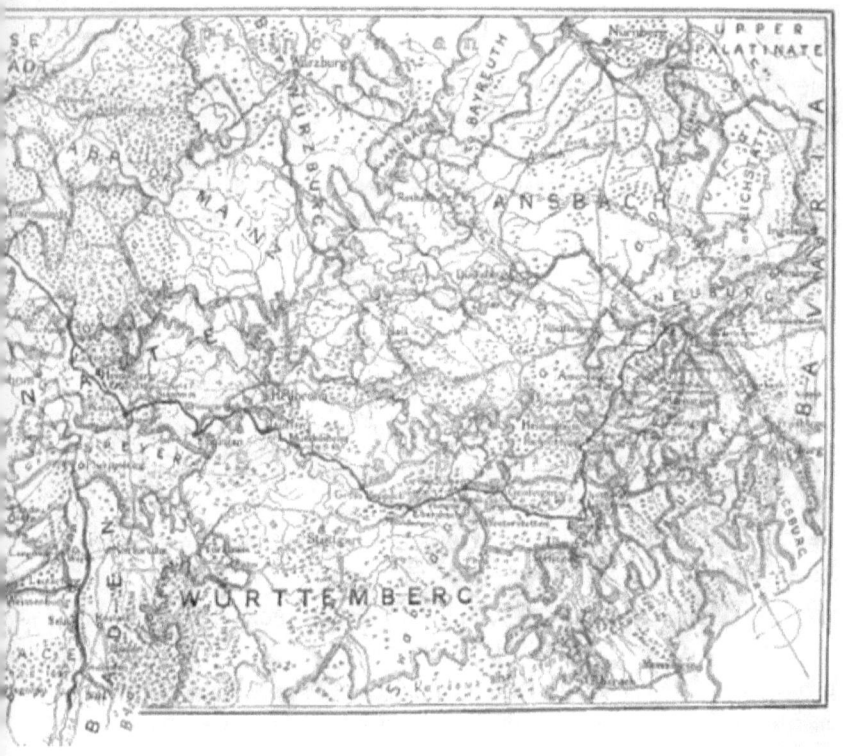

ALSO FROM LEONAUR
AVAILABLE IN SOFTCOVER OR HARDCOVER WITH DUST JACKET

ZULU:1879 *by D.C.F. Moodie & the Leonaur Editors*—The Anglo-Zulu War of 1879 from contemporary sources: First Hand Accounts, Interviews, Dispatches, Official Documents & Newspaper Reports.

THE RED DRAGOON *by W.J. Adams*—With the 7th Dragoon Guards in the Cape of Good Hope against the Boers & the Kaffir tribes during the 'war of the axe' 1843-48'.

THE RECOLLECTIONS OF SKINNER OF SKINNER'S HORSE *by James Skinner*—James Skinner and his 'Yellow Boys' Irregular cavalry in the wars of India between the British, Mahratta, Rajput, Mogul, Sikh & Pindarree Forces.

A CAVALRY OFFICER DURING THE SEPOY REVOLT *by A. R. D. Mackenzie*—Experiences with the 3rd Bengal Light Cavalry, the Guides and Sikh Irregular Cavalry from the outbreak to Delhi and Lucknow.

A NORFOLK SOLDIER IN THE FIRST SIKH WAR *by J W Baldwin*—Experiences of a private of H.M. 9th Regiment of Foot in the battles for the Punjab, India 1845-6.

TOMMY ATKINS' WAR STORIES: 14 FIRST HAND ACCOUNTS—Fourteen first hand accounts from the ranks of the British Army during Queen Victoria's Empire.

THE WATERLOO LETTERS *by H. T. Siborne*—Accounts of the Battle by British Officers for its Foremost Historian.

NEY: GENERAL OF CAVALRY VOLUME 1—1769-1799 *by Antoine Bulos*—The Early Career of a Marshal of the First Empire.

NEY: MARSHAL OF FRANCE VOLUME 2—1799-1805 *by Antoine Bulos*—The Early Career of a Marshal of the First Empire.

AIDE-DE-CAMP TO NAPOLEON *by Philippe-Paul de Ségur*—For anyone interested in the Napoleonic Wars this book, written by one who was intimate with the strategies and machinations of the Emperor, will be essential reading.

TWILIGHT OF EMPIRE *by Sir Thomas Ussher & Sir George Cockburn*—Two accounts of Napoleon's Journeys in Exile to Elba and St. Helena: Narrative of Events by Sir Thomas Ussher & Napoleon's Last Voyage: Extract of a diary by Sir George Cockburn.

PRIVATE WHEELER *by William Wheeler*—The letters of a soldier of the 51st Light Infantry during the Peninsular War & at Waterloo.

AVAILABLE ONLINE AT www.leonaur.com
AND FROM ALL GOOD BOOK STORES

www.ingramcontent.com/pod-product-compliance
Lightning Source LLC
Chambersburg PA
CBHW021955160426
43197CB00007B/142